National Systems of Innovation

Toward a Theory of Innovation and Interactive Learning

The Anthem Other Canon Series

The Anthem Other Canon Series is a collaborative series between Anthem Press and The Other Canon Foundation. The Other Canon – also described as 'reality economics' – studies the economy as a real object rather than as the behaviour of a model economy based on core axioms, assumptions and techniques. The series publishes classical and contemporary works in this tradition, spanning evolutionary, institutional, and Post-Keynesian economics, the history of economic thought and economic policy, economic sociology and technology governance, and works on the theory of uneven development and in the tradition of the German historical school.

Other Titles in the Series

Feeding The World in the 21st Century:
A Historical Analysis of Agriculture and Society
Christian Anton Smedshaug

Ragnar Nurkse: Trade and Development
Edited by Rainer Kattel,
Jan A. Kregel and Erik S. Reinert

Ragnar Nurkse (1907–2007): Classical Development
Economics and its Relevance for Today
Edited by Rainer Kattel, Jan A. Kregel and Erik S. Reinert

Techno-Economic Paradigms: Essays in Honour of Carlota Perez
Edited by Wolfgang Dreschler, Rainer Kattel,
and Erik S. Reinert

Schumpeter's Evolutionary Economics: A Theoretical,
Historical and Statistical Analysis of the Engine of Capitalism
Esben Sloth Andersen

National Systems of Innovation

Toward a Theory of Innovation and Interactive Learning

Edited by

Bengt-Åke Lundvall

ANTHEM PRESS
LONDON · NEW YORK · DELHI

Anthem Press
An imprint of Wimbledon Publishing Company
www.anthempress.com

This edition first published in UK and USA 2010
by ANTHEM PRESS
75-76 Blackfriars Road, London SE1 8HA, UK
or PO Box 9779, London SW19 7ZG, UK
and
244 Madison Ave. #116, New York, NY 10016, USA

British Library Cataloguing in Publication Data
A catalogue record for this book is available from the British Library.

Library of Congress Cataloging in Publication Data
A catalog record for this book has been requested.

ISBN-13: 978 1 84331 882 8 (Hbk)
ISBN-10: 1 84331 882 2 (Hbk)

ISBN-13: 978 1 84331 866 8 (Pbk)
ISBN-10: 1 84331 866 0 (Pbk)

ISBN-13: 978 1 84331 890 3 (eBook)
ISBN-10: 1 84331 890 3 (eBook)

1 3 5 7 9 10 8 6 4 2

CONTENTS

LIST OF TABLES

LIST OF FIGURES

PREFACE

This book has a long and complex history. Already in the late seventies, the IKE-group at Aalborg University began to integrate a French structuralist approach to national systems of production with the Anglosaxon tradition in innovation studies, in order to explain international competitiveness. This 'new combination' is reflected in the concept national systems of innovation which is at the centre of the book. The first sketches to the book, which date back to 1986, were specifically oriented towards the problems of small national systems of innovation (Andersen and Lundvall, 1988), but gradually we realised that the process of internationalisation and globalisation has made all countries 'small', and this is reflected in the final design of the book.

At several stages of the project, the Danish Social Science Research Council has given its financial support. The Research Committee, Aalborg University has funded some of the activities while our department, Institute for Production, has been consistently supportive both financially and administratively. We gratefully acknowledge the patience of these funding institutions.

During the long process, many people have commented on the general outline and on drafts of chapters at workshops and seminars. In particular, we would like to thank Carlota Perez for her often very critical but still supportive comments, at the early stage of the project, and Cristopher Freeman who is not only a co-author, but also has given us invaluable advice all through the process. We are indebted also to Gerhard Bräunling, Charles Edquist, Anders Joest Hingel, Poul Thøis Madsen, Lars Mjøset, Irene Odgaard, Jørgen Lindgaard Pedersen, Keith Smith, Lennart Stenberg and Kjell Trykkestad who, at a workshop in May 1991, commented the drafts for the book. A special thanks to Maureen O'Kelvey and Mark Elam who have tried to polish on our primitive English and who luckily could not restrain themselves from giving useful comments also to the substance.

Dorte Køster, the secretary of the IKE-group, has as always been able to solve difficult coordinative tasks in a simple and efficient way. We are grateful to her and to MA-students Keld Laursen and Ina Drejer who, in the final phase, helped a lot with the detailed editing of the chapters.

The editing process has as most activities in the IKE-group been a genuinely interactive and collective process. Björn Johnson has co-edited part I, Esben Sloth Andersen part II and Bent Dalum part III. Without their generous help the publication of this book might have had to await the turn of the century.

The editor
Aalborg, 25 February 1992

Chapter 1

INTRODUCTION

Bengt-Åke Lundvall

1.1. Introduction

Theories in the social sciences may be regarded as 'focusing devices'. Any specific theory brings forward and exposes some aspects of the real world, leaving others in obscurity. That is why a long lasting hegemony of one single theoretical tradition is damaging both in terms of understanding and policy-making. In the field of economics, the dominating neo-classical paradigm puts its analytical focus upon concepts such as scarcity, allocation, and exchange, in a static context. Even if these concepts reflect important phenomena in the real world, they only bring forward some aspects of the economic system. One aim of this book is to demonstrate the need for an alternative, and supplementary, focusing device which puts interactive learning and innovation at the centre of analysis.

Through more than a decade, a group of economists at Aalborg University, the IKE-group, has worked together studying industrial development and international competitiveness from such a perspective. This book presents results from this work in relation to one specific subject; national systems of innovation. [1]

Our choice of perspective and subject is based upon two sets of assumptions.

First, it is assumed that the most fundamental resource in the modern economy is knowledge and, accordingly, that the most important process is learning. The fact that knowledge differs in crucial respects from other resources in the economy makes standard economics less relevant and motivates efforts to develop an alternative paradigm.[2]

Second, it is assumed that learning is predominantly an interactive and, therefore, a socially embedded process which cannot be understood without taking into consideration its institutional and cultural context. Specifically, it is assumed that the historical establishment and development of the modern nation state was a necessary prerequisite for the acceleration of the process of learning which propelled the process of industrialisation, in the last centuries. Finally, it is recognised that the traditional role of nation states in supporting learning processes is now challenged by the process of internationalisation and globalisation.

These ideas are reflected in the overall structure of the book which is divided into three main parts. The first part presents the theoretical framework, the second part analyses the most important elements of the system of innovation and the third part is devoted to the opening of national systems through internationalisation and globalisation. This introductory chapter presents basic definitions, theoretical starting points, a road map for the book as a whole and, finally, references to other attempts to analyse national systems of innovation.

1.2. National Systems of Innovation

1.2.1. A First Definition

According to Boulding (1985), the broadest possible definition of a system is 'anything that is not chaos'. Somewhat more specifically, a system is constituted by a number of elements and by the relationships between these elements. It follows that a system of innovation is constituted by elements and relationships which interact in the production, diffusion and use of new, and economically useful, knowledge and that a national system encompasses elements and relationships, either located within or rooted inside the borders of a nation state.[3]

Using the terminology of Boulding, it is obvious that the national system of innovation is a *social* system. A central activity in the system of innovation is learning, and learning is a social activity, which involves interaction between people. It is also a *dynamic* system, characterised both by positive feed-back and by reproduction. Often, the elements of the system of innovation either reinforce each other in promoting processes of learning and innovation or, conversely, combine into constellations blocking such processes. Cumulative causation, and virtuous and vicious circles, are characteristics of systems and sub-systems of innovation. Another important aspect of the innovation system relates to the reproduction of the knowledge of individuals or collective agents (through remembering).

1.2.2. Nation States and National Systems

The concept, national systems of innovation, presumes the existence of nation states and this phenomenon has two dimensions; the national-cultural and the étatist-political. The ideal, abstract, nation state is one where the two dimensions coincide, i.e. where all individuals belonging to a nation – defined by cultural, ethnical and linguistic characteristics – are gathered in one single geographical space controlled by one central state authority (without foreign nationalities).

It is difficult to find any nation states, in this strict sense, in the real world. Countries differ both in the degree of cultural homogeneity and in the degree of political centralisation. In some cases it is not even clear where to locate the borders of a 'national' system of innovation. This might be true both for 'multinational' states as Belgium, Canada and Switzerland and for single-national but federal states such as Germany. At the extreme, a country might be solely constituted by a joint foreign policy with little in common in terms of it's institutional set up and culture. In such cases, the concept of a 'national' system of innovation would be of little relevance.

Most of the contributors to this book have their roots in a minority of small countries which may be characterised as culturally homogeneous and socio-economically coherent systems (Sweden, Denmark and Norway). This gives a certain bias to our world outlook (it should do so, according to our basic understanding where theoretical conceptualisation is assumed to be culturally bounded). On the other hand, it may be argued, it is quite useful, analytically, to use concepts which are archetypes rather than 'averages'. In order to bring out sharply the limits and consequences of globalisation and regionalisation, it is useful, at least as a starting point, to assume countries to be homogeneous in political and cultural terms.

1.2.3. National Systems, Globalisation and Regionalisation

Readers might ask, why we focus on the *national* level, in an era where many analysts point to an accelerating process of internationalisation and globalisation, characterised by multinational firms, loosening their relations to their home-country and entering into alliances with foreign firms. This process might actually be most advanced when it comes to the production of new knowledge and innovations in science-based technologies such as bio-technology, pharmaceuticals and electronics.

At the same time, a growing number of social scientists – often inspired by new sets of ideas labeled 'flexible specialisation', 'networking' and 'post-fordism' – have argued that regional production systems, industrial districts and technological districts are becoming increasingly important. Some authors analyse these two tendencies as interconnected and mutually reinforcing (Storper, 1991a, Camagni, 1990 and also Porter, 1990). They assume that globalisation, and international specialisation have their roots in the strengthening of specialised technological districts and regional networks.

Both globalisation and regionalisation, might be interpreted as processes which weaken the coherence and importance of national systems. In this book, we do not deny the validity of these trends. Actually, we think that they make it even more pertinent to understand the role and workings of national systems of innovation, both historically, and in the present era.

First, we believe that national systems still play an important role in supporting and directing processes of innovation and learning. The uncertainties involved in innovation and the importance of learning imply that the process calls for a complex communication between the parties involved. This will especially be the case when the knowledge exchanged is tacit and difficult to codify. When the parties involved originate in the same national environment – sharing its norms and culturally based system of interpretation – interactive learning and innovation will be easier to develop.

On the other hand, it must be recognised that important elements of the process of innovation tend to become transnational and global rather than national – and here the trend will be most important in science-based areas where the communication is easier to formalise and codify. Some of the big corporations are weakening their ties to their home-base country and begin to spread their innovative activities and to 'source' different national systems of innovation. These changes are important and they challenge the traditional role of national systems of innovation, but they do not make it less important to understand how national systems work.

When an old institutional order is threatened, and a new one is beginning to develop, it becomes critically important to understand the basic mechanisms of the old order. Without such an understanding the costs of transformation might become unnecessarily high. More specifically, the process of far-reaching European integration may run into serious problems if it does not take into account the complex interaction between institutions and economic structure in promoting innovation at the national level.

Behind the analysis lies also, as mentioned, the hypothesis that the modern nation states in the Western world – not necessarily the new states in the former colonies – have worked as 'engines of growth'. They were constituted and shaped in their present form in a period characterised by a rapid economic transformation, including the massive movement of labour from agriculture to industrial production. Their social institutions and state policies have supported such a transformation and new institutions aiming directly at economic wealth creation through innovation have been established in the course of the last century and become integral parts of national systems of production.

From what has been said, it is obvious that national systems of innovation are open and heterogeneous systems. Processes of innovation transcend national borders and sometimes they are local rather than national. Actually, this has always been the case for most national systems. The rapid industrialisation and modernisation of European countries, starting more than 100 years ago, was closely connected with an opening up of the national economies in terms of foreign trade, capital import and import of foreign ideas and experts, and already at that time the international specialisation was often reflected in a regional specialisation within the countries.

1.2.4. Public Policy and National Systems of Innovation

As pointed out at the very beginning of this introduction, one main purpose of this book is to contribute to a theoretical understanding of interactive learning and innovation. But the concept 'national systems of innovation' may also be useful when it comes to inspire public policies at the national and the international level.

First, in order to determine what governments should do in order to promote innovation, it is useful to know the specific systemic context in which a national government intervenes. Otherwise, government policies might either reproduce weaknesses of the national system or introduce mechanisms incompatible with the basic logic of the system.

Second, in the increasingly serious international conflicts about which countries are paying for (the US) and, respectively, appropriating benefits from (Japan) the investment in science and development of new technology, it is important to understand how different and very diverse national systems work. This is a point made by experts close to the GATT-negotiations (Ostry, 1990).

Third, in a world characterised by a radical shift in techno-economic foundations, the ability of national systems to cope, successfully, with change and to exploit new technical opportunities seem to be quite divergent (Freeman and Perez, 1988). Learning from the experience of foreign systems, in this respect, might be facilitated if the workings of the respective national systems as a whole are properly understood. Strategies based on naive copying may be avoided and institutional learning across national borders might be stimulated (See also chapter 14). Not least, the present development in Eastern Europe points to a strong need to develop a realistic understanding of the workings of the 'real market economies' in relation to innovation.

Actually, the concept, national systems of innovation, has already entered the vocabulary of policy-makers at the national and the international level. An ambitious effort to understand the importance of technology for economic change, was launched by OECD in 1988, as the Technology/Economy programme (TEP). When the outcome of this programme was summed up in Montreal, in 1991, the concept, national systems of innovation, was given a prominent place in the conclusions.

It was pointed out that the assignment of proper roles for, respectively, government and the private sector in enhancing technological capabilities should build upon a better understanding of national systems of innovation. Also, it was concluded that the growing international conflicts regarding the global sharing of burdens and benefits emanating from the development and use of new technology might be kept within reasonable limits only if the parties get a better understanding of the diversity of NSI's (OECD – Canada, 1991). The fact that the concept has already entered the everyday vocabulary of policy-makers makes it even more important to give the NSI-concept an analytical basis.

1.2.5. Performance of National Systems of Innovation

In order to design policies relevant for national system of innovation, it is necessary to agree upon which should be the 'desiderata' of the system (Kornai, 1971, 214 f). From the standpoint of general equilibrium theory, the main performance dimension refers to the more or less efficient allocation of scarce and given resources. A more dynamic version would point to the adaptability of the system. A Keynesian perspective would emphasise the degree of utilisation of existing resources and especially of the labour force.

At this general level, we would like to propose that the most relevant performance indicators of national system of innovation should reflect the efficiency and effectiveness in producing, diffusing and exploiting economically useful knowledge. Such indicators are not well developed today. One of the classical measures for comparing different national systems is R&D-expenditure as a proportion of GDP. There are two obvious problems with this indicator. First, it reflects only an input effort and does not say anything about what comes out of the effort. Second, R&D-expenditure is only one kind of relevant input to the process of innovation – learning in connection with routine activities may be more important than R&D.

The output measures used are more recently developed and include patents (Pavitt and Patel, 1988), the proportion of new products in sales (Kristensen and Lundvall, 1991) and the proportion of hi-tech products in foreign trade (Dalum et al., 1988). Each one of these indicators has its own specific weaknesses and it is wise to combine them in order to get a more satisfactory picture of the performance of a national system. A common weakness is that these measures do not take into account the diffusion of process technology and in order to get a more complete picture, indicators for diffusion should be taken into account (Edquist and Jakobsson, 1988).

Technical progress is not regarded as a goal in itself. The main reason why national governments engage in innovation policy is the assumption that innovation is a key element in national economic growth. Different indicators of economic growth (national income or consumption per capita) are relevant when it comes to compare systems. But such indicators will reflect factors which have little to do with innovation and, more importantly, they give little insight into how innovation takes place in different countries. One interesting observation is that different systems may develop different modes of innovation while still following parallel growth paths.[4] Bringing the different, specific innovation indicators into the picture helps to characterise the specific national mode of innovation.

1.2.6. The Normative Dimension

The choice of performance criteria and of the respective weights to be assigned to them is fundamentally normative decisions. One of the most developed attempts to come to grips with implicit and explicit value judgements in economic analysis is Myrdal (1968). He argues that as a minimum requirement economists should make explicit their value premises. Further, Myrdal actually presents a method for bringing value premises into the analysis of national economies. When studying the problems of the poor Asian countries, he choses to accept the set of value premises predominating among the national establishment in the countries studied – the ideal of modernisation.

Given the lack of alternatives, it is tempting to use a similar approach to national systems of innovation. To identify the ambitions and goals of national governments in the area of innovation is, apparently, quite easy. The public discourse is dominated by references to the international competitiveness of the national economy and to national economic growth. There seems to be a broad social acceptance in the national establishment that these are the main goals. But this is not the only relevant level to take into account.

Another level of analysis refers to the international organisations of the rich countries such as the European Community and OECD. Politicians and experts at this level are more oriented towards strengthening economic growth in their respective region and towards avoiding international conflicts within the community of countries they represent.

Finally, there is a global level of analysis, with a rather weak representation in organisational terms – the UN organisations, global environmentalist organisations etc. At this level, it becomes more obvious to experts and politicians that the long term survival of the global economy is dependent upon ecological sustainability and upon a reduction of the extreme social inequality at the global level.

We do not find it proper to adopt the set of value premises of any single one of these three levels, however. On the one hand, we consider national policies and goals, relating to innovativeness and competitiveness to be legitimate, to a certain degree. The pursuit of such goals has been an important motor behind the dramatic increase in economic wealth in the OECD-area and in some newly industrialised countries in Asia. Additionally, policies designed to strengthen the system of innovation are less of 'beggar-thy-neighbor' character than exchange rate or incomes policies.

On the other hand, we realise that some of the games related to national science and technology policy may actually be zero-sum games and that there is a growing number of examples of unpleasant trade-offs between short-term national economic growth and long term global sustainability (in terms of environment, natural resources, etc.). The national context tends to become too narrow when it comes to solving problems such as global inequity and sustainability. The value premises of the national establishment must be confronted with these broader and more long term concerns.

This is one reason, why we welcome the development and strengthening of organisations and agencies operating at the international and global level. But, as already pointed out, it might be premature to dismantle the nation states and the national systems of innovation. The on-going process of innovation changes the social conditions of citizens and regions – some for the better and some for the worse. The most important role of the nation state in this context has been to compensate the weak and to put some restraint on the strong. Without the formation of new agencies, capable of realising such a 'social dimension', a process of internationalisation and globalisation, which undermines national systems of innovation, might result in a long term social and political crisis rather than in creative destruction.

1.3. Towards a Theory

1.3.1. Innovation as a Cumulative Process

In the models of standard economics, innovations appear as extraordinary events, coming from the outside, which temporarily disturb the general equilibrium. After a process of adjustment, reflecting the work of the price mechanism, a new state of equilibrium is established. This approach might have been adequate in pre-industrial societies where innovations seemed to occur as rare and exogenous events. In modern capitalism, however, innovation is a fundamental and inherent phenomenon; the long-term competitiveness of firms, and of national economies, reflect their innovative capability and, moreover, firms must engage in activities which aim at innovation just in order to hold their ground.

One of our starting points is that innovation is a ubiquitous phenomenon in the modern economy. In practically all parts of the economy, and at all times, we expect to find on-going processes of learning, searching and exploring, which result in new products, new techniques, new forms of organisation and new markets. In some parts of the economy, these activities might be slow, gradual and incremental, but they will still be there if we take a closer look.

The first step in recognising innovation as an ubiquitous phenomenon is to focus upon its gradual and cumulative aspects. Such a perspective gives rise to simple hypotheses about the dependence of future innovation on the past. In this context an innovation may be regarded as a new use of pre-existing possibilities and components. Here, Schumpeter's choice of terminology, where 'innovations' and 'new combinations' are used as synonyms, is enlightening. Almost all innovations reflect already existing knowledge, combined in new ways.

This is, however, not to say that the step to the new combination is always of the same character. Sometimes, an innovation might be almost inevitable – the new combination might be easy to find and to realise. In other cases, it might take an enormous intellectual effort or an extremely creative mind, to identify a potential new combination. And, sometimes, the process of innovation results in radical breaks with the past, making a substantial part of accumulated knowledge obsolete. Another of Schumpeter's concepts, 'creative destruction', points to this discontinuity and it might be applied not only to the structure of production, but also to the structure of knowledge.

Nevertheless, we will put some emphasis upon the ubiquitous and cumulative character of innovation. In such a perspective the distinction made in innovation theory, between invention, innovation, and diffusion, as three separate stages necessarily becomes blurred. We also understand why it is difficult to date invention and innovation in time, and why an innovation does not stay the same throughout its diffusion. Innovation appears now, not primarily as a single event, but rather *as a process*.

A second starting point is that interactive learning and collective entrepreneurship are fundamental to the process of innovation. In his early work on the theory of economic development, Schumpeter pointed to entrepreneurs, which act individually, as the most important economic agents bringing innovations into the economic system (Schumpeter, 1934). Later, he revised his theoretical scheme, however, by giving a critical role to the collective work in R&D-laboratories (Schumpeter, 1942). In a sense, through introducing systems of innovation we pursue this trajectory from individual towards collective entrepreneurship further.

We will argue that most important forms of learning may fundamentally be regarded as interactive processes, and that together the economic structure and the institutional set up form the framework for, and strongly affect, processes of interactive learning, sometimes resulting in innovations. In the chapters to follow this general point will be illustrated at different levels of analysis.

1.3.2. Learning and the Structure of Production

One of the most important institutional innovations in the last century was the establishment of R&D-laboratories in the big private firms (Freeman, 1982, and chapter 9 in this book). Scientific activities and technical change have been brought closer together and become increasingly interdependent activities and today, the capability to innovate cannot be assessed in isolation from efforts in science, research and development. However, here, we will insist upon the fact that not all important inputs to the process of innovation emanate from science and R&D-efforts. We, thus, assume that learning takes place in connection with routine activities in production, distribution and consumption, and produces important inputs to the process of innovation. The everyday-experiences of workers, production engineers, and sales representatives influence the *agenda* determining the direction of innovative efforts, and they *produce knowledge and insights* forming crucial inputs to the process of innovation.

When bottle-neck problems are met and registered in production, or in the use of a product, the agendas of producers change, affecting the direction of their innovation efforts. Everyday-experience also increases technical knowledge and gives ideas about in which direction solutions should be looked for. Such activities involve learning-by-doing, increasing the efficiency of production operations (Arrow 1962), learning-by-using increasing the efficiency of the use of complex systems (Rosenberg, 1982), and learning-by-interacting, involving users and producers in an interaction resulting in product innovations (Lundvall, 1988).

If innovation reflects learning, and if learning partially emanates from routine activities, innovation must be *rooted in the prevailing economic structure*. The areas where technical advance will take place, will primarily be those where a firm, or a national economy, is already engaged in routine activities.[5] This basic idea is developed in *chapter 4* where the focus is upon how the national system of innovation is rooted in a national system of production.

1.3.3. Learning and the Institutional Set Up

The institutional set-up (of a specific firm, a constellation of firms, or a nation) is the second important dimension of the system of innovation. Institutions provide agents and collectives with guide-posts for action. In a world characterised by innovative activities, uncertainty will be an important aspect of economic life. Institutions make it possible for economic systems to survive and act in an uncertain world. Institutions may be routines, guiding everyday actions in production, distribution and consumption, but they may also be guide-posts for change. In this context, we may regard technological trajectories and paradigms, which focus the innovative activities of scientists, engineers, and technicians, as one special kind of institutions.[6]

One of the fundamental characteristics of institutions is their relative stability over time. They arise because, in a changing and uncertain world, agents and organisations need guidance and institutions make life more manageable and comfortable (not necessarily more efficient in any sense of this term) for them. This perspective is discussed in *chapter 2* where it is demonstrated that institutions and routines are fundamental, because they provide the stability needed for innovative efforts to take place and to be successful.

1.3.4. Product Innovation and User-Producer Interaction

One way to illustrate how the structure of production and the institutional set up, together, affect the rate and direction of innovation is to focus upon product innovations, and their roots in the interaction between producers and users. First, at the micro level, the structure of production defines sets of user-producer relationships, which condition the scope and direction of the process of innovation. Second, the institutional form which characterises these relationships – and, especially, the elements of organisation in these markets – reflects the characteristics of the process of innovation. Third, the institutional set up, once established, will affect the rate and direction of innovation. Fourth, one interesting dimension of user-producer relationships can be shown to be distance in cultural and geographical space.

Through this analysis, developed in *chapter 3*, we illustrate how the production structure, and the institutional set up jointly define a system of innovation and at the same time provide an understanding of the micro-foundation of 'national systems of innovation'.

1.3.5. Learning, Searching and Exploring[7]

Above, we have indicated the importance of learning rooted in routine activities. But, of course, economic agents and organisations also consciously invest time and resources in expanding their technical knowledge. *Searching* is another important activity, creating inputs to the system of innovation.

Organisations normally learning only from routine activities of production and distribution might engage in search activities under certain extreme circumstances. When the survival of the organisation is threatened, its members become engaged in what might be called 'desperate search'. This kind of search might begin as local search, looking for alternatives (in terms of products, processes, markets etc.) close to the ones already well-known to the organisation and, only if it is impossible to find any satisfactory solutions in this area, expanding to more distant alternatives.[8]

However, desperate search is not always very efficient. Especially when technology is science-based, complex, and changing, it becomes attractive to establish special departments permanently engaged in searching activities. Organisations with searching as their special mission might be departments for market analysis as well as R&D-departments, and – laboratories.

Searching which takes place in academic or science-oriented organisations, outside the private firms, brings forward another kind of raw material for the process of innovation. We call this kind of search 'exploring'. The most important difference between exploring and searching is that 'exploring' is less goal-oriented than profit oriented search. If we take a closer look at scientific activities we shall, however, often find that they too have a specific aim and direction. Even if the paradigms and trajectories, which determine the aims and directions of basic science, develop more according to their own internal logic and are less responsive to changes in economic parameters than innovations in private firms, the producers of basic science will, to a certain extent, be oriented towards users outside the realm of pure science. The direction of research in mathematics and logic may, for example, reflect new needs developed by computer scientists and soft-ware experts.

Exploring will, because of its weaker goal-orientation, sometimes result in outcomes, neither foreseen, nor looked for, by profit oriented organisations. This adds to technological change a dimension of dynamism and radical change, extremely important in the long run. Exploring will sometimes result in breaks in cumulative paths and create the basis for new technological paradigms.

1.3.6. Incremental Versus Radical Innovations

If innovation is rooted in learning, and learning in routine activities, we might expect all innovative activities to be incremental, and it would be rather simple to predict the direction of technical change. But we must take into account the fundamentally uncertain and disruptive character of the process of innovation. As mentioned, uncertainty rules in the process of scientific activities, and these produce, from time to time, results which where neither anticipated nor looked for. Uncertainty also rules regarding the economic impact of an innovation. A new product might fail either for technical reasons, or because it does not successfully address potential user needs. Conversely, a product originally addressed towards the needs of a small sub-set of users might later prove to be a commercial success, applicable in very substantial parts of the economy.

When distinguishing between incremental and radical innovations, we may refer, primarily, either to the technical or to the economic dimension. Some innovations, incremental in technical terms, may have a crucial impact upon the economy. This will be true for a small technical change solving a bottle-neck problem of strategical importance (the introduction of vehicles with inflated rubber wheels in agriculture did not represent any radical technical break but it had an dramatic impact upon the productivity of this sector). On the other hand, an innovation very radical in technical terms, and signalling a new technological paradigm, might for technical reasons be premature and have a very limited impact on the economy (it took the Babbage-version of the computer, obviously a radical innovation in technical terms, more than a century before it had any economic impact at all). It follows that many radical innovations will be radical only in one of the two dimensions while remaining incremental in the other dimension.

For these reasons, we assume that the process of innovation is neither totally accidental nor totally predetermined by the economic structure and the institutional set up. The analysis of systems of innovation helps us to understand and explain, why technology develops in a certain direction, and at a certain rate, but a strong element of randomness will always remain.

1.3.7. Defining the NSI – The Role of Theory and History

From what has been said, it follows that we may make a distinction between a system of innovation in the narrow sense and a system of innovation in the broad sense. The narrow definition would include organisations and institutions involved in searching and exploring – such as R&D-departments, technological institutes and universities. The broad definition which follows from the theoretical perspective presented above includes all parts and aspects of the economic structure and the institutional set up affecting learning as well as searching and exploring – the production system, the marketing system and the system of finance present themselves as sub-systems in which learning takes place.

Determining in detail which sub-systems and social institutions should be included, or excluded, in the analysis of the system is a task involving historical analysis as well as theoretical considerations.

In different historical periods different parts of the economic system, or different inter-faces between sub-systems, may play a more or less important role in the process of innovation. In the early British industrialisation new technology reflected, primarily, learning inside firms which developed and tested new production equipment, either developed in-house, or in cooperation with artisans from small workshops. The development of the new industries of chemistry and electricity at the end of the last century changed the location of the innovation-nexus and brought it closer to the R&D-laboratories of big firms.

Today, it seems as if the crucial interfaces of systems of innovation have shifted again. Radical innovations in information technology which are, themselves, science-based have put the focus upon the coupling of routine based learning to searching and R&D. 'The factory as a laboratory'– formula refered to in chapter 9 reflects these new trends. At the same time, however, more and more innovative activities have to draw upon quite different and separate sets of generic knowledge (bio-technology, microelectronics, new materials) making the process of science-based innovation, even more costly and complex.

However, the theoretical perspective is also important. The broad definition of the system used in this book reflects the importance attached to interactive learning as a basis for innovation. Alternatively a 'linear model of technical change' – where technical innovations were assumed to follow mechanically from scientific efforts and from research efforts inside firms – would define the system of innovation much more narrowly and identify it with the R&D-system.

From this background, it should be obvious that a definition of the system of innovation must, to a certain degree, be kept open and flexible regarding which sub-systems should be included and which processes should be studied. It also follows that we cannot insist upon one single approach to the national system of innovation as the only legitimate one. Different theoretical perspectives bring forward different aspects of the system.

1.4. The Elements of the System

In the real world the state and the public sector are rooted in national states, and their geographical sphere of influence is defined by national borders. The focus upon *national* systems reflects the fact that national economies differ regarding the structure of the production system and regarding the general institutional set up. Specifically, we assume that basic differences in historical experience, language, and culture will be reflected in national idiosyncrasies in:

– Internal organisation of firms
– Inter-firm relationships
– Role of the public sector
– Institutional set up of the financial sector
– R&D-intensity and R&D-organisation

International differences in these elements are important for the working of the system as a whole, but the relationships between the elements are just as important. For example both the organisation and strategies of the public sector, including its responsibility for education and R&D, and the financial sector will affect the way firms organise and form networks. On the other hand the historical specialisation of firms and networks of firms will be reflected in the public infrastructure of education and R&D.

First, we assume that the internal organisation of private firms is one important aspect of the system of innovation. Most innovations are developed by firms, and many innovation studies have demonstrated that the organisation of the flow of information, and of the learning process, are important and affect the innovative capability of the firm. The interaction between different departments engaged in respectively sales, production and R&D is one important aspect of the organisation which is attracting a growing interest in comparative innovation studies. Different aspects of the contingency of learning upon the organisation of work related to the innovation design dilemma are analysed in the chapter by Næs Gjerding (*chapter 5*).

But we also assume that inter-firm relationships are important in structuring the system of innovation. In standard economics these relationships are assumed to be characterised by competition and by pure markets. Focusing upon innovation makes it clear that cooperation between firms is a necessary supplement to competition, and one form of cooperation is the user-producer interaction analysed in chapter 4. In an increasing number of knowledge-intensive industries, other forms of inter-firm cooperation tend to become increasingly important. In the chapter by Gelsing (*chapter 6*), inter-firm interaction is presented in the context of network relationships and industrial districts, including informal exchange of technical know-how.

The public sector plays an important role in the process of innovation. As pointed out in chapter 9, it is involved in direct support of science and development, and its regulations and standards influence the rate and direction of innovation, and it is the single most important user of innovations developed in the private sector. In the chapter by Gregersen (*chapter 7*) the emphasis is put upon the role of the public sector as a more or less competent user of innovations.

The connection between the financial system and the process of innovation was strongly emphasised by the early Schumpeter and recently there has been a growing public interest in the enabling role of the financial system in regard to innovation. In the chapter by Lindgaard Christensen (*chapter 8*), the relationships between finance and innovation are analysed and interesting national differences are pointed out.

As already noted, the process of innovation is closely connected to the R&D-system; its resources, competencies and organisation. The historical development of the R&D-system and its current importance, is discussed in the chapter by Freeman (*chapter 9*). The chapter points to the need for institutional innovation in national systems of innovation.

Missing among these elements is the national education and training system. For different reasons, this extremely important element of the national system of innovation has not been been given its proper treatment in this book. There are big differences between countries in their formal and informal education and training systems which affect their innovative capabilities. This refers to the quantitative investment in education, the enrolment in science and engineering, the investment in training of skilled workers etc. Other differences are qualitative and also relate to the social norms and values reproduced by the system and to the degree of egalitarianism versus élitism in the system. An important task for future research is to integrate education and training systems and innovation systems in one single analytical framework.[9]

1.5. Opening the System

As pointed out, we do not assume the process of innovation to be exclusively localised inside national borders. On the contrary, we recognise that the process of innovation has increasingly become multinational and transnational reflecting, for example, R&D-cooperation between big firms based in different nations. Part III of the book analyses different aspects of the international relationships and takes into account that national systems of innovation are open and, increasingly, becoming wide-open.

In the chapter by Dalum (*chapter 10*), some important structural features of national systems of innovation are characterised by data on export specialisation. The long term development patterns of specialisation are analysed in terms of industry life cycles; it is shown that patterns are distinctly different country by country. The specialisation patterns are discussed in relation to structural competitiveness and in this context the strategic role of the engineering sector is emphasised.

Fagerberg (*chapter 11*) focuses upon one branch of trade theory with special relevance for the analysis of national systems of innovation, the home market theory. The relative importance of linkages between export specialisation in user- and producer industries are tested econometrically. This chapter and the one by Dalum are focused on trade patterns (arms' length trade) and do not take into account foreign direct investment and multinational enterprises.

Andersen and Brændgaard (*chapter 12*) present an analysis of economic integration from an evolutionary stand and study what might be regarded as an embryonic transnational system of innovation. The empirical case relates to the specialisation and competitiveness of the European Community in information technology and refers to some of the political efforts to strengthen the European Community in this field in relation to Japan and United States.

While these three chapters focus upon internationalisation in the form of international trade and specialisation, the chapter by Chesnais (*chapter 13*) brings foreign direct investment and multinational capital into the picture. The chapter describes and analyses how the process of internationalisation has entered a new phase of globalisation, which fundamentally changes the role of national systems of innovation. Chesnais shows that the new tendencies challenge the relative autonomy of national systems and weaken their coherence, but also give a new and even more important role to public policy.

1.6. Alternative Approaches and Methods

1.6.1. Introduction

As pointed out, the definition of the national system of innovation is dependent upon the theoretical approach and therefore it is useful to see how different authors have used the concept and to relate the approach of this book to these alternatives.[10]

Friedrich List

The first systematic and theoretically based attempt to focus upon national systems of innovation goes back to Friedrich List (1841/1959). His contribution is also interesting because it is developed as an explicit alternative to Adam Smith and his contemporary followers. List makes a distinction between Adam Smith's 'cosmopolitan' approach which puts the focus upon exchange and allocation and his own national perspective focusing on the development of productive forces. We think that this is a fruitful and interesting distinction.

The only element of List's quite complex and rich – sometimes somewhat confusing – analysis still left in modern economics is his argument for protection of 'infant-industries'. His analysis went much further, however, indicating the need for governmental responsibility for education and training and for developing an infra-structure supporting industrial development. Actually, he sketched some of the most important elements of the national system of innovation.

Christopher Freeman

The first explicit use of the concept national systems of innovation may be the one in Freeman's (1987) book on Japan. Here the concept refers both to the nation-specific organisation of sub-systems and to the interaction between sub-systems. The organisation of R&D and of production in firms, the inter-firm relationships and the role of government and MITI are at the centre of the analysis which is both historical and based upon modern innovation theory.

Richard Nelson

Almost at the same time, Nelson presented studies of the US-system (Nelson, 1987 and Nelson, 1988). The focus of the analysis was upon the combined public and private character of technology and the role of, respectively, private firms, government and universities in the production of new technology. It was shown that different industrial sectors use different methods to appropriate the benefits from their innovations.

The approaches of the two authors differ in two important respects. First, while the focus in Nelson's work is upon the production of knowledge and innovation and upon the innovation-system in the narrow sense, Freeman focuses upon the interaction between the production system and the process of innovation. Second, while Freeman applies a combination of organisation and innovation theory – which organisational forms are most conducive to the development and efficient use of new technology? – Nelson's main theoretical tool is related to law and economics – how well can different institutional set-ups take into account and solve the private/public dilemma of information and technical innovation?

The approach of this book is closest to Freeman's because we focus quite a lot upon organisational matters as related to processes of learning, but we also recognise the importance of institutional factors of the kind brought forward by Nelson's work in this area. If one should point to one specific dimension which characterises our approach, it would be the emphasis put upon interactive learning anchored in the production structure and in the linkage pattern of the system of production.

Michael Porter

The recent book by Michael Porter (1990) may be read as a work on national systems of innovation. Porter points to four different determinants affecting the competitiveness of a national industry: Firm strategy, factor conditions, demand conditions and supporting industries.

Actually, Porter refers to the constellation of determinants as a system (Porter, 1990, 75) and he argues that the level at which this system works most strongly is national (and local) rather than international and global. Our approach is akin to Porter's in some respects but different in others. One might say that the basic elements overlap but that their ordering is different.

The main focus in this book is upon explaining learning and innovation and this corresponds to the creation of qualitatively new 'factor conditions'. We regard the economic structure (including 'demand conditions' and 'supporting industries') as one important determinant affecting these processes.

The second fundamental determinant of processes of learning is the institutional set-up and this includes 'firm strategy' – including modes of cooperation as well as competition.

The most important difference between our approach and Porter's may be the level of analysis. While Porter tends to present national systems as environments to single industries involved in international competition, our focus is upon the working of the national system in its own right.[11]

1.6.2. Different Methods to Analyse National Systems of Innovation

Most discussions of national systems of innovation have been connected to one single or to a comparison of a few specific country cases. In Nelson (1992) fourteen different country specific case studies are presented. One strength of that approach is that the stories told may reflect the complex historical interplay of social, institutional and cultural factors in shaping current systems (Edquist and Lundvall, 1992). The weakness might be the lack of a common and explicit theoretical basis and the fact that the elements brought into the analysis are idiosyncratic reflecting the special interests of each author.

In this book we do not recount any specific case stories even if we refer to relevant cases in order to illustrate some general points. Instead we have tried to present a theoretical perspective which might be used in case studies and to discuss some of the most important sub-systems in the system of innovation. The price we have to pay for choosing this more general approach is a loss in terms of historical richness, especially when it comes to the social and cultural dimensions.

This is the reason why we believe that, together, this book, Nelson (1992) and Porter (1990) may give a good starting point for future work on national systems of innovation.

1.6.3. Conclusions and Open Ends

We sum up collectively in a chapter by Dalum, Johnson and Lundvall (*chapter 14*). In this final chapter we tackle some open-ended and complex policy issues relating to the theme of the book. First, we discuss in general terms the limits for public policy intervention in an economy characterised by innovation and evolution. Second, we look more specifically at what kind of policy prescriptions may be distilled from the interactive learning approach. Finally, we discuss the need for international institutional learning and the role government may play in this context.

Part I:

TOWARD A NEW APPROACH TO NATIONAL SYSTEMS OF INNOVATION

Chapter 2

INSTITUTIONAL LEARNING

Björn Johnson

2.1. Introduction

Learning processes, leading to growth in the stock of knowledge, are basic in the dynamics of a modern economy.[1] It will be argued in this chapter that almost all learning processes are interactive, influenced, regarding their content, rate and direction, by the institutional set up of the economy.

When the economy is pictured more as a process of communication and cumulative causation than as an equilibrium system, i.e. from an institutional rather than a neoclassical point of view, learning can be conceptualised as the source of technical innovation. Innovation is then, too, regarded as a process rather than as discrete events uniquely localised in space and time. It follows, it will be argued, that innovation is shaped by institutions and institutional change. It will be suggested that this process can be analysed in terms of national systems of innovation, reflecting that nations differ in terms of institutional set-ups. Furthermore, it will be argued that the relations between institutions and innovation can change, sometimes fundamentally, over time.

Institutions have a strong impact on technical change. However, partly as a consequence of the technical change they shape, a tension between technology and institutions and a pressure for institutional change is often provoked. At the same time institutions are normally quite rigid and do not change easily. The capability of national economies to cope with this problem, i.e. to learn about, adapt and change their institutional frameworks – to engage in 'institutional learning' – is important for the development of their international competitiveness.

2.2. The Heritage from Veblen

The impact of institutions on technical change is not a new topic in economic analysis. The 'institutional drag' hypothesis for example, often, incorrectly, ascribed to Thorstein Veblen, is a classic, century old theme in institutional economics. The basic idea is, that institutional factors through their inertia and rigidity retard the dynamics of technical change. Institutions are regarded as inflexible, and institutional change is supposed to be lagging behind technical change. This creates mis-match problems, which often prevent the full realisation of the productive potential of new technologies.[2]

This hypothesis has lately been revived in different versions. In the analysis of economic policy in the OECD, at least two versions of the idea that institutions retard growth have appeared in the last decade or so. In a series of publications in the latter half of the 1970's, the 'institutional sclerosis' hypothesis was formulated (Johnson, 1981). The argument went, that due to political processes leading to a growing government sector and increasing trade union powers, rigidities were being built into the economic systems of the industrialised Western world, reducing their responsiveness to price signals. At the same time, however, the need for flexible economic systems was assumed to be more pressing than ever. International interdependence was increasing, and there was a strong need for adaptations to radically changing circumstances, including rising energy prices, increasing exports from NIC-countries and new technological opportunities. A growing conflict between an increasing need for change and a decreasing flexibility was assumed to lie behind poor macro-economic performance.

In a more recent analysis of the productivity growth slow-down during the 1970's and 1980's, it is suggested that there is an 'apparent disconnection of technological progress from growth' (OECD, 1987). It is also suggested that there is a need to 'adapt the social and institutional structures to the emerging new techno-economic system'. Rigid organisational structures in firms, inflexible cooperation patterns within and between firms, and inadequate science – and technology policies are supposed to be responsible for inefficiencies in the utilisation of new information technologies. An institutional-technological mis-match is seen as an important explanation of low growth rates in the OECD-area. Similar arguments can be found in the Sundqvist report (OECD, 1988), where lags in translating potential productivity gains stemming from technological advance, especially information technology, into actual productivity gains are associated with the absence of institutional and organisational adaptation.

These examples indicate that the institutional factor is now increasingly taken into account in analyses of technical change. In a way it is not surprising, that the interest in institutional theory is growing during a period, when information technologies are becoming more and more important and information handling activities constitute a growing part of the economy. As we shall see, institutions influence, in fundamental ways, information flows and learning. These influences go through many channels and have both stimulating and retarding effects. They differ between nations and change over time, and it is utterly misleading to reduce them to sclerotic phenomena of 'lagging' and 'dragging' in the innovation process.

2.3. How Institutions Learn

In this section is it is argued that institutions at a very basic level affect all cognitive processes. It will be discussed how learning, growth of knowledge and innovations are influenced by institutions. It is convenient to start with a discussion of the character and functions of institutions.

2.3.1. The Importance of Institutions

The concept of 'institutions' has been defined in many ways. In the institutionalist tradition in economic theory, however, the common idea has been, that societies are characterised by regularities of behaviour and that these are specific to time and place. Economic behaviour is thus instituted, not because of some universal human characteristics, but rather through a process of enculturation (Mayhew, 1987). Culture, which is a local phenomena, is taken as a core concept and its role in shaping human cognitions and actions is emphasised. This was described by Commons (1931) as 'collective control of individual action' and by Veblen (1919) as 'habits of use and wont', and 'habits of thought'.

The simplest form of behavioural regularities are habits. In order to deal with the complexity of everyday life, habits are formed. They provide us with a means of retaining a pattern of behaviour without engaging in global rational calculations involving a vast amount of complex information (Hodgson, 1988). Habits are important in economic analysis, because they relate to a large set of routinised behaviour in the economy. The importance of routines in economic processes was emphasised by Veblen, who actually defined institutions as an 'outgrowth of habit' (Veblen, 1919, 241), and is now increasingly recognised in economic theory, in large part thanks to the work of Nelson and Winter (1982).

When habits and routines become general, common to groups of people, they give rise to different kinds of social regularities in behaviour, such as norms, customs, traditions, rules and laws. These may be formal and explicit as, for example, many laws and administrative guidances, but often they are informal and implicit like common law, everyday customs and moral and social norms. The common feature is that they regulate how individuals and collective groups relate to each other.

An important quality common to different kinds of regularities in behaviour is that they function as informational devices, which reduce uncertainties. They make it unnecessary to start life from scratch every day. Every possible action in relation to other people does not have to be reflected on; we act in accordance with norms, customs, rules and so on. These are often widely accepted as guidelines for social life, even if not everybody subscribes to them ideologically or politically. In this way institutions make other peoples' and organisations' actions more predictable and actually provide information. They are 'signposts' for the relations between people and people (Lachmann, 1970).

It should be observed in this connection that institutions need not be politically neutral. They often signal established power relationships between people and they do not have to be efficient or optimal in any way. It is perhaps tempting to assume, for example, that institutions are normally effective in the sense that minor decisions get routinised, while major ones are deliberately and carefully made. Douglas (1987) sees no reason for such optimism, however:

> *There is no reason to believe in such benign dispensation. The contrary is more likely to prevail. The individual tends to leave the important decisions to his institutions while busying himself with tactics and details.*

The preceding paragraphs motivate the following broad definition: Institutions are sets of habits, routines, rules, norms and laws, which regulate the relations between people and shape human interaction. By reducing uncertainty and, thus, the amount of information needed for individual and collective action, institutions are fundamental building blocks in all societies.

To avoid misunderstandings it should be mentioned that post offices, labour unions, government agencies and other tangibles which are refered to as institutions in everyday speech are also institutions under the present definition. They may be refered to as 'formal institutions'. To say that a bank is a financial institution actually means that already institutionalised acts of borrowing and lending (i.e. borrowing and lending according to certain rules, keeping reserves, respecting certain norms for interest and debt payments and so on) have been formalised and organised by the creation of a bank.

2.3.2. Institutions, Stability and Change

Institutions exist because they serve, or have earlier served, some functions. Empty institutions seldom survive in the long run (Polanyi, 1957). At the most basic level the function of institutions is, as we have seen, the informational 'signpost' function. They hold images stable enough for communication to be possible. This can be divided into different subfunctions. Institutions reduce uncertainties, coordinate the use of knowledge, mediate conflicts and provide incentive systems. By serving these functions institutions provide the stability necessary for the reproduction of society. Therefore, there are also limits to how rapidly they can change without disrupting society. Inertia is a basic feature of institutions.[3]

At the same time, however, they are important for change in society. Basically, they provide the stability necessary for change. This is also true for technical change. First, a certain amount of stability is required for innovation along established technological trajectories. This process is usually more or less routinised, since businessmen and engineers tend to agree upon the directions in which technology could be further developed. It can to some extent be handled systematically and in organised forms, and this makes more concentrated efforts and more rapid progress possible.

Second, even radical innovations, diverging from technological trajectories, depend on institutionalised behaviour. The formal and informal rules – the habits of thought – in engineering and scientific work can be regarded as time saving devices, which set free resources for more creative activities aiming at radical innovations. A certain amount of 'innovational routine' increases the ability to handle major technological decisions.

That institutions provide the stability necessary for technical change does not mean, however, that the at any given point of time existing institutional set up necessarily promotes technical progress. Institutions provide both positive and negative incentives for technical change. There are often tensions between incremental technical change along established trajectories and the capability of doing radically new things. If the institutional set-up defines an incentive system, which may favour the established trajectories, it can become very costly for the economy in terms of stagnation and loss of international competitiveness, especially in a period when a new techno-economic paradigm is emerging (Perez, 1985a).

2.3.3. Institutions and the Growth of Knowledge

It has been argued above, that institutions not only provide stability to society and make its reproduction possible, but that they also set the preconditions for different forms of social change. Basically institutions influence change through their impacts on learning.

Institutions influence the growth of knowledge in many ways and on many levels. In fact, it is impossible for an individual to think and act in any specific field of the application of knowledge without being influenced by the institutional set-up.[4] Information is culturally processed: It is never transmitted raw but is selected, arranged and perceived through institutions (Hodgson, 1988).

This is one reason why institutions cannot be reduced to simple rigidities in the process of economic change. As long as information is imperfect and costly and information processing capacities limited, the individual's perception of the world matters. Since institutions are informational devices which govern these perceptions they are at the very heart of all learning processes. Social interaction helps individuals to form a conceptual basis necessary to understand, learn and act in a complex society.

This is strikingly formulated by Mary Douglas (1987). 'Institutions think', she says. We recognise, classify, remember and forget in accordance with institutions. Particular ideas and ideals dominate in particular institutional and cultural configurations. An 'instituted community', which could be a firm or a network of firms, has a profound influence on the learning going on within it. When, for example, a firm changes its work organisation or its relations to other firms, its learning processes are, necessarily, affected.

The point is, that institutions by governing the cognitive process in a fundamental way influence all learning processes in society. Not only is learning different in different historical epoches and in culturally divergent societies with radically different institutional settings, but since culture is a local phenomena, it may also differ between more closely related societies in the same period like for example Sweden and Denmark (Edquist and Lundvall, 1992).

2.4. Institutions and Learning in the Economy

In the following the discussion is concentrated on learning in the economic sphere of society. Knowledge used in the production process is called technology, and new (or recombined or rediscovered) knowledge, introduced into the economy, is called innovation. The question is: How do institutions affect innovation through learning processes in connection with production?

2.4.1. Institutions and the Accumulation of Knowledge

Since human knowledge does not exist all by itself, but is coded into the central nervous system of human beings, which have rather limited life spans, it may (with the exception of genetically coded knowledge) easily and quickly get lost and therefore has to be stored in one way or another. (Writing it into books is obviously not enough since books have to be read and understood in order not to be meaningless). In a society knowledge is stored in many ways, and institutions are important for determining how this is done. Rules, traditions, customs, norms and even habits help to transfer knowledge from one generation to the next. Some of this knowledge will prove conducive to the further development and accumulation of knowledge, while other parts of it may retard this process by preserving unproductive habits of thought. However, without the support of institutions knowledge probably could not accumulate at all. Society would not be able to 'remember', and would soon 'forget' what it had learnt.

A system of production, consisting of more or less interrelated firms, stores its knowledge in different ways. Some is stored in 'the book of blueprints' and some in the heads, hands and backbones of the individual producers in the form of both explicit and tacit knowledge. Firms use their governance structures and routines not only to coordinate and utilise person-bound knowledge, but also to store knowledge over time, independent of the individual 'knowledge holders'.

In economic production knowledge is thus stored, coordinated, transmitted and utilised with the support of institutions.[5] But, of course, the knowledge base of production is seldom just remembered and kept as it is. It tends to change, more or less as a normal outcome of production itself. Usually we presume, for both institutional and epistemological reasons, that learning is cumulative, so that the stock of knowledge is increasing over time. This need not be the case, however. To store knowledge requires continuous reinvestments in both human and physical capital. Economic knowledge, which is not actively remembered, deteriorates. Furthermore, knowledge can be destroyed quite quickly, for example by closing down an organisation. Knowledge is, thus, changed both by learning and by forgetting.

2.4.2. The Importance of Forgetting

In fact, forgetting is neither rare nor unimportant. Knowledge which is not institutionally supported, and does not fit into a cultural context, tends to be forgotten. (Douglas, 1987). Sometimes knowledge is destroyed very quickly and veritable bursts of forgetting have occurred several times in history, as for example through the demise of great cultures. In fact, every change of scientific or techno-economic paradigm, involves a lot of forgetting of knowledge and skills.

It is quite possible that the role of forgetting in the development of new knowledge has been underestimated. The enormous power of habits of thought in the economy constitutes a permanent risk for blocking potentially fertile learning processes. It may be argued that some kind of 'creative destruction of knowledge' is necessary before radical innovations can diffuse throughout the economy. Old habits of thought, routines and patterns of cooperation, within as well as between firms, have to be changed before technical change can begin to move ahead along new trajectories. Forgetting is, thus, an essential and integrated part of learning, even if it is not always easy to separate ex ante between 'creative forgetting' and 'just forgetting'.

The role of forgetting in the growth of knowledge is closely connected to the role of shutting down old activities in economic development. Economic development can be looked upon as an unfolding sequence of transformations at many levels of aggregation. Liquidation of existing activities is often a prerequisite for the development of new ones, not only at the firm level, in the form of bankruptcies and births of new firms, but also within firms. Departments are closed down. Production of specific commodities and the use of certain processes are stopped, and so on. Such liquidations are necessary for the firm in situations, where not even intense cost hunting would bring costs down to a level where existing products could be profitably sold, and because it is necessary to redirect human and physical resources in order to introduce innovations. Closing-down of activities are thus normal and integrated parts of economic development , and as an inherent part of this, skills, competence and knowledge are forgotten and lost.[6]

Even if closing-down is part and parcel of economic innovation, it is often difficult to handle in practice. It may be difficult to shut down activities and forget knowledge into which time, effort and prestige have been invested. As a rule this will psychologically, socially or economically affect at least some persons or groups negatively. This leads to conflict which often retards the process.

The difficulties connected with creative forgetting constitute a risk for irrational lock-in of resources. Tax rules, capital markets, the character of competition and ownership and other institutional factors affect how these questions are handled. It has been argued that the exit function of the capitalist market – firms going bankrupt – is a powerful institution for economic renewal. Recently, take-overs have been seen as an important means to cut through organisational rigidities and old loyalties in order to destroy old knowledge and competence, which restrict innovation.

None of these methods are without costs. It may be necessary to have strong institutions in order to guarantee a certain amount of creative destruction of knowledge. But such institutions do not necessarily imply high levels of social insecurity and unemployment. Both learning and creative forgetting may be aided by institutions which provide social security, at least if they also simplify and facilitate class – and interest-group compromises and consensus building. A further discussion of the policy implications is developed in chapter 14.

2.4.3. Different Kinds of Learning

When discussing the impact of institutions on learning it may be helpful to take into account that learning can have different motivations. It could be the 'idle curiosity', or the 'instinct of workmanship' of which Thorstein Veblen speaks. Or some kind of prestige, like the one bestowed upon successful researchers in the scientific community. Or it could be a pecuniary motive, such as the lure of profit and the fear of loss. Usually it is a mixture of different motives. Whatever the particular motive, however, it is clear that different societies have different learning incentives. Some societies have even punished aspirations for seeking new knowledge, and have considered knowledge as something which should be preserved but not increased.[7]

It may also be useful to take into account, that there are different kinds of learning, which involve different amounts of social interaction. Undoubtedly, there is some simple, individual and isolated imprinting of immediate experiences on the memory, but this is certainly not the most important form of learning. There is also rote learning, i.e. you learn by repetition, but you do not necessarily have to understand what you are doing. This usually involves observing and learning from other people and thus involves more human interaction than simple imprinting. A lot of learning is done by feedback, which involves still more interaction. We do, try, or say something and get a response from other people which tells us something about our first action and so on.[8] Finally there is systematic and organised searching for new knowledge. This is characteristic of the modern industrialised society, with its universities, different types of research institutes and R&D-departments. It involves intense and complex forms of interaction inside the research community as well as between this and other communities and individuals.

Since almost all learning is done by some form of interaction, it is shaped by institutions. It is a social process. It is seldom done individually, without support of, or isolated from, interpersonal relations. To observe nature and learn from it in splendid isolation is a rare form of learning. Not even Robinson Crusoe was very good at that. He was mostly experimenting with and using knowledge, he had acquired earlier in a social context.

2.4.4. Learning and Searching

Four types of learning, which can be arranged on a scale of increasing human interaction, have been mentioned: imprinting, rote learning, learning by feedback, and searching. The terms learning-by-doing, learning-by-using, and learning-by-interacting (Arrow, 1962, Rosenberg, 1982, Lundvall, 1985) also refer to activities which can be placed on a similar scale of interaction. The more learning can be achieved by simple repetition, and the more it can proceed without interpersonal communication, the more easily it can be routinised. If simple forms of communication, like orders from higher to lower levels, and messages from lower to higher levels are the dominant types of communication in production, it becomes relatively easy to 'go down the learning curve'.

Technical change, however, often requires dialogue or conversation, i.e. sequences of exchanges of messages between different people in different departments and at different levels, within firms and between firms. Furthermore, the more technically or scientifically advanced the innovations, the more complicated the communication processes they usually require.

A feature of modern economies is that they seem to gradually develop their capability to learn. Both basic and applied research is increasingly institutionalised and wedded to science through universities, research institutes, R&D departments and so on. This reflects that continuous and intense 'conversation' between people with different kinds of knowledge makes the professionalisation and organisation of learning necessary. Many economic activities are explicitly aiming at increased knowledge in order to stimulate innovation, and are organised accordingly. This is a special kind of learning – a subset of the total set of learning processes – and since it is a characteristic aspect of the knowledge-based economy, it is convenient to distinguish it from other learning activities. In the following it will be called 'learning by searching' or just 'searching'.

Modern firms often search systematically and in organised ways for new knowledge to be used in production, as new processes or new products. This searching is never totally 'unprejudiced'. It is restricted and channelled in different ways. First, to the extent that technical change is a rent seeking activity under competition, searching will always be conducted under some degree of concealment, so that the results from learning in one firm are not immediately accessible in other firms. Second, the specific combination of skills, education, knowledge, and experience which characterises the personnel of the R&D department of a firm, will influence the innovation process; the problems formulated, the methods chosen, and the solutions sought. Third, because of the particular technological opportunities and bottle-necks of the firm's product area, the searching is likely to follow specific technological trajectories (Dosi, 1988b, see also chapter 4 of this book). Past investments in human capital and physical production facilities tend to keep firms on existing trajectories, and these are further strengthened by attempts to reduce risks with respect to new investments. Fourth, the dominant 'techno-economic paradigm' influences learning and searching at all levels in society (Perez, 1985a). The habits of thought created by the dominant paradigm instruct researchers how to pose their problems and choose their methods, and they also hint at possible solutions.

This does not mean that all research is just as strongly bound by technological paradigms and trajectories. Basic research in non-profit organisations, like universities, may sometimes be able to cross these boundaries and temporarily ignore the potential economic usefulness of new knowledge. This kind of less economically goal-oriented searching is an important part of the total knowledge creating system, even when it does not produce any immediately useful results.

There are, thus, at least two kinds of professional and organised searching for new knowledge: The search activities organised in close connection with production and influenced by the commodity logic of the enterprise sector, and the less profit-oriented basic (re)search activities of universities and similar organisations. The latter may be called 'learning-by-exploring' or just 'exploring'. These two kinds of searching are, however, strongly interdependent, and the borderlines between them seem to be increasingly blurred.

New knowledge is also gained from economic activities which are *not* explicitly or primarily aiming at its generation. Learning is often connected to the routine procurement, production and sales activities of the firm, and to normal communication between firms. It is, then, rather a by-product of activities organised towards other aims. This might be called learning-by-producing, indicating that its basic components may be thought of as learning-by-doing, by-using and by-interacting in relation to normal production activities. Since this is a basic form of learning, which is present also in non-searching and non-exploring economies, it can for convenience simply be called 'learning'.

Learning and searching are not mutually exclusive activities, but are more like different segments on a scale. They are interdependent, and there are many mixed forms in between. On the one hand, routinised searching is certainly a possibility in modern production, especially in production areas where technological trajectories are well-established. Routines and habits of thought are important elements in research (Dosi, 1988b). On the other hand, repetitive production activities can be consciously and systematically monitored and controlled in order to increase product quality and stimulate innovations. They can be organised in ways that increase their learning potential.

It is important to observe, however, that both learning and searching develop from within the economy. They are built into the economy and shaped through institutions of different kinds. This makes innovation an endogenous process. Of course, many innovations, especially radical ones, can not be accounted for in this way but have to be seen as exogenous acts of creation. Nevertheless, the main argument in this chapter is that the ubiquitous and cumulative character of learning, searching and innovation can only be fully understood from an institutional perspective.

Figure 2.1 (disregarding several feed-back loops and interdependences) sums up the learning argument so far and, in addition, gives a simple picture of the long and uncertain process from learning to innovation: Interactive learning,

Figure 2.1. The Relations between Learning, Growth of Knowledge and Innovation.

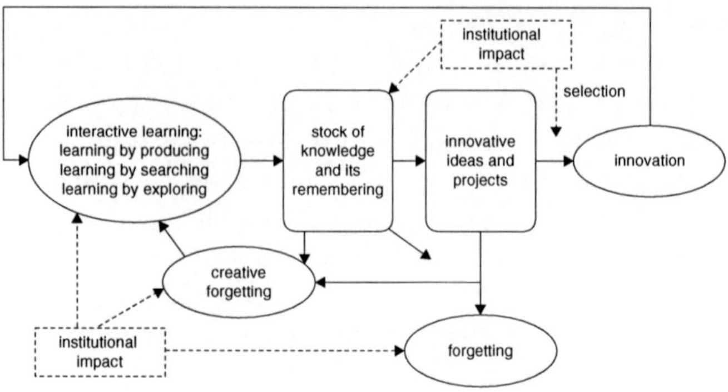

institutional impact

selection

interactive learning:
learning by producing
learning by searching
learning by exploring

stock of knowledge and its remembering

innovative ideas and projects

innovation

creative forgetting

institutional impact

forgetting

in the forms of learning-by-producing, learning-by-searching and learning-by-exploring, tends to increase the stock of economically useful knowledge. To keep this stock from deteriorating continual re-learning (or remembering), primarily 'remembering-by-doing', is necessary. The stock of knowledge tends to be diminished by different kinds of forgetting, but creative forgetting may actually establish a feed-back mechanism to learning and indirectly lead to increased knowledge. Parts of the new knowledge may under certain circumstances find its way into production in the form of innovations. This is far from an automatic process, however, which is illustrated in the figure by a 'selection mechanism' working on the set of innovative items and projects generated by new knowledge. The new knowledge has to be applicable in new processes or products, and management must realise these possibilities and have the means to exploit them. There must also be a market and an expected profit, i.e. the demand side and the appropriability possibilities are important. But even when all these conditions are fulfilled, luck and coincidental combinations of creativity may be necessary in order to take all the steps from learning to innovation. The 'flows' of learning, remembering and forgetting and the selection mechanism are all shaped by institutional factors (which will be further illustrated in section 2.4.5 below). Finally, the innovation process continually changes the conditions for interactive learning, which is illustrated by the long feed-back arrow.

2.4.5. The Roots of Innovation

Innovations are rooted both in the production structure and the institutional set-up of the economy. If innovation reflects learning, and if learning is interactive, it follows that innovation is rooted in the institutional set-up of the economy. And if learning partly emanates from routine activities in economic production, innovation must also be rooted in the prevailing economic structure, since different technological opportunities, income elasticities and linkages between industries make learning in some industries and periods much easier than in other industries and periods. Thus, both the institutional and the structural impact suggest, that the innovation process has deep roots in the history of the economy. (The structural factors, which are, largely, ignored in this chapter, are discussed in chapter 4).

A few illustrations may clarify how institutional factors influence learning. It is suggested here, that the degree to which different skills and types of knowledge are brought together to bear on each other is an utterly important factor in the learning process. In fact, this is the main reason why learning is predominantly interactive. Innovation may accordingly be viewed as basically a collective activity; an outcome of communication and interaction between people. The following illustrations reflect the increasing importance of interactive learning in modern firms, which partly follows from the development of information and communication technologies.

It may be convenient in these illustrations to distinguish between institutional factors on different levels of aggregation. It is suggested, that both the regularities of behaviour embedded in the organisational structure of the individual firm and the organised markets between firms influence learning, since this directly affects the communication and interaction pattern in the economy.[9] Learning is also influenced by institutional factors at the national level. We may think of an institutional infrastructure having an indirect but strong effect on learning and forgetting in the economy.

Communication and interaction inside firms depends on many factors. For example: Intensified quality control may lead to more efficient diagnoses of problems in production. On the job training may be designed to increase workers' abilities to identify problems. Job rotation implies that different persons with different skills observe the same production activities, thereby increasing the probability for problem identification and incremental innovation. Several authors (Aoki, 1986, 1990b, and Freeman, 1987), have underlined the importance of institutionalised communication between procurement departments, production departments, marketing departments and R&D departments and other types of established horizontal information flows.

Interactive learning, including elements of creative forgetting, may be seriously hampered if, for example, the norms and habits of workers make them reluctant to communicate and cooperate with other 'levels' of the firm. Factors like trust and legitimacy, which may depend on institutional factors like participation and job security, as well as suitable procedures for reaching compromises, are important here. Tight and intense work supervision might reduce workers' willingness to interact positively in an innovation process. Traditional barriers between different skill groups and conflicts over the distribution of power and income, both in individual firms and in society at large, tend to make communication more difficult.

Communication and interaction between firms, i.e. forward, backward and horizontal linkages and other types of out-of-firm communication and cooperation, feed much of the learning needed for innovation. Product innovation is more difficult without a feed-back of user-experiences (see chapter 3). The involvement of suppliers in manufacturing processes gives them a better idea of the equipment they are to deliver, which facilitates process innovation. Close and intense user-producer relations have proved to be effective in promoting incremental innovation in Japanese industries and a central idea behind 'technology management' (*Economist,* December, 1989). The Nordic Innovation Survey (Nordic Industrial Fund, 1991) shows, that customers are an important source of product-innovation ideas in Scandinavian firms. Universities and R&D-institutions are also frequently mentioned in this connection. The survey also shows, that virtually all large firms and most small and medium sized firms with R&D activities also engage in out-of-firm R&D-cooperation. The ability to establish, break up and re-establish out-of-firm relations and to cooperate in more or less formal networks for knowledge exchange (see chapter 6) seems to be essential for technological dynamism.

There are also many factors in the institutional system outside the enterprise sector which are important for learning. Some of these are of a basic, though sometimes intangible and informal, character and may be regarded as elements of an *institutional infrastructure.* It is difficult to single out the most important elements of this, but one should mention the educational infrastructure, including the institutions for the development of both school-bound and workplace-based skills, and both theoretical and vocational training. It is obvious, for example, that the organisation and culture of engineering schools – their heuristic routines, their norms about 'man-tool' relationships and about proper relationships between engineers, foremen and workers, their ideologies about the relations between different kinds of technical and economic competence and between science, technology and production, etc. – influence the technical learning processes also beyond the education system; in firms and organisations. One should also mention the communications infrastructure, for example the road, rail, air and telecommunication networks, and, of course, the incentive system; where, in what ways and how much does it pay to learn?

In addition, many social norms should be included in the institutional infrastructure affecting learning. One might mention norms about conflict, consensus and cooperation at all levels of the economy, which influence many institutions of economic and industrial democracy, labour market institutions, corporatist institutions and so on. The degree of 'opportunist behaviour' in the relations between different agents is also important in this context.

So far the illustrations have been of a supply side character. *The demand side*, however, remains important, even if it is often difficult to make a clear distinction between demand and supply sides in connection with technical change. Innovation is, for example, influenced by the appropriation of the benefits of innovation. Since different people and groups of people normally interact in innovation processes, the distribution of benefits and costs and opportunities and risks, influence these processes. It will influence the information communicated, the interaction undertaken and the efforts put into these activities.

The appropriation possibilities depend on norms of distribution and property rights. The question of standards, enforcement and dispute settlement for intellectual property rights, i.e. the ownership of information, ideas and knowledge, has become an area of intense institutional development. The three basic types of protection of intellectual property – patents, copyrights, and trademarks – are all important for technical learning, and have for some time been in flux, both due to a lively court activity and due to international negotiations under the GATT, to cope with new technologies like computer software and bio-technology.

The illustrations above have primarily refered to learning by producing, but the same main groups of factors that influence learning also influence searching and exploring. The role of formal institutions (in comparison with informal institutions) may be more obvious in the latter case, however.

As examples of such formal institutions we may mention 'in-house' *R&D departments*, which organise and to some extent routinise research activities (see chapter 9). The productivity of R&D departments is strongly influenced by informational interfaces inside the firm and by relations to other firms.

Extramural R&D organisations, for example at branch levels, are growing in number and illustrate the increasing importance of interorganisational communication and cooperation.

Universities and other organisations for basic research, engineering schools and so on are important parts of the formal institutional infrastructure, which affects searching in a modern economy.

Bridging mechanisms between science and technology are of crucial importance in a knowledge-based society (Dosi, 1988b). Government laboratories, public or semi-public laboratories, science parks and technopolises, where researchers from universities and private firms can meet, demonstrate an increasing awareness of this phenomenon.

The interface between science and technology involves interactions between different modes of behaviour reflecting not only differences in routines, heuristics and decision-making methods, but also in values and incentive systems. Such a clash between different modes of behaviour and habits of thought may stimulate creativity. Creative processes can be looked upon in terms of dynamic synergy between people with different information, skill, knowledge, competence, incentives and values. Such communication and interaction seems to increase the probability for unforeseen new combinations and for discoveries to occur, i.e. it may generate unexpected novelty. It may also increase the capacity to utilise such unexpected novelty, which is of course fundamental in the innovation process (Anderson, 1985). To be sure, such communication is not easy, and it is often blocked by the use of different languages and codes of communication and by different habits of thought and other cultural differences.

The examples above illustrate some institutional impacts on learning processes. They also illustrate, indirectly, that learning differs very much between countries. It is easy to see, that all these institutional factors vary substantially from country to country. From an institutional point of view it is evident that societies, which differ with respect to educational and communication infrastructures, incentive systems, the ways in which conflicts between groups and classes are coped with, ways of thinking and cooperating and so on, also learn and search differently in their production organisations.

2.5. The Importance of Institutional Diversity

A 'learning perspective' on innovation is closely related to an evolutionary perspective, in which technological change is looked upon as an open-ended, cumulative sequence of events, containing a certain element of randomness or chance. In this perspective the diversity of the institutional system and of the production structure becomes important.

It is a basic proposition in evolutionary theory that the diversity of a system affects its development. Diversity is generated by some mechanism, for example mutations in biological systems and innovations in economic systems, and a selection mechanism in combination with an 'inheritance' mechanism for remembering new traits, for example natural selection or economic competition, changes the relative importance over time of the surviving diversities. In Darwinian evolutionary theory the generation of diversity is blind and independent of the selection process. This is not the case in an economic system. Innovation is not totally random, but an integrated part of economic activity.

Generally speaking, diversity affects innovation because it affects technical, organisational and institutional learning and contributes to the knowledge base of the economy. Technical diversity means, that different product– and process technologies, representing different kinds of knowledge, are present in the economy. Diminishing this diversity means destroying parts of the economy's stock of knowledge and reducing the number of technical options, which are immediately open. It also means decreased possibilities for communication and interaction between different kinds of skills, knowledge, and competence and, thus, reduced learning possibilities. Diversity generates novelty and affects the learning capability of the economy.

There are different kinds of diversity, which are relevant from an innovation point of view: There is diversity in products and production processes, and there is diversity in modes of organisation and institutions. Diversity in the institutional system is just as important for economic change as diversity in the production structure. According to Hodgson's (1988) impurity principle pure economic systems, for example pure market economies and totally planned economies, wouldn't be viable. Some impurities in the form of co-existing structures from different systems are necessary for any economic system to operate and reproduce itself through time. Hodgson views economic systems as 'diversified pluralities' of different institutions and points out that all known economic systems in history have been mixed systems. The feudal system did not consist exclusively of serf-lord relationships, but also contained urban guilds, clerical hierarchies and markets. The Eastern European socialist economies, as long as they existed, contained market exchange and traditional forms of production and distribution alongside the system of planning, and so on. This is not just a historical coincidence, but a functional necessity. Impurities are necessary for socio-economic systems to be able to cope with change in a world of uncertainty.

Systems have to cope with disturbances and threats from their environments and from within themselves. Fluctuations in world markets, innovations, political movements, ecological stress and so on are often quite unpredictable. No system can cope with any possible kind of disturbance (the law of insufficient variety, see Hodgson, 1988), but systems with a lower degree of diversity or rather, with a lower capacity to generate new diversity, are more vulnerable. Flexibility depends on a diversity generating mechanism, and the significance of impurity is that it increases this capacity. Generation of diversity is a way to handle uncertainty and works as a shock absorber. Pure market economies would, if they existed, not last very long, because they would contain too little diversity to survive in a world of uncertainty.[10]

In addition to the structural and institutional diversity of an economy there is also a kind of 'second order' diversity. There is not only a diversity in products, production processes, organisational forms and institutions playing its part in one over-all process of technical change. There are also several local processes of technical change going on at the same time; a diversity of (modes of) innovation.

2.6. National Systems of Innovation

It is of course not at all obvious from which level of aggregation this diversity of innovation should be considered. We can think of the international economy as containing several regional innovation patterns, for example a Japanese, an American and an European one. Or we could try to identify national modes of innovation within the European economy. Or we could search for a diversity of local innovation patterns within national economies, sometimes, of course, finding that such patterns may cross national borders but still remain local in character. And we could identify enterprise-specific innovation styles as part of a 'corporate culture' and maybe even several competing modes of innovation in the same company as reported for both Japanese and American corporations (*Economist*, 7–13 July, 1990).

In this book, however, it is suggested, that it is often possible to identify 'national systems of innovation'. It is suggested, that the national economy in some important respects is a relevant environment for a system of innovation. This does not rule out, that other regional delimitations may be relevant as environments for innovation, or that some innovation activities may be rather footloose. But since nations differ, both with respect to how their institutional systems influence innovation, and with respect to the economic structure defining technological opportunities and bottle-necks, it is possible to look upon Europe, for example, as a diversity of national systems of innovation. In this context a 'national system of innovation' simply means all interrelated, institutional and structural factors in a nation, which generate, select, and diffuse innovation.

2.6.1. The Nation as a Framework for Interactive Learning

There are several kinds of institutional differences between nations which matter in relation to technical innovation. As long as we can identify *national cultures*, we should expect national differences in production and innovation. Even if neoclassical theory describes firms as rather simple input-output relations (production functions), they are in reality organisations which combine different kinds of knowledge and skills through a process of communication. Modern production is an organised process, which relies heavily upon behavioural regularities.

Culture makes nations with the same kind of economic system, for example Denmark, Sweden and Germany, different from each other, and cultural systems are governed by rules and rules about rules, including rules for breaking and changing rules. Many of these rules apply to economic production. Who can decide what? What remunerations are to be expected for different kinds of work? What efforts and what kinds of communication and cooperation will be expected in different situations? Such questions would be impossible to answer and uncertainties would take inhibiting proportions, if production was not heavily supported by different kinds of formal and informal rules. Many of the rules supporting production differ between countries and since communication within a common culture is easier than between different cultures, we should expect the differences between national cultures to have considerable staying power.

National ideologies may also be important. Lodge (Lodge and Vogel, 1987) suggests that a nation often has a rather stable, common ideology. He argues that there are ideological differences between nations; that for example Japan's national ideology is more communitarian than that of the USA, which is more individualistic, and that it is an advantage for a nation to have a coherent and adaptable ideology. Such national ideologies influence communication, interaction and learning at all levels of society.

National government obviously also matters. It imposes standards and regulations, making interaction more efficient, and it is responsible for the communications infrastructure and the formal educational system (see chapter 9).

The importance of the state basically follows from its unique power to define and supervise the institutions of property rights. Thereby it influences the total incentive system and the appropriability of technical innovations, permitting and protecting them as rent-yielding assets.

In most countries the government also has responsibility for the regulation of money and banking with important effects on the financing of innovative activities (see chapter 8), and, of course, the government regulates the level of aggregate demand and is an important buyer of new services and products (chapter 7). In all these aspects there are significant differences between nations.

2.6.2. National Performance and National System of Innovation

Differences in national economic performance motivate comparative studies, attempting to locate the sources of these differences. Recently, the interest for the Japanese system of innovation has been growing (Freeman, 1987), and it seems, as if the Japanese system has some characteristics, which are important in relation to interactive learning.

At the level of the single corporation, it has been observed that a new mode of intra-organisational coordination is emerging in many Japanese firms (chapter 5). Organisation increasingly relies upon participatory communication and cooperation between workers and shops, in contrast to traditional, more hierarchical, structures and there is a tendency to use the factory as a laboratory.

Another, more controversial, element is the, supposed, broader involvement of Japanese employees in processes of technical and organisational change.

Recently it has been suggested that this is not just an Oriental cultural phenomenon, but that 'it also reflects a rational response of universal relevance by competing firms to their changing environment' (Aoki, 1990b). Advancements in information technologies, increasing global competition in which flexibility and innovation are conditions for survival, and increasing levels of education and training of the labour force are mentioned as elements in this changing environment. This may indicate that Japanese firms have been first to introduce the elements of a new, generally valid, techno-economic paradigm.

The markets are, according to some studies, organised to a higher degree in Japan than in USA and Western Europe. Loyalty and voice are important elements in interaction, and users and producers do not change their mutual relationships, readily, when relative prices change. Japanese firms also seem to use feed-back from user-experiences far more systematically and in more organised ways in innovation processes. Furthermore, the time horizon in capital accumulation also seems to be longer in Japan, permitting a longer view on user-producer interactions in innovation processes.

The role of MITI has also been presented as an important characteristic of the Japanese system of innovation. It is interesting to note that Imai (1986) attributes the success of industrial targeting in Japanese economic policy to MITI's efforts at consensus building through promotion of intense information exchanges. Different forums for public-private consultations through so-called deliberation councils (shingikai), especially the Industrial Structure Council, seem to have been important here (Johnson, C., 1986). The high degree of communitarianism in Japan's national ideology has probably also been a supporting factor in this respect (Lodge and Vogel (eds.), 1987).

Together, these factors point to important 'communication economies'. The institutional system forms a framework for interactive and collective learning, which may give Japan competitive advantages in a period of rapid technological change. Sometimes this system is also presented as an ideal from which important parts could be copied and imported to other countries. This possibility is far from obvious, however. Institutional borrowing is a much more complicated thing than technical borrowing and it is often easier to learn from comparisons of similar systems, than of vastly different ones (Johnson, 1974). The differences between, for example, the Swedish and the Danish systems of innovation are considerable in spite of the similarities in history, culture and social policy. The earlier often celebrated Nordic model in reality consisted of several different national models, the Swedish model, the Danish model and so on, quite different both in terms of economic structure and institutional set up (Mjøse, 1986 and Edquist and Lundvall, 1992).

A recent comparison of Danish and Dutch waste-water treatment illustrates that small and not very well-known institutional differences may have important effects on innovational performance (Andersen, M.S., 1991). Environmental taxes are becoming more and more popular (OECD, 1989a). These are often looked upon as an alternative to direct administrative regulation of environmental standards. Such standards are relatively high in both Holland and Denmark. For twenty years Denmark has, on the whole, favoured direct regulation, while Holland has relied upon taxes. Both countries have succeeded in making their waste-water from industries and population concentrations significantly cleaner. Only Holland, however, has reduced the water volume, through increasing application of cleaner technologies. The Danish emission of waste-water has increased slightly over the last twenty years, while the quantity has been reduced to about twenty per cent of its former level in Holland.

The Dutch relative success is not explicable as simply a result of the polluter-pays-principle on production technologies. In addition M.S. Andersen (1991) refers to the specific institutions for the administration of the system. Four hundred year old local 'water guilds', which are corporative organs, are, together with the Rijkswaterstaat in the ministry of communication, responsible for this administration. In stark contrast to the Danish situation, Holland's long tradition in dealing with water problems and a unique combination of old and new institutions has been able to make the tax system function as a clear incentive for technological change and not just as an extra economic burden on firms and municipalities.

From the crude institutional assumptions of mainstream economics (competitive markets) follow a tendency to neglect or underestimate the institutional variety within the family of developed capitalist economies. A serious analysis of this variety is a precondition for a better understanding of the significant differences in economic performance within this group of countries, and in the present period of radical techno-economic change such an understanding may be more important than ever.

2.7. Institutional Learning in a Period of Radical Technical Change

The innovation process does not only differ between regions in economic geography. It is also subject to 'regions of time' (Boulding, 1991). Because of the cumulative character of technical learning in combination with the interdependences between institutions and technologies, it is probably impossible to find an institutional system, that would permanently guarantee an innovative economy. Institutions which stimulate innovations in one period may retard them in a later one.

A given system of institutions may affect innovations very differently, depending on the nature of the particular technologies, and on the stages of development of the technological trajectories in question. In order to be able to stimulate technical change over longer stretches of time, institutions have to change. During the Fordist growth period, for example, innovations depended on an institutional system which was very different from the one which would stimulate technical change in the present period (Perez, 1985a). In the present situation, when technological possibilities are still in a flux, and technological trajectories not firmly established, the openness and diversity of learning processes are of central importance for technical innovation. Some destruction of knowledge from the Fordist technological paradigm is necessary, and searching may have to be intensified in several directions, before routinised learning can again expand along the trajectories of a new paradigm. The flexibility of the institutional system becomes crucial.

The new information– and communication technologies represent a qualitative shift in technological opportunities, which, at least for a period of time, increases the level of technological uncertainty. This is felt at many levels. At the firm level uncertainties about investments in equipment and human capital and about organisational factors increase. At the interfirm level uncertainties about for example user-producer relationships increase, and at the national level uncertainties about economic policies become unusually high.

Some recent studies of Danish industrial firms seem to be in accordance with a hypothesis of increased technical uncertainty (Industrirådet, 1986, Broman, 1988 and Gjerding et al., 1990). In one study it is shown that in spite of an increasing awareness of the importance of interaction within and between firms in the innovation process, many firms have great problems with introducing microelectronics based production technologies. Introduction of these new technologies seems to be regarded as a kind of necessity. Often, firms are not able to form clear profit expectations in relation to innovations, but nevertheless consider them as conditions for survival. A vaguely perceived need for increased flexibility seems to be the motive behind the investments. In many cases, however, firms have not been able to handle questions of organisational change and manpower planning and education in connection with the new technologies. In some cases rapid expansions of investments in new production equipment actually resulted in decreased productivity for a period of several years in the 1980's (Gjerding et al., 1990).

It seems as if rigid habits and routines, and rigid patterns of interaction inside and between firms, can seriously hurt the ability of an economy to introduce and diffuse new technologies. A flexible institutional system, however, might bring the skills, experience and knowledge of different people, organisations and government agencies together, and get them to interact in new ways, stimulating innovation processes (Johnson, 1986, 1988). Institutional restructuring of an economy to preserve, reshape or strengthen its technical learning ability in a period of radical technical change is certainly not an automatic or costless process. Comparative studies of national systems of innovations might, however, be a way to facilitate institutional learning and clarify the possibilities of institutional borrowing between countries. (The policy implications of this will be pursued in chapter 14).

In this context it should be noted that there is a difference, and possibly a conflict, between institutionalising stable behaviour patterns and institutionalising continuous changes in behaviour. An innovative economy has to strike a balance between these two kinds of institutionalisations. An institutional system which effectively stimulates technical change may, for example, be worse at stimulating cost-efficient production methods. (The character of this dilemma at the enterprise level is discussed in chapter 5).

Learning how to learn accelerates innovation and may give competitive advantage, but there are also limits to how fast changes can be introduced without damaging the coherence of the institutional system supporting the innovation process (Johnson, 1988). Normally institutional change is rather incremental and slow because of the inertia of the many informal and culturally transmitted elements in the institutional set-up (North, 1990). As innovation is becoming more and more important, as a factor of competition, it is crucial for nations participating in the international division of labour to be able to create norms, habits of thought, ways of cooperating, job security mechanisms and so on, which reduce the social and human costs of living in a state of permanent rapid change.

Chapter 3

USER-PRODUCER RELATIONSHIPS, NATIONAL SYSTEMS OF INNOVATION AND INTERNATIONALISATION

Bengt-Åke Lundvall

3.1. Introduction

In neoclassical trade theory the so-called primary factors of production, capital and labour, are treated as strictly national assets, assumed not to cross national borders. Technology, on the other hand, is assumed to be a transnational resource, moving freely across borders. The only fundamental difference between national systems is the difference in factor proportions, and export and import specialisation reflects nothing but such differences.

One way to restate this model would be to propose a more restricted mobility of technology, and to treat investments in R&D on par with investments in factories and machinery. However, the national system of innovation would still be of very limited analytical interest in this extended model. The only new variables to be considered would be the stock and the rate of investment in R&D.

3.1.1. The National System of Innovation and the Fundamental Neoclassical Assumptions

In order to see, why the national system of innovation is a useful analytical concept, a more radical revision of basic neoclassical assumptions is necessary. In a world where agents are perfectly rational (maximisers of utility and profit, with unlimited access to information, and an unlimited capacity to gather and process information) and where all transactions take place in pure markets, with anonymous relationships between buyers and sellers, national borders play a limited economic role. In such a world, it is legitimate to assume that institutional and cultural differences between nations do not to interfere with economic processes.

In order to clarify the significance of national systems of innovation the assumptions of homogeneous and perfectly rational agents, and pure markets, have to be revised. What makes national systems of innovation important, is that markets are *organised* differently in different national systems, and that the behaviour of agents belonging to different systems is governed by different rules and norms reflecting differences in the institutional set-up, as discussed in chapter 2.

3.1.2. Introducing Innovation and Interactive Learning

Conversely, the need for a radical revision of the assumptions on perfect rationality, and pure markets, becomes clear when the focus is shifted from allocation and commodity exchange towards innovation. In a stationary world where the central economic activity is exchange of use values with constant characteristics, a theoretical construct assuming perfect rationality might be regarded as a useful abstraction. In such a stationary context it would also be legitimate to assume transactions to take place in pure markets with anonymous relationships between buyers and sellers.

An 'innovation as an interactive process-perspective' brings two crucial new elements into the analysis. The first is, of course, uncertainty reflecting change and growing complexity. Innovation involves by definition the creation of qualitatively different, new things and new knowledge. Therefore, agents involved in the creation and adoption of innovations cannot reasonably be assumed to know all the possible outcomes of their activities.

3.1.3. Differentiated Rationality in the Innovative Economy

But if rationality is bounded, we cannot insist upon homogeneity in the rules of behaviour followed by agents. If we want to specify the behaviour of agents it is not sufficient to characterise them as 'rational', any more. Behaviour must be further specified and this specification might take into account that agents differ in several respects.

Their attention might be directed differently. For example, some agents will focus upon financial variables while others concentrate upon the use value dimension of the production process. The time horizons of agents might differ; some agents might focus upon the near, while others focus upon the distant future. Motivation and effort might, even when material incentives are identical, be stronger or weaker when engaging in economic activities. The competence of agents might vary, reflecting specialised talent and accumulated learning or experience. The way a given problem is tackled might diverge and reflect cultural context and historical experience. Finally, agents might be more or less honest/opportunist in dealing with other agents. In an uncertain world it might be impossible to say, what is the most (or the least) rational behaviour from the viewpoint of the single agent. Typically, it will depend upon the context in which agents act and interact.

3.1.4. Interactive Learning and the Limits of Instrumental Rationality

The second new element, introduced by the innovation perspective, is a change of focus from a process of calculation and decision making, towards a process of interactive learning and creation.[1] If technologies were stationary it would be reasonable to assume that agents concentrate on making successful transactions, and to regard them as calculating 'Cartesians'.

Introducing interactive learning makes it necessary to reconsider the assumptions concerning the rationality of agents. If what economic agents do in the economic sphere is mainly to make decisions on the basis of price signals, assumptions presenting them as calculating and maximising individuals might catch the most important aspects of their behaviour (This is the argument of Hicks for assuming rational behaviour in the economic sphere – see Klamer, 1989). But in the knowledge-intensive economy, agents will be involved more or less permanently in processes of interactive learning sometimes demanding cooperation and sometimes involving the collective creation of complex new knowledge, and this may give rise to and reinforce other norms of behaviour.

Actually, interactive learning is seriously undermined if parties act exclusively from the view-point of calculation and maximising. (Think of the efficiency of an inter-firm cooperative R&D-lab where the scientists use most of their limited intellectual and spiritual energy on maximising the return for their mother company). Individual agents and organisations less governed by instrumental rationality and acting according to other sets of social norms including, for example, idle curiosity or mutual respect and trust will be more successful than the purely calculative ones.

However, to say that it is 'rational' (for the individual or for collectives of individuals) not to be 'instrumental' in such contexts does not dissolve the complexity of the matter. The 'efficiency' of social norms would be rather limited if they were chosen or selected just because they are rational for the individual, or for the economy as a whole. Their viability and strength reflect that they are founded in extra-economic and 'irrational' spheres of society (Elster, 1989). As pointed out by Arrow (1971), it is impossible to buy trust and if you could buy it, it would be of little value. The point to be made here is that the ubiquitous presence of interactive learning in the economy will support the viability of and reinforce social norms which transcend instrumental rationality.

Not only does innovation imply uncertainty and thus bounded and differentiated rationality. Actually, it points towards a break with a instrumental and strategic rationality. 'Discursive rationality' (Habermas, 1984) might be more typical for processes of interactive learning than instrumental rationality. This allows for a strong impact of culture on the process of economic change. Specifically, it makes it relevant to consider how different national systems foster agents with different social norms, and how this may be reflected in differences in the innovative capability of national systems.

3.1.5. Innovation, Culture and International Differences

Of course, no economist would deny the existence of institutional and cultural differences between nations. What is controversial, however, is if such differences matter when it comes to the analysis of national economic performance, and if the costs in terms of complexity and loss of generality for bringing them into view, should not be regarded as prohibitive. This chapter argues that models ignoring such differences will be misleading when it comes to explaining important contemporary phenomena in the international economy.

It will be shown that product innovations tend to take place in organised markets and in an interaction between users and producers.[2] Important in this interaction is the flow of qualitative information. Unlike price signals and other one-dimensional concepts such information cannot be transformed into 'bits of information'. Therefore communication (the development of a common language etc.) and the 'distance' between users and producers will affect the processes of interactive learning involved.

More important than geographical-physical distance will be cultural distance. For reasons already alluded to, communication and cooperation between parties belonging to different social and cultural systems will always be difficult. This will be the case especially when it comes to complex and uncertain processes like innovation. This is one fundamental reason why it is meaningful to define and analyse *national* systems of innovation. While the extension of market transactions of mature and standardised commodities may be regarded as a phenomenon coupling and bringing closer together different cultures, an increasing importance of innovation and technological competition will reinforce the importance of national and local economic systems.

3.1.6. Outline of the Chapter

The chapter is divided into three main parts. In the first part it is demonstrated why product innovation implies organised markets.

In the second part different dimensions of space and distance are introduced in relation to stable technology, incremental innovation, radical innovation and technological revolution, respectively. It is concluded that only standardised and stable technologies should be regarded as being close to the internationally, footloose technology, assumed in neoclassical models of international trade.

In the last part untraditional assumptions regarding the rationality of agents are introduced into the analysis of international user-producer interaction. What happens if national systems differ in terms of how the rationality of agents is specified? In order to illustrate the relevance of this question, two different specifications are introduced; one involving honest and trusting rational behaviour – characterising the H-economy – and another involving opportunistic and sceptical rational behaviour – characterising the O-economy.

3.2. Product Innovations and Organised Markets

Product innovations are not easily integrated in formal economic models and they have been more or less neglected in economic theory. In contrast, here product innovations will be put at the very centre of analysis. One of the themes to be discussed is how this change in perspective affects our understanding of markets versus organisations.

It should be observed that the analysis refers primarily to interactive processes where both parties are professional units (private firms or public organisations). One reason for this restriction is that 'needs' becomes a fuzzy concept when private consumers are involved (Mowery and Rosenberg, 1979).

It should also be observed that the perspective is rather abstract and that many interesting complications have been neglected. For example, it is obvious that importing units are often independent trading companies which mediate between a foreign producer and a domestic user. Here it is assumed that the buyer and the user are unified in one single unit.

Another complication not reflected in the analysis is the nature of the product; is it machinery, components, materials or services? The gist of the argument is best understood if we think of the product as a technical system such as either a component, a piece of machinery or a plant, or as a software system but, with some modifications, the approach will also be valid for materials, services and other intangibles. For example, I have argued that the relationships between universities which produce basic and applied science and industry as a user of science may be fruitfully analysed as one specific form of user-producer interaction (Lundvall, 1985).

3.2.1. Two Fundamental Starting Points

Behind what follows lies two observations. The first is that innovation is an ubiquitous process going on almost everywhere, and almost all the time. The second is that modern society is characterised by a highly developed, vertical

division of labour. Most activities aiming at innovation take place in the
formal sector of the economy, where producers produce, not for themselves,
but for others.

As we shall see, just by combining these two elementary observations, several
interesting questions regarding the institutional set-up of the economy may be
raised. Will perfect competition and pure markets – the ideal institutional set-up
for the allocation of given resources – be ideal, also, when it comes to bring
forward new ideas and materialise them into new products adapted to the needs
of potential users? Are there any mechanisms automatically selecting the optimal
combination of markets and organisations?

3.2.2. Innovation as a Collision between Needs and Opportunities

The scientist who develops new instruments for his own use, in order to be able
to pursue a specific experiment in his laboratory, knows better than anyone else,
which needs the instruments should address and satisfy. He/she will also have a
better insight into the new use value characteristics of the resulting innovation
than anyone else. Here insights about needs and technical opportunities are
combined in one single person.

The R&D-laboratory engaged in the development of new process
equipment, and the production department in the same firm, are already, in a
more difficult situation. A reciprocal flow of qualitative information, with
regard to technical opportunities and user needs, must connect the two
departments. How to efficiently organise this relationship is not a simple matter
(see also chapter 5).

But the problem of organising co-ordination and exchange of qualitative
information will be even more difficult, when the innovating producer
and the potential user belong to two different organisations, separated by
a market. Therefore, it seems paradoxical that such a large proportion of
innovative activities measured both as input (the proportion of R&D, oriented
towards product innovations, registered in the OECD-statistics), and as
output (proportion of important innovations, used by firms and sectors,
separate from the innovating units – see Pavitt, 1984), aim at or result in
product innovations. How can the producer know the needs of potential
users, when markets separate users from producers? And, how can the
potential user get information about the specific characteristics of a new
product?

In order to answer these questions it is useful to proceed step by
step, starting with the pure market, as presented in standard economic
textbooks.

3.2.3. The Pure Market and the Transaction Cost Approach

It is obvious that product innovations would be rare and accidental, if markets were characterised by anonymous relationships between producers and users. Producers would have difficulties in observing new user needs, and users would lack qualitative information on the characteristics of the new products.

Although the pure market is presented as the ideal norm in the neoclassical analysis of allocation, it represents an institutional set-up, hostile to innovation. The neoclassical theoretical scheme is perhaps best understood as reflecting an economy, where innovation is a marginal and accidental phenomenon, only affecting process technology. In such an economy, the pure market might survive. And, conversely, pure markets would effectively block product innovations, and reinforce the stationary character of the economy.

Another way to analyse the institutional implications of product innovations, would be in terms of transaction costs.

When new products are continuously introduced in markets, fundamental uncertainty would prevail. This uncertainty would be built into the commodity itself and information impactedness/asymmetry, reflecting that the producer knows more about the characteristics of the new product than potential users, while lacking knowledge about user needs, would be a typical phenomenon.

As a consequence, according to the original Williamson-approach to transaction costs (Williamson, 1975), we would expect vertical integration to take place whenever product innovations are frequent and important. Product innovations would disappear, as they were gradually transformed into process innovations through vertical integration. This analysis leads us, as did the pure market assumption, to believe that product innovations are unimportant and infrequent.

Fundamental for this conclusion is the Williamsonian assumption of 'opportunism' (self-seeking behaviour with guile) as a generalised, or at least frequent, type of behaviour. It is opportunism which gives rise to prohibitive transaction costs in situations characterised by uncertainty. The general validity of this assumption will be discussed later in this chapter.

3.2.4. The Organised Market as the Institutional Response

Paradoxically, in the real world, product innovations are not rare, and efforts to develop such innovations are common. How come? The simple answer is that most markets are not pure and characterised by anonymous relationships between buyers and sellers. Most markets involve an element of mutual exchange of qualitative information, and sometimes by direct cooperation between users and producers, in the process of innovation. The relative importance of product innovations indicates that most markets are organised markets. This implies that modern economies are 'mixed' in a fundamental sense; not only does the private sector coexist with a large public sector; the relative success of the market economies in terms of technical progress reflects, not the purity of the markets, but rather their impurities.

The most important elements of organisation constituting the organised market are exchange of qualitative information, cooperation, hierarchy and mutual trust. These characteristic elements imply that the relationships are durable and selective. It also follows that the elements of organisation will be strongest in those markets which are characterised by on-going change in technical opportunities as well as user needs.

The most basic function of the user-producer relationships, in relation to product innovations, is to communicate information about both technological opportunities and user needs. The user and the producer will gradually develop a common code of communication, making the exchange of information more efficient. To leave a well-established user-producer relationship becomes increasingly costly, and involves a loss of information capital.

Sometimes, the relationships between users and producers will involve direct cooperation. For example, a user might invite a producer to take part in solving a specific problem within the organisation. Cooperation might take place at different stages: while defining the problem, while developing the solution or while introducing it in the user organisation.

User-producer relationships will often involve elements of power and hierarchy, and the direction of the innovations will reflect, who is the dominating party. But in most user-producer relationships, we find other social elements besides hierarchy and dominance. Without a certain degree of loyalty, mutual respect of each others' autonomy, and mutual trust, transaction costs would, as already pointed out, become prohibitively high and vertical integration would take place.

It follows from what has been said that user-producer relationships tend to be durable and selective. As pointed out, it takes time to develop efficient codes and channels of information. This might be even more so, when it comes to establishing relationships of dominance, trust, and common codes of conduct. In order to obtain economies in the exchange of information, and in order to develop working, hierarchical relationships and mutual trust, the number of producers and users connected must be limited, and this implies that user-producer relationships must be selective, connecting to each other subsets of all potential users and all potential producers.

The main reason why markets tend to become organised pointed to here is innovative activities. It follows that the intensity, and the character of user-producer relationships, might be very different in different parts of the economy. In parts where product technology remains almost constant, the relationships might become close to the ideal of the pure market. In other areas, a high degree of complexity and radical change in technologies might result in a complete and formal, vertical integration. But in between these two extremes, we should expect to find the vast majority of real markets, each one including varying elements of organisation.

3.2.5. Why Not Just Process Innovations?

But how can innovative activities aiming at product innovations survive? What are the relative advantages of organised markets as compared to the pure market and the pure hierarchy? Here, it might be useful to repeat an argument put forward by Arrow (1974). According to Arrow, the formation of an organisation might be regarded as a process involving both growing efficiency, and growing inflexibility. The positive effect from an extension of the organisation is that information exchange is likely to become more efficient, through the development of common codes and channels of information. The negative aspect of bringing more and more activities into organisations is that the activities get 'locked in' into a net-work of communication codes and channels, difficult to adjust when faced with radical change in the environment.

Here, I shall argue, first, that the organised market might be regarded as a compromise, taking into account both the advantages of acting collectively – in our context, primarily, to exploit the fruits of learning by interacting – and the costs of rigidity. The organised market represents a degree of rigidity necessary to produce innovations, but a rigidity of a lower degree than the one represented by the pure organisation.

Second, we must take into account, how vertical integration affects the participation of the integrated units in interactive learning, taking place outside the pair of integrated units. Integrating a producer, will give a user more direct access to technological know-how. And, at the same time, the integrated producer will get more direct access to knowledge about the changing needs of this particular user.

But the price paid for these intimate relationships might be high, in the long run. Users and producers not integrated will be reluctant to give away sensitive information to the pair of integrated units. Non-integrated users will be reluctant to surrender information about their strategic bottle-neck problems to a producer integrated with a competitor. And, non-integrated producers will be unwilling to give away their most advanced technical know-how to a user unit integrated with a competing producer.

As a result, the input to the process of innovation from interactive learning becomes specialised and limited in scope. Thus, there is a trade-off between the short term advantages of a closer interaction between the integrated units, and the long term cost of their isolation from the broader process of interactive learning involving several, formally independent, users and producers. The informal organisation, characterising the organised market, is less exclusive in this respect, and keeps open a more encompassing network of information, cooperation and interactive learning. This is one reason, why firms may prefer to accept relatively high 'transactions costs' in the organised market rather than join a pure hierarchy, locking them into a much more narrowly defined space for interactive learning.

This somewhat functionalist explanation of, why organised markets tend to survive, and make product innovations possible should be complemented in two respects. First, we must discuss the compatibility of the organised market with the behaviour of individual agents. Second, we must ask if the functional perspective implies that the actually existing institutional set-up is optimal, satisfactory or unsatisfactory.

3.2.6. Opportunism and Transaction Costs

If agents acted opportunisticly, we would expect organised markets to become transformed into hierarchies. The efforts put into product innovation, and their frequency in the real world, may be regarded as evidence that agents restrain their opportunistic tendencies – at least when participating in processes of interactive learning. Actually, there might be several, good reasons for such a restraint.

First, existing institutional set-ups such as legal or informal systems of rules and norms may induce individual agents to act honestly (Milgrom, North and Weingast, 1990). The establishment of such institutional set-ups may be analysed and explained as a 'rational' response to high transaction costs.[3]

An alternative would be to assume that honesty reflects social norms characterised by a certain relative autonomy in relation to economic rationality. People are not honest (only) because it pays them to be honest, and the social norms prevailing are not there (only) because they increase the efficiency of the economic system. This is the stand-point taken by Elster (1989). There are many socialising processes in Western society aiming at giving the individual a propensity to feel shame when lying and being dishonest (the ten commandments of the bible, the rules against cheating in school etc.). It would take an extreme interpretation to regard these processes and institutions (including religion) as just 'rational' attempts to reduce transaction costs.

But, it is obvious that most institutions which have been established in order support honest behaviour – including an informal reputation system – are costly in terms of time and resources, and these costs may be regarded as 'transaction costs' for the market system as a whole. It is also obvious that the need for such institutions and their costliness will vary with the social norms prevailing in the economy.

3.2.7. Are Established User-Producer Relationships Always Satisfactory?

A related question refers to the functionality of the existing institutional set-up, in terms of markets, organisations and organised markets. Above, some reasons why agents might prefer organised markets both to vertical integration and to pure markets were mentioned, and we have argued strongly that user-producer relationships are necessary prerequisites for product innovations. However, these arguments do not imply any mechanism of selection, which guarantees that the actual network of user-producer relationships is optimal or even satisfactory. In another context, I have pointed to two different characteristics systematically fostering unsatisfactory innovations (Lundvall, 1991).

One of them is asymmetrical power relationships between users and producers, resulting in biased technical change. When producers dominate both in terms of financial resources and in terms of technical competence, there is an inherent tendency to develop costly innovations not well suited to the needs of users. This seems, for example, to be the case when a few big producers produce systemic capital equipment for a large number of small users (dairy factories, cement factories, nuclear plants). But the dominance of a few big users may also give rise to unsatisfactory innovations. The US automobile industry, and its interaction with domestic producers of machine tools, seem to illustrate this kind of mechanism.

The second characteristic is the inertia characterising user-producer relationships. This problem will be most severe in periods of technological revolution, bringing fundamental changes in technological opportunities, and in user needs. In such a period, the prevailing pattern of user-producer relationships will adjust sluggishly to the emerging new needs and opportunities.

3.3. User-Producer Interaction in Space and the Character of Technical Change

We are now prepared to discuss the spatial aspect of user-producer interaction, and how it relates to the character of technical change. First, the concepts of 'space' and 'distance' will be discussed and then we will introduce a taxonomy of technical change, and attempt to interpret it in spatial terms.

3.3.1. Four Dimensions of Space

In the present context, it is useful to operate with four dimensions of space; economic, organisational, geographical and cultural. As we shall see, there are important interconnections between these four dimensions. For example, a wide gulf between users and producers, in one of these dimensions might be possible to overcome by closeness in one of the other dimensions.

Economic Space

Economic space relates to how different economic activities are located in the system of production. In an extended input-output table (a table where deliveries of capital goods are included and where organisations, producing science and technology, are represented as sectors), the economic distances between different activities are indicated by the prevailing set of input-output coefficients.

Organisational Space

Organisational space refers to horizontal and vertical integration. In the traditional analysis, the 'organisational distance' between economic activities is presented as discontinuous. Either there is full integration, and the distance is zero, or there is no integration, and the distance is infinite. Introducing organised markets, and the possibility of more or less distant relationships between divisions in conglomerate corporations, allows for a continuous concept of organisational distance.

Geographical Space

Geographical space can be measured unequivocally in terms of distance, when activities can be assigned to distinct locations. This dimension of distance might be more or less relevant, depending upon which types of interactions are studied, and the systems of transportation and communication prevailing. Measured in terms of costs and/or time, an economic-geographical space might be constructed related specifically to the kind of interaction in focus.

Cultural Space

Cultural space is a loose and multidimensional concept, but it relates to important characteristics in the real world. Especially when studying learning processes and communication processes involving complex and ever-changing messages, this dimension is important. As demonstrated in chapter 2, the general institutional framework – including norms and codes – represents a context for communication, and individuals and organisations will decode information in accordance with this context. When cultural differences are present, certain types of messages will be difficult to transmit and decode. Complex and ever-changing messages, combining explicit information with tacit assumptions regarding mutual obligations, will often be required in interactions involving innovative activities. Here, cultural differences between user and producer may block the interaction.

This is one reason why nations still play an important role, as economic entities, with a relative autonomy. In some dimensions, the cultural distance between domestic agents and organisations is considerably less than the distance to foreign ones. Certainly, a cultural convergence towards an American lifestyle in the post-war period has weakened the impact of cultural distance, but the fact that national languages, and national differences in the institutional set-up, persist implies that this factor cannot be ignored.

Interconnections between the Dimensions of Space

As mentioned, different dimensions of space and distance are interconnected in a complex way. Economic space does not play any independent role in our analysis. Actually, the unit of analysis discussed so far, the user-producer dyad, is defined as, the combination of units, as close to each other as possible, measured in this dimension.

Organisational space has already been discussed in relation to vertical integration and organised markets. Here, it will be confronted with geographical and cultural space. It is obvious that a short organisational distance may substitute for geographical and cultural proximity. The multinational corporations tend to develop their own internal channels and codes of information, and they may also develop a specific, transnational, corporate culture. Why this type of substitution will take place in the form of vertical integration – eliminating markets for product innovations – will be discussed in the last section of this chapter.

3.3.2. The Character of Technical Change and Interaction in Space

How does the character of technical change affect the relative importance of spatial, cultural and organisational distance between users and producers involved in interactive learning and innovation? In this context, a distinction will be made between four different forms of technical change: stationary technology, incremental innovation, radical innovation, and technological revolution. These distinctions are based upon the taxonomy developed in Freeman and Perez (1988).

Stationary Technology

First, let us assume that technological opportunities and the needs of users are fairly constant. The engineering activities taking place in firms and institutions will gradually develop norms, standards, and terminologies giving a full description of the technology.[4] A high degree of standardisation means that communication between a user and a producer can be performed over long distances, and it might even be transformed into 'bits' of information, cheaply transferred between computers by telecommunication. In this case, distance – geographical as well as cultural – will play a very limited role, and mainly reflect the costs of transportation and telecommunication. This is the case, where industries become virtually 'foot-loose'. Activities may be located anywhere, and one should expect 'comparative advantage', in terms of the relative scarcity of factors of production (defined in a broad sense), to play the decisive role in determining the spatial division of labour.

Perhaps we might argue that some pre-industrial societies were technologically stationary for periods, but when analysing modern knowledge-intensive economies and societies, this case is primarily a theoretical construct and may be regarded just as a reference for the other, and more realistic cases.

Incremental Innovation

Second, let us assume an user-producer interaction, where incremental innovation is an on-going activity. The codes and channels of information developed must be flexible in order to take into account the change in technological opportunities, and the change in user needs. Stable user-producer relationships will develop in order to overcome uncertainties on both sides of the market. The drive towards standardisation will be countered by recurrent changes in the technology. Messages will be complex and changing, and the information cannot readily be translated into 'bits', transferable by telecommunication. In this case, distance will play an important role. Being close to advanced users will form a comparative advantage for the producers, and vice versa.

In small open economies, we find many examples of patterns of specialisation, which reflect comparative advantages based upon such a close interaction between competent users and producers. Dairy technology in Denmark, wood cutting and metal working technologies in Sweden and technologies related to shipping and fishery in Norway have all developed in a historical process of interaction between industries, where users have been export-oriented, and for this reason quite competent and demanding. This kind of interaction has resulted in lasting, strong positions in the world market for users as well as producers. Such industries, often forming parts of national, industrial complexes, or clusters, are not footloose. On the contrary, they base their comparative advantage upon geographical and cultural proximity Andersen et al. (1981b) and chapters 4 and 11 in this book discuss the importance of linkages and of home-markets for international specialisation.

Radical Innovation

The third form of technical change to be considered is one of radical innovation.[5] A radical change in technology implies that the codes developed to communicate a constant, or a gradually changing, technology will become inadequate. Established producers which follow a given technological trajectory will have difficulties in evaluating the potentials of the new paradigm. Users will have difficulties in decoding the communication coming from producers, developing new products built according to the new paradigm.

In this case, geographical and cultural distance might play an even more important role than in the case of incremental innovation. The lack of standard criteria for sorting out what is the best paradigm, implies that 'subjective' elements in user-producer relationships – like mutual trust and even personal friendship – will become important. In an experimental phase, the lack of communicability might make 'hands-on-experiments' necessary for potential users. In this phase, face-to-face contact between users and producers might be necessary in order to communicate new technological opportunities and user needs. The accelerating growth of 'Silicon Valleys' around the world may be interpreted in these terms.

A new cluster of users and producers might be 'footloose' ex ante – small accidents may determine where the first units are located – but, ex post, they will become strongly rooted in regional or national networks of user-producer relationships, giving them a comparative advantage in national and international competition. Interesting modelling exercises, which illustrate stochastic allocation in space, when increasing returns are involved, have been developed by Brian Arthur (1988). One important source of these agglomeration effects which might explain Silicon Valley phenomena is the need for proximity between users and producers, in the phase of radical innovation.

What role will multinational corporations play during such a phase? Vertically integrated, multinational corporations may be quite resistant to new technologies, and ideas emanating from new paradigms. This might, to a certain degree, be compensated for by a long-term perspective and by strategic planning, which takes radical technical change into account. In the field of microelectronics, the biggest computer firms were quite slow in recognising the potential of the new paradigm – the PC-technology. The current activity of multinationals in the field of biotechnology (Chesnais, 1988a) might reflect a learning effect from that experience.

In a later phase, when the new paradigm has proven its worth, it becomes, of course, an attractive field for take-overs and investment. The flexibility in space which originates in the peculiar form of organisation characterising multinational corporations facilitates simultaneous location in several Hi-tech strongholds, and the sourcing of innovations from such strongholds. The broader analysis of internationalisation in chapter 13 shows that globalisation, as a new phase of internationalisation, challenges the traditional role of national systems in this respect

Technological Revolution

Finally, the implications of a cluster of basic, radical innovations is to be discussed. A basic innovation, is defined as one with a potential use in most parts of the production system. Microelectronics and potentially biotechnology reflect basic, radical innovations in this sense. Micro-electronics may be used in almost all production and administrative processes in a modern society, and they are important components in many new consumer goods.

In our framework, the most important consequence of such a cluster is that it tends to break up the traditional network of user-producer linkages, and to constitute the basis for new user-producer linkages. This will affect vertically integrated corporations as well as organised markets. In both cases, inertia and the costs involved in breaking up existing, and establishing new codes and channels of information, will tend to cement the existing structure of user-producer relationships. The force of resistance might be strongest in those areas where the interaction has been most effective in establishing strong poles of competitiveness, both on the user side and on the producer side.

Such a 'technological revolution' may have a drastic impact on the spatial division of labour. Regions and countries which are 'late-comers' may get a competitive edge before regions characterised by historically rooted networks of users and producers (Perez and Soete, 1988). The radical changes in the global localisation of manufacturing; shifting production from the 'Atlantic region' –Western Europe and the eastern part of US – towards the 'Pacific region', reflects such a mechanism.

Such processes of reallocation of labour and production in space may persist both at the global and the local level. But this does not imply that industries have become 'footloose'. Rather, it reflects that the roots of old industries in historically established networks have become too strong, and that new industries are now in a process of rooting themselves in new networks.

3.3.3. Empirical Illustrations

In some of the literature on industrial networks, a distinction is made between domestic and international user-producer relationships. The empirical results suggest that national borders still matter in this context.

1. The study by Håkansson (1989) shows that 80% of all inter-firm cooperation activities aiming at innovation, and involving user-producer interaction, are domestic (op.cit., 110). Local and district relationships are not very frequent, however (less than 20%). This supports the hypothesis that systems of innovation tend to remain national rather than regional or transnational, but it should be taken into account that the firms studied were small and medium sized.
2. In a comprehensive study of user-producer relationships, which focused upon British, German and Swedish firms, the characteristics of domestic relationships were compared with international relationships (Hallén et al., 1987). The authors test a series of hypotheses, and one of the main conclusions is worth quoting in extenso:

> The results thus reveal a basic difference in the working of business relationships in domestic versus export markets. The strength of export relationships develops as far as the product exchange requires, i.e. initial adaptations are made and information exchanged to cope with these. However, in domestic relationships the adaptations in addition to this constitute a viable framework for expanding interaction processes, which both permits and requires more information exchange and new adaptations . Thus a cyclical strengthening of the relationship is obtained. (op.cit. , 36)

It is important to take into account that the firms in this sample were big, internationally oriented, manufacturing firms. Thus, the conclusion should be expected to be valid, a fortiori, for less internationalised units. Again, the result supports the assumption that national borders matter.

3.4. Introducing Differently Specified Rationality in International User-Producer Interaction

I have argued that 'cultural distance' might have an important impact upon the patterns of national and international user-producer relationships and upon innovation. Culture is a broad and vague concept, and it might be useful to go into some detail with an illustration of, how and why culture invades the core of the neoclassical economic system; the market and the rationality of agents.

In this last section, the focus will be upon what happens when one of the core elements in the economic system – the rationality of agents – is invaded by culture. How will international differences in the specification of the 'rationality' of agents affect national performance? What are the implications of internationalisation for the process of innovation, when rationalities are specified differently between national systems?

3.4.1. Homogeneously Specified Rationality

In standard economics, all agents are assumed to be equipped by one single rationality. Even when the assumption of hyper-rationality is challenged, all agents are assumed to follow one and the same set of behavioural rules. In this respect, the owner of the hot-dog stand on the corner is assumed to be identical with the management of IBM. It is assumed that motives, ambitions and competence are the same. One, and only one, specification of rationality across agents is an assumption economists are very reluctant to sacrifice, when introducing more realistic assumptions into their models. One reason is that without it mathematical models would become less neat, and aggregation more complex.

Kornai is one of the few economists who has explicitly questioned the principle of one single specification of rationality, and pointed to concepts making it possible to operate with differently specified rationality (Kornai, 1971, 174–75 *et passim*). Another contribution has been made by Peter Allen (1988). In his very interesting model on fishery in Canada, it is differentiated between fishermen who are either 'Stochasts' or 'Cartesians'.

3.4.2. Honest Agents vs. Opportunist Agents

One consequence of introducing 'opportunistic behaviour' – agents who pursue their own interests with guile – is that a further specification of rational behaviour becomes necessary. We might specify the behaviour of 'rational economic men' (REM) either as building upon honesty and trust or as characterised by opportunism and lack of mutual trust.

In order to illustrate the importance of international differences in rationality, the distinction between opportunism and honesty will be used as an illustrative example. There are several other documented, interesting, international differences between agents which are rooted in national social norms and culture. The time horizon might be short or long term, and their attention might be directed towards either financial variables or use value aspects of production. My reason for choosing opportunism as the illustration here is that it cannot be reduced to a question of different 'preferences'.[6]

Let us assume two co-existing systems; one populated by honest agents (Hon-REM system), and the other by opportunist agents (Opp-REM system). If an agent tries to behave opportunistically in the Hon-REM system, the sanctions in terms of exclusion from further interaction might be very tough. If, on the other hand, an agent in the Opp-REM system tries to behave honestly, and expecting others to follow suit, he would come out as the loser. The others would not believe in his good intentions, and his own expectations would not be fulfilled. In both systems, the single agent would be best off obliging to the dominating form of behaviour, and in this sense both systems are REM-societies; they are both compatible with consistent goal-seeking behaviour.

What determines if a system becomes Hon-REM or Opp-REM? Theoretically, the question might be analysed through game theory, comparing the viability of cooperative vs. conflictual rules of behaviour (Axelrod, 1984). In the real world, the dominance of either honesty or opportunism at the national level will reflect historical, and perhaps even an heritage from pre-capitalist developments. As demonstrated by Arthur (1988), small historical events may impose a dominance of one single technology, when increasing returns are involved. Similar mechanisms might be at work when social norms become established at the national level.

3.4.3. Coexisting Subsystems with Differently Specified Rationalities

What characterises the two different systems? Here, the focus will be upon how transaction costs and interactive learning involving users and producers are affected. In Table 3.1, the two subsystems are contrasted in these respects.

The fact that opportunism results in transaction costs is well-known from the work of Williamson (1975). Agents, acting with guile, will create an atmosphere of mutual distrust between users and producers and as a result it will be very difficult and expensive to formulate, and monitor contracts acceptable to both parties. As a response to opportunism, costly institutions, such as an intricate legal system and extensive control mechanisms, may be developed to cope with opportunistic behaviour.

Table 3.1. **Sub-systems Characterised by Different Rationalities**

	Opp-REM	Hon-REM
Transaction costs	High	Low
Learning capability	Low	High

In the system where agents are governed by social norms which direct them towards honesty and trust, the transaction costs will be more limited, and the need for special institutional arrangements will be less. The high transaction costs will make vertical integration a much more common phenomenon in the Opp-REM system and, ceteris paribus, at any point of time we would expect the degree of vertical integration to be higher in the Opp-REM system; a smaller proportion of the flow of products would involve market transactions.

But the negative impact upon interactive learning might be even more dramatic, and also more difficult to counteract through institutional design. It is extremely difficult to engage successfully in interactive learning, if both parties act with guile. Generally, processes of learning will be stimulated by an environment, characterised by honesty and mutual trust. (The strong sanctions against pupils who cheat at school, and the strong expectations of teachers to be truthful reflect this fact).

Again, lack of trust might be overcome by vertical integration. But integration will not guarantee a high learning capability. As far as intra-firm relationships involve opportunistic agents, the negative impact upon learning will remain. It may be possible to direct opportunist agents to pursue repetitive operations, and to use economic threats to force them to perform simple tasks. But it is much more difficult to force them to engage in processes of complex and interactive learning. So, even if transaction costs could be reduced through vertical integration, the effect of integration upon learning would be more dubious.[7]

3.4.4. International User-Producer Relationships Involving Differentiated Rationality

Within a national system, users and producers who belong to different subsystems, might get involved in interaction. The opportunist producer will be looking for honest and trusting customers whose honesty and trust he can exploit. But within national systems, the professional user who is a honest and trusting customer will develop methods and techniques to identify and avoid domestic opportunist producers. Information sharing between firms, which belong to the same industry, regarding the trustworthiness of different producers will often be efficient, especially in a small country, and in areas where few potential producers are involved.

Let us now assume that two national systems differ in terms of the rationality governing the behaviour of agents in the two systems. How will interfirm relationships develop between an economy dominated by opportunism (the O-economy), and another dominated by honest and trusting agents (the H-economy). The agents of the H-economy would become seriously disappointed with the behaviour of the agents from the O-economy. The agents from the O-economy would not be able to understand the behaviour of the agents from the H-economy. If both sets of agents stick to their original pattern of behaviour, transaction costs would become extremely high, and interactive learning involving partners from the two systems would remain very restricted and limited.

The other possibility involves 'institutional learning' and adaptation. The H-firms may differentiate their behaviour and begin to act as opportunists in their interaction with the foreigners from the O-system, while sticking to honest behaviour domestically. This would not reduce transaction costs, nor would it increase the potential for interactive learning at the international level. And, gradually, selective opportunism may become generalised, and include domestic transactions. If such a version of 'Gresham's law' were at work, any small germ of opportunism might spread and contaminate the global economy as a whole.

Alternatively, the firms from the O-system might learn to behave honestly, when they interact with H-firms, while sticking to opportunistic behaviour at home. In this case, we might get lower transaction costs and a higher learning capability in international user-producer relationships than in the ones internal to the O-system. Axelrod's (1984) experiments, confronting different rules of behaviour actually point in this optimistic direction, showing how a simple and, potentially, cooperative 'tit-for-tat'-rule tends to win the game.

All the most probable outcomes would involve high transaction costs, and low interactive learning capabilities. To overcome this problem vertical integration would be a frequent result. Instead of international user-producer interaction we tend to get multinational corporations. Instead of sales between users and producers of different nationality we tend to get commodity flows across national borders, but inside the same corporation.[8]

3.4.5. Implications at the International Level

High transaction costs and a low learning capability at the national level, are serious problems which might reflect the presence of opportunistic behaviour, inside the national economy. But we can now see, why they become even more severe when agents from different nations are involved. In order to identify and cope with opportunistic agents, it is extremely important to know, and understand, the culture, the language and the codes of conduct of the other party. In cases of disagreement it is also important to understand, and have equal access to, institutions solving legal problems. These observations might inspire a reassessment of different phenomena in the world economy:

– the dominating role of multinational corporations
– the problems for small firms to internationalise
– the limits of internationalisation

- the importance of product standards and standardisation
- the impact of the single European market upon innovation and growth

Important reasons why multinational firms tend to organise such a large proportion of the international commodity flow are that user-producer relationships which involve foreign users are expensive in terms of transaction costs, and that opportunism and international differences in rationality will tend to block interactive learning. If this is the case, the formation of multinational firms may be regarded as a 'second-best' response to this problem.

National firms will have problems when they enter international trade with commodities characterised by technical change, because of high transaction costs and a low capability for interactive learning. Many of these firms have developed their specific competence and products, in an interaction with competent and demanding domestic users. As they become oriented towards export niches, and weaken their ties to the domestic economy, they might lose their innovative capability, and they will also be burdened by high transaction costs. In national systems (Denmark, Ireland, Portugal, Australia) which have few multinational champions, the competitiveness of the whole economy will suffer for the reasons given above.

We can also see why internationalisation, and the dissolution of national systems of innovation, must be regarded as a contradictory and complex process. Multinational firms will often represent institutional frameworks less flexible than organised markets. A process of internationalisation based upon multinational corporations might actually weaken the innovative potential not only of single national systems, but also of the global economy as a whole.

This analysis in terms of interactive learning and transaction costs indicates the importance of standardisation. Especially when international institutional differences are involved, technical standardisation becomes crucial for the pattern of international user-producer relationships. Standardisation between countries in terms of business procedures, technology and product quality, reduces the uncertainty of foreign users, and limits the room for opportunism on the producer side. Standardisation reduces transaction costs and in some cases it might stimulate international interactive learning.

The European Single Market is interesting, in the light of the foregoing discussion. Obviously, this project aims at a standardisation in terms of products and technology. If the project becomes a success in this dimension, we should expect uncertainty and transaction costs to be reduced. However, its impact upon the process of innovation is more difficult to evaluate (for a further discussion of this theme see chapter 12). The specific designs of standards might be crucial in this context. A more fundamental question is the long term trend in the rationality of economic agents at the European scene.

Is the single market project in its long term perspective designed to influence basic social norms and cultural values, as these are reflected in the rationality of economic agents?

In the last part of the book we shall return to some of these issues. The purpose of this chapter has been to indicate in a preliminary way, starting from an analysis of user-producer interaction, the relevance of 'national systems of innovation'.

3.4.6. Empirical Illustrations

The cultural and institutional differences analysed in the literature on innovation are mostly refering to differences between Japan and United States. Some of this literature supports the importance of institutional and cultural factors which relate to the organised market and to differentiated rationality:

1. There are important differences in inter-firm relationships between the US and Japan. Japan is characterised by closer and more long-term user-producer relationships (Freeman, 1987, 49 ff, and Dertoutzos et al., 1989, 99 ff).
2. The Japanese inter-firm relationships are characterised more by loyalty and trust and at the same time the Japanese economy is characterised by a lower degree of vertical integration than the US-economy (Dore, 1986).
3. The work by Mari Sako (1989) who compares inter-firm relationships in the printed circuit board industry in Japan and UK, points to radical differences in how industrialists in the two countries regard and organise user-producer relationships. While UK-strategies are relatively focused upon flexibility, price competition and pure market relationships (both a high degree of vertical integration and a predominance for short-term contracts, anonymous relationships and limited cooperation), the Japanese strategy involves a much stronger element of organisation in organised markets (low degree of vertical integration, long term relationships, social bounds and strong cooperation).

These observations may be interpreted as support for an assumption that rationality is differentiated between countries. In Lester and Crocker (1987) the authors point to Japanese 'cultural and institutional constraints on opportunistic behaviour' in connection with their international comparison of interaction between users and producers involved in the development of nuclear plants. However, it would be a simplification to reduce these differences to the juxtaposition between opportunism in the US and the UK, and honesty in Japan. The presence of honesty and trust in Japan might be quite selective, and refer primarily to members of the same industrial group.

Generally, there is a strong need for systematic international comparative studies of countries closer to each other in terms of geography and culture than the US and Japan. Such studies should aim at understanding international differences in the organisation of markets, the specific rationality of agents and the impact of such differences on the process of internationalisation.

Chapter 4

APPROACHING NATIONAL SYSTEMS OF INNOVATION FROM THE PRODUCTION AND LINKAGE STRUCTURE

Esben Sloth Andersen

4.1. Introduction

Studies of national systems of innovation (NSI) often focus on the R&D system. This chapter will argue that less conspicuous production and sales/purchase activities are an alternative and, in many ways, more adequate point of departure. More specifically, the claim is that by shifting attention to the production and linkage patterns of nations a whole set of questions is raised and much can be said about rates and directions of innovative activities.

This chapter will develop this claim in several steps. First, the basic approach and the analytical elements of the analysis of NSI are sketched (section 4.2) and the background of the approach is discussed (section 4.3). Then the two sides of the approach are treated: production structure and 'simple' learning (section 4.4), and linkage structure and interactive learning which includes the special case of development blocks and their structural tensions (section 4.5).

4.2. The Basic Approach

Behind the production and linkage approach to NSI is the postulate that most of what is normally classified as 'innovation' is closely related to existing products and processes. We find first of all that new possibilities are often discovered as more or less unconscious by-products of production and sales activities. Second, more ambitious and conscious searching for and learning about new products and processes quite often start with the problems of existing products and processes, which may be conceptualised as two lists of possible demand specifications accumulated since the last shift of product or process: one list containing errors, repair problems and larger breakdowns and another list of ideas and wishes for new features, facilities, performance measures etc. Such lists (which may only exist in the memory of engineers) are clearly connected to the existing structure of production and to user-producer linkages. Third, in many simple and subtle ways the existing traditions influence the criteria by means of which new ideas are judged.

These aspects of continuity of innovation may be seen as a result of 'bounded rationality' leading to localised search in the space of (technological and marketing) alternatives. Provided we accept this kind of world-view, we are imposing upon ourselves a certain conception of NSI. First of all, the name of the game is variety-creation and variety-selection within a given pattern of industrial specialisation. The resulting changes in competitiveness may lead to contractions or expansions of industries but normally not to jumps in the basic industrial structure. Second, the search rules of firms and their privileged access to alternatives found by lead-users are basic characteristics of NSI. We are, therefore, urged to look for possible national characteristics of search rules and lead-user access. They may be founded in the overall institutional framework, especially the national idiosyncrasies of financial systems, national inter-industrial networks and educational systems. Third, corporate R&D is seen as the outgrowth of less conspicuous search activities (related to general learning and the accumulation of knowledge) and it may be discussed in terms of very general search heuristics (cumulative, random, radical, etc. search strategies). The scale and scope of R&D is influenced by national traditions and national systems of taxation. Fourth, our conception of the role of public R&D and systems of technology protection and transfer can also be developed from the linkage perspective.

4.3. Background of the Approach

A long series of discussions and modelling exercises can be developed within the broad limits of the production and linkage approach to NSI. We will soon explore some of these possibilities. However, it may be helpful to start with some of the background and the typical dilemmas of the approach. This is especially important since the approach may be seen as an attempted resolution of the conflict between structural and evolutionary modes of explanation in the analysis of technical or 'techno-economic' change. The delicate problems of combining these two modes of thought may be easily forgotten and the concrete articulations of the approach may end up with a purified version of one of the components.

4.3.1. The Problems of Growth Pole Analysis

Let us start with an example of the uneasy relationship between evolutionary and structuralist approaches: the growth pole theory of Perroux (1955 and 1969). The idea behind the theory is taken from Schumpeter's (e.g., 1928, 30 ff) discussion of the direct and indirect effects of a radical innovation. A major innovation may be seen as creating the basis for a whole series of more or less adaptive decisions during a shorter or longer epoch of time. Some of these are performed within existing routines while others are innovative, but supposedly of an adaptive and incremental character ('clusters of innovation'). Such sequences of decisions may be captured by the notion of growth poles in the industrial system consisting of propellant industries (the primary, 'autonomous' innovators) and impelled industries (showing adaptive response, including 'induced' innovation). The development power of a nation is to some extent dependent on the existence of propellant industries and many national policies can be understood as attempting to monopolise the resultant forces of development. Perroux is thus clearly sketching a production and linkage approach to national (and regional) systems of innovation.

But this was not clear to all his followers (see Brookfield 1975, 105 ff). Many of them were not interested in the 'laws of succession' but rather in the 'laws of coexistence' between the different parts of the industrial system. Here they could use the fact that Perroux stated his ideas in terms of industries and that he suggested the application of input-output analysis to the phenomenon of growth poles. They translated the theory into an input–output language with (temporarily) fixed technical coefficients in the following way: large technical coefficients can be taken as proxies for important 'linkages' or propelling forces; 'industrial complexes' are parts of the industrial system connected by strong 'linkages'; the cores of the 'industrial complexes' can partly be found by means of the inverted input-output matrix which shows the direct and indirect inputs used for one unit of output of each industry of the industrial system. The policy prescription for development was then to invest in important core industries which for one reason or another were not present in the nation under consideration. The rest of the industrial system would then be constructed or renewed by means of the propellant forces from the core industry which was also the core in a NSI. However, this translation of Perroux's argument is, unfortunately, radically wrong. The tight 'linking' of industries revealed by the input-output tables of the most advanced countries has no necessary connection to growth poles. On the contrary, it probably indicates a 'mature' situation with routine deliveries and few possibilities of change and development.

The sketched formalisation of growth pole analysis led to a boom in its application in regional and development economics. But the success was quite short-lived because the studies had little to do with change and innovative investment strategies and much more with the interdependence of a well-established industrial system. This led to a neglect of Perroux's concentration on disequilibrium and on the character of the exploration of the space for investment possibilities which constitutes the foundations of the whole approach.[1] Furthermore, major problems were created because of the too-ready translation of the search space connected to economic decision-making into a space dominated by geographical or national distances, a translation which clearly neglected Perroux's (1950/1969) original warnings. The boom ended in 'immense confusion', mainly because of a neglect of the fact that

> ... *the activity creating a growth pole was essentially a sectoral and geographical disturbance not because of its larger than average size, nor because of its higher multiplier, but because it was [... a radical]* innovation. (Brookfield, 1975, 93)

The most important conclusion of the story of growth pole analysis appears to be the necessity of making very explicit the basic assumptions. The widespread, non-evolutionary modes of thinking and inappropriate analytical tools may otherwise provide a propensity to drift away from the assumptions and end up in confusion and even nonsensical statements. To avoid this it is important to emphasise the assumptions concerning the aspect of discontinuity in the analysis even if assumptions of a good deal of (probabilistic) 'continuity of development' are a necessary precondition for the analysis.

4.3.2. An Evolutionary Framework

The articulation of basic assumptions is probably not enough to strengthen the evolutionary side of the analysis. Another means is to propose explicit tools for this part of the analysis. Here the basic point of reference is still Nelson and Winter (1982). Their analysis is central to the present attempt to articulate the production and linkage structure approach to NSI. But the present upsurge in evolutionary analysis may be so strong that there is a danger of 'crowding out' the structuralist aspects of analysis in much the same way that evolutionary aspects were squeezed out of growth pole analysis. Actually, we will see that the attempt to systematise evolutionary theory by Nelson and Winter allows little room for the structurally-oriented analyses these authors have presented elsewhere. Even Nelson's model of uneven economic development across economies (Nelson and Winter, 1982, 237 ff) is kept in a highly stylised form with little coupling to many parts of the schema of evolutionary analysis. The reason is, of course, that the explicit account of routine-behaviour, the search for new routines and selection mechanisms introduce a great deal of complexity into both discussions and models which has to be counterbalanced by simplifications in other parts of the analysis.

Nelson and Winter's aim is to deal with the totality of the process of economic evolution including the mechanism of transmission (in terms of routine behaviour), the mechanism of variety-creation (in terms of search for new routines) and the selection mechanism (in terms of dynamic market processes or 'Schumpeterian competition'). Their book contains a verbal analysis of these mechanisms as well as a series of specialised models and simulations which incorporate and study different versions of the mechanisms. One of the central models deals with an industry with a homogeneous product but with the possibility of different and changing production routines in different firms. The development path of the industry is described in terms of a Markov process. Figure 4.1 describes the computational structure which determines (probabilistically) what happens in each period. Each period has

Figure 4.1. The Computational Structure[2] of a Simple Simulation Model of Nelson and Winter (1978, 1982, chapter 12–13; cf. Gerybadze 1982, 129).

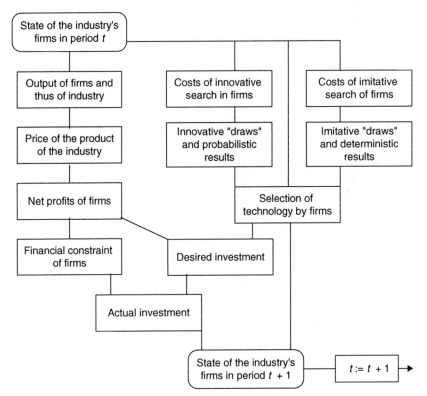

inherited a state of the industry from the former period. The state is defined in terms of the size of the physical capital stock and the productivity of capital in each firm.

The computational steps in the figure describe how the state of the industry in the next period is found. This involves firstly a simplified economic process in the industry whereby the output, price, profits and financial constraints of firms are found by taking into account the given cost and demand conditions, the capacity utilisation rules of firms and the behavioural rules of banks.

Secondly, there is a process whereby new production techniques are found. In the particular model, firms are always involved in search for new production techniques and their search costs are defined by fixed relationships to their capital stock. Through imitative search the firm may be able to get access to the present best-practice routine of the industry. In innovative search, things are more complicated. Here the firm explores a space of possible production routines which are defined in terms of capital productivity.[3] The probability of achieving a result is dependent on search costs. In the 'cumulative technology' version the productivity of a result (a 'draw') is most likely to be near to the present technology (localised search), while it is only dependent on exogeneous factors in the 'science-based' case. When the search of the period is over, the firm decides which routine to use: the one inherited from last period or the results of the imitative or innovative search. If the routine is changed, it will influence total productivity in the next period (disembodied technical change).

Thirdly, we have the investment decision. Desired investment depends on the relationship between price and unit costs with the improved technology compared with a target mark-up factor. Actual investment must be between zero and the financial constraint. Together with the stock inherited from previous periods (minus depreciation) we now have the capital stock of the next period.

This evolutionary model is just an example since 'a vast array of particular models can be constructed within the broad limits of the theoretical schema' (Nelson and Winter, 1982, 19). Therefore, we should not be constrained by the concrete model specifications but should see that

> ... *the analytical vantage point of an evolutionary theory reveals things from a different angle. After one gets used to that viewpoint, it turns out that much of what is seen is familiar. However, previously unnoticed features of the familiar objects become apparent* (Nelson and Winter, 1982, 414).

To what extent this is the case with respect to NSI is, of course, what concerns us in the present context together with the question of which aspects of NSI the framework is pushing into obscurity. These questions will be dealt with in the following.

4.3.3. Growth Poles in the Evolutionary Framework

At present we will see the model in Figure 4.1 as a paradigmatic example of evolutionary analysis and ask to what extent it allows the inclusion of a richer structural set-up. Can it, for example help to formalise the evolutionary aspects of growth pole analysis which were 'crowded out' by too much structure and determinism?

The immediate answer to this question is negative. Nelson and Winter's 'laws of succession' make the paths followed by individual firms interdependent for two simple reasons. First, total output of the industry determines price which determines profitability which, in turn, is one of the factors determining investment. Second, the firm may imitate the best-practice routine found in the industry in a given period. But in growth pole theory firms are influencing each other in many other ways. Special emphasis is put on 'vertical' supplier-producer relationships rather than intra-industrial relationships, new products are considered just as well as new processes, and so on. Thus the types of relationships covered by Nelson and Winter and Perroux are quite distant from each other.

But at a deeper level there is much more similarity. To see this we need to sketch a modified version of the Nelson and Winter model. Let industry C be the one which supplies the capital goods for industry D, the one described in the Nelson and Winter model. The disembodied change of the routines of industry D has already been described. But let us assume that the capital stock puts limits on the radicalism of change in production routines while new types of physical capital allow us to use a broader set of new routines. Thus, the innovative D-firms will have the possibility of creating a 'list' of routines which are not feasible in the present period. The existence of such 'lists' would radically ease the search conditions of the C-firms, but at the same time equal access to the 'lists' would delimit their relevance for creating competitive advantages for specific firms.

However, the 'lists' do not exist in practice because they are difficult to establish and involve a lot of tacit knowledge. But if there is a well-established 'linkage' between two firms belonging to different industries, there is a large probability that the C-firm will find out about non-feasible routines of industry D. If the C-firm is also active in search for new product-variants, there is some probability that it will discover a machine-type which makes the D-routine feasible. When presented to them, the new machine will be acknowledged by D-firms as having superior characteristics and being worth a higher price than ordinary machines.

But why should D-firms allow the search in their factories for non-feasible routines? If the question should be answered in isolation and if the machine became immediately available to all D-firms, there would be no reason for helping C-firms. But C-firms may be asked whether a new routine can be performed in connection with existing machines and they may be involved in modifying existing machines. Furthermore, a new C-product is normally produced at a small scale in the beginning and the 'linked' D-firm(s) may benefit from early access to the new machines. From a modelling viewpoint these practices greatly complicate the tasks, but in principle they may be integrated into the Nelson and Winter framework.

With respect to growth pole analysis the discussion of the interplay between C- and D-firms is illuminating. There is nothing of the automatic mechanisms of input-output analysis but an unbalanced interface between two industries. If industry D represents the core of the growth pole, there will be a rapid exploration of the space of production routines and a lot of non-feasible ideas. In such a situation we may find zero or even negative search costs in industry C because D-firms become involved in machine development and propose new specifications for selected C-firms and are also involved in the rapid debugging of the new C-products. Actually, the D-firms may choose to become involved in C-production but this case will not be discussed here.

4.3.4. Problems with Structures

An important difference between evolutionary and structuralist approaches seems to be the different ways in which they treat 'structures', like, for example, market structures or national specialisation structures. The structuralists treat these as *structures*, i.e., relatively stable phenomena which may help to explain more flexible phenomena. The evolutionists (and neoclassical economists) often treat 'structures' as relatively flexible *patterns* to be explained by other factors. This fundamental difference may help us to understand why the two components of, for example, growth pole analysis behave like a mix of oil and water.

A similar controversy has developed over national specialisation structures. Here there is a long-standing tradition of explaining trade specialisation patterns by the factor endowments of the nation. The underlying assumption appears to be that the specialisation pattern is relatively flexible while the factor endowments and other explanatory variables are stable characteristics of nations. This assumption has been challenged. Different kinds of 'structuralists' (e.g., of the Latin American brand) have argued that the specialisation pattern of a nation is in reality a rather inflexible *structure*, at least in the weakly developed areas. For such areas the specialisation structure is a major explanation of the factor endowments and for the (poor) overall economic performance.

Other economists have moved in the same direction, but within the traditional framework: parts of the specialisation pattern may be explained by other parts of the specialisation pattern which are supposed to reflect special

Figure 4.2. Some Relations between Technological Development and Specialisation Structure.

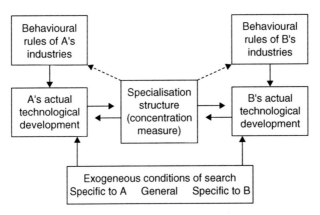

factor endowments. In the same fashion one can probably argue that the existence of a growth pole core within a nation is an asset which explains other parts of the specialisation pattern. But also national R&D and education systems may be considered as being more readily available for local firms than for foreign firms. The former obtain competitive advantages by utilising these opportunities just as when they utilise other abundant factors of production.

In Figure 4.2 the discussion over the specialisation structure of two nations, the 'domestic' economy A and the 'foreign' economy B, is sketched in an evolutionary style. The basic line of the evolutionary argument would start from the behavioural rules and the search conditions and move via the actual technological development of the industries (e.g., C and D) to the specialisation pattern as reflected in Balassa's export specialisation figures (see part III). But we will show below that the specialisation structure may also be taken as the starting point of the analysis which determines the actual technological development and even influences the behavioural rules of the industries. Even certain aspects of the search space are influenced by specialisation but this relationship will have to await further research.

4.4. Production Structure and 'Simple' Learning and R&D

To start with, the production pattern of a nation may influence the long-term behaviour of the central variables of the national economic system (technical change, competitiveness, employment, GPD per capita, etc.). This version of the 'structural' explanation of national competitiveness will be followed by other versions of the theme that 'production and linkage patterns matters'. In all cases a main purpose is so make explicit some of the propositions about innovation and international specialisation which appear to be underlying the 'structural thesis'. The result is a series of propositions which are intended to provoke two types of reactions. First, the propositions should be criticised and refined. Second, they may be taken heuristically as a preliminary set of assumptions for empirical studies and model-building exercises related to the production and linkage structure approach to NSI. The propositions are mainly formulated at the industry level while the underlying dynamics are studied in terms of the heterogeneous firms of the industry. The full resolution of the structural-evolutionary dilimma is left for future studies.

4.4.1. Learning as the Outcome of Production in a given Industry

There is a tendency for systems of routines to become hierarchical so that changes of routine take place within the framework of unchanging meta-routines. One basic meta-routine at the industry level may be formulated as 'keeping doing what you do best' or 'cobbler, stick to your last'. This allows for more restricted kinds of innovation. Once in a while there is a break-up of an apparently irreversible absorption into a certain state in the state space (a radical innovation of the Schumpeterian type) but we have more to say about the process following such a radical innovation (see section 4.5). In any case we emphasise the differentiation of the broad business term of 'innovation' so that certain searching and learning activities are seen as leading to 'incremental innovations' within the framework defined by a more or less 'radical innovation'.

The structural conservatism which is reflected in a stable specialisation pattern is not only founded on acknowledgement by the economic actors of their own bounded rationality but also in more binding reasons for path-dependency and 'lock-in-ness'. A simple version of this self-reinforcing specialisation takes its starting point in Arrow (1962) which brings into focus the idea of 'dynamic economies of scale' or 'learning-by-doing'. It was his basic hypothesis

> ... that technical change in general can be ascribed to experience, and that it is the very activity of production which gives rise to problems for which favourable responses are selected over time. (Arrow, 1962)

The cumulated results of experience may thus represent major barriers against shifting from one field of specialisation to another since the beginner will start at a lower level of productivity than the established firms.

In Arrow's formulations we find the elements of a theory of minor innovations ('favourable responses') related to 'problems' of production which may help to explain the rate and direction of an important part of the innovative activities within NSI. The pure example of such a learning process is given by the Horndal steel-mill which for two decades had an annual increase in its labour productivity (nearly 2% p.a.) without any investments (Lundberg, 1961, 130 ff). However, one should note that many studies show rapid decreases in the learning effects of a *given* line of productive activity; it is structural change and investment in new machines which secure the continued reproduction of the conditions for high rates of learning.

There are good reason to believe that industries differ with respect to the 'natural trajectories' of learning and minor innovation (Nelson and Winter, 1982, 258 ff). Furthermore, it should be noted that, according to the assumptions of behavioural economics, short-term pressures on the economic actors are central to the transformation of learning possibilities into technical change. And these pressures may differ markedly between nations (Tylecote and Demirag, 1991). Under such conditions a specialisation pattern becomes, at best, a local optimum for the decision makers: even if they would be better off when placed in another pattern they can/will not perform the intermediate steps which would create this pattern. In principle, this difficulty may be overcome with the help of a highly developed financial system. In practice bounded rationality represents a major determinant of historicity and hysteresis in the specialisation of nations.

These ideas may be summarised and developed at two levels: first, in terms of homogeneous industry aggregates and second, in terms of industries consisting of explicitly heterogeneous firms. The first level may be expressed in terms of the following propositions:

(a) The specialisation pattern of a nation is relatively stable. Large parts of it are stable for decades, but once in a while 'jumps' (i.e., relatively rapid changes) take place.

(b) This relative stability does not exclude and is actually dependent upon trajectories of learning and minor innovations which reflect the gradual evolution within the given framework of specialisation.

(c) There are major differences in the possibilities of learning and minor innovations between different industries in a given period of time. These differences may sometimes be described in terms of industries which have to different degrees 'moved down the learning curve' or reached different 'stages of the product life cycle'; but they may also be due to more global changes in technology and demand.

(d) The learning and innovation effects of different specialisation patterns are important determinants for differences in the overall competitiveness of nations measured in terms of the balance-of-payments-equilibrium growth rate.

These propositions are closely related to each other. The stability of the specialisation structure (a) is largely dependent upon static and especially dynamic economies of scale (learning-by-doing, etc.) (b). The relevance of this stability for the effects of the specialisation pattern on national performance is partly due to the differences between branches with respect to learning and minor innovations (c). Nations with similar propensities to transform learning possibilities into technical change will show differences in productivity performance due to differences in the specialisation structure. Whether these differences will influence profitability and industry growth depends on, for example, elasticities of demand and supply. Thus proposition (d) needs further specification: a learning-enhancing specialisation structure cannot be exploited and upheld in the long run unless the institutional set-up of the nation is appropriate for this purpose (see chapter 2).

4.4.2. The Evolutionary Foundations of Learning-by-Doing

The modelling exercises of Nelson and Winter (1982) concentrate on a single industry consisting of explicitly heterogeneous firms. While these firms are producing a homogeneous product they are searching for production routines of higher productivity than the ones they use in the present period. As mentioned in chapter 2, 'searching' may be considered as a special case of 'learning' which is especially demanding with respect to social interaction. However, in the present context it is more convenient to consider 'searching' as one aspect intrinsic in all 'learning activities' while memorising represents another aspect. In the simple but classical learning experiments we have first search in a space of alternatives, then the reinforcement of specific behaviour by different kinds of rewards. This method of trial-and-error (or rather trial-and-success) is firmly built into Nelson and Winter's framework and its formulation in probabilistic terms should not conceal its close relationship to Arrow's ideas (which are formalised in terms of deterministic equations). One may simply argue that Arrow is operating at a higher level of aggregation than Nelson and Winter. But the focus of the latter at the micro-foundations of production-near aspects of NSI brings forward a whole set of questions which are not reflected by Arrow's growth story and model.

There is another reason why many have overlooked the close but difficult relationship between Arrow's 'learning-by-doing' and Nelson and Winter's 'search' for new and better routines. The reason is that Nelson and Winter, by following the behavioural school, take seriously the problem of routine-transmission. Thus they (1982, 99 ff) must deal with the conservative aspects of learning and remembering by, e.g., talking of 'remembering-by-doing' as the major way in which firms preserve their routines. From this starting point, change of routines becomes a problem to be studied rather than the more or less automatic outcome of (creative) practice in the sense of Dewey and Arrow. In this vein Nelson and Winter prefer studies which

> ... *do not treat learning as somehow an inevitable and uninfluenceable consequence of doing. Rather, learning is viewed more actively, and it is apparent that resources can be applied to learning.* (Nelson and Winter, 1982, 258)

To emphasise this point, the search aspect of learning activities are called R&D and treated as a separate activity of firms which may be expanded (or contracted) independently of production activities. But it should be underlined that 'R&D' is just a name used by Nelson and Winter for activities whereby a firm may (intentionally or unintentionally) get access to new productive routines. Real R&D activities are primarily treated in terms of a 'science-based industry' while more learning-like 'R&D' activities are treated in a 'cumulative technology' case.

In a modified form Nelson and Winter's analysis of the evolution of a single industry may illuminate some issues concerning NSI. The primary modifications are to subdivide the firms of the industry into a national and a foreign subset, to assume that the two 'economies' are equal with respect to, for example, factor endowments, and to assume that the industry is only of marginal importance to the overall economic process of both 'economies' (in order to avoid some of the complexities of international economics). In such a context we may discuss and study how differences in R&D spending rules, financial evaluation methods of innovative projects (including pay-back periods), and possibilities of imitation (including different modes of enforcing patent regulations and nationally-bounded industry-pools of knowledge) will influence competitiveness and investment in the long run. Such characteristics of NSI are clearly important (and will be treated in subsequent chapters) but still they miss some of the core concerns of the present book.

But the modification of the Nelson and Winter framework points to a question of more general interest to the present argument: the 'topography' of the search space and the selection space. This term is used as a metaphor to suggest the conditions under which the search for new routines takes place.

> *The topography of innovation determines what possibilities can be seen from what vantage points, how hard it is to get from one spot in the space of possibilities to another, and so forth.* (1982, 229).

We have actually included one or more new dimensions into this landscape to the extent that the search involves contacts and information flows across national borders. This is especially clear when we talk of imitation and selection. But even in the case of innovation search we will often have to consider the economic, geographical and cultural dimensions of space discussed in chapter 3.

Actually, we find that even the organisational dimensions of space are nearly absent in the argument of Nelson and Winter except in the discussions of imitation. But even in this case all firms are equally near or far from each other. This idea may be a relevant abstraction in many discussions. But it is quite far from the visions behind the present argument and it represents a radical delimitation of the concept of 'locality' in the argument of Nelson and Winter which is especially clear if the search and selection spaces are taken together. To use a metaphor: there are no 'Galapagos Islands' in their topography and thus no chance of developing and testing new variants under specialised conditions before they are tested in the more hostile environment of the mainland.

The task of the topography of Nelson and Winter is much more modest. It is mainly described in terms of total productivity created by productive routines and emphasises the distance and search costs involved in obtaining new routines. In this context the production routine of a firm is upheld until it finds a more productive routine. If the firm is following the metaroutine of satisficing conservatism, it will not search for new routines unless its profitability falls beneath a certain level. The rationality of this behaviour is founded on the assumption that only 'localised' search (and thus minor productivity gains) is likely to be successful while at the same time this search (and the implementation of its results) are still costly and uncertain. This specification of firm behaviour may be challenged and the firm may be seen as performing a permanent and production-near search (and learning), but this alternative view only underlines the 'localised' character of the activity and thus the very small probability of great jumps of productive performance. However, if the firm finds a new and more productive routine, it still increases its competitiveness within the given selection environment, profitability is increasing and there is a possibility for increasing its production capacity and market share.

When describing the evolutionary path of the firms of a given nationally located industry, it is important to note that this path is not only dependent on the adaptation of a global fund of knowledge. Competitiveness is also dependent upon a good deal of 'localised' learning, innovation and diffusion of knowledge (see figure 4.2). By 'localised' we mean national and more or less industry specific. This kind of localised search may help to conserve national idiosyncrasies in the pattern of specialisation. In this case we are not dealing with a global 'lock-in-ness' into a specific technology (as discussed by David (1985, 1988) and Arthur (1988)) but with a lock-in of national firms/industries due to, for example asset specificity and the difficulties of entering well-established industries where an especially huge amount of tacit knowledge becomes a major barrier to entry. The empirical arguments can be found in disaggregate studies of trade specialisation of industrialised nations as is revealed in the OECD trade-by-commodities statistics (see chapter 10).

4.4.3. Back to Industry-Level Analysis

The analysis may reveal new problems if it is expanded to cover many industries and not just a single one. Here we will mainly talk in terms of industry aggregates rather than collections of individual firms. At this level of analysis we may say that even if two industries have the same overall rate of growth, one may be characterised by big productivity increases while we only see small effects in the other. This observation may partly be described in terms of different degrees of sectoral 'maturity' with respect to production and products. The degree of maturity cannot be discussed solely in terms of the 'life cycles' of the industries since there are obvious natural and technological differences with respect to problem-solving. There is an old tradition among economists of pointing out that the potential for productivity growth is smaller in some industries than in others. Such cases are discussed in the literature on dynamic increasing returns to scale.

But there are many other factors which determine the number of new problems and 'favourable responses' created by a given rate of growth. Productivity change takes place in each industry both as a function of investment and as a function of learning-by-doing within the branch and disembodied transfer of knowledge from other branches (and other knowledge sources). Even under such conditions there are good reasons to believe that there are major differences in learning capabilities between different industries of the economy. But even if the possibilities of learning and productivity gains were evenly distributed among industries, actual production-dependent learning would differ between branches because of differing income elasticities of demand (and the inflexible response to establish new industries). In other words, an increasing world income is divided non-proportionally among the different product categories and, therefore, we have an additional reason why branches have different possibilities of learning and productivity growth (see Pasinetti, 1981, Thirlwall, 1986 and Dosi et al., 1990).

4.5. Linkage Structure and Interactive Searching and Learning

4.5.1. On the Structural Character of Some Interfirm Relationships

The linkage aspect of the production and linkage approach to NSI is closer to the underlying vision than the production and learning-by-doing aspect. Here we emphasise that the economy of a nation may also be seen as a network of interfirm/interindustry relationships, i.e., the flows of commodities, labour and information knitting the system together. Thus the question of why the network is relatively stable becomes crucial to us. Is it really appropriate to label part of this network the linkage 'structure'? If so, have the relatively stable parts of the network any relevance to innovation? Neoclassical analysis normally presupposes an extreme degree of flexibility in the relationships of the economic system, and therefore exchange relations are not a part of the 'structure' of the system. Nelson and Winter are primarily discussing routines and routine-creation internal to the firm and not bound to interfirm relationships. The idea may rather be seen as a special case of Williamson's (1985) transaction cost analysis but he has not developed much interest in the problems of technological development.

The neglect of the structural character of some interfirm relationships is closely connected to the neglect of product innovation in most of the theoretical literature. The flexibility of the interfirm network presupposes the exchange of standard products which may, according to an old tradition of generalising from primary products, be called commodities. The underlying assumption, which is seldom formulated explicitly, may be understood as defining an 'ideal type' of interface between the producer and user of a commodity (Andersen, 1991). We may call it an interface constructed according to the principle of commodity abstraction. This principle may be discussed in relation to the model of the interaction between machine producers of industry C and machine users of industry D (section 4.3.3).

The disequilibrium-ridden interface, where a lot of product innovation may take place in the machine-producing C-firms if they get access to the problems and ideas of their customers, is not ideal from many points of view. Especially, we see that a lot of information is needed to deal with new machines and with their diffusion to competitors and customers. A substantial part of this information cost may be avoided by using the principle of commodity abstraction. According to this principle, standardised and information poor seller-buyer relationships should be constructed in order to reduce the information burden put upon the parties. The buyer of a product should be able to consider the product as a 'commodity' which lives up to well-defined standards and has a well-defined price. The advantage is that the necessary knowledge is diminished and thus the buyer is helped to avoid running into a complexity limit (Hayek, 1948). Similarly, the seller can avoid the need for impossible amounts of knowledge as long as he accepts the interface specification. For example, he does not need to know anything about the buyer if he wants to change his production process—as long as he does not change the interface. This principle is clearly pointing at an ideal state which can only be reached approximately in real life.

If interfirm relationships are designed according to this principle, they become quite flexible. What is inflexible and routine-like is the interface specification. Actually we may easily see a lock-in into such an interface because of a kind of vicious circle. The more the principle of commodity abstraction is followed, the less information it transferred between producers and users, and the more difficult it becomes to redesign the interface.

But this stability may once in a while come under serious pressure. Let us say that the D-firms become connected to a growth pole but at the same time have developed a fixed interface *vis-à-vis* the C-firms. They find themselves faced with a rapid expansion of their production and they are generating much new knowledge about possible routines which are not feasible because of existing machine-types. Perhaps they are even induced to develop their own machine production. But there is an alternative. That is to uphold a certain ability of changing interfaces, even in relatively stable periods. In other words, the firms are to a large extent engaged in the fixed type of interface but they are at the same time upholding some interfaces which are organised according to the principle of interactive learning in product innovation. According to this 'ideal type' principle informal and information rich seller-buyer relationships should be developed because they are necessary in the development of a loosely defined 'proto-commodity' and in the beginning of its transformation into a well-defined 'commodity'. This principle is necessary in the evolution of new products and branches. And some products may even remain in their unfinished and information-rich form. But this kind of relationship between sellers and buyers means heavy information costs for both parties and makes frequent negotiations necessary.

It is important to understand that both principles are presupposed by the linkage approach to NSI. In a way the first principle is the rule while the second principle is the exception. The first principle is necessary for mass-production but also for all kinds of decision-making in a complex economy. The second principle is necessary for creating products which are first constructed according to loose buyer specifications and by means of anything you can lay your hands on (in French: *bricolage*) on the producer's side. Later the product (as well as the related processes of production and consumption) undergo a process of debugging and routinisation. It is in these early steps of the process of 'commoditication' that we argue that intranational relationships between firms/branches (and final customers) have their special role to play (see below).

4.5.2. Propositions on Linkages and Learning

The idea of product innovation by means of interactive learning may be seen as a generalisation of Arrow's (1962) analysis of learning-by-doing. In this case, learning-by-doing is really learning-by-using new products (chapter 3, Lundvall, 1985 and Rosenberg, 1982, chapter 6). One might also speak of a kind of knowledge accumulation founded in the trials and errors connected to the use of the product. In the case of computer programs such knowledge accumulation will often take the form of a list of errors and major problems ('bugs') and another list of new facilities which may be important to the user. This learning and knowledge accumulation is (to a large extent) located in the using branch and some of its results can be implemented without changing the machinery or the programs (disembodied technical change). Other results concern the improvement of machinery/ programs. If we assume a strict division of labour, such ideas cannot be implemented without a product development in the machine producing branches or in the programming houses. These branches are, furthermore, the main suppliers of knowledge about the technological possibilities for such improvements.

There is thus a clear need for informal relationships and, therefore, the interface between the two parties cannot be fully frozen. And we will find linkage-effects which are not fully accounted for by the exchanges of commodities and money, not even if we include commodified information.

It is well-known that such a state of floating limits between firms/industries is not necessarily permanent. Sometimes limits may be 'frozen' according to the principle of commodity abstraction. Furthermore, the possibility of establishing and retaining the information-rich 'interfaces' between firms/industries may be especially common when we study intranational relationships.

One of the reasons is that it is easier to organise nationally these kinds of informal but contract-like relationships which presuppose a certain degree of reciprocity. The problem is, of course, how to agree upon and secure 'reciprocity' in extremely informal matters and here the closer-knit network and the cultural norms of the nation may help. Thus the innovative relationship between two firms/industries should not only be described in terms of 'interdependent learning' or 'learning-by-interacting'. We should also emphasise that crucial learning results may take the form of tacit knowledge which is only brought into a more precise form through the interaction of the two firms/industries. This is a major reason for national processes of interactive learning (see chapter 3).

In the present context it has been argued that the structural character of inter-industry relationships is related to transfer of learning results and their relevance for innovation. This implies a set of propositions concerning the relationships between firms/industries in the process of innovation and special consideration of relationships where both parties are located within a national framework (see chapter 3):

(e) Even if many interfirm/interindustry relationships are of a flexible character, there exist a subset of relationships which are relatively stable and function as information-channels.

(f) The transfer of preliminary learning results (relevant to innovation) normally takes an informal character. To a large degree this transfer takes place in some of the relative stable inter-industrial channels. These channels connect innovative producers and their 'lead users' (von Hippel, 1988).

(g) Information channels tend to have a life history which makes them less and less suited for innovative communication. Because of this rule, the creation or re-creation of information channels is central to innovative performance.

(h) Intranational relationships are normally better than international relationships as means of transferring semi-formal and informal information.[4] By 'better' we mean that the transfer is not as strongly filtered and disturbed in intranational as in international channels.[5]

(i) The creation of new channels of the innovative type is easiest between members of a national production system. Thus the national framework may help to develop a creative response to new international conditions (and even to a new techno-economic paradigm).[6]

(j) Differences with respect to the character and amount of national linkages between producers and lead-users lead to differences in the overall competitiveness of nations (see proposition (d)).

These propositions are closely related to the core concerns of this book (see chapters 1, 2 and 3). They are partially drawn from the 'stylised facts' of our investigations into Scandinavian socio-economic evolution (including the agro-industrial case). At the same time they provide a central element in the understanding of NSI. However, since they are treated elsewhere in the book, they are presented in a condensed form in the present chapter.

4.5.3. Development Blocks and their Structural Tensions

We are now prepared to return to the growth pole analysis (section 4.3) and to the question of how the different elementary propositions fit together in an approach which is both structuralist and evolutionary. We will discuss how events are kept together in a sequence of evolutionary steps or, perhaps, a cascade of events. This becomes especially clear at the border of the approach, at times when the specialisation structure of a nation cannot be taken for granted and 'jumps' take place. Here we will consider the interaction of jumps and more regular phenomena in terms of Dahmén's (1950/1970 and 1988) idea 'development blocks'.

When moving from the automatic and continuous learning outcomes of a given set-up towards more and more radical 'jumps', we are approaching the 'ideal type' of innovative entrepreneurship in the classical Schumpeterian sense. However, even Schumpeter saw the autonomous innovation of the entrepreneur followed by less conspicuous, induced innovations, and induced innovations are in turn inducing other innovations. If we follow this immediate network of related innovations (not including those related to the increase in general demand) we have a 'block of development', to use a term of Dahmén (1950/1970 and 1988). The borderlines of this 'block' are quite vague so a notion of 'clusters of innovative investment projects' may be more appropriate. However, we follow Dahmén and use the term 'development blocks', which combines a Schumpeterian 'push' with a Schmooklerian 'pull' of innovation.

The whole discussion leans heavily on the Schumpeterian analysis of two 'ideal types' of economic decision-making related to innovative entrepreneurship and the administration of given possibilities. The two related strategies may be termed the Cartesian and the stochastic strategy (Allen, 1988). The Cartesian strategy is characterised by calculations with reference to a set of economic values which are supposed to represent the experiences of a more or less stationary, non-evolutionary economy. These kinds of investment decisions are clearly irrelevant to actors who are trying to make a profit by doing something radically different. Here is needed an *ex ante* calculation which cannot fully refer to the *ex post* evaluations of earlier projects. If the actors who are dealing with these kinds of decisions refer to the old routines, their projects will fail. These routines are, furthermore, related to 'vested interests', hostile to the new projects. To judge whether there is a possibility of making a profit through a radical break with these routines implies a short-cut through the fundamentally non-computable aspects of the analysis of the investment. Here the innovator is referring to a new system of economic values which in part is only existing in his own mind. Innovative projects involve a good deal of gambling and 'animal spirits'.

The propositions presented in section 4.5.2 may help to develop an analysis from such foundations. On the other hand, the ideas of Dahmén et al. may help to combine the structural level and the actor level of analysis more clearly than it has been done in sections 4.4 and 4.5. This combination leads to a new set of propositions (plus extra definitions) which represent a reinterpretation of earlier discussions on the disequilibrium dynamics of development blocks, based on new results on networks and evolutionary processes:

(k) The establishment of a development block takes place in a context where there are some adaptable branches and/or certain traditions of entrepreneurship. The thinking about the evolution of the development block presupposes that the initial state of the system is relatively well-defined, even though it is not possible to define it in terms of general equilibrium.

(l) The establishment of the core of the development block can then be seen as bringing into the system a jump in the degree of disequilibrium, starting a sequence of structural tensions and their partial resolution (Dahmén, 1988). In other words, the core innovation creates directly and indirectly a whole set of new niches, some of them filled by chance or by innovative jumps.[7]

(m) The development block is not only discernible *ex post*, as certain relationships between historically recorded innovative activities in related (supplier or customer) branches, but also *ex ante*, as an element of the investment calculus of the pioneering innovators (Schumpeterian entrepreneurs). The conception of a 'development block' in relation to investment decisions does not necessarily become confirmed by *ex post* accounting but it clearly influences real activities.

(n) The existence within a national economy of development blocks which are at the same time 'immature' and well-established will strengthen its overall competitiveness and 'development power' (see propositions(d) and (j)).

It is clear that the core concept in the above propositions is that of 'structural tensions' and their temporary resolution. It is this concept which presupposes a possibility of defining an initial 'equilibrium' with a certain degree of resolution of tensions. On this basis it is possible to consider a sequence of structural tensions and their partial resolution. Or, in Dahmén's (1988, 6) words:

Uncompleted blocks are usually indicated by price and cost 'signals' on various markets. This could mean low current profits, or even losses, in some areas but also promising prospects, if the steps necessary to complete the blocks are within reach. Less anonymous impulses may also come from actors in economic life, where, as we know, there are widespread networks of relations and contacts outside what theoreticians call a 'market'. In both cases the challenge is in 'gap filling' which tends to eliminate structural tensions but may also lead to new tensions by overshooting, as technical and other solutions sometimes run ahead of the immediate goal.

These formulations may appear to be applicable to all interactions between producers and lead-users but the idea of 'gap filling' relates mainly to more radical innovations. Especially we should emphasise that the decisions to 'fill in the gaps' are by no means automatic. This can be seen from Dahmén's (1988, 5) example of a development block from the classical history of the British textile industry with the sequence of innovations running from weaving to spinning and back to weaving during a 50-year period. However, we may also develop the discussion in terms of 'national sectors of production'. Such an example of structural tensions and linkage effects in relation to the engineering industries (including machinery and electronics) is depicted in Figure 4.3 (GRESI, 1976, Dalum et al., 1981).

These sectors may be regarded as proxies of parts of the learning and innovative activities within a nation. From this viewpoint data collected according to the scheme seems to allow a rough classification of production structures (and NSI) according to their 'comparative advantages' with respect to inter–sectoral linkages (Figure 4.3). Such a classification was proposed by French economists in the 1970's on the proposition that for a given nation and a given period of time it is often one of the linkages (or, one pair of linkages) which has the dominating investment–inducing and innovative potential. In other words, it is here that we find the most innovatively fruitful structural tensions. In this vein it has, been argued for example that Germany is

Figure 4.3. Forward and Backward Linkages within Parts of a Production System and Possible National Strongholds of the 1960's.

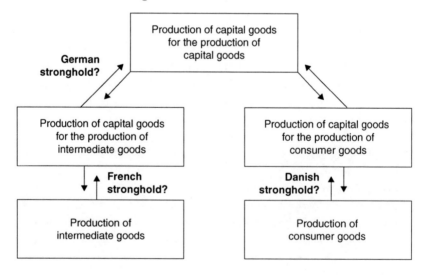

particularly specialised in general capital goods in interplay with capital goods for the production of intermediary goods (such as power stations and steel mills) because innovative performance is especially strong here, and *vice versa*. On the other hand, France has been strong in both the construction and operation of plants for intermediary goods while Denmark has been strong in some types of machinery for the agro–industrial complex and certain other consumer goods industries.

The aggregated view of 'interdependent innovations' does not answer the question of how to judge the relative importance of branches at different steps of the vertical chain of production processes in the determination of the performance of NSI. The controversial question appears to be whether comparative advantage comes from upstream engineering goods or whether the derived innovative ideas spring mainly from downstream innovations. However, it is not difficult to combine these two conflicting views. To do so, it is convenient to argue in relation to a more simple 'product life cycle' model.

In the beginning of the life of a major new product or a branch of industry there are structural tensions between users' needs and producers' production of the product. This 'transformation problem' between the attributes of the product conceived by users and the production characteristics confronting the producers is more or less solved through a series of debuggings and introductions of new product features. If this series of tensions finds a relatively stable solution the structural tensions are rapidly transferred to the interface between producers and their suppliers of intermediate goods and production instruments. Here we find a 'transformation problem' which is in many ways similar to the first one. A series of tensions and subsequent solutions may end up with a relative balance between the vertically related links in the production chain. But a new tension may also build up due to overfilling of the 'gap' or new tensions in the next step of the chain. However, the pioneering spirit around the development block is to a large extent dependent on supernormal growth rates in demand and investment and supernormal profits. And they cannot be upheld forever. Overall techno-economic evolution will sooner or later move the centre of entrepreneurial interest to another area.

Structural tensions may also be discussed in terms of innovation decisions. In the Schumpeterian universe there are basically two types of actors: the innovative entrepreneurs who try to *create* changes and the actors who passively adapt to changed situations or go out of business. Similarly the problem of 'gap filling' can be seen from two points of view. First, the innovator may try to take into account the subsequent 'gap filling' (innovations and investments by other parties) when judging the profitability of his own innovation.

He might even get involved in broader areas of the development block. Thus
Schumpeter (1939, 319) points out that in the last century in the US

> ...*a railroad [company] opened a region, built elevators, prepared many things for the
> would-be farmer, sometimes even furnished instructions about products and methods.*

This clearly points to a notion of an *ex ante* development block which is part
of the expectations and even planning around an innovation.

Second, there is a case where an innovation is already introduced and a
structural tension is revealed somewhere in the related vertical chain of
production and use. Thus the introduction of railways created huge profits in
many related branches and pointed at innovative possibilities. In this way the
development block revealed itself *ex post facto*. But in this situation the pioneers
among the 'gap fillers' had to take a chance, relate their calculations to guesses
and not only old routines and fight 'vested interests' which were partly hostile
to the new projects. In other words, much 'gap filling' is more or less innovative
and involves a kind of gambling. Thus there is in Schumpeter's and especially
in Dahmén's universe a twilight zone between innovation and routine activities
which seems to be of special interest for the discussion of NSI.

Finally, the situation may be one where the gap has been filled out.
According to the Schumpeterian interpretation, a radical transformation
is now taking place. The innovative entrepreneurs are becoming 'mere
managers' and this is an irreversible process. Fortunately, there is a chance that
'new men and new firms' come on to the scene. Another possibility is that large
corporations try to internalise both roles.

Let us try to develop the sketched argument at the national level. Here we ask
whether the overall 'business situation' is characterised by a whole set of
immature but strong development blocks (where new innovative opportunities
continue to pop up) or whether the dominant development blocks have reached
a state of saturation and, perhaps, overaccumulation. The first situation implies
a positive 'transformation pressure' upon the national economy while the
second situation sooner or later implies forced adaptation or 'creative
destruction'.

With such a description of the 'business situation' with respect to innovation,
adaptation and destruction, it is possible to evaluate macroeconomic policies
from a Schumpeterian stand-point. The basic industrial dynamics may, for
example, explain an economy's response to exchange rate policies. If the basic
'development power' of the NSI is strong, then the economy will be able to
respond strongly and innovatively to an undervalued currency while this is not
possible in a saturated economy. One might think of the Japanese as opposed
to the British experiences. But it is perhaps more interesting to compare

Sweden (where a whole set of development blocks appears to have become relatively mature during the 1960's) and Finland (where maturation occurred much later.) Such examples give many possibilities for studying the different effects of, for example devaluations and monetary and fiscal policies in different 'business situations' (Dahmén, 1988). For example, we have the Swedish model of economic policy, including a promotion of industrial transformation through a squeezing of profits in the weak sectors and labour market flexibility. This model was developed in a situation of strong 'development power' but later it seemed less appropriate.

There is, however, another possibility of transforming the micro- and meso-oriented discussion of development blocks to macro-economic performance. Semi-permanent sectoral strongholds of NSI may be interpreted in terms of innovative tensions between two sectors which are not just 'filled' but also reproduced due to, for example, a continued technological revolution in the national capital goods sector or long-term and strong world market pressures upon the consumer goods sector. Therefore, some interfaces in the national system of production and innovation may remain characterised by an immature and pioneering spirit for relatively long spans of time.

4.6. Conclusions

In this chapter we have formulated and discussed a set of propositions and some models which seem to define and apply a production and linkage approach to NSI.

The propositions of the chapter may be divided into three groups. First we have a set of propositions which postulates the importance of production and linkage patterns for learning and innovation ((b), (c), (e) – (g), (k) – (m)). Together they point towards systems of innovation (SI) in relation to production and exchange. These propositions may help to keep the readers' attention upon the production and linkage-related aspects of the process of innovation even though the very notion of NSI tends to draw interests in many other directions.

The second set of propositions ((h) – (i)) postulates that *national* linkages are of importance for innovative performance at the micro- or meso-level. To many this idea is provoking but it should not be forgotten that it is implicitly present in many arguments around NSI. The emphasis upon the importance of national linkage patterns for competitive advantage is part and parcel of much technology-policy-making of international organisations, government offices, trade unions and many business firms. The present framework is intended to help make such ideas more precise and to judge their possibilities and limitations. This is especially important with today's internationalisation of technology, communications and decision-making procedures and the related question of the future importance of the national production and linkage pattern for NSI.

The third set of propositions ((a), (d), (j), (n)) postulates that the processes within nationally bounded SI are of importance for overall national performance. These propositions have been included for reasons of completeness but they have only been dealt with in passing (see part III for further evidence). Thus there is at present no room for evaluating different national technology policies in the context of the production and linkage structure approach to NSI. However, it should already be clear that policy analysis should be performed with at least the same care as academic studies in the area. The confusion created by the neglect of the assumptions of growth pole analysis was just as much related to (regional and developmental) policy analysis as to theoretical and econometric studies.

If the propositions presented in the chapter are judged to be relevant, the question is which tools are available for conducting studies and discussions in the direction indicated. The negative answer is already given: tools like Leontief's (static) input-output analysis and Arrow's growth model with automatic learning effects are not sufficient and may be misleading. What is missing are tools which are usable for expressing some of the basic Schumpeterian and evolutionary insights. The chapter has tried to persuade the reader that the analytic and model builder tools of Nelson and Winter (1982) are highly relevant, even in relation to the complex processes of the state-transformation of a national economy. In this connection NSI may be defined as one of the forces which influence the behavioural rules and the search space which, in turn, is a partial determinant of the sequence of changes in the production and product routines of firms.

The chapter is basically analytic. However, the policy perspectives should not be forgotten in a period when 'new windows of opportunity' may for a while open up for many countries (Perez and Soete, 1988a). Sooner or later major new 'niches' created by the new IT-oriented techno-economic paradigm will be occupied and the production pattern may regain its fixed character. In the meanwhile ideas of learning, lead-users and development blocks may help to avoid the total dominance of one-sided prophecies of the 'Decline and Fall of National Systems of Innovation'. There is also some room for a study of the 'Rise, Fall and Possible Resurrection of National Systems of Innovation'.

Part II:

A CLOSER LOOK AT NATIONAL SYSTEMS OF INNOVATION

Chapter 5

WORK ORGANISATION AND THE INNOVATION DESIGN DILEMMA

Allan Næs Gjerding

5.1. Some Initial Questions

As argued by Johnson in chapter 2 of this volume, learning 'is the basic force behind technical innovation'. Learning is moulded by the operation of institutions reflected in the regularities of behaviour, which can be observed at different levels of aggregation within the economic system. This chapter focuses on the process of learning at the micro level with reference to the relationship between learning and work organisation and argues that the processes of intra-firm learning are contingent upon the type of work organisation in which learning takes place.

In order to evaluate the validity of this argument, one must ask: What are the institutional configurations of the type of work organisation in question, and to which type of learning do they relate in a contingent manner? Exploring the answer to this question is not at trivial matter, neither theoretically, nor empirically. Firstly, the answer cannot be obtained solely on the basis of the conceptual framework developed in part I of this volume, because the question touches upon issues requiring the application of organisation theory. However, this is not a problem, but an opportunity of inter-disciplinary cross-fertilisation, which will penetrate the discussion in this chapter. Secondly, the answer depends, obviously, upon the character of the specific case we are investigating. And thirdly, the question can be posed at several levels of aggregation, and the perspective need not be restricted to an individual firm or an operating unit, but may easily incorporate the most common principles of work organisation within an industry, a production system, or even a national system of innovation.

The aggregation level of this chapter is *the management system*. The management system will be defined as the common general organisational principles of a national system of innovation guiding the organisation of work at the factory level. Thus, the management system is perceived as a set of signposts for (1) the relationship between management and subordinates, (2) the mutual adjustment of actions taken by subordinates, and (3) the relationship between subordinates and the process of physical production in which they are engaged. Exploring the functioning of this set of guidepost's involves a number of questions: What is the overall management approach? What are the logistic principles of production? What type of human resource management is employed? What is the degree of intrafirm specialisation? And what are the implications for the decision-making process?

The answers to these questions, which will be dealt with in turn, are of some interest, not only to theoreticans, but also to industrial practitioners and politicians, who take an interest in the factors affecting the competitiveness of firms. Competitiveness at the micro level is unquestionably related to (1) the process of learning influencing product innovation and thus the product portfolio of the firm, and (2) the process of learning influencing process innovation and thus the relative efficiency of the firm. This chapter discusses how these processes are moulded by the contingency of learning upon work organisation.

5.1.1. A New Model of the Management System?

Following the methodology of chapter 2, it may be argued that the contingency of learning upon work organisation is both nation-specific and time-specific: It is nation-specific, because the set of signposts reflects enculturation, which differs between national systems of innovations; and it is time-specific, because changes of the techno-economic paradigm alter the principles of the management system. Thus, an analysis of the contingency of learning upon work organisation must consider the interplay between cultural values inherent in the national system of innovation and the management system, as wll as the interplay over time between technical and organisational change.

None of these perspectives are frequently addressed in the innovation literature. However, the present wave of technological change associated with the transition from the fourth to the fifth Kondratieff (Freeman and Perez, 1988) highlights the importance of these perspectives, if one wishes to understand the factors determining the development of competitiveness at the intrafirm micro level. The advent of the fifth Kondratieff introduces a number of new management principles (Perez, 1989b) including the combination of flexibility, short lead times, high product quality, and productivity as the competitive nexus of the firm of the 1990's (Gjerding, 1992). Regarding the principles of work organisation, *humanware* and 'giving wisdom to the machine' (Shimada, 1991) has been described as a prerequisite for exploiting the opportunities of reconciling manufacturing efficiency with manufacturing flexibility offered by the development and diffusion of microelectronics and information technology (OECD, 1988).

These competitive configurations are highly similar to the stylised facts of what might be termed *the Japanese management system* (Leibenstein, 1987, Urabe, 1988). The Japanese management system (JMS) comprises the *best-practice organisational technique* of the Japanese system of production, and in my view, much is to be learned from the contingencies of learning upon work organisation in this system, since the organisational principles in question represent important features of what is gradually becoming the best-practice organisational technique *of the world*. Thus, this chapter analyses the questions posed above with the JMS as the principal point of reference. In doing so, I attempt an analysis in the Weberian sense, in which two ideal-types are contrasted with each other, the one being the Japanese management system representing the best practice of the fifth Kondratieff, the other being the management principles of ideal-type Fordism representing the best practice of the fourth Kondratieff.

5.1.2. A Few Words of Caution

The existence of stylised facts about the JMS and the impressive success of the Japanese national system of innovation have induced many Western analysts to argue that an appreciation of Japanese organisational principles should induce an imitation of the characteristics of the JMS. This piece of advice partly reflects an argument by analogy: Since the Japanese have been so cunning in imitating the technical innovations of the West, the West could do likewise regarding the organisational innovations of the East. However, while the imitation of technical innovations in many instances is troublesome and sometimes haphazard, the imitation of organisational principles is an even less straightforward and unequivocal process, since organisational innovations tend to diffuse slower than technical innovations: The transfer of non-trivial institutions from one cultural setting to another, i.e. institutional borrowing beyond the level of institutions of the most simple nature, requires institutional learning (chapter 14 and Johnson and Lundvall, forthcoming), and historical evidence indicates that the development of organisational principles of work at all levels of aggregation tends to follow a natural trajectory within the national setting (Kogut, 1991). Thus, as argued by Johnson in chapter 2, institutional learning between national systems of innovation is more likely to occur, when the systems have common characteristics, than in cases of great disparity.

So, while the JMS, according to the stylised facts, might be said to represent, presently, the best-practice organisational technique of the world, one must be careful to infer that this technique can be easily transferred to other national systems of innovation. In fact, we might expect that nation-specific adaptations of the Japanese organisational technique will create a range of organisational techniques, all of which represent some sort of best-practice. The last section of this chapter is devoted to the question of cultural barriers to the imitation of the organisational principles of the JMS with special reference to the Nordic countries.

5.1.3. The Hypothesis of this Chapter

In order to handle the questions posed above, analysis will be guided by an important question, which elucidates the differences in the contingency of learning upon work organisation between the JMS and Fordism: How do firms reconcile the need for persistence in the pursuit of organisational goals and the need for change in the pursuit of organisational survival? This question, which is at the core of behavioural theory, has been restated as the *flexibility-stability dilemma* (Zaltman, Duncan and Holbek, 1973) and later the *innovation design dilemma* (Holbek, 1988), which will be described in the following section. I will argue that the two ideal-type management systems under scrutiny in this chapter differ with respect to how they resolve this dilemma, especially in the use of uncertainty-absorbing techniques and the kind of problem-solving undertaken.

In order to validate my *argument*, this chapter examines an underlying *proposition* and a *hypothesis* derived from this proposition. The proposition and the hypothesis are inspired by the distinction between 'rational' and 'natural-system' explanations of organisational behaviour proposed by Gouldner (1959) and elaborated by Thompson (1967). Rational models of explanation result from a *closed-system* strategy and natural-system models from an *open-system* strategy for studying organisations,[1] and both strategies are found in real-life management principles for structuring complex organisations in order to cope with uncertainty related to technology and environment by 'creating certain parts specifically to deal with it, specialising other parts in operating under conditions of certainty or near certainty' (Thompson, 1967, 13).

I pose the following *proposition*: While the work organisation principles of the ideal-type Japanese management system emphasise the integration of different parts of the work organisation and equip each part with organisational possibilities and opportunities to deal with uncertainty created by technology and by the activities of other parts of the work organisation, the principles of ideal-type Fordism aim at a sequential nature of the production process stressing that each part should be sealed off from the contingencies created by the other parts. Thus, the logic of the work organisation principles of the JMS and Fordism may be defined as an open-system and a closed-system logic, respectively.

With this proposition as my point of departure, I state the following *hypothesis*: An open-system logic as opposed to a closed-system logic is applied more frequently in the ideal-type Japanese management system than in the ideal-type model of Fordism. In the former case, the propensity to engage in problem-solving activities of a productive nature as opposed to reproductive problem-solving (March and Simon, 1958) is higher.[2] Furthermore, while search processes of a problematic nature (Cyert and March, 1963) obviously are found in both cases, opportunistic surveillance (Thompson, 1967) occurs more frequently in the JMS.[3]

Before engaging in the examination of my proposition and hypothesis, I would like to focus the reader's attention on the notion of the innovation design dilemma. There are two kinds of innovation involved in the notion of the innovation design dilemma: *Technical* and *organisational* innovation. Unfortunately, they have mostly been studied separately within the domain of innovation theory and organisation theory, respectively. However, both the growing volume of literature on the merits of the JMS and the strand of literature on the pervasiveness of microelectronics and information technology highlights the importance of matching technical and organisational innovation. This theme pervades the analysis to follow.

5.2. The Innovation Design Dilemma

Briefly put, the innovation design dilemma relates to the transition from the *initiation* stage of an innovation, in which the gathering and processing of new knowledge is a salient feature, to the *implementation* stage, where rules of procedure, i.e. activity programs, are developed. The initiation of an innovation is triggered by an intraorganisational perception of a *performance gap*, i.e. a discrepancy between the goals pursued and the goals attained, or between what organisational members are doing and what they think they should do, as Zaltman, Duncan and Holbek (1973) put it. The recognition of a performance gap stimulates a process of search for alternative solutions, the attachment of possible consequences to each solution, and the decision to adopt or reject what has been found. During the implementation stage, the first solution meeting some minimum criteria of performance is implemented. Thus, the decision-making behaviour advocated by Zaltman et al. (1973) is a satisfying one in the sense of March and Simon (1958, 140):

An alternative is satisfactory if: (1) there exists a set of criteria that describes minimally satisfactory alternatives, and (2) the alternative in question meets or exceeds all these criteria.

The analysis of how the innovation design dilemma is resolved in the JMS as opposed to the solution entailed in Fordism will rely on (1) the contingency proposition that the structure of the organisation is critical to the efficiency of the organisation's information-processing capability at the various stages, and (2) the cybernetic proposition that the organisation may be perceived as a set of elements linked and coordinated by the communication flows of the information critical to the function of the organisational activities. This combined approach suggests that the transition from initiation to implementation might be impossible, unless the organisation reconciles the need for stability required to perform present activities with the need for change in order to preserve organisational survival.[4] Thus, the character of the dilemma depends upon the knowledge-acquisition structure of the organisation, and the formalisation and centralisation of information flows and problem-solving activities. In fact, the innovation design dilemma might be described as a hybrid proposition consisting of two dilemmas: The dilemma of diversity and the dilemma of formalisation and centralisation, both caused by features intrinsic to the Fordist approach to management requiring a high degree of intra-firm specialisation.

5.2.1. Diversity

Following Hage and Aiken (1970, 32–33), diversity may be defined in terms of

> ...the level of knowledge and expertise in the organization. There are two complementary aspects...: the number of occupational specialties in an organization and the degree of professionalism in each.

A great number of occupations in the organisation creates a diversity of values and perspectives, which serves as an impetus for change, because diversity enlarges the set of signposts for action and thus makes the organisation more receptive to technological and organisational opportunities, which might be perceived during the initiation stage and discovered and refined during the implementation stage. For instance, Hage and Aiken (1970, 33–38) argue that any occupation will try to demonstrate the necessity of its organisational role by seeking new ways to improve organisational performance. Furthermore, a high degree of professionalism facilitates learning, because professionalism entails an emphasis on the acquisition of knowledge inducing the members of an occupation to keep abreast of the latest developments in their field.

However, while conducive to learning and search, diversity entails a number of possible conflicts, all important to the formation of consensus in the organisation through communication processes. Some examples: Code scheme barriers may exist, e.g. interface problems between marketing and production concerning a new product, since each unit possesses its own focus of attention such as marketability in the case of the marketing unit and manufacturability in the case of the production unit. Furthermore, the impact of an innovation on the social relations in the organisation might be regarded as a threat to the established structure of power and hierarchy, leading to resistance to change, not only during the substages of initiation, but also during the process of implementation. Especially, a not-invented-here-syndrome might be at work, e.g. because the idea that a certain organisational structure is unique for attaining a specific goal could lead to 'the belief that alterations in the organisation would dissipate this uniqueness' (Zaltman et al., 1973, 87).

5.2.2. Formalisation and Centralisation

The degree of formalisation and centralisation is negatively related to the initiation of an innovation and both negatively and positively related to the ensuing implementation.

The negative relation occurs, because rules 'set limits not only on what men do but also on what men think' (Hage and Aiken, 1970, 43). A high degree of codification will limit the set of signposts and thus the flow of innovation proposals during initiation and the flow of adjustment proposals during implementation. Rules are intended to secure conformity and rely on the implicit assumption of decision-makers that the rules represent the best method of achieving a certain behavioural response. The organisational members subject themselves to the behavioural pattern imposed by the rules, and thus a high degree of formalisation and centralisation is only efficient in cases of routine activities.

The need to break away from routine activities occurs, when a performance gap is perceived by the organisational members. In this case, the individual member is confronted with conflicting role expectations, because he is supposed to reduce the performance gap while at the same time performing his activities according to established rules and procedures (Zaltman et al., 1973, 139). Thus, a low degree of formalisation might be needed to initiate and implement solutions to the performance gap. However, in order to avoid role conflicts and the ensuing organisational tension, a 'singleness of purpose is required' (ibid., 140), which is especially conducive to the process of implementation. But at the same time, a high degree of formalisation and centralisation limits the number of communication channels, and decision-makers might never be informed about occurring problems.[5]

In sum, a high degree of centralisation might hamper the information gathering and processing capability of the organisation, which is a critical factor to both the initiation and implementation of innovation. On the other hand, during the implementation stage a clear and strict line of authority and responsibility is needed to create consensus and avoid conflicting role expectations.

5.3. The Japanese Management System

Many impressive stories about the successes of the Japanese management system at home and abroad can be told: The ability of Honda to set up and expand productive facilities to such an extent that Honda within three years became the sixth largest automobile manufacturer in the USA (Insley, 1989); the sad tale of Xerox, who invented the modern copy machine, but at the end of the 1970's had lost their competitive edge, because Japanese competitors were able to produce at 50% of the manufacturing costs, needing only half the number of employees in research and development with half the product-development time compared to Xerox (Dertouzos et al., 1989). Similar cases can be found in consumer electronics, semiconductors and computers.

The instances of Japanese firms superseding their Western adversaries indicate that the adversaries have gradually become the victims of the very principles, which constituted the Fordist success of the fourth Kondratieff. This has been argued to be especially the case in the USA, while countries offering alternatives to mass production, such as Germany and Sweden, have been more successful in developing work organisation principles more coherent with the opportunities offered by the present techno-economic changes. But the existence of mass production is just one part of the story, and it certainly does not explain why Japan has experienced an impressive economic performance at the very heart of mass production, the automobile industry. An explanation of this phenomenon must rely on a comparative analysis of differences in the contingency of learning upon work organisation principles.

These differences might partly be explained by the differences between *myopic* and *dynamic* systems (Pavitt and Patel, 1988) of innovation. It seems reasonable to suggest that the fallacies of the Fordist management system are rooted in a focus on short-term financial performance partly associated with the interconnectedness of capital and management;[6] the lack of a technically and organisationally skilled workforce; the treatment of the workforce as a commodity and not as a long-term investment; the neglect of the importance of close cooperation between design and manufacture; the application of narrow job boundaries; and the fear of delegating authority downstream to the shopfloor level.[7] Conversely, it seems reasonable to suggest that the best-practice standard of the Japanese management system is rooted in the absence of these stylised facts of Fordism. The remaining part of this section, which is devoted to the five questions posed in section 5.1, elaborates on some of these and other features, and places the contingency of learning upon work organisation within the framework of the Japanese national system of innovation.

5.3.1. The Overall Management Approach

Following Freeman (1987, 1988), the Japanese success can partly be explained by the learning effects of the principle of *reverse engineering*, which has been conducive to the perception of the entire production process as an integrated system, enacting the use of the factory as a laboratory displaying close relationships between job functions and the flourishing of horizontal information flows. Concomitantly, product and process design is regarded as an integrated activity, and incremental product innovation, incremental redesign of production processes, and a continuous emphasis on quality control has increased product quality and productivity rates considerably. Thus, continuous improvements of the product portfolio and the relative efficiency of the firm are the most likely outcomes of reverse engineering.

Shimada (1991) has described the JMS as an *integrative* model as opposed to the *confrontational* model invoked by the principles of Fordism. While the confrontational model 'is designed to minimise the influence of human variability upon the performance of the production system', the integrative approach accepts that 'human variability affects significantly the performance of the production system' and 'performance of the system will depend critically on human factors and vice versa' (ibid., 460).[8] This argument is in line with the notion of *peoplism* applied by Itami (1988, 28), to whom peoplism is

...a way of thinking in which the employees (or at least long-time employees) are regarded as the de facto 'owners' of the firm, because they supply the most precious resource – human resources.

The sharing system is an important facet of peoplism: Income shares tend to be equalised, not only horizontally, but also vertically in the organisational hierarchy, and thus the relationship between power and remuneration is weak, creating a feeling of equality among employees. The tendency towards equalisation of incomes finds its equivalent in the distribution of power, where even shopfloor workers, contrary to Fordist practices, are equipped with considerable discretion over technology and the production process.

Implications for the Hypothesis

The integrative model, based upon an appreciation of human resources, delegation of authority, and the importance of engaging in learning processes, requires that frequent and open-minded communication takes place along vertical and horizontal channels of information. The exercise of discretion places a heavy coordinative burden upon the single employee, and learning processes involve the communication between peers at all levels. Thus, homoeostasis (self-stabilisation) is an important feature of the integrative model, and the closed-system logic of Fordism, which relies on the minimisation of functional inter-relations in order to remove contingencies creating uncertainty, is rarely found. Discretion at all levels, and the combination of horizontal and vertical communication in order to facilitate coordinating and learning, create fluid boundaries between tasks, jobs, and units, implying an open-system logic. This feature is more clearly spelled out in the paragraphs below.[9]

5.3.2. Logistic Principles: The Application of the Kanban System

The fact that processes of enactment are frequently addressed in American and European management literature is very symbolic. Coordination of the production flow in ideal-type Fordism is usually obtained through a 'push' system relying on central production planning with precise and specific instructions running down the production line. Conversely, the just-in-time practice applied in the JMS can be described as a 'pull' system (Shimada, 1991), where the output level of an operational unit is determined by the level of demand occurring downstream.

Just-in-time is the strategic core principle of the *kanban* system (Urabe, 1988) aiming at stockless production, and high quality and productivity rates.[10] Following Aoki (1990a), the main logistic principle of the kanban system may be described as the combination of (1) central tentative production planning providing a general guide-line for a specific period of time, and (2) local discretion over technology within the framework of the guide-line according to local demand stimuli. The functioning of the kanban system is highly dependent on horizontal information flows communicating knowledge of intrafirm demand, product defects, and machining problems. The system thus forces the employee to respond flexibly and rapidly to changes in intra-firm demand, and to exercise control over local emergencies. The employee must subject himself to self-management and self-inspection, and is, furthermore, encouraged through experience to make minor modifications to the production process in order to secure smooth operation. In this case, incremental innovation is likely to occur.[11]

Implications for the Hypothesis

The application of the kanban system, which is an important organisational innovation compared to the principles of the Fordist management system, provides first rate product quality, eliminates waste (muda) and stimulates continuous improvement of production processes (kaizen), because it is designed to reveal problems rather than to override them in a Taylorist fashion (Roos, 1991). The single most important kanban feature is the flow of horizontal information in order to detect and prevent obstacles to local activity programs. This might have at least two important effects: (1) The search for efficient solutions is enhanced, thus pushing the limits of criteria for what may be regarded as satisfactory solutions to performance gaps. This contributes to a growth in the relative efficiency of firms employing the kanban system. (2) The accumulation of experience induces the employee to perceive possible causes of future local emergencies and anticipate needs for local program changes. As a result, problemistic search will occur more frequently in the JMS than in ideal-type Fordism, and the same applies to opportunistic surveillance, 'the organizational counterpart to curiosity in the individual' (Thompson, 1967, 151). While solutions to emerging problems might be obtained through consultation with experienced peers, solutions to anticipated problems might be harder to get at. In this way we might expect a greater frequency in the JMS of not only reproductive search, scanning the 'organisational memory' for nearly-finished solutions, but also productive search, constructing new solutions from new knowledge and information (March and Simon, 1958, 117).

5.3.3. The Human Resource Perspective

The differences between the human resource perspective of the JMS and Fordism, respectively, is clearly spelled out in an Anglo-Japanese comparison of the use of CNC machine tools made by Whittaker (1990), who focuses on differences in the human/machine interface.[12] The Japanese managers held a *technical approach* to the use of CNC, i.e. they viewed CNC as a computer with a machine tool attached to it, and thus as a device which would function provided correct programming was undertaken. The British managers held a *craft approach*, i.e. they viewed CNC as a machine tool with a computer attached to it and emphasised the ability of operators to ensure smooth machining. In manning the machines, the Japanese managers emphasised the ability of the employee to learn programming, while the British managers emphasised machining experience. As a result, programming and operating tasks tended to be intertwined in the Japanese case, leading to broad job classifications, and separated in the British case, maintaining narrow job classifications.[13]

The technical approach of the JMS, as opposed to the Fordist craft approach, is associated with a high degree of continuous on-the-job training and retraining (Freeman, 1987) and with the acquisition of diagnostic skills through participation in quality control, notably in the well-known quality circles (Whittaker, 1990). Employees are regarded as important 'agents of change' (ibid.), and contrary to the Fordist practice, where on-the-job training typically takes the form of a short instruction within a narrow task range, the best-practice Japanese on-the-job training focuses on learning through experience, where newly-hired employees often are supported by full-time teachers and by team-leaders (Shimada, 1991). These arrangements are conducive to the development of company-specific skills, which display themselves through incremental process innovation (Urabe, 1988).

Implications for the Hypothesis

While learning-by-doing plays an important role in the productivity growth of ideal-type Fordism, the most important efficiency element in the human resource perspective of the JMS might be said to be learning-by-doing-*and*-interacting contributing to incremental process innovation. This reflects the integrative approach and the peoplism addressed earlier. The organisation of intra-firm education and training serves as an impetus to the exchange of experience and information between the members of the organisation and is likely to stimulate both problemistic search and opportunistic surveillance to a higher degree in the JMS than in ideal-type Fordism.

5.3.4. *The Degree of Intra-Firm Specialisation*

Intra-firm specialisation relates to two dimensions: The vertical division of labour between hierarchical levels and the horizontal division of labour between job functions. Within each dimension, standardisation of tasks take place. Scientific management, administrative management, and the Weberian bureaucracy are prototypes, where standardisation in both dimensions is performed to the smallest economically feasible unit. Opposed to this, in the JMS the 'unit of standardisation is not the job function of an individual worker, but rather a group of job functions performed by the team of workers' (Roos, 1991, 107). Employees are organised in teams assigned to a cluster of interconnected jobs among which the team members rotate, and the boundaries between jobs are extremely fluid and ambiguous (Aoki, 1990a). As a consequence, where the number of job classifications may be very large in ideal-type Fordism, the job classification system in the JMS confines itself to a few, broad job classes (Shimada, 1991).

The broad, team-oriented, rotation-structured job classification system (1) avoids the development of 'property rights' in the job, because it is very difficult for the employee to identify himself with a special assignment (Leibenstein, 1987), and (2) builds flexibility and multi-skills into the workforce, which makes it easier to redeploy the workforce 'as circumstances change' (Lincoln, 1990, 11). Thus, the JMS trades off lower economies of specialisation with higher economies of multi-functionality and attendance to local emergencies resulting in dynamic efficiency based on 'collective learning by workers and encouraging semi-autonomous problem-solving and adaptation to local shocks by the versatility of workers on the shop-floor' (Aoki, 1990a, 277).

Implications for the Hypothesis

Lincoln (1990) argues that a high degree of task specialisation and engineering refinement characterises many Japanese firms. At a first glance, this point of view seems contrary to the Aokian description mentioned above. However, this opposition is misleading, because task specialisation and job specialisation do not refer to the same dimension. A high degree of task specialisation and a low degree of job specialisation might be completely reconcilable, since a job can comprise a number of different tasks, which can all be subjected to rigorous standards. If the range of tasks within a certain job is rather large, the job cannot be described as specialised, even though the single task might be specialised. In this case, the job consists of a number of specified programs, but the employee employs an array of programs and might even be authorised to exercise some discretion as to which program (activity) he will attend presently. Thus, the Aokian analysis may be retained, and consequently the degree of intra-firm specialisation in the JMS is supportive of the hypothesis of this chapter by the same argument as the ones proposed in paragraph 5.3.2. and 5.3.3.

5.3.5. The Decision-Making Process

Actually, the preceding analysis has described a range of important facets of the decision-making process, and, consequently, this paragraph will restrict itself to the hierarchical structure of the JMS. One of its most striking features is that the tendency towards equalisation of remuneration is accompanied by a tendency towards equalisation of status reflected in the absence of visible status symbols such as uniforms, cafeteria facilities, and so on. The equalisation of status between blue collar employees, white collar employees, and managers, has 'contributed towards the elimination of the status barrier in communication' (Urabe, 1988, 13), and is especially manifest in the decoupling of status and job responsibility. Contrary to ideal-type Fordism, a promotion in status ranking is determined by a seniority principle and signals the location of the employee in the status hierarchy, but not necessarily in the management hierarchy (Lincoln, 1990).

The cooperative style of decision-making may be exemplified by (1) the *ringi* practice, which denotes the circulation of an innovation proposal from any level of the hierarchy, (2) the *nemawashi*, which denotes a process of informal consultation across formal hierarchical levels, and (3) the quality circles. These processes, which combine formal and informal bottom-up decision procedures aimed at creating consensus, are important devices in the focusing of attention. Together with other kinds of formal and informal meetings and with the existence of bulletin boards issuing information on the economic and technological performance of the firm (Shimada, 1991), they not only facilitate the communication of innovation ideas, but also aid implementation through the creation of consensus.

Implications for the Hypothesis

The equalising and cooperative style of decision-making, relying on information networks between peers and between employees and their immediate superiors, with whom they socialise (Leibenstein, 1987), is an unavoidable outcome of the overall management approach. It contributes to organisational learning and facilitates reproductive problem-solving and problemistic search. Furthermore, bottom-up oriented decision procedures such as the *ringi* practice, which is a simple way of communicating ideas, might stimulate the desire of entrepreneurial employees for engaging in opportunistic surveillance and thus enact productive search.[14] In sum, one might expect a larger degree of employee commitment to the firm in the JMS than in ideal-type Fordism.

5.4. The Hypothesis Revisited

Table 5.1 combines the definitions of search and problem-solving activities presented earlier with reference to the behavioural theory of the firm, and relates this combination to the notion of routine versus non-routine activities. The resulting outcome is a continuum stretching from routine to gradually higher forms of non-routine activity. The north-west quadrant represents a situation, where search induced by a problem aims at surveying knowledge related to alternative solutions in the neighbourhood of present activities. The direction of search is restricted to current knowledge and current ways of thinking about problem-solving. We might perceive this as a routine problem-solving activity focussed by established heuristics. If the alternatives found do

Table 5.1. **A Routine/Non-Routine Perspective on the Relationship between Search and Problem-Solving**

	Problemistic Search	Opportunistic Search
Reproductive problem-solving	Routine	Quasi non-routine
Productive problem-solving	Non-routine	Non-routine

not represent a satisfactory solution, the search activity moves to areas of alternatives not familiar to the organisation, thus becoming more and more non-routine, as expressed in the south-west quadrant.

The north-east quadrant describes a situation, where agents try to predict future problems and alternatives for solving these problems by applying knowledge already present in the organisational memory or familiar to the agent. The attempt to anticipate problems implies non-routine behaviour, because it involves the creation of new activity programs, but these programs are perceived by the aid of known heuristics and, in effect, only represents an incremental change of existing activities. Thus, the combination of opportunistic search and reproductive problem-solving reflects a quasi non-routine activity. If the direction of opportunistic search implies the application of new knowledge unfamiliar to the agent, the activity moves down to the south-east quadrant, gradually becoming more and more non-routine.

Restating the initial hypothesis in terms of Table 5.1, we may conclude from the evidence presented in the preceding section that a relatively higher frequency of work organisation related problem-solving and search activity in the ideal-type Japanese firm than in the ideal-type Western firm could be found in the south-east corner.[15] Relying on broad job classes, extensive job rotation and transfer of employees between teams as opposed to narrow job classes, virtually no job rotation and a stationary work situation, the JMS-firm is better suited than its ideal-type Fordist adversary to stimulate non-routine search. This opposition is enhanced by the self-management and self-inspection principles of work station conditions as opposed to the specialisation and externally controlled work station conditions in the Fordist regime. The pull-system of information and material flows as opposed to the Fordist push-system might enhance the relative performance of the JMS-firm *in all kinds* of search and problem-solving activities.

Thus, the principles of work organisation in the Japanese management system seem highly appropriate to overcome the innovation design dilemma inherent in the Fordist regime. During the initiation stage, knowledge-awareness processes are likely to take the direction from the north-west to the south-east corner of Table 5.1. The procedures of participation, and formal and informal consultation, are likely to create consensus during the substage of formation of attitudes and simplify the decision substage. Implementation is highly facilitated due to rapid and frequent feedbacks of information. The human resource approach, effective information management, group-centered organisation principles, and flexibility within broad job classes combined with stability obtained through specialisation of tasks, are all features creating favourable conditions for overcoming the dilemmas of complexity, formalisation and centralisation.

5.4.1. The Logic of JMS and Fordism

As mentioned in section 5.1, the overriding logic of the JMS work organisation as opposed to the Fordist work organisation is that of an open system as opposed to a closed system. While an open-system logic permits inter-relations between functional units and allows human variability to affect the physical production system, a closed-system logic advocates minimisation of functional inter-relations in order to remove contingencies creating uncertainty. The ideal-type closed-system-logic work organisation seals off the single unit, at least the technological core, from contingencies, creates specific uncertainty-absorbing subunits, and relies to a large degree on learning-by-doing as a source of problem-solving and search. The ideal-type open-system-logic work organisation allows contingency-related uncertainty to influence the organisational activities as a mechanism of enacting opportunistic surveillance and productive search based on learning-by-doing-*and*-interacting.

At a first glance, it seems reasonable to propose that the two types of organisational logic involve a very different set of intra-firm cultural values. An open-system logic emphasises the ability of the employee to participate in cooperative activities, handle uncertainty, overcome organisational role conflicts, and anticipate future contingencies, while a closed-system logic emphasises the ability of the employee to restrict himself to individualised routine activities guided by stable activity programs, and refer contingency-related problems to superiors. Thus, one might hypothesise that the open-system-logic organisation is characterised by a low degree of *uncertainty-avoidance* in the sense of Hofstede (1980a, 1980b), and vice versa for the closed-system-logic organisation.[16] Furthermore, one would expect the distribution of power to be more equal in the former case than in the latter, and collective action as opposed to individual action to take more prominence in an open-system-logic organisation, while individual action predominates in the closed-system-logic organisation.

Although this description seemingly applies to the two systems in an ideal-type sense, it might, however, not be valid in actual national settings. In fact, drawing on Hofstede's cultural analysis,[17] some important qualifications may be added to the above description of the JMS work organisation. These qualifications, elaborated below, have important implications to the point made earlier that much is to be learned from the Japanese Management System. The chapter concludes with a brief discussion of this question with respect to the abilities of the Nordic countries, illustrated by Denmark and Sweden, to apply JMS work organisation principles, hypothesising that Nordic firms might be in a very favourable position to adopt the best-practice organisational techniques emerging during the present transition from the fourth to the fifth Kondratieff.

5.4.2. Applying JMS: Cultural Perspectives and Hypotheses

Studying the management system of an industrialised country, a Western observer, inspired by ideal-type Fordism, would, typically, expect to find an alignment of social status and discretion, of remuneration and social status, and of remuneration and discretion. However, the previous analysis indicates that these alignments may not be found in the case of the ideal-type JMS. Due to the application of the seniority principle, the distribution of discretion and the distribution of social status within the organisational hierarchy do not have identical or nearly identical shapes, because the distribution of social status would tend to be much more unequal than the distribution of discretion. Furthermore, the level of remuneration is only related to the level of social status and the level of discretion to a very limited degree. The Western observer would get the impression of a work organisation comprising (1) a tendency towards equalisation of incomes, (2) a large degree of participation and discretion at the horizontal level based on a feeling of collectivity among organisational members, but at the same time (3) a tall social status hierarchy.

What are the cultural implications of this, and how does these implications fit the description of the ideal-type system-logic proposed above? Following Hofstede (1980a, 1980b), the cultural underpinning's of the JMS would comprise a very strong tendency towards uncertainty-avoidance, a relatively strong tendency towards collectivist values, and a very high degree of tolerance towards power distance.[18] Consequently, the average organisational member of the JMS would accept a great power distance within a collectivist framework minimising the possibilities of role conflicts. Interpreting this result with respect to the three points mentioned just above, the Western observer would get the impression of a work organisation in which (1) organisational members perceive themselves as important parts of the organisation, (2) feel that their effort are appreciated because they have the opportunities of discretionary action within a framework of low income differentials, (3) accept a high degree of unequality regarding social status and (4) are, relatively unequivocally, aware of their organisational roles within a turbulent intra-firm environment. Eventually, the Western observer would end up with the conclusion that the efficiency of the, apparently volatile, JMS work organisation is conditioned by a collective framework with relatively clear social demarcation lines and organisational roles.

Thus, we might propose that the application of teamwork combined with the uneven distribution of social status, reflecting overriding social values of collectivity within a tall social status hierarchy, create an *informal social organisation* characterised by a high degree of uncertainty-avoidance, within the boundaries of which the interaction between individuals is performed according to a rather narrow prescription of acceptable social behaviour. Consequently, the JMS set of organisational roles, which at a first glance seem broad and relatively ambiguous, is subjected to tight social control. It seems arguable that the incentives to engage in opportunistic surveillance and productive search, described earlier as some of the most important merits of the JMS work organisation, are, to a certain degree, triggered by a well-established set of social expectations demanding the individual to engage in these activities, otherwise exhibiting deviant behaviour.

Although the close relationship between a formal set of broad and relatively ambiguous organisational roles and an informal set of narrow and relatively unambiguous social roles is extremely contributive to efficiency, it might, at the same time, represent the *Achilles' heel* of the JMS work organisation, for two reasons, at least: First, the level of efficiency is vulnerable to changes in the set of social roles within the informal organisation. Such changes may be induced by intra-firm processes, e.g. by the emerging tendency towards the abandonment of the seniority principle in many Japanese firms reported by Whittaker (1990), or by extra-firm processes, e.g. through overall changes in social values. Second, the relative competitive strength of the JMS is bound to be eroded, in the future, as competitors learn from the Japanese experiences, partly as a result of catching-up through organisational learning in the way argued by Kogut (1991) and Johnson and Lundvall (forthcoming). The 'rate of erosion' may increase, depending on the *dynamism* of the relationship between the formal and the informal organisation within the structural configurations of these competitors.

What is meant by *dynamism* in this case? Well, the relative efficiency of the JMS work organisation depends, apparently, on informal tight social control of the discretionary actions taken within the formal organisation. Tight social control limits the tolerance of the organisation towards deviant behaviour and thus the initiative taken by the individual organisational member. Consequently, a process of organisational learning, pushing the limits of what is regarded as acceptable deviant behaviour, may create new possibilities for discretionary behaviour within the overall strategic framework of the organisation. Organisational learning of this kind would, arguably, contribute to the relative efficiency of the work organisation *vis-a-vis* the ideal-type JMS work organisation through changes of the relationship between the formal and the informal organisational structure of the work organisation.

This conclusion has important implications for the process of imitation of the JMS work organisation principles within the Nordic countries, e.g. Denmark and Sweden. According to Hofstede (1980a, 1980b), the cultural underpinning's of these two countries may be described as comprising a rather weak tendency towards uncertainty-avoidance, a relatively strong tendency towards individualistic values, and a rather low degree of tolerance towards power distance, and we may, therefore, infer that the informal social organisation of an average ideal-type Nordic work organisation would be quite the opposite of the informal social organisation in the JMS case, exhibiting relatively wide limits to acceptable deviant behaviour *vis-a-vis* the JMS. Consequently, it seems reasonable to propose the hypothesis that the dynamism between the formal and the informal organisation might be, *ceteris paribus*, stronger in the former case than in the latter case, and that opportunistic surveillance and productive search within the framework of a flexible set of heuristics for routine activities would proliferate, relatively, in the former case.

However, the two terms 'might be' and 'ceteris paribus' are chosen deliberately. Dynamic organisational learning, changing the relationship between the formal and the informal organisation, depends on the nature of the match between the formal and informal organisations in question, and would be prevented in cases where the formal organisation is, more or less, structured according to Fordist principles, thus exhibiting an organisational focus of attention emphasising unity of command based on vertical information and communication linkages rather than horizontal information and communication linkages. Such cases might be described as cases of a mismatch between the formal and informal organisation, from the dynamic learning point of view, and are, arguably, commonly found phenomena in the Nordic management system largely inspired by the cultural diffusion of, primarily, American management principles. For instance, in Denmark there is no tradition for effective human resource management, emphasising a close and lasting relationship between employees and the firm with a continuous on-the-job and vocational training (Gjerding et al., 1990), and, although widely recognised as a serious problem, the development of industrial policy in these areas only shows weak signs of improvement. In Sweden, where these problems are, to a larger degree, relatively absent, and where the consultative cooperative bargaining style at the labour market is somewhat replicated at the firm level, the present pattern of socio-economic development points, seemingly, to the dissolution of the 'social contract' between capital and labour (Edquist and Lundvall, 1992).

However, at the micro level, empirical evidence suggests that consultative principles of management are steadily diffusing in the two countries (Glimell, 1989, Bévort et al., 1991), propelled by large and medium-sized firms, to some extent as the result of the development of new management principles inspired by the Japanese experiences. It might seem that the political and socio-economic development at the macro level is traded off by learning processes and a change in the rule-of-thumb of strategic planning at the micro level. Unfortunately, to an impatient observer, the magnitude and results of this diffusion must await future research and the test of time.

Chapter 6

INNOVATION AND THE DEVELOPMENT OF INDUSTRIAL NETWORKS

Lars Gelsing

6.1. Introduction

In part I of this volume, it was argued that interactive learning in national systems of innovation (NSI) is strongly affected by the specific institutional set-up (chapter 2) and the specialisation in production structure (chapter 4). In chapter 3, the notion of user-producer interaction was introduced as a critical parameter for innovative success thus forming a micro-foundation for innovative industrial complexes and an important determinant for the performance of NSI's. The interaction between firms in user-producer relationships is not the only important type of interactive learning in innovative processes. In chapter 5 the interaction between various departments and functions within the firm were discussed.

Introducing now the notion of 'industrial networks', we set out to specify further, conceptually, the relationships between NSI's and industrial complexes/development blocks on the one hand and user-producer relationships on the other. The application of the network concept can serve as a qualitative as well as a quantitative specification of the micro-structure and micro-behaviour in NSI's.

However, the national level of systems of innovations will not be explicitly analysed in the present chapter. Its focus is on conceptual problems and on empirical illustrations mainly from Danish and Swedish industry. In this context, it should be mentioned that the concept of industrial networks also applies to international relationships (Imai and Baba, 1991). International industrial networks and inter-firm alliances will be discussed in chapter 13.

Using the concept of industrial networks as a description of sub-systems of national and international economic systems raises some fundamental questions as how to define and identify networks? Following Eric von Hippel's (1988) contributions on the importance of customers (users) in the innovation process and the notion of collaboration between producers and 'lead users' we get a rough picture of the need for a further specification of the notion of user-producer interaction. The discrimination between lead-users and users in general is only the first step in the right direction.

In any modern economic system every firm has a number of relations to suppliers and customers and not all relations to external units are of equal importance for the innovative activities of the firm in question. A number of anonymous transactions of standard components to market prices has little or no effect on the innovative capability of the firm. On the other hand, as we shall see relations to competitors (horizontal linkages) may be quite important for the innovative process – a type of collaboration mostly omitted in standard economic textbooks. In what follows we will make a distinction between two types of industrial networks:

the trade network – where focus is mainly on linkages between users and producers of traded goods and services and
the knowledge network – where focus is on the flow of information and exchange of knowledge irrespective of its connection to the flow of goods.

However, it should be made clear that the distinction is mainly analytical in the sense that often the trade networks and the knowledge networks will overlap, but in extreme cases they can be totally separated.

The concept of 'industrial networks' has become widely used in the last few years and for good reasons, but being as wide and open as it is, the concept needs further clarification before it can be used as a powerful tool in economic analysis.

6.2. The Network Concept – Other Approaches

While some authors have used concepts similar to 'industrial networks' to characterise the production structure within a region (Brusco, 1982 and Russo, 1985), others especially sociologists have contributed substantially in analysing the purpose and effects of networking by focusing on parts of networks or specific types of networks. Aldrich and Whetten (1981) deal with the relations between a focal organisation and its surroundings using the concept of 'organisational sets' which refers to two organisations and the relation between them. Granovetter (1973 and 1985) analyses the information value in personal networks consisting of mainly strong and weak ties respectively. In Granovetter's famous emphasis on the benefits of weak ties one finds at least a partial explanation of the general interest for networking as an analytical object. A company can benefit from the loose ties in networks by getting access to information that would be impossible to get without such ties.

However Granovetter (1985) expresses some doubt as to the effects from loose networks. While a loose network may provide participants with large amounts of information, the information obtained tends to be of little use because of a lack of established information codes. Information from tight networks is more restricted in volume but tends to be better suited to the needs of the receiver.

The International Marketing Group at Uppsala University has since long used the network concept explicitly (Håkansson, 1987) to analyse industrial marketing and industrial development. In the IM-group version of networking, the inter-relatedness between relations in industry takes on an important role. Although their definition in our view needs further clarification, the IM-group has presented a number of very interesting studies of networking in Swedish and European industry which we will turn to below.

The merits of industrial network analysis has been summed up by Håkansson (1989, 170). Network analysis 1) 'focuses on events and developments *between* companies and organisations rather than – as more traditional analysis – looking chiefly at events within the companies', 2) emphasises 'specific relationships as opposed to the more usual focus on general relations between international, national and regional developments...' 3) focus on dynamics. 'A network is never stable or in balance, but is always changing in all kinds of ways'. These three elements: the focus, the specificity and the dynamic character will also apply to the studies refered to below.

6.3. Industrial Networks – Further Definition and Identification

Any network basically consists of nodes and relationships. In the present context, the nodes will be industrial firms and their innovative partners, be it suppliers, customers, private and public consultancies and, not to forget, competitors.

From a broad industrial organisation point of view, we may place industrial networks as an institutional form between 'markets and hierarchies' designed to overcome well known weaknesses of these forms. Such a definition is not producing much clarification, but further clarification is not a simple task. In order to develop a useful definition it seems necessary to specify further a) the number of participants (nodes), b) their degree of symmetry, c) the degree of standardisation, the frequency and duration of exchange and d) the degree of interdependence of relations. This will be done below.

6.3.1. Number of Participants

While a maximum number of participants seems irrelevant, a lower limit will be dictated from the very need to separate networks from organisation-sets and dyads (e.g. the user-producer relations). When to determine who is inside and who is outside the network, the focus should be on activities tying participants together. Neither formal contracts nor joint-ventures are necessary in order to constitute a network. From this potentially informal character of networks it follows that any single firm may participate in several distinct networks reflecting the various fields of interest and activities of the firm.

6.3.2. Symmetric and Non-Symmetric Relationships

Relations between participants will be influenced by the specific characteristics of the partners in a number of dimensions: their access to resources (size, established network etc.), their degree of specialisation, their position in the value added chain, their degree of internationalisation and their organisational culture – just to name a few of the most important. The networks may consist of firms which are tied together by user-producer relations (non-symmetric) but may also consist of firms with another kind of mutual positions, e.g. competing firms which are symmetric in relation to their position in the value added chain. This notion reflects the fact that competing firms sometimes do cooperate in the innovation process. This is illustrated by the case presented in section 6.5. At least in principle, networks may exist without any user-producer relations at all.

6.3.3. Standardisation, Frequency and Duration of Exchange

When firms communicate through market channels with other firms and with consumers as end users the information must be standardised (stick to a given code), the frequency may be high (in regular advertising) but the duration of each interaction will be close to zero. The anonymous market transaction is a number of flashes where buyer and seller get a short glimpse of each other followed by a longer period in the dark. The kind of information transmitted in market transactions is connected to prices and quantities.

The communication that deserves the label 'networking' is mostly unstandardised (standardised information and tangible products can be provided much cheaper through other channels), the frequency will be considerable and so will duration. Unstandardised information exchange between participants with considerable frequency for some time indicates mutual thrust whether already established or becoming so.

6.3.4. Interdependence of Relations

One point which may appear of little importance at a first glance, but which has important implications for empirical analysis, is the role of interdependence of relations. To illustrate the point we may look at the relationships between the three firms A, B and C. Let us assume that we find relations between B and C and between A and C. We may now distinguish between two types of networks. If there is a specific relation between A and B, e.g. a (longer lasting) flow of goods and services or a sustained exchange of non price/quantity information, we will name the network *a closed triplet* If we find no direct relations between A and B we will name it an *open triplet.*

Any network may consist of several closed and open triplets as well as relations of other types. In a recent study (Gelsing, 1990), 'closed triplets' were used as a way of defining the object of network analysis, while in the works from the Uppsala network group more indirect relations between firms A and B will qualify as networks (Håkansson, 1987). According to this approach, it is likely that the supply from C to B of goods or services will affect either C's ability to supply A or A's willingness to buy from C, and therefore it is argued the relations between C – B and C – A are adequately interrelated to make them qualify as network relationships.

In empirical analysis, the overall purpose of the study will ultimately decide whether one should apply the closed or the open triplet when defining the limits of the network. If the purpose is just to demonstrate the existence of the network, the precise limits of the individual network is of minor interest and in this case an open definition will do. If the purpose is to analyse the network-process and how relationships between networking firms differ from relations between firms outside networks, a closed definition will be needed.

Finally, it is necessary to specify the activities to be focused upon in order to be able to pin-point the borders of a network. Is it technical development projects, 'old boys networks', shared production equipment, shared procurement, shared marketing or shared knowledge accumulation (collective learning) etc.? This implies that there will be considerable overlap between various networks both for a group of firms and for the individual firm. In short, for empirical analysis it is necessary to specify further the focus chosen.

Figure 6.1. Types of Networks.

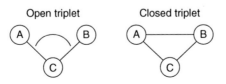

The specification to be made here refers to the distinction between trade networks and knowledge networks. The trade network consists of relations between users and producers and the flows of information is connected to flows of commodities with a certain price. The knowledge network focuses on the flow of information irrespective of its connection to the flow of goods. The knowledge network approach must pay equal attention to information exchange between users and producers on the one hand and between competitors on the other.

Cooperation among competitors is a paradoxical phenomenon but its importance is supported by empirical findings. Eric von Hippel devoted a chapter to 'cooperation between rivals' (von Hippel, 1988). He characterised this structural relationships not as knowledge networks but as 'informal know-how trading'.

The informal proprietory know-how trading behaviour I have observed to date can be characterized as an informal network that develops between engineers having common professional interests. In general such trading networks appear to be formed and refined as engineers get to know each other at professional conferences and elsewhere. In the course of such contacts, an engineer builds his personal informal list of possible useful expert contacts by making private judgements as to the areas of expertice and abilities of those he meets. (1988, 77)

To underpin his argument von Hippel deals with the following three questions based on his own empirical material. Is it valuable know-how, that is being exchanged? Are the firms in question really rivals? Is it trading? The answer to the first two questions is 'yes'. Concerning the third question von Hippel found that the exchange of information is highly restricted but not by a price mechanism. It is a 'barter-relationship' where information is disclosed only when information of similar value is likely to be given in return (op cit., 1988, 82).

One possible reason for the development of knowledge networks in industry may be the specialisation process. Even when belonging to the same branch of industry any two firms will tend to differ in the chosen equipment, the market segment, the distribution, the quality control etc. and thus they may allow engineers to exchange information with colleagues in competing firms. In short the result of specialisation is that the resources of firms differ and therefore two manufacturers of similar products like Volvo and Renault can cooperate in car-engines. In section 6.5 we will refer to an example with cooperation between two manufacturers of mobile celullar telephone equipment.

6.4. Allocation of Industry and the Development of Regional Industrial Networks

When discussing why and how networks affect firm behaviour and especially, how they affect the innovative capabilities of industrial firms it is useful to place network-analysis into a broader model of industrial development as the industry-life-cycle model presented in appendix 6.1.

Here industrial development is divided into four main phases: the innovative, the competitive, the oligopolistic and the decline phase and characteristics of the four phases are described in terms of patterns of localisation, importance of proximity, growth and finally technological development.

The content of the four phases is more or less 'standard' and will not be treated further here.[1] The interest will be directed towards the changing role of networks in this admittedly broad picture of the phases of development of industries.

6.4.1. Networks in the Industry-Life-Cycle Model

In the innovative phase, which attracts primary interest in this context, networks tend to be informal, for instance networks of old colleagues and engineers with a common background and interests, entrepreneurs with an unspoiled fascination of new applications of technical ideas into products. In most cases, the early start of an industry will be local and based on a minimum of local demand for the products in question. This is inferred from the fact that the typical entrepreneur is too preoccupied with her product to do any serious market research. An important exception is when the industry is strongly research-induced. Then the take-off may be located in different regions depending on the location and diffusion of the critical scientific break-through. If this break-through is local the shift from local to international markets for the new industry may occur very rapidly as the employees of such new firms – some of which will come from research institutions – have already established international communication networks and know how to use them.

Locally oriented entrepreneurs characterises phase 1 of the model. When the industry has reached a certain degree of maturity, the process of establishing relations to distant companies – establishing international networks – will accelerate. But in phase 1 uncertainty will be overwhelming and the access to local suppliers will be very convenient in order to solve the various unstandardised and unforeseen problems.

Some branches of industry will tend to move into phase 2 where official and non-official standards begin to guide the development and other competitive

Table 6.1. **Expanding the Innovative Stage**

Stage of Industry Parameter	Innovative	Innovative
	1.A: 'Swarming'	1.B: 'Strategic Networking'
Localisation pattern	Close to existing pools of high-skilled labour/ founders residence	Dependence on local networks is reduced or transformed from user-producer networks to knowledge networks
Importance of proximity	Agglomeration economies are high. Attraction point: innovative centres.	Reduced. Increasing search cost for international best-practice partners (colleagues, lead-users etc.)
Growth	High growth rates. Employers from established firms form spin-off firms	High but unstable. The transformation of best-practice knowledge into new products is uncertain. Spin-off is reduced by increasing knowledge arriers to entry
Technological development.	Product innovations have primacy. In many cases production equipment is modified by the user.	Product innovations have primacy

parameters such as scale-economics will become important. Other branches, such as electronic component industry continue for decades to have room for entrepreneurs. The maturity of such a segment of industry characterised by continued innovation will show itself in the development of business relations where firms and groups of firms will try to plug into international networks. They will however be less attracted to 'least cost sites' because their primary potential is their innovative capabilities and not so much their cost efficiency.

In branches of industry like electronics, which has maintained its dynamic characteristics for at least three decades, a further distinction of the first stage is called for. A distinction may be made between a stage 1.A where industry is characterised by massive entrepreneurial activity and a stage 1.B where a smaller number of established firms have a more planned R&D-activity and concentrate their resources on further product development, but still giving less attention to cost efficiency than a phase 2 industry.

While networks in phase 1.A may be expected to be open and relatively spontaneous in respect to the selection of members and content, the networks one would expect to find in phase 1.B would be characterised by strategic planning and they would be more exclusive, have more formal organisation etc.

This distinction would also be expected to affect the economic resources invested in network activities and the geographical and cultural distance between members of the networks.

A general weakness of phase- and life cycle-models is exposed when the analysis goes a step further than just to present the stages and the very simple dynamics between them. The model does not take into account the differences between the industrial branches and there is not even an approximate indication of the time-span for each phase.[2]

We will conclude that a further specification of the phases, as shown for the first phase, is called for. The merits of the model is primarily analytical but it presents a rough picture of a very complex process.

6.5. Industrial Networks – Some Illustrations

The empirical evidence to be presented comes mainly from three studies. A study of networking in more than 120 Swedish manufacturing companies (Håkansson, 1989), a Danish study of the cooperation in electronics in North Jutland (Brændgaard and Gelsing, 1987) and another Danish study on cooperative innovation in industry based on cases from North Jutland (Gelsing, 1990).

Håkansson (1989) is a very rich empirical study and we will only refer to some results, which are important for our main thesis here; namely the importance of the analytical separation between trade networks and knowledge networks. The study reveals results on cooperative relationships with customers, suppliers and colleagues/competitors in at least four dimensions: 1) frequency of personal contact, 2) revealed results from collaboration, 3) the expected results and 4) the duration of collaboration.

While the most frequent form of cooperation is the cooperation between producers and users, the cooperation between competitors seems qualitatively not to be weaker than vertical cooperation. The results on the first three dimensions sum up to the conclusion that interaction with colleagues/competitors is equally intense, equally effective and with as rich perspectives as the interaction with customers and suppliers. The duration of supplier/customer relationships are only a fraction longer than horizontal relationships (Håkansson, 1989, 111–118).

6.5.1. Danish Studies

The two Danish studies differ considerably with respect to the data and the method used. The *first* (Gelsing, 1990) is based on seven case-studies of companies within the metal-working and electronics industry and their partners in specific development projects. The data on cooperation patterns were collected in 37 interviews with company representatives from as many companies and institutions. The selection of the seven companies was based on the following criteria: The company should have 1) its main activities in the metal-working or electronics industry, 2) a general reputation of being 'innovative', 3) more than 20 employees, 4) four years or more in the business and 5) production and sales department as well as a development function/department on location.

The selection of partners was made after the first seven interviews were finished and the criteria were the estimated importance of the partner for the development project in question.

The *second* study (Brændgaard and Gelsing, 1987) had a more explorative nature. The purpose was to map the cooperation pattern within a particular industry (electronics) in a particular region (North Jutland). The data were collected through 17 interviews 'on location' with company representatives of as many companies.

For the group of innovative industrial companies in the metal-working and electronics industries there is a clear tendency to build lasting relations to suppliers, customers, competitors and technological institutes. These companies spend considerable resources in building up and maintaining these relations. Relations are mainly established with 'agents', that are already known to the company and are mainly effective in solving the problems they were meant to solve. Companies seem less successful in the long term control of innovative activities.

In six out of seven cases these relationships form informal innovative industrial networks defined as closed triplets as mentioned in part 6.4.

In the North Jutland electronics study (Brændgaard and Gelsing, 1987) the network was described in terms of *informal knowledge contacts* between the technical staff in different firms. This last network was established over the last two decades without any specific industrial policy stimulus other than the establishment of a Department of Electronic engineering at Aalborg University; and the detailed study on commercial and non-commercial flows between firms concluded that personal contacts forming a knowledge network was an important resource for the development performance of this group of firms. A business service centre has been established recently within a new science and business park in the region and several electronics firms have started projects in the science-park.

DC-Development as an Example

Especially one network between two quite successful electronics firms and the Department of Electronics at Aalborg University deserves attention. The two firms have been competing actively both in their product markets (cellular mobile telephones) and in their demand for skilled labour. Even within the industry they were thought of as very unlikely partners. But when market opportunities began to change radically with the agreement on standards for a pan-European mobile telephone network in 1992–3 and competition was expected to increase because of the creation of a larger market, the two firms formed a joint development firm and placed it in the science park only a few minutes walk from the third part: The Department of Electronics.

The purpose of the joint project is to develop a number of highly complex integrated circuits that must qualify to given standards and allow for miniature equipment. The development project was split up into several smaller parts and divided among the members of the network. When the components are produced each firm can apply them in a product as they seem fit. Then the competition on function and design can begin.

In this example the network-model is used to make it possible for two smaller firms to carry out a development project that would be far too expensive for any of the firms on their own. Siemens, Ericsson, Motorola, Nokia-Alcatel and others have similar projects but with much bigger resources behind.

On the other hand it takes some size to launch a development project containing say 200 man years over a five year period.

All the innovative industrial networks mentioned above are also open and informal in the sense that one participates because of genuine interest and mutual trust and not because of contractual commitments. If a firm wants to build knowledge in a new field, nothing in the already established network will prevent it from doing so except resource constraints. This is a feature which contributes flexibility. On the other hand, activities like DC-Development tend to be better suited for some kind of formalised agreements. This may take the form of mutual R&D-ventures, subcontracting, mutual marketing and training programmes etc.

Another common feature of the network is that it contributes to the competitiveness of small and medium-sized firms. Firms below 20 employees compete successfully on the global market assisted by local service centres and colleagues. Furthermore the networks contribute considerably to regional employment.

The development of industrial networks is strongly affected by the entrepreneurial tradition in the regions in question. The tradition for cooperation is not equally developed in all regions. Furthermore the empirical evidence suggests that the conditions for the development of innovative networks will be different from industry to industry depending upon among other things barriers to entry. Finally, a part of the explanation will rest upon the specific industrial history as in the case of the electronic industry in North Jutland, where the spin-off of a number of small firms from a pioneering firm has had a considerable influence on the development of the network.

6.6. Perspectives on National Systems of Innovations

As argued above the industrial structure of a nation will have an impact on the types of networking which are established. The size structure of firms will also affect the tendency to apply networking as a method of handling the relations to the environment. But structure of firms is also a dependent variable, explained partly by the entrepreneurial activity in the nation. A high frequency of entrepreneurial firms (young firms) will develop a firm culture based mainly on private ownership and personal informal contacts while the opposite structure (larger/older firms) will tend toward more formalised cooperation. In both cases private companies will be attracted to the network-model of interaction because of its flexibility and because it affects the firms degree of self determination only to a limited extent.

Again, the entrepreneurial activity is affected, among other things, by the division of labour between manufacturing industry and business service and by how industrial policy discriminates between small and larger firms. In a national system of innovation with a highly developed technology service infrastructure one should expect a strong tendency to use networking while another national system where entrepreneurial activity is blocked by legal, economic and structural obstacles should show less networking activity. The NSI's of Denmark and the other Scandinavian countries will tend to be of the first kind while the US system seems to be closer to the second category (Rosenberg, 1982).

6.7. Summing Up

Above we have discussed the phenomenon of industrial networks in relation to industrial innovation. One has to admit that this discussion probably raised more questions than it presented answers. To a certain degree it reflects the complexity of the issue i.e. the level of analysis which 'unfortunately' has to make jumps from the theory of firm behaviour to 'stylised facts' of national systems of innovation.

A well known solution to the analysis of complex issues is simplification. In this case simplification is not an easy task because the study of networking always involves a mix of structure and behaviour. And if one leaves out the dynamics, much of the 'exotic flavour' will disappear.

If not simplification then specification is called for, if the study of industrial networks shall become capable of answering some of the questions raised here. We have suggested some dimensions in which industrial networks may be specified. The dimensions were rather straight forward:

- Number of participants.
- Symmetric and non-symmetric relationships.
- Standardisation, frequency and duration of exchange.
- Interdependence of relations.
- Industry characteristics.

Based on empirical findings we can conclude that industrial networking is a non-trivial phenomenon. Today networking is a well known phenomenon among technicians and top management in industry. In industrial policy programmes to promote networking are now becoming frequent. Denmark, Sweden, Spain, Portugal, even the US where 'industrial policy' is a curse and, not to forget, Italy where some claim it all started have networking programmes today.

For the analytical purposes further specification is necessary. In more general terms, the study of sub-systems in the national innovation systems must be based on empirical evidence designed to answer specifically the questions raised (industrial development blocks/complexes, growth poles vs. industrial networks and knowledge networks). The more or less impressionistic views on the degree of network structures in Japan vs. USA/Europe raise more questions than they answer (Sable, 1987 and 1990). The present lack of specification is not well suited for reaching conclusions and answers (Thomson, 1989).

On the other hand well specified and detailed empirical analyses tend to narrow the focus and studies like the ones referred to in section 6.5 certainly call for generalisation.

Appendix 6.1. **A Neo-Schumpeterian Model of Industrial Development**

Stage of Industry Parameter	Innovative	Competitive	Oligopolistic	Decline
Localisation pattern	Close to existing pools of high-skilled labour/ founders residence	Firms are attracted to least cost sites (labour, land, taxes etc.)	If early: relocation is retarded because market strategies are better implemented from old centres. If late: reorganisation of industry to less unionised labour	Close down operations in old industrial regions. Modernised plants in new regions.
Importance of proximity	Agglomeration economies are high. Attraction point: innovative centres.	Proximity to competitors/ colleagues less important. Prox. to producers of equipment of some importance	Firms operate on larger in- and output markets. Internal division of labour and level of information up.	Low
Growth	High growth rates. Employers from established firms form spin-off firms	High. Minimum optimal scale increases and spin-off becomes rare.	Low. Markets are increasingly organised and negotiated.	Negative
Technological development	Product innovations have primacy. In many cases production equipment is modified by the user	Products are standardised. Process development aimed at economies of scale.	Product differentiation (fashion) and process development dominates	Product development suppressed by short-term profit dispositions. Process developments are rare.

Chapter 7

THE PUBLIC SECTOR AS A PACER IN NATIONAL SYSTEMS OF INNOVATION

Birgitte Gregersen

7.1. Introduction

In a period characterised by increasing internationalisation and transnational political regulation the traditional role of *national* government in relation to industrial policy and technology policy is challenged. In this context it becomes important to understand which role the public sector has played in the past and can play in the future in relation to innovation and technical change within nations.

In many ways, the central role of the public sector in creating, maintaining and developing modern national systems of innovation is comparable with the one played by a pacer in a bicycle race. If public sector demand in both qualitative and quantitative terms races ahead it loses contact with the innovative capability of national suppliers. On the other hand, if public sector demand slows down too much, national suppliers may slow down their process of renewal and stick to pure routinising. As optimal pacing in a bicycle race requires a mutual understanding between the racing cyclist and the pacer, optimal pacing leading to an upgrading of national systems of innovation requires a mutual understanding between the public and private participants in interactive learning and searching processes.

In many countries the public sector actually tries to play the role of a pacer via technology programmes, public procurement policies, and so on. Sometimes it succeeds, and sometimes it fails or comes out with only modest success. In this chapter we will try to specify circumstances under which the public sector participates in innovation processes as a competent pacer stimulating long term positive learning effects, internal as well as external to the public sector, and circumstances where public sector activities seem to have inhibited innovativeness in both the public and the private sectors.

The direct and indirect participative roles of the public sector in creating, maintaining and developing modern national systems of innovation are very complex and many-sided and can, of course, not be fairly portrayed in a single chapter. The main emphasis here is put on the public sector as a pacer through its role as a *user* and *regulator* paying less attention to the public sector as a *producer* of crucial R&D and human resources. This is taken up in chapter 9 of this book, where Freeman analyses the role of R&D in national systems of innovations. The general discussion of the pacer role will be illustrated by some exemplary case material drawn mainly from Denmark and the other Nordic countries.

In most countries technology policy programmes have hitherto been dominated by a technology push strategy. The purpose has been primarily to support high-tech producers directly, paying less attention to the user side. However, innovation studies (e.g. Rothwell and Zegveld, 1981, von Hippel, 1988, Porter, 1990) have shown that an effective supplementary national strategy might be to strengthen the demand side in quantitative and qualitative terms. 'Competent users' being able to communicate their needs in a form, which makes it possible for producers to adapt and develop high-quality products reflecting such user needs is an essential basis for dynamic interactive learning (Lundvall, 1985). The public sector itself is a very large and important user of various products necessary to support production and fundamental human needs, and especially in a period where a combination of technical uncertainty and market uncertainty tends to restrain the development of new products and processes the potential effects of an innovation oriented procurement policy reflecting competent user needs appear to be great.

Despite the fact, that the public sector is one of the most important users of many innovations, this sector has in general not attracted much attention in the literature on technical change and economic theory. This also holds for analyses studying user-producer interrelationships and interactive learning. Two important and interrelated exceptions from this analytical obscurity are the many interesting studies of public procurement and regulation in relation to domestic military and telecommunications industries.

These studies of the innovative effect of public procurement and R&D spending in relation to the military area and its 'set-off' on civilian industries seem to show great variations concerning the potential positive effects over time both among nations, among the national industries, and among the individual military programmes (e.g. Kaldor, 1981, Braun and Macdonald, 1978, Rothwell and Zegveld, 1981, Reppy, 1990). For instance did the US semiconductor industry benefit to a much higher degree than the UK semiconductor industry in the 1950s and early 60s' from a relatively huge, sophisticated and lucrative military market. However, since the mid-60s' the civilian market for electronics in the US as elsewhere has increased its relative share and has now far outstripped the quantitative and qualitative importance of the military demand except within very specific areas with no or very limited potential civil application.

It is indisputable that public military procurement and military R&D spending – be it relatively large as in the US and UK or relatively small as in Japan and most small welfare states including Denmark – should be an important part of our understanding of the role of the public sector in various national systems of innovations, although it is still controversial to what degree it is a benefit for the economy as a whole. While this the *national* part of the 'national system of innovation' concept is especially strong and important in relation to the military area, we will not discuss this special case further in this chapter. Our case material is mainly collected from various non-military welfare fields including environment protection.

Most theoretical and empirical analyses of incentives to innovate or adopt new products and processes stress the drive for profit and growing market share and thereby exclude the public non-profit activities from the dynamic dyads of innovative users and producers. From many of these innovation studies we know that the ability to innovate and adopt new technology within a given techno-economic paradigm differs between industries and firms depending on the technology in question, firm size, the capital, time and human resources required as well as the environment in which the firms are operating such as market conditions and relations to suppliers and users. To grasp and analyse such similarities and dissimilarities in ability to innovate and adopt new technologies Pavitt (1984) among others has employed useful categories for firms and industries within the *private* sector, but we still lack a counterpart covering the *public* sector based on innovation studies within this part of the economy. Or in other words, we cannot be sure that the mainly private sector based innovation theories and studies hold for the public sector too. In section 7.2 we discuss such possible differences between the private and public sector in the ability to innovate and adopt new technology.

In section 7.3 we stress the interaction between the public and the private sector based on two different main pacer roles played by the public sector in relation to learning and searching processes: interactions based on the public sector as a user of innovations and interactions based on the public sector as a regulator. Although these and other roles often occupy the stage simultaneously they are here treated separately.

7.2. Public and Private Stereotypes

Public sector organisations are often portrayed as bureaucratic, ineffective, parasitic monsters in contrast to flexible, effective, productive private firms.

One of the key words has been 'system defects' as an explanation of an assumed ineffectiveness of the public sector. Murray (1987) mentions various examples of such claimed 'system defects' in the public sector. First, *economists* have focused on the absence of free market forces which may have several negative implications: The 'real' demand is unknown, which either leads to over-production or rationing. The fixing of prices is uncertain, and without the drive for profit there is no motivation for adjustment and rationalisation of the production. There is a lack of dynamic efficiency in the Schumpeterian sense, and a lack of innovative capability. Second, *public choice theorists* have stressed that decisions taken in the public sector are not 'pareto optimum', since the majority can control the minority. Third, contributions from *organisation theorists* have pointed to elements such as ineffective organisation and management, rigid wage contracts, inadequate cost awareness and obscure and blurred goals. According to Murray, there is one important common characteristic of these statements: They are all *hypotheses* due to a striking lack of empirical analysis, and they compare *assumptions* about the public sector to an *ideal abstraction* of 'perfect markets' and a presumed economic rationality prevailing in the private sector (Murray, 1987, 16).

As described in chapter 3 by Lundvall and chapter 4 by Andersen, one of the fundamental assumptions behind the interactive learning concept is the interrelationship between production, use and innovation. If such an interrelationship is assumed to be present also where public sector institutions participate as users, producers or suppliers, the distinctive characteristics of the underlying goal orientation or rationalities of this participation may influence both the innovative capability and the orientation of the learning processes. In other words, public sector demand dominated by social, political, strategic or military goals or rationalities may stimulate or restrain innovation, and perhaps even pull or push innovation processes in certain directions. Studies of public performance oriented procurement in connection with the military area especially have demonstrated how offensive or defensive national military considerations may outstrip any economic rationality in the sense that product quality in terms of performance, reliability and accuracy clearly exceed cost considerations in importance. In other parts of the public sector innovation diffusion may be facilitated due to the relatively high degree of openness of procedures where detailed product and process information are less strategic or proprietary.

Following this line of argument that different rationalities or goal orientations may influence the pace and direction of interactive learning and searching processes, one important question is, which types of rationality are then to be found when the public sector participates and how do they affect the innovative capability of this sector?

One interesting attempt to answer this question is made by van de Donk and Snellen (1989). They pictured government policy as situated between four rationalities. *Political rationality* implies that government actions and decisions (for instance in relation to public procurement and regulation) reflect the – at any time – dominating political and economic interest groups or coalitions. *Legal rationality* means that government policy must have its foundations in law ensuring equality before the law and legal security due to the independent position of the legal establishment with respect to politics. *Scientific rationality* (or 'paradigmatic rationality') is to a certain degree sector specific and related to individual professions or social-scientific disciplines. In public sectors dominated by technical disciplines as within the technical infrastructure areas (e.g. electricity, communication, railway systems, water-supply) we can expect agents to give their highest priority to technical security and quality, while medical, human and social professionalism and rationalities are expected to prevail in public welfare institutions like hospitals, institutions for old age- and child care. *Economical rationality* implies that budgetary cycles put restrictions on government policy. Since the mid-1970s' the economic restrictions on many public sector activities have been severe as compared to the 'happy 60s'.

The four rationalities are presented above without interdependency. However, in real public institutions and government policy formulation these archetypes often interrelate and concrete policy outcomes will mostly reflect a mix of the various rationalities. The mix of the cocktail may of course differ from sector to sector, from case to case, and from period to period. For instance in a study of the introduction of new computer technologies in American local government it was political rationality in the shape of reinforcement politics that was found to be the crucial component rather than economic or technical rationality (Danziger et al., 1982). Strategies developed and implemented by the central edp-departments came up with technical solutions reinforcing the technical and organisational structure and power of the central edp-departments. Contrariwise, in those (rare) cases where the user departments (e.g. social services department, revenue department) were the project originators, the technical and organisational solutions promoted, reinforced the computer capacity of the user departments at the expense of the central edp-department. In another study of the diffusion of computer-based systems (including WP) in Danish local government during the late 1970s' and the beginning of the 80s', budget restriction was found to be the prime restraining factor (Brændgaard et al., 1984). Often computer-based systems, legislation and administration proceed hand in hand. Complex and changing legislation within, for instance, the social and fiscal area demands large computer-based systems for their administration at both the local and central administrative level. On the other hand, the use of computer-based systems may be restricted by legislative ties as is the case in relation to the composition and physical placement of central computer files. In other cases, as for instance in relation to environment protection, short-term economic rationalities may more frequently today than previously take the back seat thanks to increasing environmental awareness and consciousness among producers, consumers and politicians.

According to van de Donk and Snellen the four rationalities distinguishes public administration from private enterprise. This distinction, however, is based on the assumption that private enterprises in principle may limit themselves to economic rationalities and to a certain degree scientific rationalities. As discussed previously in this book (see Part I) and in other institutionalist and evolutionary approaches (e.g. Nelson and Winter, 1982) this assumption may be an unrealistic simplification. Few would argue that legislation of various kinds does not affect the strategies of private firms. Also the concept 'political rationality' may, in the broad sense as we have used it above, be relevant for our understanding of activities going on in and between private enterprises. The distinction between public and private organisations may then be rather a question of finding significant patterns in the way these various rationalities are interrelated, than a question of one, two or four rationalities being relevant. Arguments for this statement may be found in Lane (1988), who, in a way, is less 'categorical' in his distinction between public and private organisations.

From a comparative analysis of public and private management Lane argues, that in a mixed economy it may be difficult to distinguish, clearly, between public and private leadership, because 'each appears to work with a multiplicity of goals, facing a complex environment where several interests look for participation and many rules restrict behaviour' (Lane, 1988, 61). However, he concludes, that in a mixed economy there are still fundamental differences between public and private management especially along two dimensions as illustrated in Table 7.1 below. The one dimension is the well-known classical one concerning *goal orientation*. The second dimension is the *environment*, within which the two types of organisations operate. The traditional image of public organisations is type I, whereas that of private is type IV.

Table 7.1. **Public and Private Leadership**

Orientation	Environment	
	Stable	Unstable
Public interest	I	II
Private interest	III	IV

Source: Lane, 1988, 61.

According to this image, public organisations tend to work in a more stable or less unstable environment than private organisations. The 'market conditions' or the relations to the consumers or clients differ between the two types of organisations. The relations to consumers or clients of the public organisations are often authoritative without possible exit whereas the relation of private organisations to their consumers is dependent upon market demand where exit for both the producer and the consumer is a possibility.

Private organisations attempt to maximise or satisfy a private goal function, whereas public organisations have to respond to the public interest defined by a political body being the government or the electorate. As previously indicated, public interest may often consist of a multiplicity of conflicting goals or rationalities, qualitative in nature which may be more difficult to quantify or evaluate than a dominating profit orientation in private organisations.

If we then substitute the goal orientation dimension in Table 7.1 with a dimension capturing the orientation towards innovation, which is the prime focus in this book, we can illustrate the traditional image of innovativeness of public and private organisations as follows.

According to this traditional image public organisations tend to be of type I, whereas private organisations mainly belong to type IV. Lack of competition (e.g. stable environment) together with bureaucracy in the Weberian sense (e.g. functional specialisation, rules and procedures to ensure uniformity and continuity, impersonality of interpersonal relations, hierarchy of authority, and technical qualifications forming the basis of employment and promotion) is assumed to put a brake on the innovativeness of public organisations and stimulate conformity and standardised routine solutions. Contrariwise, the spirit of entrepreneurship in the Schumpeterian sense (e.g. personal growth, creativity and initiative) together with competition (e.g. unstable environment) force private organisations toward continuous innovation.

The framework developed by Daft (1982) may help to introduce some light in this gloomy picture of innovative capability in public bureaucracies. The point of departure is that all organisations, be they public or private, organic or mechanistic, or hybrids, have to handle the stability-change dilemma (as described in Chapter 5 by Gjerding) by facilitating both routinisation and

Table 7.2. **Public and Private Innovativeness**

Orientation	Environment	
	Stable	Unstable
Routine	I	II
Renewal	III	IV

novelty but they solve this dilemma in different ways depending upon the type of innovation typically needed and the environmental context.

The question of bureaucracy versus nonbureaucracy should not be answered upon our biases for nonbureaucratic forms of organization, but on the needs of the organization for stability versus change and on the ability of the structure to meet those needs (Daft, 1982, 160).

With a minor transcription we may conclude that the question of public versus private innovative capability should not be answered with reference to our bias towards competitive forms of organisation, but on the needs of the organisation for stability versus change and on the ability of the structure to meet those needs.

Many traditional public welfare institutions related to personal services like old age homes, kindergartens and schools, but also public administrative institutions like tax authorities and social services departments have during the 1980's found themselves in a very unstable environment with frequently changing laws and severe financial cuts. Also public hospitals have in recent years faced increasing uncertainty in both the technical and the administrative environment creating an urgent need for special organisational changes. Some of these institutions, especially the administrative parts, have tried to respond to the changing environment by introducing new information technologies. However, many of these public administrations have run into problems due to both a lack of internal 'computer-knowledge' and a lack of organisational change towards a more organic type of bureaucracy, which seems more suited to take advantage of new information technology.

It is important to stress that the degree of uncertainty of environment may shift over time. Since the micro-electronic revolution and the shift in techno-economic paradigm, the pressure for both technical and administrative innovations has been increased in private as well as public organisations, but without comparative studies we have no particular reason to believe a priori that public institutions may do worse than private ones in the long run.

7.3. Public-Private Interactions

In this section we will switch our focus from a discussion of possible distinctive characteristics between public and private organisations in relation to innovative capability to a discussion of how *interactions* between the two sectors may stimulate (or restrain) innovation. We thus turn our attention from a discussion of stability versus change or routine versus renewal *inside* public institutions or private firms to a discussion of how *interaction* based on stability, standardisation and routinising inside public institutions under certain circumstances may stimulate and under other circumstances inhibit change, renewal and innovativeness in private firms. We will also discuss the opposite situation where change, instability and renewal of public sector activities under certain circumstances inhibit and under other circumstances promote innovativeness in private firms. In other words, we will try to locate situations or circumstances where the public sector has acted either as a professional or as a more amateurish pacer for the private sector using public demand and regulation as political tools.

We start the discussion in section 7.3.1 with four examples sketching how the public sector may perform as a pacer under various circumstances. Section 7.3.2 discusses more generally the regulation tool in relation to innovation, and section 7.3.3 focuses on public sector demand.

7.3.1. Four Illustrations of the Pacer Role

Table 7.3 illustrates four different outcomes of interactions between public users and private producers.

Type I illustrates a situation where a high degree of stability in both the technical and administrative environment combined with a routinised behaviour among public users tends to lull the private suppliers to sleep. The public market is secure and stable and the suppliers set the pace. Examples can be found within traditional public procurement areas where a monopolistic or monopsonistic domestic or local supplier structure typically prevails as for instance public transportation, or municipal standard wastewater treatment plants.

Type IV illustrates the opposite type of interaction between public users and private producers. A high degree of instability in the technical and administrative environment forces public users to be innovative, pacing innovativeness among private suppliers. Illustrative examples are the wide diffusion of new public waste-handling routines based on recycling and eventually combined with restrictive regulations on packaging as in Germany. The growing need for sustainable solutions to the escalating waste-handling problems all over has initiated re-thinking and a renewal process among technicians, administrators, lawyers (and even economists) in public sector institutions (especially at the local level)

Table 7.3. **Public-Private Interactions**

Demand from Public Users	Innovativeness Among Private Producers	
	Routine	Renewal
Routine	I	II
Renewal	III	IV

in Denmark, Sweden, Netherlands, Germany and other high-income countries. More and more private producers respond with new low- and non-waste-products with greater recycling possibilities and more environmentally compatible products and production processes. Another encouraging kindred example of progressive public sector pacing is the rise of the Danish windmill industry despite an originally strong resistance from the established power stations. However, using old instruments such as taxes, rates, and dues on the conventional energy sources together with public R&D funding and subsidising the development and use of 'alternative' energy sources, the Danish Energy Ministry has converted the concessionary energy companies to a more conciliatory attitude towards windmills and other 'alternative' energy sources.

As indicated by Type II, it is not necessarily the case that the classical virtues of public bureaucracies in the form of market stability, technical standardisation and administrative routinising lull the domestic suppliers to sleep. In fact, if demand is characterised by long term stability, technical standards are set at a high level, and work-procedures are routinised and widely spread among public users, the innovative 'inclination' and capability among domestic private producers may be stimulated. The Danish hearing-aid industry obtained international strongholds (today about 2/3 of the world market) as a result of optimal pacing combining high level technical standards and knowledge within the electro-acoustics area with a solid home market based on public subsidising (Jørgensen, 1986). Another well-known example of this type of interaction between public (or semi-public) users and private producers is the development of national telecommunications industries as convincingly described by Grandstrand and Sigurdson, 1985. In their study of the Swedish telecommunication industry they show how public 'routinising' in the form of technical standardisation, price setting, procurement and market regulations combined with R&D subsidising made the foundations for not only a strong *domestic* tele-industry – as has been the case in most developed countries – but also an industry with *international* strongholds. Thus, routinising (to a certain degree) among the public users may sometimes be a precondition for renewal among private producers.

Public-private interactions of Type III illustrate situations where a high degree of market uncertainty is combined with a forced process of renewal of administrative routines among public users may inhibit long term innovativeness among private suppliers. The Danish public demand for wastewater treatment plants contains an illustrative example on Type III-relations (Gregersen, 1988). Since the early 1970s' Danish municipal investments in wastewater treatment plants have been rather unstable and fluctuating. In the first half of the 1970s' investments accelerated. Then investments declined rapidly in the period of the late half of the 1970s' to the late 1980s' when once more investments accelerated. This stop-and-go policy made long-term planning of the suppliers' R&D activities very difficult. During the period of cuts in the late 1970s' and early 1980s' many engineers and experienced marketing experts in established firms had to reorient their efforts and ambitions from advanced wastewater technology for the home market to technically less advanced water treatment plants for less-developed countries. Another consequence was debilitation of the users. Due to the cuts in the public sector since the late 1970s' local government have been unable to maintain their technical expertise in administrative departments and on the operational plant level. Local government is now forced to rely entirely on the suppliers and the private consulting engineers. The base for future dynamic interactive learning has thus been clearly weakened.

Despite the stop-and-go policy, some Danish suppliers actually developed international strongholds within biological wastewater treatment technology in the late 1970s' and the first half of the 1980s'. The explanation of this has however more to do with the 'Type II interaction'. These innovation processes started in a period when increasing environmental awareness among politicians and their voters caused stricter environmental regulation and, no less important, caused an expectation among the suppliers of a more or less stable tendency towards stricter future legislation on both domestic and international markets. This combination of sticks and carrots in the form of a stable tendency for stricter future regulation and possible first mover advantages stimulated research activities among some of the central domestic suppliers. The patented advanced methods for biological removal of nitrogen and phosphorus from wastewater, BIO-DENITRO and BIO-DENIPHO, were developed in that period by Akvadan in cooperation with the Department of Environmental Engineering at the Technical University of Denmark. Also the development of the oxygen meter by Danfoss, improvements of the active sludge treatment process by Krüger and several other technical improvements within wastewater treatment technology belong to this period when strict public regulation paced the domestic suppliers ahead of their international competitors.

One general conclusion from these examples is that *maintaining* the successful pacing of domestic suppliers over time is a difficult task. It seems to require that both quantitative and qualitative demand change under stable conditions, and that user-qualifications and technical standards are maintained at a high level. However, even if these conditions are fulfilled there is, of course, no guarantee of interactive learning leading to fruitful innovation.

7.3.2. Pacing Private Firms Using Regulation as a Stick

One important difference between the public and the private sector is the ability of public authorities to define the 'room of innovative manoeuvre' for both private and public sector organisations by setting up standards, Patents Acts and various other regulatory procedures to protect and control innovation and diffusion of new products and processes. The instrument of regulation has many strings, but one may roughly distinguish between one category mainly aiming at economic efficiency and another focusing at other goals. In the first category we find regulations in the form of standardisation and Patents Acts. In the second category we find regulations aimed at environmental protection, consumer and worker safety. The main focus in this section is on regulation of the second category.

Since the 1950s and 1960s', various national and international regulations covering nearly all kinds of products and processes have emerged. Environmental regulation acts with quantitatively defined emission rates, regulations on time of rest for truckdrivers, restrictions on the introduction of new drugs and pharmaceuticals and several consumer goods, rules for the mesh size of fishing nets, standardisation of communication equipment, just to mention a few examples. Regulation in this strict sense of making rules and procedures for innovation and diffusion may serve either the producer or innovator (as for instance the patent system), the user (as for instance regulation concerning drugs and pharmaceuticals) or the environment and natural resources (as for instance emission rates or fishing quotas).

Most of the academic literature on regulation and innovation has seen this interplay as a kind of input-output process, where regulation either stimulates or restrains the rate of innovation and diffusion. One may find several case studies supporting each statement, depending on the sort of regulation, the type of innovation and the kind of industry in question. (For an overview of the literature on regulation and innovation see for instance Rothwell and Zegfeld, 1981). By counting the number of new products introduced and the time delay from invention to marketing due to approval restrictions, studies on the effects of the growing regulation within for instance the drug and pharmaceutical areas have pointed out the restraining facets of the interrelationship. By similar studies, the stimulating facets have been shown especially within military, health and environment protection areas.

One may of course question the methodological base for many of these case studies on the interaction between regulation and innovation. One fundamental problem concerns the difficulties in isolating the effects of regulation from all the other firm internal and external factors effecting learning and searching processes. Another methodological problem is related to the analytical level, which has typically been the single innovation or the single firm. When the analytical level is the single innovation, it is of course difficult to draw more general conclusions for other kinds of innovations taking place in another period or at another location. When the analytical level is the single firm, the effects of a specific regulation on the overall economy, consumer behaviour or long term knowledge accumulation in the national system of innovation are excluded. A third kind of problem, similar to that of adding apples and pears, arises when different types of innovations are put together and measured along the same time axis.

In short, most of the studies done within this area hitherto have focused on how regulation affects the *rate* of innovation and diffusion.

Regulation has rarely been considered as a positive means of technical control e.g. through stimulating new forms of technological response rather than simply restricting the operation of the marketplace. The whole issue of regulation, therefore, has been conceptualized as a post-innovation check on undesired side-effects rather than as a tool for directing technology towards socially desirable ends (Irwin and Vergragt, 1989, 58).

Irwin and Vergragt (1989) introduce an approach to study the *inter-relationships* between regulation and innovation based on a more complex socio-technical perspective. Innovation, regulation, and their interaction have to be seen as a product of 'social and institutional negotiations' at every level (1989, 63). In their 'interactive model of regulation-innovation' the form of regulation affects the corporate response, and the character of that response will affect future regulation. Thus, innovation and regulation are part of the same social and technical process.

As the model indicates, the form of regulative intervention can be manifold, and so can the corporate response. The extent of necessary organisational, technical or economical changes and responses may be dependent on both the technical characteristics and the timing of standards and vice versa. For instance emission limits for nitrogen and phosphorus may correspond to existing or dominating best practise techniques or they may within a certain time span require the development of radical new products or processes as in the case of the 'Montreal-protocol' from 1987 demanding a total stop in year 2000 for the use of CFC (freon) in industrial processes and products like home freezers, refrigerators, sprays and several others.

The mode of enforcement, for instance to what degree the combination of regulative sticks (taxes, rates and dues) and regulative carrots (subsidies and development contracts) is open to objection, will influence the outcome of the regulation-innovation interaction too. Many exceptions to specific emission dues or repeating exemptions to passed respites – as for instance has been the case in relation to the realisation of the Danish 'water-environment action plan' from 1987 – may of course influence the search intensity towards new technical solutions negatively.

Figure 7.1. The Interactive Model of Regulation-Innovation.

REGULATION	INNOVATION
Technical characteristics and timing of standards	Economic changes - rate of innovation - production/product cost - effects of competition - profit/turnover statistics
Mode of enforcement	
National/international coverage	
Anticipatory/reactive character	Organizational changes - staffing - priorities - lobbying
Product vs. process control	
State of the "knowledge base"	Technological changes - new responses - effects on product cycle

| Effective characteristics of regulatory action | → | Changes in safety policy |

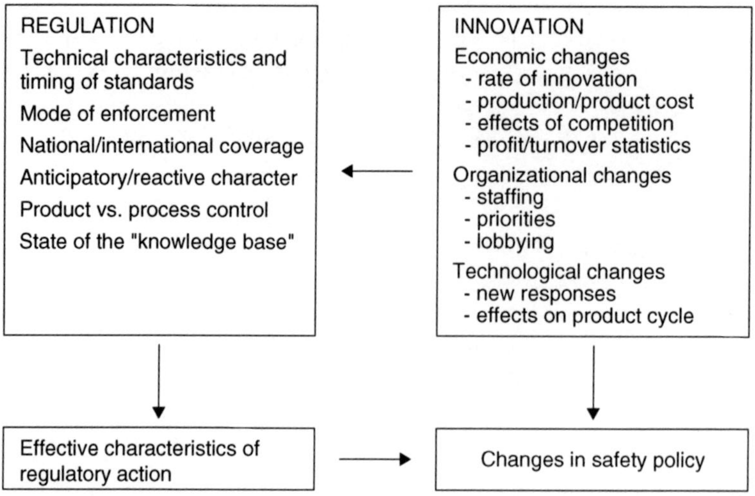

Source: Based on Irwin and Vergragt (1989, 62).

National or international coverage of the regulation may also influence competitiveness of the firms concerned. In the short run, international competitiveness of some individual firms may decline as a result of strict national environmental regulation. In the long run, such regulation may give international comparative first mover advantages to the same firms concurrently with environmental regulative tightening in other countries. This is, for instance, clearly the philosophy behind the Danish regulative initiatives on CFC's, which put a deadline for the use of CFC a couple of years before the 'Montreal-agreement'. To support the Danish development of new CFC-free products and processes the Government has set up a specific R&D programme on CFC-free production, indirectly financed by a CFC-tax.

Regulation may be reactive or proactive in character. Hitherto environmental regulation has in most countries mainly been reactive in character in the sense that the dominating environmental protection activities have been leaning against an 'end-of-line' philosophy as for instance municipal wastewater treatment plants or high chimneys with smoke filters. A more, but not fully alternative proactive strategy is pre-treatment at the source of pollution, for instance industrial wastewater treatment. Proactive regulation stimulating low- and non-waste technologies are still only dawning in most countries despite their ecological superiority.

Regulations may refer to individual products or entire manufacturing processes. Regulations and standards may be formulated in terms of products or process specifications or they may be formulated in functional terms (for instance strength, durability, speed, or compatibility). It is important to notice that the type of regulation and standardisation will influence the direction of future search activities. If for instance standards are formulated in functional terms rather than in terms of product or process specifications, the search activities may be more open-ended and less bounded within existing trajectories.

If there is a widespread disagreement about the environmental assessment results of a specific regulation among experts (e.g. the state of the 'knowledge base' is unstable) – the strategic behaviour of the organisations affected by the regulation may be influenced too. The affected firms may see their chance to loosen the regulations and the following control activities may be less consistent.

Two general propositions are put forward in the interactive model of regulation-innovation above. The *first* is, that the type of regulation affects the potential innovative outcome and the *second* is, that success, where regulation paces private firms to innovate, depends on social and institutional negotiations among qualified agents and experts within both the public and the private organisations involved. We may expect to find the most positive and encouraging successful illustrations of regulation-innovation interaction when the regulation instrument is used with a certain professional 'fingerspitzengefühl' in areas where competent public demand prevails.

7.3.3. Pacing Based on the Public Sector as a User of Innovation

Public sector demand affects innovativeness in the private sector directly through its size and quality. In modern national systems of production and innovation public demand is considerable. According to Dalpé, government markets represent between 10-15% of total production in most industrial countries (Dalpé, 1989). An European Commission study of public sector procurement has estimated total public purchasing (government and public enterprises) to about 15% of GDP in 1984 for the EC as a whole, but with important country variations ranging from 12% in Germany to 22% in the UK of which government purchasing contributed half (WS Atkins Management Consultants, 1988).

There are of course variations in the share of government markets between different product areas. In areas such as food products, consumer electronics and miscellaneous metal products, government markets account for only a minor percentage of the total market. Within areas, such as transport equipment and computers, the public sector market is large and growing. In other areas, such as environmental protection, medical equipment and infrastructure products and services, government markets in most countries account for the major part. In relation to a long term upgrading of national systems of innovation it is important to stress this variation between product areas, because the market share of public sector demand seems to be dominating and increasing especially in the growing markets for high-tech products based on new information technology or biotechnology.

The *quantitative* side of the demand is a very central ingredient in an analysis of how the public sector as a user explicitly or implicitly may stimulate, inhibit or orient innovativeness among private producers. Firstly, a certain quantitative demand is a necessary precondition for private firms investing in R&D-activities. Within many product areas, the public sector is the first user of innovations, patents and products (Dalpé and Debresson, 1989). As indicated above stable government home-markets may be essential not only from an infant industry perspective, but also in relation to the long term maintenance of obtained international strongholds. Secondly, the market position of the public sector is important for the ability of the public sector to play the card of demand pressure. Such potential public demand pressure may not always be fully exploited due to possible shortcomings in the coordination of time and demand specification among the many small and scattered users operating on the local government level. The solution to such coordination problems is of course the establishment of various types of institutionalised cooperation as for instance state discount on public purchases, common advisory committees or specific publicly owned suppliers like the Danish Municipal Software House (Kommunedata) providing administrative information systems for local government. However, while a lack of coordination and exchange of experience among users may reduce the demand pressure and thus weaken potential interactive learning processes between public users and their suppliers, extended institutionalised cooperation may on the other hand contain a risk of lock-in of technical and organisational solutions. As indicated in section 7.3.1, balancing routinising and renewal processes certainly is a difficult task.

The importance of the *qualitative* side of demand has in recent years obtained increasing attention in innovation theory and empirical analyses. There are two interrelated aspects of qualitative demand reflecting the degree of user-participation. The one is concerned with user-led innovations where users innovate or where users participate directly in the innovation process. It is well documented that competent users play such direct participative roles in some innovation processes (von Hippel, 1976 and 1988, Lundvall, 1985). The other aspect is concerned with user-led innovations, where competent users formulate user needs or demands, but leave the 'enterprise' to the suppliers. Along this line, as mentioned earlier in this chapter and in chapter 3, studies of processes of innovation and diffusion of new products and processes have indicated, that a lack of competence amongst users may weaken long term innovativeness among suppliers and/or inhibit optimal or efficient use of new technological opportunities (e.g. Lundvall, 1985, Gregersen, 1988, Gjerding et al., 1990).

While most of the innovation theory and studies with economic roots have hitherto mainly emphasised innovation processes in the private sector, several of the case studies of competent user-involvement in innovation processes actually deal with professional users within the public or semi-public sector, as for instance does the classic study by von Hippel of user-dominance in the development of scientific instruments for hospital and university labs, and the studies of government procurement in relation to areas such as defence, hospitals, telecommunications and environmental protection. The conclusion, that qualified users are important in innovation processes based on dynamic interactive learning, is general in the sense that it holds for all user types, be they private or public. However, as indicated in section 7.2, the specific goal orientation towards public interests, where other than 'simple' private monetary profit and cost rationalities dominate, distinguishes public sector institutions from private firms in relation to possible user-pacing of suppliers. When public sector demand is primarily driven by military, political or social goals and secondarily by cost considerations, 'quality and performance oriented procurement' tends to favour innovation (Dalpé, 1989). The development of for instance the Swedish telecommunications industry (especially Ericsson) illustrates how standardisation combined with public procurement may form an innovative platform for world-wide competitiveness. The development of the Danish hearing aid industry, the Danish wind-mill industry, and the Danish environment industry are other illustrative examples of how standardisation, regulation, welfare schemes and public subsidising under certain circumstances (e.g. a qualified and stable home market) may pace socially desirable innovations from the private sector.

7.4. Conclusion

In many industrial policy recommendations the distinguished role of the public sector and governments is to create a 'dynamic industrial environment' in which private domestic firms may flourish. The practical content of this support or dynamic industrial policy is manifold. It range from taxes, direct subsidies, public education and training facilities, public R&D institutions, infrastructure facilities, financial support, regulation, standards, to public procurement. In general, these policies have hitherto mainly been regarded as a domestic concern, but along with the on-going transition of the nation based systems of production and innovation towards international and transnational systems of production and innovation follows a corresponding transition on the political stage, where transnational political regulation increasingly narrows the scope of national politics. These subjects are the main focus in Part III.

The internationalisation process certainly challenges the traditional role of the national public sector, but it does not render it superfluous. As indicated in this chapter, the public sector can play an important role as a stabilising and stimulating pacer in a situation where the private sector is confronted with extremely unstable environments.

First, successful public sector pacing requires both maintenance and renewal of learning processes *inside* the public sector. It implies that resources inside the public sector must be channelled continuously to maintain and develop user qualifications at a high level. The direct effects of the on-going privatisation and cuts in traditional public welfare activities as health care, social security, education and environmental protection are in the first hand reduced level of services, but a more indirect threat may be a debilitated capacity for renewal of central parts of the national system of production and innovation in the long run due to lack of competent demand from users in the public sector.

Second, successful public pacing requires both maintenance and renewal of interactive learning *between* the public sector and the private. The case-material presented in this chapter supports the conclusion that such positive learning processes are facilitated if both the quantitative and the qualitative public demand change under stable conditions, and technical standards are maintained at a high level. Despite the on-going 'deregulation debate', our case-material indicates that the regulation instrument may be a rather effective means to pace socially desirable innovations from the private sector if the preceding social and institutional negotiations take place among qualified agents and experts within both the public and the private organisations.

Chapter 8

THE ROLE OF FINANCE IN NATIONAL SYSTEMS OF INNOVATION[1]

Jesper Lindgaard Christensen

8.1. Introduction

One of the most important institutional conditions for the process of innovation is the possibility of financing the process. This is not just a question of getting finance cheaper in one country compared to another. Rather there are some *national*, institutional factors in financial systems, which are important to firms, when they need to obtain finance for their investments in new technology. One might argue that the concept of a *national* financial system has apparently become less and less relevant due to internationalisation, deregulation and globalisation of financial markets in recent years. However, in spite of these trends there are still differences in the financial systems which are crucial to take into account.

Risky investments in innovations are often initially financed internally. This goes especially for large companies, whereas small and medium sized firms may have less possibilities for self financing. However large companies also increasingly tend to use external finance. Higher R&D costs and shorter life cycles for most high technology product, make technology based firms more dependent on external finance. Underneath this very general statement however there are important differences, not only between the financial strength of firms, but also between countries. In some countries there is a stronger tendency to finance investments internally, and this makes firms less dependent on external finance.

In the following discussion the focus will mainly be on external finance. My main purpose is to show that institutional differences between national financial systems are important to financing innovation. Even though it is an extremely important part of NSI, the financing of the education system will not be dealt with. In some contexts the theoretical problems treated will present themselves differently if the financing is by equity rather than debt, but for the sake of clarity the terminology will be kept as 'lender-borrower' throughout the chapter.

Investments in innovation imply more uncertainty than ordinary investments. This goes both for the market uncertainty and in particular the technical uncertainty. In addition, learning processes in production and consumption are somewhat longer for a new product and possibilities for security are worse than for known products.

Uncertainty and the profit/risksharing can be an obstacle to innovation projects if financial institutions are risk adverse.[2] But an acceptable level of knowledge can reduce the problems of uncertainty about a project and the persons undertaking it, and this will ease access to finance. One way to provide this information and confidence is by repetitive contracts between a borrower and a lender, accumulating knowledge through interactive learning. Thus, learning is indeed very important in finance as well. Another way is to create financial institutions suited to accumulate and diffuse knowledge already generated, and to support the creation of new knowledge. Different institutional set-ups of financial systems will support or limit the development of these relations between the lender and the borrower,[3] and this is the more precise topic of this chapter.

To analyse this problem, I shall discuss some theoretical points, with an emphasis on the learning aspects of financing innovations. As both the personal relations between the borrower and the lender and the level of the national system will be dealt with, the discussion will have both a micro- and a macro aspect, but as will be evident, the systemic factors do have a feed back on micro behaviour. Then, some of the theoretical points will be illustrated by outlining some of the characteristics of the financial systems in selected countries. This is not meant to be an adequate historical analysis of the credit systems in the different countries. It should rather be seen as examples illustrating how the innovative capability of nations may be limited or supported by the functioning and institutional set-up of financial systems. Finally, the theme is discussed in the light of current trends in the development of financial markets.

8.2. Theoretical Considerations on Finance, Information and Technological Change

Schumpeter was one of the first to discuss the importance of credit in the process of innovation. According to Schumpeter, the entrepreneur is the driving force in the process of innovation, but it is necessary that he can convince the banks to provide him with credit to finance the innovation (1934, 69). Schumpeter considers the lenders' judgement of the borrower to set the limit of credit expansion, and the contribution by Schumpeter to this aspect of innovation theory is still enlightening.

8.2.1. Borrower-Lender Relationships

As briefly mentioned in the introduction, different access to information is a substantial characteristic of the relation between the lender and the borrower. In the traditional perfect market approach to the analysis of financial markets, services are bought and sold in an anonymous manner, and the only information transfer consists of signals given by movements in prices. If the capital market actually worked in this manner, there would be no need for financial intermediaries – borrowers would obtain their loans directly from depositors. But real markets are organised and do not function without friction due to informational constraints. In addition, part of the loan contracts are traded outside the organised market. Instead decentralised trading between a borrower and a lender takes place, and distance between the borrower and the lender in centrally organised markets is replaced by close relationships in various forms.[4] The reason for this is that these relations can alleviate problems of obtaining finance, monitoring and screening the applicants; all problems which stem from the asymmetries in information.

But what is a 'close relationship', what is actually learned in the interaction, and why should a firm or a bank be interested in sustaining the relations?

8.2.2. The Content and Stability of the Relationships

Uncertainty takes on a twofold dimension in the relationship between the lender and the borrower. The lender has to analyse the borrowers project, but this is not all. He also has to make a decision as to whether the borrower himself is to be trusted. Asymmetric information may result in credit rationing, and to avoid this, confidence and trust in the other parts' conception and fair use of information is crucial.[5] This is a substantial element of what is built up in the interaction, and what constitutes the relationships.

A prerequisite for efficient information exchange is common channels and codes of information, effectively distributed and understood. The specific channels and codes will reflect the cultural, geographical and organisational differences between the borrower and the lender. Once information channels have been established through a learning process, there is an unwillingness to pay the price of building up new relations, which implies new series of learning processes (Arrow, 1974, 19).

Another kind of knowledge, which is accumulated through the learning process, is insight into different cultures and logics. In banks and firms, respectively, different kinds of competence are built, such as financial management skills versus technical competence. The established relationships will be preserved, if exchange of information and competence at a satisfactory level have developed. But not only the specific competence is relevant in this respect. Equally important is the mutual understanding of the way of thinking in the industry and financial world. A certain degree of social and cultural coherence thus facilitates the establishment and maintenance of relationships between users and producers of financial services.

On the lender side, specific knowledge about the technical aspects of the project and the industry in general will be generated. On the other side, the borrower will learn about prices for funds, different financial instruments, and financial innovations relevant to corporate finance. In addition, the fund raising ingenuity, that Schumpeter (1934) and Penrose (1980, 37–39) characterised as essential to the entrepreneur, will improve.

Borrower-lender relationships does, of course, change over time and between the projects. The mutual dependency is influenced by increased competition in the financial sector, changes in the self financing ability of the firm, establishment of financial departments in firms, etc.

Many advantages of these stable relations could be mentioned. The development of the relationships is not just development and accumulation of knowledge about a single innovation project. As the borrower becomes better to articulate financial needs concerning investments in technological change, the lender might be able to develop financial innovations to meet these needs. On the other hand, there is a danger that these stable relations might result in inertia and a resistance to change. The decentralised way of getting finance might be less than socially optimal, compared to a more or less automatic lending using standard procedures. In addition, there may be economies of scale in information gathering and monitoring in a centralised, organised market with special agencies for mitigating informational imperfections.

8.2.3. The Irrelevance of Interest Rates

With this discussion in mind (and the one in chapter 3), we are ready to give some additional comments on the propositions in section 8.2.1.

The functioning of financial markets is not easily compared with that of markets for physical goods. There are several problems with applying the conventional perfect market theory to financial markets (Christensen, 1991). In particular, there is no general clearing mechanism in the market for credit. The direct application of traditional models would mean, that interest rates should equilibrate the demand and supply for loans and provide information to the agents about changes in supply and demand. However, there are several reasons to question this picture. The credit is often created in a decentralised manner between borrower and lender, as described above, and here all talk about market clearing is irrelevant.[6] In addition, the impossibilities of full information in screening and monitoring borrowers make it irrelevant to use interest rates to equilibrate the loan market. For instance, there may be an adverse incentive effect if banks raise interest rates to get rid of bad borrowers. In that case, some borrowers might be willing to undertake very risky projects with a high rate of return, but correspondingly high probability of default. Similarly there may be an adverse selection effect from raising interest rates. Borrowers with low-risk projects may leave the loan market and the average project becomes more risky. Risk premium will then increase, causing still more safe projects to leave the market etc. Therefore, interest rates are not used to clear the market. Instead credit rationing is imposed.[7]

It follows from this that the problems with adverse selection and moral hazards can be reduced by reducing asymmetries in information. This can be done by close screening and monitoring, providing incentive structures and signalling. The institutional set-up of the financial system will determine how these functions are undertaken and how effective they are. This is one explanation of why financial intermediation occurs: the costs of information, and the varieties in costs of monitoring, verification etc. explain why institutions for providing these services exist, and the differences between financial institutions reflect comparative advantages in different modes of information processing and combination. The possibility of economies of scale in these activities is the reason for the existence of banks.

The borrowers will avoid transaction and searching costs for the security in a long term connection to a lender, even if the loans are a bit more expensive. On the other hand – at the lender side – a few percentages above average interest rates, are virtually unimportant, as the down-side risk is much larger than the up-side gain. In other words, the money lost in a too risky project will never be compensated by a limited overpricing of a few other contracts.[8] Consequently, lenders prefer rejecting applications if they are too risky, rather than raising interest rates.

The time horizon in financing investments is perhaps more important to innovation projects than interest rates. The duration required to develop the project is highly uncertain as is the introduction in the market. If lenders are expecting a return in the short term, this may pose problems for innovation projects. The tendency to short-termism has been discussed intensely, and national differences have been pointed out,[9] Differences also arise in the information exchange between lender and borrower, according to the time perspectives and institutional set-up of financial systems. If lenders trade their shares in a fluctuating manner, they are more concerned with diversifying investments and risks than with obtaining information on how the firm is doing in the long run, and how they may be able to influence decisions. This information is, of course, relatively more expensive the more the portfolio is diversified and then the emphasis tends to be on the short term value of assets and possibilities of arbitrage, instead of long-term growth and technological development (Tylecote and Demirag, 1991). The consequence for technology financing is a pressure on projects to show results in a period of time that may be inexpedient to innovation. Indeed firms employ different pay-back periods depending on the expectations on the development of competing technologies and cost of capital. Furthermore, they are dependent on the type of investment. Thus, Hall (1991) argues that in sectors without rapid changes in technology and without the large complexity in investments, the time pressure is not as heavy as in other sectors. Also on the national level, differences in pay-back periods exists (Silverberg, 1990, 182). These are rooted in the historical, cultural and social characteristics of the society (Tylecote and Demirag, 1991), and tends to limit the importance of the level of interest rates.

8.3. The Development of Institutions of Importance to Financing

In this, largely explorative, section, I shall try to outline how the institutional set-up forms a framework for processes at the microeconomic level. Even though stable borrower-lender relationships may reduce uncertainty in innovation projects, there will always remain an element of uncertainty. In uncertain and non-stationary environments individuals and firms will try to accumulate knowledge generated through trial-and-error processes of searching and learning. However, this search is not totally random, and one of the selection mechanisms of technologies is the financial system. On the other hand, financial systems change in response to the environment, and this dichotomy – the selection function of the financial system and the inducement to changes within it – will be the major issues to be discussed in this section.

8.3.1. Selection Function of Financial Institutions

As shown by Dosi (1982) and Freeman and Perez (1986), processes of searching are often guided by technological paradigms and trajectories. This path-dependency of searching is a means of reducing uncertainty but it is not cost free. The lock-in effect on learning and searching processes reduces the likelihood of exploring alternative potential trajectories.[10] In financial institutions the credit decisions for innovation projects are often dependent on individual judgement, but as far as it is possible, they (including governments) also try to create a choice set and set up objective criteria for giving credit. However, innovation projects rarely fit a schedule-like set of rules to allocate credit and to select among projects because of the generic diversity in the sample of innovation projects put forward to a potential lender.

Diversity in the sample of innovation projects, in financial institutions and in behaviour of individuals, firms and institutions, is a prerequisite for learning processes. How should financial institutions learn about innovation projects and develop financial innovations if the projects were all alike? How should organisational flexibility develop without diversity in behaviour, not to talk about the flexibility and division of labour of the financial system towards financing innovation projects in different stages? Thus, even though a certain degree of social and cultural coherence between the borrower and the lender is important to the development of stability in borrower-lender relationships, the diversity in modes of behaviour between the lender and the entrepreneur, at the same time, induces dynamics.[11]

Provided learning is cumulated in financial institutions errors in the selection of projects may also increase the future capability to select, provided the learning is cumulated in financial institutions. We are here at the very core of different functioning of financial systems. In some institutional set-ups, the cumulative learning in credit institutions and among borrowers is the main way of increasing allocation efficiency, whereas other kinds of systems tend to rely more upon a one-period selection function. Later, I shall specify these propositions somewhat.

8.3.2. The Role of Government

Governments have the possibilities for exploring new, promising technological trajectories without the same dramatical financial consequences, as if a private firm or investor uses a large share of their capital on a project, which eventually fails. Many projects are too risky for an individual, but in government funding the risk spreading is complete, and high risk premia can be avoided. This is one reason why the targets for government programs are often in the early stages of innovation projects, where failure rates are high. Basic research and general education are also primarily government financed because there are no direct prospects of returns. This is only the direct investments. Equally important is the way governments conduct industrial policy. An interventionist versus liberal mode will also inevitably lead to a different set-up of financial systems (Rybzinsky, 1984).

8.3.3. The Impact of the Macroeconomic Setting on Learning Processes

The processes of interaction between the borrower and the lender described above do not of course, take place with the same effectiveness over time and in space. Differences in the attitudes of the borrower and the lender as well as external factors like the degree of uncertainty prevailing, alternative sources of finance, financial innovations and competition from other financial institutions have a major impact on whether the learning processes are intensive in time and space. In some countries and periods of time the ability of the financial system to meet financial requirements and develop/take advantage of productive learning processes will depend on the flexibility and specialisation of the financial institutions. The ability of the system to develop in order to preserve and stimulate links between borrowers and lenders and to diffuse generated knowledge is a substantial characteristic of a national financial system able to support technical innovations.

Changes in the speed and diffusion of innovations also have impacts on the whole economy, and influence relationships between borrowers and lenders. In periods with radical breaks in technology and implementation of a new technological paradigm, the effects will be diffused throughout the whole economy and the financial sector will be facing a much larger number of borrowers who applies for external capital for investments in new technology. If the financial sector sticks to traditional lending procedures the industry will run into difficulties with long term finance. It is crucial for the effectiveness of national systems of innovation, that the financial system possesses enough channels of information, effective processes of learning, social and cultural relations to the firms and a certain willingness to take risks in order to make an effective selection.

8.4. Characteristics of National Financial Systems and their Impact on Innovative Capability

8.4.1. Analytical Framework

Financial systems can be defined as institutional arrangements for the transformation of savings or credit to investments, and for advicing firms. Therefore, financial systems may differ in the way this transformation is undertaken and in the institutions undertaking it. More specifically, financial systems are different in the division of labour between financial institutions, the degree of concentration of these and their size relative to the economy as a whole, the instruments used in the financial sector and the relation to the corporate sector – including the classical distinction of capital structure of the firms and degree of self financing.

Starting from this definition, financial systems may be grouped according to two criteria. One is the relative importance of financial markets and financial institutions in the transformation of savings to investments. Another is the role of governments in this process and in the regulation of the financial markets as such. Financial systems will here be grouped into three distinct categories:[12]

a) A market oriented system, where funds are allocated through a developed capital market with perfect competition and little government influence
b) A credit based system, where financial institutions – mainly banks – transfer savings to investments and with heavy government control and regulation and
c) A credit based system dominated by financial institutions with little government intervention.

Even though this grouping draws upon Zysman (1983), the analytical emphasis is complementary. The key problem for Zysman is that governments have to recognise the specific character and function of the financial system in order to undertake adequate policies considering the function of the financial systems. In the following, the focus will be on the ability of different kinds of financial systems to support the generation and diffusion of innovations and the learning processes discussed in section 8.2.

The categories a–c demand some further explanations.

8.4.2. Archetypes of Financial Systems

The Capital Market Oriented System

In the capital market oriented system a relatively large part of the transformation of savings to investment takes place through a highly competitive capital market. Much capital allocation takes place through variations in the prices of funds, whereas credit based systems are to a larger extent characterised by credit rationing.

The institutions and financial intermediaries are highly specialised, but so numerous that prices are determined by market forces. Firms are supplied with long term capital partly by the developed capital market, and the role of banks is limited to the provision of short-term capital or to linking the firm with potential funds. The US and the UK have been said to be capital market based financial systems.

The performance of this kind of system can be evaluated by different criteria. The ability to support the various borrower-lender interplay described in section 8.2, is weak in this system for several reasons. First, communication is mainly one-way leaving the borrower without any opportunities of convincing (many and anonymous) lenders about the merits of his project.

Second, the volatility of the stock market implies that funds move from one asset to another, which limits the possibility to build up codes and channels of communication. Furthermore, the risk assessment might be determined not by the future, long-term potentials of the firm, but rather by the psychologically determined peculiarities of the stock market.[13]

Third, interactive learning processes are hampered by the fact that the valuation of the firm's assets is not made in connection with a single project but in relation to the performance of the company as a whole. In principle, it is possible to get access to funds for financing a dubious project, as long as the company is doing well in other fields. In companies with several different products and projects, the single project will have a kind of anonymity when raising funds from the capital market.

Credit Based System Influenced by Government

In this system, long term capital is provided mainly through loan markets where some prices are controlled by government. Government discriminates between institutions allocating funds in order to influence the flow of capital to areas with high priority. The relative importance of the capital market is small.

Due to the relatively small importance of complementary markets, owners do not engage in buying and selling of stocks to the same degree as in the capital market based system. If something goes wrong owners stay with the borrower and try to influence him by taking part in the management, introducing restrictions on loans etc.[14] But this kind of intervention is even more important at the aggregate level – i.e. the government 'voice' on financial institutions. An important – but often overlooked – aspect of this kind of system, is that the institutional set up resulting from the regulation of the financial markets is generally accepted. Without this confidence in the institutions and their performance, the stability and efficiency of the institutions is likely to be small.[15]

Even though France and Japan differ in many respects – also compared to the groups indicated above – it is possible to characterise them as credit based financial systems influenced by government. In both countries technological and industrial development is heavily influenced by government, and one of the means of influence is the control of the financial system.

Credit Based Institutional System

This system differs from the ones mentioned above in that financial institutions influence prices independently of government. Government does not intervene in the market to any large extent except for pursuing open market operations and establishing general rules. The stock market is of little importance, and loans or stocks are not easily accessible to the company. In this system the ties between industry and finance are also very strong. The firms are not only dependent on the banks, because of their role as intermediaries to the stock market and other forms of finance, but the banks often control a considerable part of the votes in the company. The German financial system is generally taken as an example of this type of system.

Predictions of Characteristics of Financial Systems

The better possibilities for obtaining loans in the two credit based systems indicates a lower degree of self financing of firms in this type of system. The higher degree of debt relative to equity in these systems provides an incentive for borrowers to monitor and to keep in close contact with lenders, and we expect a closer relation to banks in this system. The degree of concentration is also expected to be higher in this system because of the less developed market for exchange of control – the stock market.[16] This has implications for the type of owners in the two systems. Whereas the entrepreneur, and more active ownership, is likely in established firms in credit based systems, we would expect a higher degree of 'punters' – that is traders in shares with the only purpose of maximising portfolios – in the capital market based system. Take-overs are likely to be more frequent in this system as well.

Obviously this crude classification does not reveal all interesting international differences, and the distinctions between the systems ought to be taken with some reservations. In spite of the variations within the categories, there are however some stylised facts, which manifest themselves, when actual financial systems are compared. Table 8.1 summarises expectations to how the different types of financial systems would look like.

Let us now take a look upon how these expectations are fulfilled.

Table 8.1. **Stylised Facts of Financial Systems**

Type of System	Capital Market Based	Credit Based Government	Credit Based Institutions
Degree of self financing	High	Low	Low
Role of banks in external fin.	Small	Large	Very large
Ties between industry and fin.	Weak, anonymous, standardised	Strong, known, non-standard	Strong, known, non-standard
Way of influence	Exit	Voice	Voice
Debt /equity ratio	Low	High	High
Concentration of Credit + owner-ship	Low	High	Very High
Cost of capital	Low	High	Very High

8.4.3. Comparing Actual Financial Systems

Sources of Financing

Certainly self financing is the most common form of investment financing, but there are large differences in the degree of self financing, and even within the external finance there are differences across countries in the way firms finance, investments. In Table 8.2 these proportions are shown.

From these figures[19] a number of conclusions can be derived. First, the main source of financing is – not surprisingly – retentions. Mayer (1990, 318) shows, that this is also the case if we look specifically at small and medium sized firms, although these firms are considerably more reliant on external finance than large firms. Second, the countries classified as capital market based financial systems, the UK and the US, do have the expected higher ratio of self financing to external finance. Third, the figures confirm that the term 'capital market based system' ought to be used in a cautious manner. Rather than a dominance of capital markets, the net financing figures show that all the countries in the sample are bank-oriented to a greater or lesser extent, if the relative share of external capital to firms determines how the system is classified. However, this rather controversial conclusion would probably be modified if the figures were divided into short term and long term capital supply. Fourth, another controversial conclusion is that German banking is not as dominant as maintained. Loans do not account for a large proportion of external financing to firms compared to the other countries. However, this conclusion must also be modified because German banks are extensively involved in other sources of external finance to firms. In addition, there are large variability in the figures for

Table 8.2. Unweighted Average Net Financing of Non-Financial Enterprises 1970–85[17,18]

	US	UK	Germany	France	Japan
Retentions	85.9	102.4	70.9	61.4	57.9
Capital transfers	0.0	4.1	8.6	2.0	0.0
Short term securities	0.4	1.7	−0.1	−0.1	N.A.
Loans	24.4	7.6	12.1	37.3	50.4
Trade credit	−1.4	−1.1	−2.1	−0.6	−11.2
Bonds	11.6	−1.1	−1.0	1.6	2.1
Shares	1.1	−3.3	0.6	6.3	4.6
Other	−16.9	3.2	10.9	−1.4	−3.8
Statistical adjustments	−5.1	−13.4	0.0	−6.4	N.A.
Total	100.0	100.1	99.9	100.1	100.0

Source: OECD, Financial Statistics part III, 1990 and Mayer (1990, 310).

small and large firms (Edwards and Fischer, 1991). Fifth, the securities market is of very limited importance in the period of observation. Only the US bond market is of any significance.

The rather long time span ending 1985 that is used for this important table motivates a closer look at more recent data in relation to some of the other predicted stylised facts of financial systems.

The Role of Bank Credits in External Financing of Firms

A credit based – or 'bank oriented' – financial system would typically have a large degree of bank credits in relation to other types of external capital to firms. In Table 8.3, bank credits to firms are calculated as a percentage of total liabilities. Attention should be directed towards the strictly quantitative character of this comparison. In reality the organisation of the financial systems is equally important. For example, segmentation of the financial system and bank specialisation affects the functioning of the system, as may differences in how much banks are oriented towards financing industry, special kinds of industry or even special technologies.

The recent data on the size of bank loans relative to other kinds of debt support the pattern outlined in the a priori classification of financial systems. The credit based financial systems can, according to Table 8.3, be sorted out and capital market based systems (UK and US) identified. Thus 21.42% and 30.05% of liabilities in French and Japanese firms are bank credits in 1988, while the figures for the two capital market based countries, the US and the UK, are 8.73% and 11.45% respectively. The development of the share of bank credits in external finance shows a rather stable pattern, but if national trends are to be deduced, it is that the importance of banks has increased in the UK financial system in the last few years, while it has decreased in France and Japan.

Table 8.3. **The Relative Importance of Bank Credits in Financing Industry. (Short and Long Term Bank Credits**[20] **as a Percentage of Total Liabilities in Industry**

	US[21]	UK	Germany	France	Japan
1984	8.13	16.57	N.A.	28.09	34.50
1985	8.41	15.39		26.11	34.37
1986	8.99	11.16		25.11	34.40
1987	8.55	9.54		22.89	31.92
1988	8.73	11.45		21.42	30.05
1989	8.95	13.79			

Source: OECD, Financial Statistics, part III, 1990.

The Capital Structure of Firms in Different Financial Systems

The development in debt-equity ratios for the countries discussed are shown below. We expects to find higher d/e-ratios in countries classified as credit based financial systems. The main argument for this is related to the close relationships between lenders and borrowers in these countries. Financial institutions allow firms a higher d/e-ratio because monitoring of the firms is easier (and more necessary). Another argument is the difficult access to funds on the capital markets for some firms. Both in terms of gross and net debt-equity ratio these predictions are shown to be valid. D/e-ratios in the US and UK are significantly lower than the average (the difference is even more pronounced if calculated on a net basis). The development of the ratios indicates a tendency towards convergence of financial systems, as the ratios of US firms increased from a low level and the ratios of France and Japan decreased from a higher level. This is so using both measures.

In addition to the relationships between borrowers and lenders, the concentration of credit and ownership structure in firms is important to take into account when explaining differences in capital structure. Variations in ownership structure provide different incentives to choose debt or equity. The monitoring function may also be different dependent on the ownership structure, as may the mode and degree of intervention in case of financial distress and risk of default. Thus, capital structure is a reflection of some of the institutional properties of financial systems and the just mentioned ownership structure.

The Cost of Capital

One would expect the countries with the lowest level of financial intermediation to have the lowest cost of capital, provided intermediation is

Table 8.4. **Capital Structure in Firms**

	US[22]	UK	Germany	France	Japan
1982	0.32	0.53	0.59	0.72	0.77
1983	0.33	0.52	0.58	0.72	0.76
1984	0.36	0.52	0.57	0.71	0.75
1985	0.38	0.51	0.56	0.70	0.74
1986	0.40	0.51	0.51	0.67	0.72
1987	0.42	0.51	0.60	0.64	0.71
1988	0.47	0.51	0.60	0.63	0.70
1989	0.45	0.53	0.60		

Source: OECD, Financial Statistics part III, 1990.

Table 8.5. Cost of Capital in Different Countries. Research and Development Project With 10 Year Payoff Lag. (Returns Requested)

	US[23]	UK	Germany	Japan
1984	20.3	24.4	14.6	7.7
1985	20.2	25.4	13.9	9.2
1986	16.8	18.9	13.2	9.4
1987	18.2	20.6	14.4	8.4
1988	20.3	23.7	14.8	8.7

Source: Explaining international differences in the cost of capital, quarterly review, summer 1989.

costly. In addition the small debt proportion in the firms should make external finance cheaper. Apparently it is the other way around. In Table 8.5 countries with an extensive net of financial institutions, like Japan, are at the low end of prices, as opposed to countries with direct financing, like the US and the UK According to Table 8.5, capital for investment in a British R&D project with a ten year pay-off period had to provide a return nearly three times as high as the same project in Japan.

Let us save an explanation for later because this seeming paradox becomes explicable if we take a closer look upon the institutional set-up of the financial systems and the way these institutions work.

Functions of Financial Institutions in Different Countries

In *Japan* the way the financial system supports technological development is through government influence but compared to the case of France the government influence is more coordinative and indirect. Of course, the finance-industry relationship in Japan cannot be properly described without mentioning MITI (Ministry of International Trade and Industry). MITI has had a powerful coordinative role in the postwar period sustained by its influence on price and quantity of credit, and in this regard the creation of financial institutions was a major step towards a coherent industrial policy, using the financial system as a means of allocation. Loans from government were important, but equally important was the interest rate control, which limited destructive competition and stabilised business atmosphere for financial intermediaries. Thus, industrial growth was encouraged by developing the banking system and the indirect way of financing (as opposed to a capital market based financing), which made loans easily accessible for small firms with large growth potentials (Suzuki, 1990, 22 f).

Today 123 government bodies implement long term economic goals like financing risk intensive or unprofitable industries; rescuing and restructuring old industries and developing new key industries (Mullinuex, 1987, 74). In general, the financial system is very segmented and different institutions are highly specialised, both concerning the terms of lending, size of companies, and sector. For instance, ten different government agencies finance small and medium sized enterprises in special industries, where a general, social benefit can be expected. In recent years, the Japanese financial system has gone through major changes. The trend is forward more securitisation and liberalisation.

In *France*, the indicative planning procedure assures national goals for production in key industries, and heavy government influence on credit allocation is an important way of achieving the fulfilment of the national plan. Government has special institutions for this credit allocation and in addition some of the largest banks have been nationalised. As the Ministry of Finance has significant influence on the capital market, the level and structure of interest rates are also influenced by government. Lately, the banking sector has been deregulated, and steps have been taken to improve the supply of venture capital (Derian, 1990, 6–7).

As in Japan, the *US* financial market is rather segmented. In the 1980's deregulation has led to concentration of capital in national commercial and investment banking institutions, making it still more difficult for small, local firms to get their projects financed. This is due to national banks' lack of experience with industrial banking and their specialisation in short term lending (Cox, 1986, 38). In general, long term lending is scarce, and legislation prohibits commercial banks to go into investment banking.

However, some US government agencies have been established to support lending for special purposes or to small businesses but in general, they are not directly involved with the borrower. Instead, they give loan guarantees or they lend to special institutions, which relend the capital. In the military sector, however, government funding of R&D is substantial.

The lack of a close borrower-lender contact limits the development of stable, long-term relationships. One exception to this general picture is the story of venture capital development in the US, which illustrates that the development of financial institutions for financing technological change is a mutual learning process leading to accumulation of skills (Bullock, 1983).

Borrower-Lender Interaction in the Financial Systems

Let us now return to the unexpected relation between the low costs of capital and the high level of financial intermediation. The main explanation of this financial cost-intermediation paradox is the role these institutions play in mitigating informational constraints. The favouring of selected firms or branches, and the associated accumulation of knowledge and monitoring skills within institutions reduce uncertainty and monitoring costs, and enable firms to borrow relatively cheaply. In recent studies, Hoshi, Kashyap and Scarfstein (1989 and 1990) compared the performance of Japanese firms with close relationships to a bank with firms loosening these relationships during the deregulation of the Japanese financial market. They found that investments in firms, which kept their relations to the bank (Keiretzu), where less constrained by liquidity than in the other group of firms. Furthermore, the costs of financial distress were reduced through this close relation. Obviously, the wide range of specialised financial institutions, the overall guidance and social acceptance of MITI, the personal and economic coherence between finance and industry, imply a high degree of interaction between financial institutions and industry. Indeed, these are an important part of the Japanese success story.[24]

Similarly, this feature has been said to be an important explanation to the good performance of the German industry. Historically, the German tradition of strong banking influence in the process of industrialisation goes back to the middle of 19th century.[25] In the German financial system of today, commercial banks – or rather 'universal' banks – are important in credit allocation. Through their privileged access to capital market banks are intermediaries to other forms of financial capital than loans. According to Cable (1985) bank representation on company boards reduces informational asymmetries and monitoring costs. However, Edwards and Fischer (1991) argues that the aggregate figures for external finance do not show a dominance of banks and the large firms (who primarily have supervisory boards) are primarily internally financed. Banks, and government grants, are important in financing small and medium sized firms. In addition, even though the proxy vote system enables the three large banks in Germany (Deutsche Bank, Dresdner Bank, Commerzbank) to control a large part of the votes, then the actual evaluation of the management is not particularly close.

On the other hand, the institutional features of the German system makes take-overs difficult as opposed to the case in the UK and the US Frequent changes in ownership may disrupt possibilities of building reputation and long-term relationships (Franks and Mayer, 1990), and there is still a close involvement of banks in the development of industry.

At the other extreme, the ownership structure in the US and UK does not provide the same information exchange, and neither the same incentive structure. The many anonymous and disengaged shareowners in the US have provoked a debate of 'the punters of capitalism' (*Economist*, May 5th, 1990). The problem is that the old-style entrepreneur is disappearing, and is replaced by diverse shareholders who take little interest in the development of the firm, except for the short term prices of their shares. This kind of passive ownership reflects the conflict in logic of, respectively, the financial and the industrial world.[26]

8.4.4. Stylised or Real Facts of Financial Systems?

Comparing the predicted and actual characteristics of financial systems both confirms expectations and shows some deviations from expectations. In particular, the term 'capital market based' financial systems is perhaps somewhat exaggerated. Truly, the securities market are more important in the countries that have been placed in this group than indicated, but one could argue, that all the countries in this study are more or less bank oriented, as bank loans are the main source of external finance in all countries.

In addition, the development shows a tendency towards convergence of the systems, and this apparent blurring of lines between the archetypes, may reflect an increasing internationalisation in some countries. The question is if this is beneficial for the national industry and technology.

8.4.5. Advantages of Anglo-Saxon Selection Mechanisms

What has been said so far may sound biased towards the advantages of credit based financial systems. However, there are some disadvantages of these systems as well as some merits of the capital market based systems. In the credit oriented financial system, it is easier to accumulate knowledge and develop competence to judge projects. However, in times of rapidly changing technologies it may be difficult to take advantage of this and to build up lending routines and new sets of criteria for lending. In the capital market oriented system there is not the same build up of routines, because there are not so many institutions to cumulate what is learnt. The lack of routines may sometimes be an advantage in a volatile environment because routinised behaviour may be hostile to innovation because it prevents exploring new ideas.

Thus, the centralised market may have some advantages in terms of a high degree of flexibility. But flexibility is also dependent on the variety of financial institutions, and their capability to adapt to new states of the environment. To overcome information problems, intermediate institutions also develop in capital market based systems to a certain extent. These can be special agencies for advicing investors wishing to invest in technological projects, junk bonds, venture capital firms, credit rating agencies, and banks functioning as links between the capital market and the firm.

In conclusion, one may argue, that these systems have their respective advantages in two different ways of supporting technological change. One (the credit based) could be termed the learning mode, where development of, and development within, the financial institutions are essential. The other (capital market based) has its strength in one-time selection, and here the market mechanism is the main way of selecting between projects (see also Dosi, 1990).

Even if this is a basic difference between the systems, there is also an element of selection in the credit based systems. The financial institutions in these systems are based upon accumulation of skills to select between projects, but the institutions themselves are also selected. The selection mechanism may be competition, or government choice or creation of new financial institutions.

This process of shaping the financial system and selecting institutions is not always easy to display, and the need for historical studies of institutional development is not widely recognised. Especially, it is often overlooked, that sometimes the important features are not only what exists and what did happen, but in particular what did *not* happen. In addition, the importance of informal institutions must be taken into account when explaining the present systems. Legislation is, in other words, not the only factor shaping financial systems. Rather the development of financial institutions is rooted in the culture, history, and interaction with industrial development in the nations. After World War II, the US occupation authorities, changed the Japanese legislation along US lines and prohibited the 'zaibatsus'. If legislation was the only important thing in the development of financial systems, the Japanese system ought to look like the system in the US, and 'keiretsus' would not be present. As shown above this is not the case.

8.5. National Financial Systems and Future Perspectives

The role of finance in national systems of innovation has been discussed, underlining the importance of learning processes and the borrower-lender interplay at the micro level and technological and institutional change at a higher level of aggregation. Different types of national financial systems, supporting technological investments, have been evaluated and used as illustrations of the theoretical discussion. It was found that the financial system does make a difference when comparing possibilities for financing innovations in different countries. The claim has been, that some of the problems with obtaining finance are information dependent, and that credit rationing could be reduced through close relationships between borrower and lender. Financial systems differ in this respect. Some types of system mainly select projects through a central market, while other systems are more directed towards institutions selecting projects. The question remains as to what the future development and the on going changes of financial systems will bring in this respect.

Several new trends in financial markets can be identified. One is the general tendency towards convergence of the different types of financial systems. The credit based systems are developing towards the capital market based system, and to a lesser extent, vice versa. (Other trends may be named deregulation, internationalisation, despecialisation, financial innovations, disintermediation and increased competition pressure. These processes are, of course, interdependent and vary in intensity across nations.[27]

At least a few plausible effects on borrower-lender relations and innovation financing can be deduced from these trends. Deregulation has led to despecialisation and diversification of activities in financial institutions, and disintermediation reduces the role of financial institutions. The latter trend, for obvious reasons, hampers borrower-lender relationships, but this may also be an effect from deregulation, despecialisation and diversification. The point is that skills in new areas of activity need time to develop, but the development in the financial sector is very rapid, and perhaps too fast to allow competence to be built up, before financial institutions enter new fields of activity and expose themselves to greater competition pressure.

The global deregulation of financial markets similarly leads to new financial innovations and internationalisation in terms of different types of direct mechanisms of financing, entry of foreign banks and possibilities of getting finance abroad.

The entry of foreign banks has by itself speeded up the diffusion of financial innovations, as they bring with them new financial products and know-how already tested in other markets. In other words financial innovations are not only developed through an interaction between other financial institutions and the national industry but also through an interaction with financial systems and markets in other countries. This is a modification to bear in mind, when talking about a national system of financing innovations, although the impact should not be exaggerated and generalised.

Now, what do these trends mean for the possibilities of stimulating interactive learning processes in the national financial systems for the purpose of supporting technological development? This question is, of course, a very difficult and complex one to answer, but as discussed in section 8.4, the advantages of the capital market based system are not the generation of lender-borrower relationships and the provision of long term capital. It can be questioned, if the development actually fits into the European and Japanese national systems of innovation, or if it is a more or less independent development in the global financial system without connection to the industrial and technological development in the specific nations. In addition, it is plausible that nations have specific technological development and that they also have their own speed of technical change. Can the global process of deregulation, integration and homogeneity be adjusted to such country specific needs?

The problem may be that the nations with credit oriented financial system are changing too fast. The national financial systems have been built in interaction with industrial development and government policy measures through many years, and institutions for coping with specific, national problems have developed. A radical change in financial systems during a short period of time calls for an adequate institutional framework to be built in the same period, if the advantages of the specificities of national systems are to be upheld. Thus, the stability of the financial system, the ability to reduce asymmetric information through close relationships between firms and banks, the accumulation of knowledge in specialised financial institutions, the longer time horizon in investments and the ability to handle financial crises in firms without take-overs,[28] may be merits of the old national systems worth keeping for the price of homogeneity and integration.[29] However, they will not be kept, if the old institutions are torn down without replacement.

In a Paper on Take-Overs Franks and Mayer (1990, 215–216) Conclude That

...it may not be possible to provide managers and employees with adequate incentives to engage in long-term investments. As a consequence, investment in R&D and training may suffer. In this regard, the case for harmonization across members of the EC is open to serious question....Not only will continental Europe be subject to an unfamiliar (and apparently unwelcome) form of restructuring but also, in the process, the stable relations that have existed between investor and firm be extinguished.

Therefore careless deregulation is not the road to follow if financial systems are still to serve the needs of national industry and finance innovations. Rather it is the reduction of uncertainty in industrial investments and the encouragement of special, national financial innovations, which are suited to the national financial system and the kind of industrial and technological development in the nation, that should be the political assignment.

This indicates that the connection between the development of the financial system and industrial and technical change has to be maintained. One possible way to deal with this problem and reduce that of asymmetric information, is to create more specialised financial institutions.[30] If these e.g. lend to one sector of the industry, it is plausible that they will have a better ability to provide a qualitatively improved advising, screening and monitoring of potential borrowers inside that sector.

In the Words of Colin Mayer (1988, 1183):

The distinctive feature of successful financial systems is their close involvement in industry. A primary characteristic of a market based system is an arm's length relation between investor and firm.... The fundamental challenge that faces any institution or government that can affect the practice of finance is to encourage the emergence of closer relationships and to direct the wealth of talent that has now been concentrated in British financial institutions into direct participation in corporate activities. In the process, the apparent attractions of intensifying competition in financial markets may have to be resisted. The benefits of competition may only be attained at the expense of longer term economic prosperity.

In addition to advocating market segmentation and warning against too extensive despecialisation, there are limits to integration, which are necessary to recognise as long as the nation state exists. In reality, the internationalisation process does have its own boundaries beside the political ones. For example, despite entry of foreign banks, national banking systems are persistent.

However, the reality is that national financial markets remain separated from each other, do continue alongside international markets, and do continue to matter... national institutions have primary access to national savings because the retail banking networks in place are difficult to push aside....Global banking remains, for the most part, wholesale banking. Even then the evidence is substantial that the behaviour of global financial institutions in international markets is shaped primarily by national regulation and national trade flows (Zysman, 1990, 27).

This is on second thought, and with chapter 3 of this book in mind, not that peculiar. Confidence in national banks will usually be higher when norms, language, regulation etc. are national. In other words, the access to first order savings is important for competition between domestic and international banks, and the national level of savings and degree of intermediation will have an impact on the conditions for competition between national and foreign banks.

Chapter 9

FORMAL SCIENTIFIC AND TECHNICAL INSTITUTIONS IN THE NATIONAL SYSTEM OF INNOVATION

Christopher Freeman

9.1. Introduction

As we have seen in earlier chapters, the concept 'National System of Innovation' may be used in two senses: in a *broad* sense it encompasses all institutions which affect the introduction and diffusion of new products, processes and systems in a national economy; and in a *narrow* sense it encompasses that set of institutions which are more directly concerned with scientific and technical activities. This book is mainly concerned with national systems in the broad sense and has stressed the importance of the interactions between the production system, the users and innovation. In this chapter, however, we focus more on the narrower set of formal institutions and attempt to outline some major stages in the evolution of these institutions.

Chapter 1 has pointed out that flexibility in the economy does not only derive from market institutions. This chapter shows that the capacity to adapt to major changes in technology has depended historically on the development of a network of scientific and technical institutions, both in the public and private sectors. Whereas chapter 7 has focused mainly on the role of the public sector as *user* of innovation, this chapter concentrates more on its role as *producer*.

In the early days of the industrial revolution contact between science and industry was certainly already important (Musson and Robinson, 1969) but it was largely on an individual basis and not on a systematic, continuous basis. Firms were very small and science was largely the province of individual enthusiasts, loosely linked in scientific societies and in national academies. Nevertheless, already Adam Smith clearly recognised the great importance of scientific activities from direct observation of contemporary economic developments in Europe.

The expression 'scientist' had not yet been invented but Adam Smith (1776, 8) spoke of

> ...*philosophers or men of speculation, whose trade is not to do anything but to observe everything, and who upon that account, are often capable of combining together the powers of the most distant and dissimilar objects.*

He already pointed to specialisation in science ('peculiar tribes' of philosophers) and to the advantages of this specialisation for the accumulation of knowledge.

Adam Smith was also very well aware of the importance of innovative and inventive activities within firms, even though they, too, were largely conducted on an individual basis. He pointed out that improvements in the design of machines were made both by the specialised producers of machines and by their users. Thus, even though the expression 'Research and Development' had not yet been invented, both scientific and inventive activities were certainly important from the earliest days of industrial capitalism. The 'partnership' between inventors and financial entrepreneurs was a particularly important legal form of early company organisation in Britain, as in the case of Watt and Boulton with the steam engine. This may have been one of the decisive organisational advantages of British firms in the early period of the industrial revolution. The capacity of skilled craftsmen to make high quality prototypes was also an essential condition for the innovative successes of the British machine tool industry.

As technology became more complex public sector activities became much more important and firms grew larger. This chapter argues that institutional innovations in the formal science-technology system accompanied major changes in technology and that a strong interaction between technical and institutional innovations is a fundamental feature of contemporary economic development as well as of previous waves of technical change. First it will deal with the origins of industrial R&D and other institutional innovations from the 1880's to the 1930's. In the next section it will deal with the empirical evidence on patterns of innovation in the period of high growth following the Second World War. Finally, in the concluding sections it will discuss the changing pattern of R&D in relation to computer technology and various social innovations in Japan and other countries.

9.2. The Loss of British Technological Leadership

Just over a century ago two of the most important institutional innovations in the science-technology system were introduced in Germany and in the United States: the 'in-house' industrial R&D laboratory and the 'Technische Hochschule' or 'Institute of Technology' for the professional education of engineers. Both were a response to the increasing complexity and scale of the newer technologies emerging in the electrical and chemical industries in the second half of the 19th century and both greatly increased the scope and effectiveness of product and process innovation in those industries and in others. Together with a cluster of other technical and social innovations they enabled Germany and the United States to displace the erstwhile technological leader – Great Britain – in the period leading up to the First World War (Freeman, 1987 and 1990).

Historians of 19th century industrial technology and economic development have noted that whereas British industry maintained a productivity lead in the *older* established industries, this lead was lost by the end of the 19th century in the *new* technologies. Arthur Lewis (1978) particularly stresses this contrast in his historical account.

The failure of Britain to achieve technological leadership (and productivity leadership) in the new industries (electric power and motors; organic chemistry and synthetics; the internal combustion engine and automobiles; precision engineering and the assembly line) was *not* due in the first place to a failure of scientific discovery or even of radical innovation in Britain. On the contrary British scientists and inventors, from Faraday to Swan made an outstanding contribution to the development of electricity.

The really important point about Britain's loss of technological leadership in the 1880's and 1890's was not that Britain ceased to make scientific discoveries or radical innovations, but that British institutions proved incapable of *diffusing* these innovations, of scaling them up and of using them in a wide variety of new applications based on electrification of other industrial sectors, as well as households. It was the *institutional* innovations in the narrower sense in the German and American science-technology system which enabled German and American industry to exploit the generally available new scientific knowledge far more effectively than British industry in the years before the First World War. And it was the slowness of institutional innovation in the wider social system which further hindered the pace of technical change in Britain. Other smaller European countries, such as Sweden and Switzerland, were also quicker to adapt their institutions.

It was above all the increasing availability of considerable numbers of professional engineers and other skilled people which gave the decisive advantage to German and American industry. Hobsbawn (1968) estimates that Germany was producing 3000 graduate engineers *per annum* by 1913, whereas Britain was producing only 350 in all branches of science, technology and mathematics. In the first half of the 19th Century, with the older mechanical technologies it was possible to train good engineers by a combination of practical on-the-job experience and night school, but with the newer technologies it became more and more necessary to provide full-time professional formation and a curriculum which related scientific principles to practical applications.

Pavitt (1991) has argued that the contribution of basic research to economic performance is often under-estimated because analysis has concentrated on 'output' measurement in terms of scientific discoveries, publications, citations and so forth. Of equal or greater importance is the indirect contribution through the education of scientists, who as a result of their scientific training are able to perform a variety of activities in industry which they otherwise could not perform so well or even at all. Over the last two centuries industrial technologies have become increasingly science-related and less dependent on pure empiricism or craft skills of hand and eye. The training of engineers themselves increasingly incorporates physics, chemistry and now even biology, whilst physicists, chemists and biologists are often working as engineers and managers as well as in the narrower roles of scientists. Investment in basic science is not just a luxury designed to produce scientific papers although this is a necessary part of good scientific training. It is also an essential contribution to technological capability in a wide range of industries and services.

Schumpeter (1939) already recognised this point in his historical account of the rise of the big German electrical combines, AEG and Siemens, from the 1890's to 1914:

> *Electrical technology had, at the beginning of our period, become an applied science which it was possible to learn and to develop in laboratories and schools. A considerable part of the men who currently rose to fill the, very roughly, 40,000 to 50,000 leading or semileading positions in the industrial organism of Germany had that sort of training, at least to the extent of being able to understand and apply readily what was suggested by the scientific engineer, many being scientific engineers themselves. Many so easily found avenues to wealth and advancement within the existing big concerns that to try to set up new ones would have been mere waste of energy for them. Vigorous and varied enterprise thus went on under the almost immediate impulse of the technical departments of those concerns, the entrepreneurs being largely employees and monopoly positions of individual gadgets being incessantly won or lost in the course of a race which, though never displaying the formal properties of perfect competition yet produced all the results usually attributed to perfect competition* (Vol.1, 440).

As Schumpeter saw, the professional internalisation of the development of new products and processes gave an advantage to large oligopolistic firms. By 1914 each of the German electrical giants employed more than 50,000 people and the US industry was dominated similarly by two giants: General Electric and Westinghouse. The in-house R&D laboratory, starting in the German chemical industry in the 1870's was the formal institutional innovation which enabled both the new giant chemical firms and the new giant electrical firms to develop a stream of new products and processes. It provided a method for the regular and systematic improvement and scaling up of these products and processes, taking into account new scientific developments outside the firm, as well as the experience of users and the requirements of the entire technological system.

No British electrical firm, on the other hand, employed more than 10,000 people before 1914 and most were dependent on American or German technology. The early scientific discoveries and innovations by men such as Swan (light bulbs), Parsons (turbines) or Ferranti (alternators) did not lead to market dominance comparable to that of the German and US concerns. In fact the main firm, the British General Electric Co., was headed by a German immigrant, Hirsch, even though he was a fervent supporter of Joseph Chamberlain and the protectionist wing of the Conservative Party.

Leslie Hannah (1983) in his lecture on the failure of British entrepreneurship pointed out that the success of foreign investment in Britain could be traced back to this period of electrification. Schumpeter, too, ascribed the loss of British economic supremacy at this time to a 'failure of entrepreneurship'. But, as his own account (1939, Volume 1, chapter 5) makes clear this weakness in entrepreneurship was not simply a question of genetic failure, or of fatigue in the British stock of entrepreneurs but was closely related to professional skill, to a change in the nature of entrepreneurial activity and to the availability of more profitable investment opportunities for British entrepreneurs in the Empire in mines, plantations, railways and infrastructure. In many years before 1913 overseas investment amounted to more than half of net British capital formation, so that net domestic capital formation was far lower than in Germany or USA (Lewis, 1978). There was a certain tendency not merely to neglect engineering but to look down on industry as in some way socially inferior compared with the professions or the way of life of the aristocracy.

It was not only in professional engineering education and in the new in-house R&D activities that British industry lagged behind German and US industry, there were many other institutional innovations which facilitated the emergence of a new techno-economic paradigm in those countries, whilst its spread was retarded in Britain. Not only could the new in-house R&D Departments in German industry draw upon a good supply of qualified engineers and technicians from the 'Technische Hochschulen', they could also interact with researchers in many of the German universities and increasingly with strong Government Research Institutes. The 'Physikalische und Technische Reichsanstalt' set up in 1887 was not simply a strong Standards Institute but was an active research organisation, which was the model for the Kaiser Wilhelm Institutes set up at the turn of the century. Germany was thus the first country to develop the network of formal professional research and technical organisations, which became characteristic of all industrial countries later on, as they in turn assimilated and developed the new technologies. It was not until more than a decade later that Britain set up the National Physical Laboratory and the lag was greater for many other institutional changes.

The new 'national system of innovation' (in the narrow sense) comprised university laboratories (since Liebig's innovation in German chemistry departments and the introduction of the PhD as a research degree), in-house R&D laboratories in the leading sectors of industry and quality control and testing facilities in other industries, national standards institutes and national research institutes and libraries, a network of national scientific and technical societies and publications, all supported by a growing supply of qualified people from the educational system and a thorough industrial training system for a variety of craft and technical skills. With varying time lags other European countries and Japan followed Germany in developing these national networks of scientific and technical institutions. Nowhere could industry develop and use the new technologies without a national system of innovation to provide supporting services and skilled people even when the technology was mainly imported.

In the United States too, a comparable set of institutional innovations and developments led to the emergence of a similar network of scientific and technical activities in the closing decades of the 19th century. The scientific developments were not so strong as in Germany, nor were the national research laboratories or the industrial training system, but US industry enjoyed the great advantages of a huge flow of skilled immigrants from Europe and of a very rapid growth of general and technical education, as well as the Institutes of Technology in the higher education system. In the United States also, private contract laboratories headed by outstanding inventors and scientists, such as Edison and Tesla played an important transitional role in the late 19th and early 20th Century (Hughes, 1989).

It was not, therefore, just a question of a 'spirit of entrepreneurship' which explained the difference in the innovative performance of British industry on the one hand or German and US industry on the other. It was a different social climate related to changes in the national system of innovation, which meant that it was possible for a new type of technical innovative entrepreneurship and incremental technical change to flourish in Germany and USA, but not to the same degree in Britain. Those European countries, such as Sweden and Switzerland, which imitated the German educational and institutional innovations, also began a rapid catching up process, which enabled them too, to overtake Britain in the new technologies and to develop strength in specialised industries using electric power, but related to local resources and user interactions.

Thus, when Papachristodolou (1988) speaks of the 'heroic' period of the Swedish inventor-entrepreneurs, and similar accounts of American industry stress the extraordinary qualities of Edison as an inventor or Carnegie as an entrepreneur, they are of course correct as far as they go. But a more complete account of socio-economic development must take into account also the changing institutional climate, which made it possible for these and other innovative entrepreneurs to recruit certain types of professional managers, certain types of skilled workers and certain types of engineers, and to combine their contributions in novel ways and so to make a success of innovative enterprises. The rapid growth of these firms at the end of the 19th century and in the early 20th century was not simply a feat of individual will, but was dependent on a complex process of institutional change of which these individuals were themselves to a large extent also the product. The dominant management culture in Germany was 'Technik' and in USA too, management in the large concerns became specialised and professional, though with less emphasis on the quality of technology than in Germany and greater emphasis on standardisation for a large market. A combination of institutional lags, complacency induced by earlier successes, social attitudes unfavourable to industry and alternative opportunities for profitable investment delayed these changes in the British system.

9.3. The Growth of the R&D System and Patterns of Innovation

Although in-house R&D has been described by Whitehead as the greatest single invention of the 19th Century and was already well established in the electrical and chemical industries by the time of the First World War, it was during the *Second* World War that R&D became established as the most essential activity for advancing military technology. This culminated in the Manhattan project, with its awesome demonstration of the power of a massive R&D project to take fundamental discoveries in physics and to use them to develop by far the most destructive weapons ever known. But even before the atomic bomb, the Anglo-German competition in radar technology, was employing thousands of skilled scientists and engineers, and was decisive for the British success in the 'Battle of Britain'. The development of radar, of the V1 and the V2, and of nuclear weapons were only the most spectacular examples of what had become an R&D intensive war on both sides (Jones, 1978). The accelerated development of computer technology for code-cracking, aircraft design and ballistic calculations was another development with enormous long-term consequences.

The contribution of scientific research to military success was so obvious that the social climate in the post-war world was highly favourable to the rapid expansion of the R&D system and other types of scientific and technical activity. Ideas, which before the War had seemed Utopian and visionary, now became acceptable. In his pioneering work on the 'Social Function of Science', Bernal (1939) had estimated that all R&D activities in Britain before the War amounted to only about 0.1% of GNP. He thought that in the United States and the USSR they accounted for a proportion of GNP about two or three times as high as in Britain, but even so he advocated a *tenfold* increase in the scale of R&D world-wide. Such an increase was in fact achieved in most of the industrialised countries in the thirty years which followed the Second World War (from about 0.1 – 0.3% to about 1 – 3% of GNP). Most Third World countries, however, still have much lower levels of R&D (Table 9.1).

The obvious consequences of military R&D not only served to enhance the prestige of R&D generally, in particular they legitimised a massive increase in the role of *government* expenditure on R&D. The report by Vannevar Bush on 'Science, the Endless Frontier' (1946) was influential in the setting up of the National Science Foundation in the United States and similar social innovations in most countries meant that university research expanded very rapidly in the 1950's and was put on a relatively stable foundation with regular public funding over and above the support of teaching activities.

The pattern of in-house industrial R&D which had emerged during the 'Third Kondratieff' wave (1880's to 1930's) affected primarily a few key leading industrial sectors, especially electrical equipment and chemicals. In other industries and services, technical change took place of course, but more as a result of external impulses, the work of suppliers or the incremental improvements introduced through accumulated experience and interaction with markets. It was during and after the Second World War that the specialised R&D Department became a characteristic institution in most branches of manufacturing in the leading countries, although R&D intensity continued to vary enormously between sectors (Pavitt, 1984).

R&D was never, of course, the only source of technical change. As we have seen, many other scientific and technical institutions are essential for an effective national system. Within industry the Design and Drawing Office continued to be an important source of technical innovation in many branches of mechanical engineering and in vehicles and was only gradually integrated with R&D, more narrowly defined. Many incremental innovations continued to be made by production engineers and by shop-floor workers without any necessary reference to R&D (Hollander, 1965). These changes were a major source of productivity improvement. As illustrated in many other chapters, the process of learning by interacting with users, as well as learning by doing, was another major source of technical innovation.

Table 9.1. **Countries R&D Expenditures, R&D as a Percentage of US R&D[A], and R&D as a Percentage of GNP. (Constant 1982 Dollars in Millions)[B]**

Country	R&D	R&D/US R&D[C]	R&D/GNP
Argentina (1981)	$ 1,087.3	1.4%	0.4%
Australia (1985)	1,718.0	1.8	1.1
Austria (1987)	1,310.1	1.3	1.3
Belgium (1983)	1,441.5	1.7	1.5
Brasil (1985)	1,448.0	1.5	0.7
Burundi (1984)	3.1	D	0.4
Canada (1986)	4,877.0	4.9	1.4
Cent. African Rep. (1984)	1.4	D	0.2
Chile (1980)	139.6	0.2	0.4
Columbia (1982)	43.0	0.1	0.1
Congo (1984)	0.1	D	D
Costa Rica (1982)	2.8	D	0.1
Cyprus (1984)	1.8	D	0.1
Denmark (1985)	707.4	0.7	1.3
Egypt (1982)	57.7	0.1	0.2
Ecuador (1979)	43.6	0.1	0.4
El Salvador (1984)	36.0	D	0.9
Finland (1987)	1,235.6	1.2	1.7
France (1987)	13,728.0	13.6	2.3
Germany, West (1987)	19,370.7	19.2	2.8
Greece (1985)	102.7	0.1	0.3
Guatemala (1983)	43.1	0.1	0.5
Guyana (1982)	0.9	D	0.2
Iceland (1986)	24.8	D	0.8
India (1984)	1,482.1	1.6	0.9
Indonesia (1983)	286.2	0.3	0.3
Iran (1985)	217.9	0.2	NA
Ireland (1985)	132.5	0.1	0.8
Israel (1983)	637.2	0.8	3.0
Italy (1987)	7,394.3	7.3	1.5
Japan (1987)	39,117.8	39.0	2.9
Jordan (1987)	32.1	D	1.0
Korea, South (1983)	1,307.9	1.6	1.1
Kuwait (1984)	223.2	0.2	0.9
Madagascar (1980)	7.7	D	0.2
Malawi (1977)	2.1	D	0.2
Mauritius (1985)	1.5	D	0.2
Mexico (1984)	881.3	1.0	0.6
Netherlands (1985)	3,099.8	3.2	2.1
New Zealand (1985)	203.9	0.2	1.0
Nicaragua (1985)	10.0	D	0.3
Nigeria (1977)	235.2	0.4	0.3
Norway (1987)	1,007.1	1.0	1.9
Pakistan (1984)	$100.1	0.1%	0.3%

(*Continued*)

Table 9.1. (*Continued*)

Country	R&D	R&D/US R&D[C]	R&D/GNP
Panama (1975)	5.6	D	0.2
Peru (1984)	42.5	D	0.2
Philippines (1982)	61.2	0.1	0.2
Portugal (1984)	71.7	0.1	0.4
Qatar (1984)	1.6	D	D
Rwanda (1984)	2.2	D	0.1
Saint Lucia (1984)	4.2	D	3.0
Seychelles (1983)	1.8	D	1.3
Singapore (1984)	93.3	0.1	0.5
Spain (1984)	1,762.4	1.9	0.5
Sri Lanka (1983)	8.5	D	0.2
Sudan (1978)	18.9	D	0.2
Sweden (1987)	3,967.4	3.9	3.0
Switzerland (1983)	2,131.1	2.5	2.3
Taiwan (1983)	505.1	0.5	1.1
Thailand (1985)	115.3	0.1	0.3
Trinidad and Tobago (1985)	52.7	0.1	0.8
Turkey (1983)	116.2	0.1	0.2
United Kingdom (1986)	13,764.7	14.0	2.4
United States (1987)	100,823.0	100.0	2.6
Venezuela (1984)	180.1	0.2	0.4
Yoguslavia (1985)	315.8	0.3	0.8

A. Most current year available.
B. Foreign currency conversions to US dollars were calculated with OECD purchasing power parities for the following countries: Belgium, Canada, Denmark, France, West Germany, Italy, Japan, Korea, The Netherlands, Norway and United Kingdom. All others were calculated using IMF average-for-period par/market exchange rates. Constant 1982 dollars are based on US Department of Commerce GNP implicit price deflators.
C. Percentage is calculated using US R&D in the reporting year of the foreign country.
D. Less than 0.05 percent.
Notes: The above data should be used only as an estimation of the relative R&D standing of nations. Although there is a fairly high degree of consistency in the data reported by the OECD, data for countries reporting to UNESCO are less comparable. This is principally because of differences in national statistical collection capabilities and definitions. Additionally, some R&D/GNP percentages are R&D/GDP. As long as these factors are taken into account, such differences do not preclude international comparisons. Again these caveats are less applicable to OECD data.
Source: NSF, 1989.

Numerous other *external* sources of scientific and technical ideas were important (Table 9.2).

Nevertheless, the R&D department became the main point of entry for new scientific development and the main focus for the development of new products and processes in most branches of industry. The dominant

***Table 9.2.* Sources of New Technology**

(1) In-house research, design and development
(2) Experience in production, quality control and testing
(3) Experience in marketing and feedback from users
(4) Experience in plant design and construction and feedback from contractors and suppliers
(5) Scanning of world scientific and technical literature, patents and other information sources
(6) Recruitment of engineers and scientists
(7) Contact with university science and engineering faculties
(8) Contact with government research organisations
(9) Consultancy arrangements with (7), (8) and independents
(10) Acquisition of other firms or mergers
(11) Joint ventures
(12) Cooperative research arrangements
(13) Licensing and cross-licensing of new products and processes and know-how transfer agreements
(14) Contract research
(15) Other

technological style of the quarter century following the Second World War was a 'Fordist' mass and flow production paradigm taking advantage of big scale economies in production and design and using vast quantities of cheap energy and materials. The new synthetic materials were mainly developed by the R&D-intensive large chemical firms; the new sources of energy by the oil industry and the nuclear power industry; the household durable goods, such as television, radio and washing machines by the R&D-intensive electrical firms; the new machinery by a combination of R&D activities and design activities in the engineering industries. The cold war meant that the extraordinarily high R&D-intensity of the aircraft, electronic and other weapons industries was maintained (Table 9.3).

The enhanced role of the professional R&D Department found its expression not only in the order-of-magnitude expansion of R&D activities, but in the selection of R&D as the focus for regular national and international statistics and 'League Table' type comparisons. As the authors of the 'Frascati Manual' recognised from the outset (OECD, 1963), R&D was only one part of a whole complex of scientific and technical activities which contributed to technical change. But despite spasmodic efforts these other activities, such as design, information services, exploration, testing and so forth have never been systematically measured in the same way as R&D. Only in Eastern Europe were these activities regularly measured together with R&D. However, lack of measurement certainly does not mean lack of importance.

Table 9.3. **Distribution of Industrial R&D Among Selected Manufacturing Industries: 1985 or 1986 (Percent)**

Industry	France (1985)	West Germany (1985)	Japan (1986)	United Kingdom (1986)	United States (1985)
Total industrial R&D	100	100	100	100	100
Electrical equipment	25	26	18	31	22
Machinery and computers [A]	8	11	21	11	14
Chemicals and allied products	17	21	16	18	1
Motor vehicles	10	15	14	7	9
Aerospace	19	7	B	17	23
Professional and scientific instruments	1	2	3	2	7
All other industries [C]	20	18	28	15	15

A. This category includes general machinery as well as office, computing, and accounting machinery. Data for Japan for this category and equipment are NSF estimates.
B. Less than 0.5%.
C. Including non-manufacturing industries.
Sources: National Science Foundation (1989).

The picture which emerges for the OECD countries therefore is a very incomplete one and can in no way be taken as providing a map of all inventive and innovative activities. The characteristic pattern of R&D which became available on a comparable basis for many countries in the 1960's is nevertheless an important part of the jig-saw, provided it is seen in its broad historical context and the missing parts of the jig-saw are not forgotten, just because the quantitative measures are still lacking.

Typically, most OECD countries have a rather skew distribution of R&D with a heavy concentration in the largest firms. In the larger countries, 100 firms usually account for about two-thirds or more of total industrial R&D. There is some national variation but usually *industrial* R&D accounts for between 60 and 70% of total R&D (GERD), performance, universities for between 10 and 20% and government and 'non-profit institutes' for the remainder. In terms of *source* of funding the government share is larger, especially in those countries (US, UK, France) where there is a heavy military R&D programme. But in all countries government is the main source of funds for fundamental research and for a significant proportion of civil applied research as well.

From all this it is evident that in the 20th Century the growth of R&D activities was associated with the process of concentration in the economy more generally and with an increased role for the nation-state as contractor and as source of funds. But in emphasising the role of the 'techno-structure' in the large US Corporation Galbraith (1969) overstates the degree of 'planning' and marketing manipulation which is possible and belittles the role of small firms and users. Technical innovation, especially radical innovation, remains an uncertain business even for the largest corporations. Market acceptance cannot be guaranteed nor can technical success. Moreover, small firms still retain advantages in certain types of innovation.

UK empirical evidence (Pavitt, Robson and Townsend, 1985) shows that although large firms account for about two-thirds of all innovations, the smallest firms nevertheless contribute a significant fraction (over 15%) and that this fraction is much higher than their share of R&D expenditures. Wallmark and McQueen (1988) found that small Swedish firms contributed about 20% of important Swedish innovations from 1945 to 1980. The R&D statistics understate the contribution of small firms because they do not measure satisfactorily the part-time work of non-specialised individuals and groups. As in the 18th and early 19th centuries, when they predominated everywhere, small firms often do not find it worthwhile to have specialised departmental structures. Moreover, the inventor-entrepreneur who establishes a firm with the objective of exploiting an invention is still a significant phenomenon. Such entrepreneurs may often transfer the results of university or government R&D to their firms.

However, even though Jewkes et al. (1958) were right to reject the extreme position that large corporate R&D no longer left any place for inventive activities of the small firms in the 20th century, their own evidence actually confirmed that the role of large corporations had grown enormously. Whilst university inventors or small firms often made a major contribution in the early stages of *inventive* work, the majority of the case studies in their book actually show that development costs were so high that in the end large firms took over, so that they accounted for about two-thirds of the actual *innovations*.

The Jewkes study and other similar work on invention and innovation is important also in confirming that for almost any major innovation, whether made in small firms or large firms, there are numerous inputs from a wide variety of different sources. The more detailed studies commissioned by the National Science Foundation (1969 and 1973) in Project TRACES showed conclusively that it is virtually impossible to consider any major innovation as the work of a single individual or a single organisation. There is always a long trail of earlier scientific and technical contributions, made over previous decades and even in the last few years of development activity, there are almost always inputs from other firms, from potential users, from universities and from government institutions. There are also of course inputs from abroad but the ability to gain easy and rapid access to local sources must be one of the most important advantages conferred by an efficient national innovation system.

This applies both to R&D institutions and equally to other institutions such as scientific and technical information services, patent offices, standards institutes, precision components for prototypes, test facilities and so forth.

Indeed, many studies of success and failure in innovation have concluded that the capacity to communicate and interact with a variety of external agencies is one of the main ingredients of success. Cultural and social factors mean that *national* sources of interaction are exceptionally important in this process. Perez and Soete (1988b) have demonstrated how great is the cost disadvantage of firms in the Third World lacking such national networks. A number of studies have shown that inputs from fundamental research institutions often continued to be important, even in the later stages of development work (e.g. Gibbons and Johnston, 1974). The institutions involved in scientific and technical activities (the 'national system of innovation' in the narrow sense) should therefore be viewed as a *network* and a one-sided emphasis either on individual people or on individual institutions fails to capture the true nature of innovative entrepreneurship, which is essentially a process of *combining* multiple inputs. In particular the contribution of science is often under-estimated (as in the American Defence Department Project HINDSIGHT) because of the time lags and as we have seen the frequently indirect mode of input, often through the education system. The experience of Silicon Valley and similar concentrations of innovative entrepreneurs demonstrate that relationships of trust and intimate dialogue with suppliers, scientific institutes and various supporting institutions depend on both geographical and cultural proximity (Saxenian, 1991, Freeman, 1991). This must cast some doubt on some theories of 'globalisation' as well as on the real nature of 'free riders'.

Of course, the variety of scientific and technical inputs varies enormously with the nature of the innovation. Studies such as HINDSIGHT or TRACES or the work of Saxenian were concerned with radical innovations or new systems which did indeed depend on numerous sources. But as we move across the spectrum towards minor innovations and incremental innovations, clearly there is less need for such a large variety of sources. The individual engineer or worker on the shop floor can indeed make suggestions for product and process improvements, which involve little or no contact with any outside sources, and often no contact is sought or needed with the firm's own R&D department. However, even at this end of the spectrum the institutional context cannot be ignored. The type of improvements which are made will relate to the education and training, as well as the work experience of the individuals involved. Whether their suggestions lead anywhere will depend on the industrial relations within the firm and on the extent to which suggestions are welcomed and rewarded. Similar considerations apply to the innovative ideas and proposals of users. Thus the *national* environment continues to play a major role in all types of innovation.

The variety of different types of innovation accounts for some of the apparent contradictions in the empirical work on innovation. At one time in the 1960's and early 1970's it was fashionable to claim that:

1. Innovation was mainly a demand or market-led activity;
2. Most ideas for innovation did *not* come from R&D, but from other parts of the firm or from customers;
3. Basic research (or even any *research*, as opposed to *development*) was a waste of resources for the firm, since it could not lead to profitable innovations.

Mowery and Rosenberg (1979) provided a valuable corrective to some of these simplistic propositions by showing that most of the empirical surveys which were cited did not in fact support these propositions, but rather pointed to a complex interaction between the 'supply' side (R&D labs, scientific and technical institutions) and the 'demand' side (potential and actual users, marketing organisations, etc.). Clearly, when it comes to incremental improvement type of innovations, the experience of users is bound to be extremely important and will often predominate as a source of ideas for innovation. But in the early stages of radical innovations it is the contribution of scientific and technical institutions (in our time, especially from R&D organisations) which tends to predominate, even though of course the R&D people often do have some conjecture of a potential future market or application. In some cases scientific research has its own trajectories which lead only later to marketable applications. Thus, for example, the laser, which today has innumerable applications in industry, was once thought of as 'an invention in search of applications'. When Crick and Watson discovered the Double Helix they were not thinking of the market, but in the 21st century bio-technology may well be the strongest influence on technology and markets in both agriculture and industry. A recent study of several innovations emanating from a Dutch national laboratory (the TPD) showed that none of them started through market demand, but rather had to overcome conservative resistance in industry.

This points to an extremely important conclusion: when there is a radical discontinuity in technology systems the role of the S and T network becomes exceptionally important. But when the main direction of technical change is the improvement and diffusion of a familiar technology, the interaction with users becomes more important. As we have seen, the R&D network itself came into existence because new products, such as synthetic dyestuffs or electric motors, could in no way emerge from the incremental improvement of existing natural products or of steam engines (or from user experience).

Electrification, when it was first diffusing in the 1880's and 1890's could not be handled by simple trial and error techniques. It required a certain fundamental background in physics and new types of instruments and test equipment. It still does. But as the technology has become completely familiar, the necessary skills have become very widespread and as the successive generations of products have become more 'user-friendly' and safer, then what would have once been thought of as very radical leaps in product design tends to be thought of as 'incremental' (Perez, 1988).

When there is a pervasive radical change in technology, which we may describe as a change in 'techno-economic paradigm' (Perez, 1983), then the institutional changes in the science-technology system will be especially important, and access to a national network for information and advice is essential. Electrification was one such change and the contemporary 'computerisation' of factories, offices, design and research laboratories themselves is another. In the 21st century bio-technology may lead to another such paradigm change. The final section of this chapter explores some of the institutional changes in the science-technology system which are associated with paradigm change.

9.4. The Newly Emerging Pattern of Institutions

Earlier chapters in this book have discussed various types of institutional change and have emphasised the importance of 'learning' processes for institutions as well as individuals. Changes in the institutional framework came about for a variety of reasons but the main reasons are the following:

1) People have ideas to improve existing institutions and to invent new institutions and are able to muster enough political support to make changes.
2) The existing institutions are unable to cope with new problems or the growth of old problems or can no longer function effectively because of changing circumstances.

Changes in technology stimulate institutional change for both these reasons. Inventions, such as the telephone and the typewriter, made it possible for many bureaucratic institutions to function in a somewhat different way. The same is true of FAX and the word processor today. On a much broader scale the rising living standards made possible by technical change facilitated the introduction of a variety of 'social services', including health services and many related new institutions. On the other hand, technical innovations can sometimes have such dangerous side-effects on the environment and human beings that new institutions are needed to regulate and control these adverse effects and to reduce the risks. This list could be expanded almost indefinitely. It is obvious that there is a continuous interaction between technical, organisational and social innovations. But to make sense of this complex myriad of interactive changes we have to distinguish between various types of technical change.

The big systemic changes in technology (changes in 'techno-economic paradigm') tend to provoke correspondingly big changes in institutions, and conversely some institutional innovations are particularly favourable to the introduction and diffusion of new technologies. Perez (1983) has described this process of mutual adjustment as one of achieving a good 'match' between institutions and technology. She describes the downturn and depression phase of the long waves in economic development as a prolonged trial and error process of search for the type of institutions which could make a good match ('regime of regulation' in the terminology of Boyer (1988) and his colleagues). This search process is painful and conflict-ridden as of course there are various social and political alternatives, which may be supported by various interest groups.

In these terms the 1970's and 1980's may be viewed as a prolonged process of social adjustment to the potential and to the characteristics of the computer revolution in technology. We shall not develop here the argument that the convergence of major innovations in computers, micro-electronics and telecommunications has generated a wave of technical change which is affecting all industries and services. This has been thoroughly argued elsewhere (e.g. Perez, 1985b). Here we shall take this for granted and will examine only the effects of this paradigm change on the R&D system and related scientific and technical institutions. We shall also examine what types of change in these institutions might make for a 'good match' in the sense of facilitating the introduction and diffusion of the technology and a return to high rates of productivity growth and employment. Our starting point will be the problems which were developing in the 1960's with the 'old' regime of R&D and innovation and the stresses experienced in that regime as a result of the new wave of technical change.

Before going any further we should note that, purely in terms of productivity growth, the previous system worked rather well. In these terms the 1950's and 1960's were probably the fastest period of sustained economic growth which the world has ever experienced. Together with the big expansion of education and training, the network of scientific and technical institutions did indeed make a major contribution to this achievement (Fagerberg, 1987).

However, as with steam technology in the late 19th century there were limits in the 20th century to the continued growth of productivity and profitability under the energy-intensive Fordist regime. The strains began to be felt not only in terms of the availability and price of energy and materials inputs, but also in work organisation, in diseconomies of scale and in diminishing returns to R&D along the old technological trajectories. Baily and Chakrabarti (1988) have shown in their detailed studies of American industrial sectors the close connection between falling productivity and a slow-down in innovation. In chemicals there was a particularly sharp drop in the number of product innovations, but in electric power and in machine tools, the effects of Wolf's Law of diminishing returns to investment in technology were also apparent.

Some of the institutional problems associated with this decline of innovation in the chemical, energy and mechanical engineering industries and some of their difficulties in adjusting to a change of techno-economic paradigm can be clarified by looking at 'failed' attempts at innovation. Studies of failure, both with the older technologies and with the new ones are particularly helpful in exposing some of the difficulties, weaknesses and stresses of the institutions involved in innovation, especially the R&D departments.

When we examine studies of failure, particularly project SAPPHO, (Rothwell et al., 1974) but also the more recent work of Martin Lockett (1987) on information technology, then three points emerge with particular force:

1) The commonest and most persistent cause of failure was in the relationship between 'producers' and 'users' of an innovation, even when they were both nominally part of the same organisation, as in Lockett's studies or in many of the chemical process innovations in the SAPPHO project. (see chapter 3)
2) A related and equally serious problem was the lack of adequate 'horisontal' communication and cooperation between R&D Departments, Production and Marketing within the firm. (see chapter 5)
3) Finally, internal communication problems were often compounded and aggravated by external communication problems. As we have seen, almost every significant successful innovation has involved inputs from a wide variety of different scientific and technical sources, as well as from users. A good external network is therefore vital for innovative success, including of course, access to university research, as well as other institutions. (see chapter 6)

All three of these common causes of failure are associated with the specialisation and professionalisation of R&D and may also be affected by the geographical and organisational isolation of the R&D department. Very often one of the advantages of smaller firms lies in much more flexible and rapid communications.

Because these difficulties were so common in the 1950's and 1960's, various attempts were made at institutional changes which would minimise the problems. These ranged from regular rotation of people between Departments to joint management teams, joint seminars, relocation of groups, and sabbaticals. Probably Japanese firms went further than most others in promoting this type of institutional change. Many observers have commented on the high degree of 'horisontal integration' between research, design, development, production and marketing. Aoki (1986) has contrasted this horisontal information flow characteristic of Japanese firms with the vertical information flow characteristic of the large hierarchical American corporation. Baba (1985) has described the Japanese approach as 'using the factory as a laboratory'. The tradition of 'reverse engineering' in some sectors of Japanese industry facilitated this horisontal integration, because design and research groups had to cooperate very closely with production engineers to imitate a foreign design and improve it (Freeman, 1987).

In the light of these weaknesses in the 'old innovation system', it is clear that the change of techno-economic paradigm makes institutional change in the R&D system essential. It also facilitates some of the most desirable changes. Since the new technology confronts most firms with a radical break in their previous trajectories, the need for information from external sources becomes even more crucial. Even giant firms like IBM which have been rather self-sufficient in their R&D and have resources greater than many small nation-states, have been obliged to enter into a whole series of collaborative arrangements in R&D, because no firms can possibly cope single-handed with the full range of interrelated developments in the computer and telecommunication revolution and the speed at which they are taking place. Consequently a feature of the R&D scene in the 1980's has been a rapid proliferation of new agreements and consortia, often international in scope for collaboration in R&D projects and programmes (Freeman, 1991). These are frequently promoted by governments, which again, following the Japanese precedent, have acted as brokers in setting up various types of R&D consortia, especially in Information and Communication Technology (Arnold and Guy, 1987).

The design and re-design of customised software is essential for computerised systems of all kinds and since the information revolution affects service industries even more than manufacturing, this means that the old pattern of manufacturing as R&D-intensive with the services lacking R&D has broken down. But the new types of service innovation based on computer systems are based on software design and development which is not always classified as formal R&D. Moreover, these service innovations, like other innovations in communication systems, generally involve networking with hardware suppliers, users and other institutions.

Some of the new consortia and networks involving both hardware and software are simply between firms with complementary abilities in technology or a common interest in a new field. But frequently they also involve universities and some of the government programmes in USA and Europe, as well as in Japan, deliberately set out to stimulate joint projects between industry and universities. Many new institutions have developed to cope with the ICT revolution and they are transforming the information systems, the R&D process, the role of government and of universities. Such arrangements are even more important in biotechnology where the links between basic research and industrial applications are even more intimate. At the same time there is a tendency in the largest and most powerful firms, again especially in Japan, to build up their own in-house basic research laboratories as well (Gregory, 1986). These tendencies are not mutually exclusive but on the contrary represent two aspects of the same process: the growing convergence of science and technology.

What all of this means is that 'networking' is now becoming of critical importance for effective innovation (see also chapters 5 and 6). It applies not only to collaboration within and between the scientific and technical institutions, but to collaboration between firms (especially suppliers of software materials, sub-systems and components), and between firms and users (Lundvall, 1988). Information and communication technology greatly facilitates networking by making it technically feasible to use common data banks, transmit data and design drawings in seconds anywhere in the world, pool patent data, and share search costs. Thus the technical change both determines and is determined by the new institutional environment in an interactive process (see the special issue of *Research Policy*, Vol. 20, No. 5, 1991).

The importance of informal networks, of combining diverse inputs, of access to specialised skills and facilities, of social attitudes and of other national institutions mean that *national* systems will continue to be a powerful influence on the relative performance of local firms. But through the growth of international investment in R&D by MNC's, some of the strongest firms are able to gain access to the advantages of several of the strongest national systems. The possible effects of this internationalisation are the subject of chapter 13 by Francois Chesnais.

Part III:

OPENING NATIONAL SYSTEMS OF INNOVATION: SPECIALISATION, MULTINATIONAL CORPORATIONS AND INTEGRATION

Chapter 10

EXPORT SPECIALISATION, STRUCTURAL COMPETITIVENESS AND NATIONAL SYSTEMS OF INNOVATION

Bent Dalum[1]

10.1. Introduction

The following contains a comparative analysis of some important structural background features of national systems of innovation (NSI's). The sample is limited to 21 OECD countries. The empirical source is OECD's Trade by Commodities (foreign trade by 'visible' goods).[2] This kind of data can only serve as an incomplete illustration of the conceptual framework derived in earlier chapters. However, the material offers some advantages worthwhile to exploit, e.g. time series covering more than a quarter of a century. Certain features of international export specialisation will be used as indirect proxies of more general economic development patterns of the OECD countries.

In chapter 4 the so called 'structural thesis' emphasises (domestic) production and linkage patterns as important determinants of substantial shares of not only non-professionalised learning and innovation, but also professionalised R&D. The arguments stress the incremental character of innovation and its path dependency. The changes of products and processes – it was argued – follow trajectories, to a large extent determined by inherited production and trade patterns. History matters; present and future innovation possibilities are highly dependent on existing structural features of the economy. Structure, as a reflection of history, matters.

It is no simple task to illustrate this line of reasoning, let alone to deliver outright empirical proofs on an international comparative basis. However, some of the 'propositions' of 4 may be confronted with empirical evidence. In the empirical part of this chapter it will be shown that the international specialisation patterns of the OECD countries fruitfully may be analysed in terms of *life cycles*. It will also be shown that these patterns, as the main rule, have been characterised by distinctly *different features country by country*, and that these features do not appear to converge in spite of increasing internationalisation. Finally, a highly aggregate structural variable will be used as an indicator of the 'strength' of the NSI's over time.

The chapter will take as its point of departure (section 10.2) recent developments in the theory of international trade. The question will be raised whether these developments satisfactorily incorporate the impact of the dynamic disequilibrating forces of technological change. In section 10.3 the concept of structural competitiveness is discussed as a transmission mechanism between export performance and domestic economic activity. Finally, section 10.4 contains the empirical survey of the specialisation patterns of 21 OECD countries.

10.2. Recent Developments in Trade Theory – Technical Change and Disequilibrium

The orthodox Heckscher-Ohlin-Samuelson (H-O-S) model has more or less been unrivalled as the standard textbook case until the mid 1980's. Two strands of research, both initiated by 'real' or political problems, have, though, led to a more realistic approach, often referred to as 'New trade theory'.

The very existence of intra-industry trade (IIT) calls for extensions of the simple H-O-S model. Its assumptions implicitly exclude the existence of the phenomenon in contradiction to empirical realities. Greenaway and Milner's (1986) survey of the field covers most dimensions of New trade theory, i.e. Neo-Heckscher-Ohlin models (identical products); Neo-Chamberlinian and Neo-Hotelling models; models incorporating oligopolistic competition (in identical as well as various kinds of differentiated products); and multiproduct as well as multinational firms.[3]

The second phenomenon calling for further development of trade theory has been the attempts to analyse the micro and macro effects of economic integration, especially the effects of the European single market from 1993 (see also chapter 12). The EC Commission initiated a major research effort, 'The Cost of Non-Europe', with the explicit purpose of establishing the foundation for claiming a large growth potential from the removal of non-tariff barriers to trade, such as technical trade barriers, border formalities etc. Previous studies had shown fairly small effects of different integration projects, typically with less than 1% increase in GNP.[4] These studies were normally based on the standard H-O-S framework assuming perfect competition, non-increasing returns to scale, etc. The Cost of Non-Europe project has, however, adopted most of the developments of New trade theory, and the effects of economic integration are significantly stronger than those found in earlier studies.[5]

According to Smith and Venables (in EC Commission, 1988b, Vol. 2) the effects, at the microeconomic level, have been derived from models based on partial equilibrium allowing for imperfect competition, mainly caused by product differentiation and economies of scale. The EC Commission was aware of these limitations and emphasise that three important dynamic factors have been omitted from the calculations: 1) technical innovations caused by increasing competition, 2) dynamic economies of scale (learning by doing) and 3) new business strategies of European enterprises leading to the emergence of truly European companies. The Commission concluded that the results 'are unlikely to be overestimates of the potential benefit of fully integrating the Community's market' (EC Commission, 1988a, 20) – i.e. taking these dynamic factors into account would have increased the potential benefits (for further discussion on economic integration, see chapter 12 by Andersen and Brændgaard).

However, it is not evident that the dynamic mechanisms referred to *a priori* will result in increasing economic benefits of economic integration – at least not for all participants. In the case of Cost of Non-Europe the welfare gains are calculated at an aggregate EC basis.

Theories of vicious circles of divergence of regional fortunes resulting from market integration exist, but so do alternative theses that point to more balanced or indeterminate outcomes; the latter theses including important recent developments in the analysis of trade between industrialized countries (EC Commission, 1988a, 21).

These recent developments are the New trade theories. But the former theses (theories of vicious circles of divergence) represent an important strand of analysis – too important to ignore.

In their book on technical change and international trade, Dosi, Pavitt and Soete (1990) divide recent developments of trade analysis in two groups. The first, 'Neo-classical extensions – the *Revisionists*', is mainly based on relaxing some of the strong assumptions of the pure H-O-S framework, such as allowing for economies of scale, differentiated products, non-identical production functions between countries and even effects of multinationals. The models may usually be characterised as partial equilibrium models – with a high degree of conceptual rigour. The New trade theories, referred to above, belong to this group. The emphasis of the second group, 'Less pure theory – the *Heretics*', is on international differences in innovative activities and the lack of equilibrium mechanisms in the international or intersectoral adjustment process believed to be of significant importance in understanding international trade patterns.

A central feature is also the cumulative character of technical change, which may lead to vicious or virtuous circles of economic development at the aggregate level.

In spite of more or less hostile attitudes from part of the established profession, the Heretic approach has gained ground among the general public in the 1980's. Proponents of the view that technical innovation is a major factor behind successful long term economic performance have gained considerable ground.

Increasing trade tensions between Japan, Europe and the US have given considerable impetus to this kind of analysis in the US.[6] The 1992 Single Market project; the wave of mergers, acquisitions and strategic alliances; and the major European research programmes (such as Esprit, Race and Eureka) have often been discussed as means for creating technological strength and, accordingly, international competitiveness in European companies vis-à-vis their US and Japanese competitors. However, the basic textbook versions of international trade theory are still dominated by, usually minor, modifications of the H-O-S framework.[7] The lack of conceptual rigour of the alternatives is still a major inhibiting force within the profession.

Dosi, Pavitt and Soete (op. cit., 26–27) summarise the Heretic approach in terms of the following features:

1) International differences in technological capabilities are fundamental in explaining differences in levels and trends in exports, imports and income per capita of each country.
2) General equilibrium mechanisms of international and intersectoral adjustment are weak. Growth rates are often balance of payments constrained. The relevant international adjustment mechanism is world market share – transmitted to domestic macroeconomic activity through foreign trade multipliers.
3) Level and change of market shares between countries can be explained by country-specific absolute advantages or disadvantages.
4) Technology is not a free good. It is, on the contrary, often cumulative, path dependent, local, firm specific and privately appropriable.
5) Allocative patterns of international trade have dynamic impacts, which may either lead to virtuous or vicious circles of economic development.

The dichotomy between convergence and divergence is related to the characteristics of the main technologies on the one hand (across countries and across firms) and 'strategies, context conditions and history' on the other (which vary with companies and countries but across technologies). In their interpretation, the technology factor reflects two dimensions. Innovations, whether of product or process technology, leading to divergence; and diffusion pointing towards convergence between firms and countries. The *national context* has a significant role to play in determining long term growth:

Once the cumulative and firm-specific nature of technology is recognized, its development over time ceases to be random but is likely to be constrained to zones that are closely related technologically to existing activities. If those zones can be identified, measured and explained, it is possible in principle to predict likely future patterns of innovative activities in firms and countries. (op. cit., 85).

Like the approach presented in Part I of the present book, it is important to make structural analyses country by country as a precondition for discussions of future growth potential. Dosi, Pavitt and Soete's approach concentrates more on the economic effects of the technology factor *per se* on trade and growth patterns. National context variables are among the determining factors of technology. The NSI approach focuses on what constitutes national systems of innovation; the economic effects of qualitative differences between them; and may contribute, potentially at least, to lay the foundations for the relevance of *national policy efforts*. The two approaches are not mutually exclusive; they are complementary with significant overlaps.

On countries' technological activities Pavitt, Dosi and Soete (1990, 102) summarise the following four empirical characteristics – based on detailed and internationally comparable patent data (at the industry and firm level):

1) Small countries are more technologically specialised than large countries.
2) Stability in the technological specialisation pattern of each country over time.
3) Specialisation patterns are distinctly different from country to country.
4) The significant importance of relatively few (large) firms on country patterns.

The Heretic approach leads to a dynamic view of the economic development of countries. Theories of vicious or virtuous circles of economic development are too important to be ignored as is common in various New trade theory approaches – or eventually reserved exclusively for the study of development features of Third World countries. However, the transmission mechanism from countries' technological performance characteristics to their economic development in general is far from simple. The concept of structural competitiveness may serve as a helpful tool.

10.3. Structural Competitiveness

International competitiveness is usually applied as a vague, though intuitively plausible, concept – often without any clear analytical foundation. Empirical studies of competitiveness have most often been carried out by government bodies in their quest for a rationale for short term policy interventions to tune macroeconomic performance, especially balance of payments problems.

Traditionally, the focus among economists has almost exclusively been on unit wage costs, in many countries even without taking productivity into account. Most analyses of competitiveness take as their point of departure a simplistic logic based on assumptions of perfect competition in world markets. Growth in relative (unit) wage costs leads to increasing prices, which lead to decreasing market shares. Competitiveness is only dependent on price factors in this line of thought. Non-price factors such as product quality, after sales services, marketing, etc. are ignored. Prices are for all practical purposes determined by (unit) wage costs and exchange rates. In less rigourous versions profitability is emphasised. Decrease in wage costs leads to increase in profitability, which again allows firms to invest more in R&D, product innovation, marketing, etc. to conquer market shares.

Already in the late 1970's several studies raised serious doubts on the validity of simplistic wage cost/export performance relations (e.g. Kaldor, 1978 and Christensen et al., 1978). Kaldor demonstrated an apparently 'perverse' relationship between relative unit labour costs and/or relative price variables and export performance – as measured by world export shares for 12 OECD countries 1963–75. Ten years later Fagerberg (1988a) developed and tested an econometric model of competitiveness for a sample of 15 OECD countries for the period 1960–83. In his model the proxy for competitiveness is the rate of growth in world export shares. The explanatory variables are five factors: 1) the technology gap measured by relative per capita income; 2) growth in national technological activity measured by patenting activity; 3) investment efforts measured by the investment/GDP share; 4) demand growth measured by growth of world trade in constant prices; and 5) wage costs measured by relative unit labour costs. Fagerberg found that the main factors influencing competitiveness are growth in technological activity and the investment effort variables. The cost factor also affect competitiveness 'to some extent but less so than many seem to believe'.

Dosi, Pavitt and Soete (op. cit.) also present econometric studies in their analysis of international competitiveness. At the conceptual level the point of departure is the term structural competitiveness,[8] which is basically synonymous with absolute advantage (as opposed to comparative advantage). They model structural competitiveness in terms of the determinants of export performance (market shares) along the following lines,

$$X_{ij} = f\left(T_{ij}, C_{ij}, O_{ij}\right)$$

where T is an indicator of technological capability; C is a cost indicator; O is an industrial organisation variable (domestic market structure, ownership structure, degree of concentration etc.); and i and j represent industry and country, respectively. Total export performance of a country may then be aggregated to Xj. Like Fagerberg's, their empirical analyses are primarily directed towards cross-country intra-industry studies. Their results are in accordance with Fagerberg's.

The ambitions of proponents of the Heretic approach to build alternative models are, though, still far from being fulfilled at the present stage. Although the framework in chapter 7 of Dosi, Pavitt and Soete is a step towards an integration of trade theory and disequilibrium open economy macroeconomics, the transmission mechanism between trade performance and domestic activity is discussed in terms of a highly stylised two-sector two-country model. The components are on the one hand an 'innovation' versus a 'Ricardian' commodity sector; on the other the innovating North *vis-à-vis* the South (cf. Krugman, 1990). Innovation in the North and its subsequent diffusion to the South represents the engine of growth.

A radical critique of the relevance of the concept of competitiveness of nations as such is expressed by Porter (1990, chapter 1). He argues that discussions of why some nations are successful and others not, in international competition focus on the wrong question. According to Porter, the right question

Figure 10.1. Porter's Diamond.

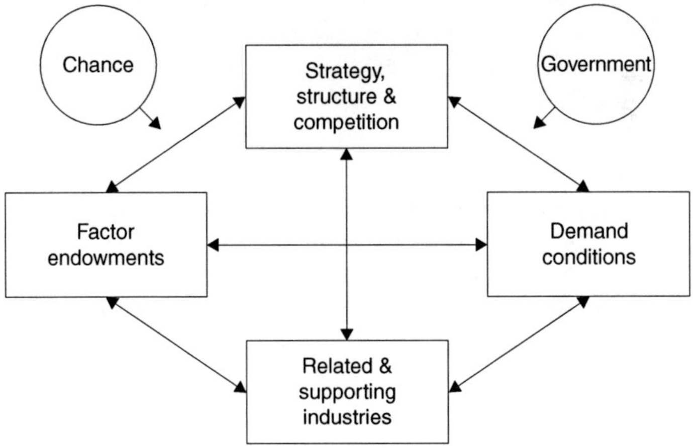

Source: Porter, 1990.

is, 'Why does a nation become the home base for successful international competitors in an industry?' or 'Why is one nation often the home for so many of an industry's world leaders?' In his terms competitive advantage of a nation consists of those national attributes that foster competitive advantage of some of its industries.

From a methodological point of view, his analysis is highly different from those mentioned above. His empirical analysis is based on 10 success industries in 10 different countries (i.e. around 100 cases). At the statistical level, the performance criteria for success are world export shares higher than the national average. Porter's work contains no coherent econometric models of competitive advantage, but his 'diamond-model' contains some features of interest for the analysis of national systems of innovation.

His framework represents an interesting revival of the Dahménian development blocks (cf. chapter 4 of the present book) in terms of nation specific clusters of industries. The 'diamond' consists of four determinants of competitive advantage. *Factor endowments*, including infrastructure in broad terms, is the realm of the standard comparative advantage version of trade theory and most analyses of international competitiveness of nations in terms of comparative costs. *Strategy, structure and competition* contains the dominant analytical approach in his previous work (Porter, 1980 and 1985), in which the framework of traditional industrial economics was extended to include company strategies as a major determinant.[9] Emphasis on the positive effects of domestic rivalry on international competitive advantage is another important factor.

The other building blocks represent extensions of his previous work. *Demand* features, such as size and qualitative characteristics, exert a major influence on competitive advantage. Especially the qualitative features of domestic demand are emphasised – following the line of thought of Linder (1961), Vernon (1966) and Andersen, Dalum and Villumsen (1981a, 1981b).[10] Finally *related and supporting industries* exert a major influence in creating external economies highly beneficial to international competitive advantage. Here Porter draws on Hirschman's (1958) linkage approach; the Swedish network approach in international business represented by the 'Uppsala School' (see e.g. Johanson and Mattsson, 1989); and Dahmén's (1950/70, 1988) concept of development blocks. The importance of user-producer relations as the micro counterpart of 'industrial complexes' elaborated by Lundvall (1985, 1988) and Andersen et al. (op. cit.) is also a part of the foundation of Porter's eclectical framework.

The 'diamond' is characterised as a mutually reinforcing system. Porter does not accept the concept of national competitiveness, as expressed by e.g. a few quantitative indicators (e.g. wage rates and exchange rates). The competitive advantage of nations may be analysed in terms of their clusters of industries.

> *The basic unit of analysis for understanding national advantage is the industry. Nations succeed not in isolated industries, however, but in clusters of industries connected through vertical and horizontal relationships. A nation's economy contains a mix of clusters, whose makeup and sources of competitive advantage (or disadvantage) reflect the state of the economy's development.* (Porter, 1990, 73).

However, this aggregation principle (the mix of clusters) is not followed by Porter himself in the final chapters of his book. The analysis of 'how entire national economies progress in competitive terms' (1990, 543) – by means of his Rostowian concept of stages of competitive development of nations (developed in his chapter 10) actually tries to answer some of the same wrong questions, that he initially warns us about.

This lack of consistency in aggregation principle raises problems about Porter's conclusions on the salient features of the economic development patterns of the ten analysed nations.[11] However, Porter's 'diamond' brings important conceptual and empirical insights to the analysis of the dynamic development of clusters of industries.[12]

Although a Porter inspired mix-of-clusters approach, despite the critical comments, may have been a useful tool for a deeper understanding and empirical comparisons of NSI's, the remainder of this chapter will restrict its efforts to an analysis of a few highly stylised features of long term economic development at the macro level. As a challenge for future research, the mix-of-cluster approach may fruitfully be reformulated and integrated in the present NSI framework – as part of its micro-to-meso foundations. At the present stage, however, we stick to a lower level of ambition by discussing *factors behind* the development of aggregate statistical proxies for structural competitiveness of nations, such as market shares.[13]

As mentioned, the transmission mechanism between increase in export performance (e.g. market shares) and domestic economic activity may be approached by Keynesian open economy macroeconomics, as done by Thirlwall (1986). The key link is foreign income elasticity of demand of a given country's exports. Products with high growth rates in world trade may be assumed to be proxies for exports with high income elasticities. Comparisons of export structures, country by country, may serve as indirect indications of qualitative characteristics of the pattern of income elasticities (*vis-à-vis* foreign demand), which again may function as a proxy for the structural competitiveness of an economy. The export specialisation patterns to be analysed in the next section represent a condensed quantitative measure of relative export structures.

10.4. International Specialisation Patterns and National Systems of Innovation

At a highly aggregate level, Figure 10.2 illustrates some important structural changes in OECD trade (in current US $).[14] Foreign trade statistics are available for fairly long term comparisons of the countries. Our trade database contains the 4-digit SITC value data for each of the OECD countries for selected years 1961–87. In the present analysis the detailed information has been aggregated to the five broad sectors shown in Figure 10.2: 1) products based on natural resources; 2) oil and gas; 3) chemicals; 4) engineering products (electrical and non-electrical machinery, electronics, transport equipment); and 5) products from so called 'traditional' manufacturing industries (manufactures of metal, furniture, clothing etc.)

The most salient feature of structural change of OECD exports, thus measured, is the long term decrease in the share of natural resource based products versus the increase of engineering products. However, chemicals, oil and products from traditional industries also increased their shares. The corresponding annual growth rates *in current US $* are shown in Table 10.1. In the 1960's engineering, chemicals and products from traditional industries showed double-digit growth rates, significantly higher than those of oil and natural resource based products. This pattern was highly disturbed in the 1970's by the effects of the first oil crisis. Exports of oil and gas had the

Figure 10.2. Export structure – 1961–87.

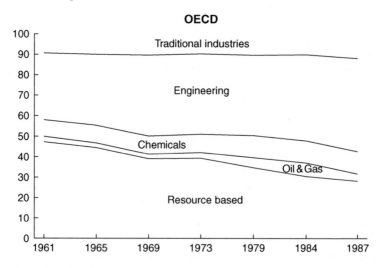

Source: Own calculations based on OECD figures.

Table 10.1. **Annual Growth Rates of OECD Exports (Current US $)**

	1961–69	1973–79	1979–87	1961–87
Engineering	11.2	15.0	7.4	13.9
Chemicals	10.5	18.2	5.8	13.3
Traditional industries	10.2	16.0	7.2	12.7
Oil & gas	7.0	25.0	1.9	12.9
Natural	6.7	12.9	3.2	10.7
Resource based				

Source: OECD; see also appendix to the present chapter.

highest annual growth rate at 25% in 1973–79 – also reflected in the growth rates of the other main groups via price increases of their input. Finally, in the 1980's the previous ranking of the growth rates from the 1960's was reestablished, although at much lower growth rates.

Although the growth rates for the whole period 1961–87 at first glance appear fairly equal, the breakdown in subperiods clearly indicates the presence of three high growth sectors – engineering, chemicals and products from traditional industries – and one 'laggard', natural resource based products. The growth rates of the high growth sectors were, however, fairly similar in the two 'normal' periods, although engineering was growing slightly faster than the others. Thus, it does not appear reasonable to distinguish between the importance of the three sectors on purely quantitative grounds. Theoretical reflections are demanded.

10.4.1. Neoclassical Analysis of Development Patterns

Let us, as a point of reference, return to the standard neoclassical approach. One of the most outstanding empirical efforts to test the empirical validity of the Heckscher-Ohlin theory is presented by Leamer (1984). The very first lines of his preface states:

> *The micro half of international economics is surprisingly sparse in empirical work. It is difficult to name another substantive field in economics in which theorists make such great efforts to identify the unending stream of logical possibilities, and in which so little effort is made to attach empirical probabilities to their many models.* (Leamer, 1984, xiii).

In most of the exposition, the models and their assumptions are carefully presented and discussed; and the empirical material is overwhelmingly comprehensive. Leamer's book has, thus, already become a 'classic' reference in textbooks. However, when we turn to his analysis of development patterns of countries some concepts are not clearly stated. In chapter 4 he presents and illustrates empirically a neoclassical 'ladder of development' model (op. cit., 86–87), which takes as its point of departure a division of products according to different factor intensities. Total trade is disaggregated into ten sectors – two primary products, four crops and four manufactured goods. The trade patterns for the first six are assumed to be determined by the prevalence of natural resources in each country ('land'), while the four manufacturing sectors are assumed to be determined by characteristics attached to capital per man and skill ratios. The four sectors are: 1) LAB, labour intensive products, with low capital intensities and low skill ratios; 2) CAP, capital intensive products and 3) MACH, machinery, both with moderate levels of capital intensities and skill requirements, though with slightly higher capital intensities for CAP and slightly higher skill ratios for MACH; and finally 4) CHEM, chemicals, with high capital intensities and skill requirements.[15]

The development model focuses on net exports of the four sectors as the dependent variable.[16] LAB represents the lowest degree of development. 'The next rung up the ladder' (Leamer, op. cit., 86) is represented by CAP, which requires more capital compared to the low skill intensity of LAB. 'The more advanced countries, which are abundant in skills and capital, stand at the top and export' MACH and CHEM (op. cit., 86). Net imports of all sectors represent the lowest degree of development. The next stage is net exports of LAB and net imports of the other three; followed by net imports of LAB, net exports of CAP and net imports of MACH and CHEM – and so forth.

Although net exports of MACH as well as CHEM was above described as a feature of the more advanced countries, the presentation and interpretation of the empirical material leaves no doubt that Leamer ranks net exports of CHEM as the highest stage of development. In 1975 France and Japan are ranked at level 5) at the development ladder with net exports of *all four* sectors. Germany and the UK are at level 3) because they were net importers of LAB and net exporters of the other three, indicating that they had switched out of comparative advantage in labour intensive products. At level 2) you find Switzerland and the US as net importers of LAB and CAP and net exporters of MACH and CHEM. The highest stage of development is represented by the Netherlands as net exporter of CHEM and net importer of the other three sectors.

When we look at the development in the rankings between 1958 and 1975, some fairly surprising features turn up as well. Sweden was a net importer of all four sectors in 1958 and ranked below such countries as Denmark, Portugal, Spain and Yugoslavia, who were net exporters of LAB. Sweden was put at level 9) together with Afghanistan, Burma, Canada, Egypt, Finland, Honduras, Ireland, Nigeria, Peru, Turkey and 30 others – primarily developing countries. Sweden, though, has managed to climb up the ladder between 1958 and 1975 as a net exporter of MACH and net importer of the other three – 'thereby catapulting itself into the group of industrialised countries' (Leamer, op. cit, 98). The Swedish development may have been caused by a minor change in the trade balance for MACH between 1958 and 1975, indicating that net exports is a performance indicator with problems for long term analysis. The sign of a trade balance is obviously sensitive to small changes when exports and imports are of approximately the same size.

Another, in our opinion, counterintuitive feature is the treatment of Japan. In 1958 Japan was ranked at level 4) with Italy as net importer of CHEM and net exporter of LAB, CAP and MACH. In 1975 Japan is ranked at level 5) although it has become a net exporter of all four sectors. This downgrading does not at all appear to be an obvious feature of the Japanese economic development in this period.

Although Leamer's work as the rule is characterised by a high degree of rigour, this is not the case in his ladder of development approach. And it leads, in our opinion, to highly dubious results. Below we shall try to sketch another approach, which also will be illustrated by a comprehensive amount of empirical data. The approach to be presented is, admittedly, characterised by lack of conceptual rigour. The results, however, do not appear to be counterintuitive.

10.4.2. The Engineering Sector as the 'Engine of Growth'

The framework of the previous chapters of this book points toward an approach to development different from Leamer's. Chapter 4 stresses the importance of domestic production and linkage patterns for the rate and direction of innovative activities. To analyse the character of these structural preconditions on an international basis, we shall compare export specialisation patterns by means of Balassa's (1965) Revealed Comparative Advantage index (RCA) as an indicator of the relative export structure for each of the OECD countries, assuming that export structure is a relevant proxy for domestic production structures. Balassa's RCA index shows the relative share of a sector in a given country's total exports compared with the relative share of the sector in total OECD exports. The weighted index for each country in each year is by definition 1.[17]

Chapter 4 also indicates the importance of the domestic capital goods sector and its interdependence with production of intermediate goods and/or final consumption goods (cf. Figure 4.3 in 4). An important feature of a NSI is, accordingly, its capability to develop products that are used as process technology in other industries – at the initial stage in the same country, later on internationally. The capability to introduce commercially successful capital goods is conceived as one of several possible indicators of the 'strength', so to speak, of a given system of innovation. To sustain long term growth, the evolution of a capital goods sector is seen as an important, though not sufficient, condition. Given the significantly increased openness of most OECD economies since the late 1950's, a more restrictive condition for successful long term economic performance could be the presence of an *internationally competitive* capital goods sector.

It is, however, no easy task to construct a proxy for the capital goods sector – having the character of the 4-digit SITC classification in mind (see also Dalum et al., 1981). We have, for pragmatic as well as theoretical, reasons chosen the engineering sector as the relevant proxy for the 'engine of growth' in postwar growth of the OECD countries. Cornwall (1977) used that term for the entire manufacturing sector in his analysis of the dynamics of growth in the 1950's and 1960's. We find that capital goods *and* consumer durables ('American way of life products' such as consumer electronics, domestic appliances and motor cars) *together* may constitute the most appropriate 'engine of growth' sector – at least until the late 1980's. The engineering sector, as defined in the appendix, appears to be a reasonable proxy for this 'engine'.[18] It is important to note that chemicals are not classified as capital goods. According to our framework, chemicals are mainly intermediate products (e.g. synthetic materials) or, often non-durable, consumer goods (e.g. pharmaceuticals).

10.4.3. Development in the Specialisation Patterns of NSI's

The present chapter includes a series of diagrams of the specialisation patterns of 21 OECD countries, 1961–87, in terms of the five sectors already shown in Figure 10.2 and Table 10.1. The diagrams contain, though, only the Balassa RCA indices for four of the sectors. The oil and gas aggregate is omitted from the diagrams because of its volatile behaviour in the period. For the majority of the countries, oil and gas amounts to only a small share of exports, except in the case of Norway and the UK where two diagrams are shown – one including oil and gas, the other without. It should be noted that the oil and gas sector is included in all calculations; it has only been omitted in the graphic representations.

Three categories in Table 10.2 summarise relative stability versus change of the specialisation patterns in terms of radical change, no change and some change. In the diagrams it is striking that only a few countries are characterised by radical change. Four countries belong to this *first group*. The dramatic increase of oil exports is a simple explanation of the UK and Norwegian presence in that group. The Japanese and Irish patterns have also changed significantly, but for other reasons. Japan has emerged as one of the strongest NSI's in the world and has challenged the US technological lead in a fairly large share of manufacturing

Table 10.2. **Change of Specialisation Patterns 1961–87**

Radical Change	No Change	Some Change
Japan	West Germany	USA
Ireland	Sweden	Belgium-Luxembourg
	Switzerland	Denmark
United Kingdom	Netherlands	Finland
Norway	France	Spain
	Italy	Portugal
	Canada	Turkey
	Austria	Greece
	Iceland	

Source: OECD; see also appendix and enclosed diagrams to the present chapter.

industries. Japan has, thus, been the home nation for the emergence of a large number of MNE's, which today are among the global leaders in their respective fields.[19] Ireland has, on the other hand, mainly been characterised as a host country for foreign MNE assembly and chemical plants; and no significant technological innovation capability appears to have emerged in Irish manufacturing. The lack of 'indigenous' innovative development forces appears to be a major problem.

The *second group*, with no significant qualitative change in specialisation profiles during the period, is the largest. Nine countries belong to this group: West Germany, France, Switzerland, Sweden, Austria, the Netherlands, Italy, Canada and Iceland. Their present profiles emerged before the beginning of the 1960's.

In between we find the *third group* of eight countries with some, though not fundamental, changes in their specialisation profiles. The US RCA index for products from traditional industries of more than 0.9 in 1961 decreased significantly until 1979, and hereafter it increased to slightly more than 1 during the 1980's. Belgium-Luxembourg has become more specialised in chemicals from 1970, and Denmark in traditional industries from 1969. The initially less developed Finland and Spain and the still less developed Portugal, Turkey and Greece may also be included in this group.

This brief survey may lead to the idea that NSI's run through life cycles. Most of the stable countries of the second group may be characterised as mature NSI's, whether they are large and highly developed or have been locked-in in a peripheral trajectory of development (e.g. Canada and Iceland). But among members of the first and third group, several pronounced features may be taken as clear indications of life cycles.

The specialisation profiles of some of the less developed OECD countries reveal systematic development features. At the beginning of the 1960's, Turkey,

Greece, Portugal and Spain were characterised by specialisation in resource based products, exclusively. During the following period they became specialised in traditional industries as well. In the case of Spain and Portugal, this happened already in the mid 1960's, while Greece and Turkey reached that stage in the late 1970's and early 1980's, respectively.

Among these four countries, Spain is the only one to have approached a higher stage of development. Specialisation in traditional industries (probably mainly based on low wage costs) peaked in the early 1970's, while specialisation in engineering has increased steadily since the early 1960's, although it was still significantly below 1 in 1987. The dependence on natural resource based exports was still far from a finished stage at the end of the period. Spain nearly reached a specialisation index of 1 in chemicals in the mid 1960's; followed by a decrease until 1973; and a steady increase 1973–87.

This analysis, compared with Leamer's framework, does not indicate that the Spanish specialisation profile in chemicals can be taken as any indication of a high rating of the Spanish NSI on an economic development ladder. Cheap labour costs and, perhaps of more importance, less restrictions on setting up highly polluting chemical process plants, are probably the main explanations. These features indicate a low stage on the development ladder. However, the other features of the Spanish pattern exhibit what we may call a stylised case of an OECD country at an early stage of a development trajectory, which, potentially at least, may point towards a virtuous circle of development – i.e. Spain has not been entirely locked-in in a purely peripheral pattern *vis-à-vis* the developed European countries. The increasing and subsequent decreasing specialisation in traditional industries and the long term increase in the specialisation index for engineering, although from a very low level, point in that direction. The steady specialisation in natural resource based products 1961–87 is not necessarily an indication of a low level of development. That feature has also been present in such developed countries as France, Sweden, Austria, the Netherlands, Belgium-Luxembourg and Denmark.

It is an interesting feature that some of the small developed countries, such as Denmark and Finland, have followed a pattern with some of the same characteristics.[20] Apart from chemicals, Finland has followed the Spanish pattern to some degree – i.e. an increasing and subsequently decreasing specialisation in traditional industries and a long term increase in engineering. Denmark, on the other hand, has been characterised by a long term increase in specialisation in traditional industries and a decrease in engineering since 1973.[21]

As far as chemicals are concerned, Denmark and Finland have been increasingly specialised in chemicals over the long term. At the best of our knowledge, the chemical industries of these two countries have mainly emerged as results of indigenous innovative forces in their NSI's and not as a consequence of low cost locational advantages.[22] Thus net exports of or high specialisation in chemicals does not appear to be a relevant indicator of a high stage of development of a country.

This line of reasoning may be further substantiated at the other end of the sample. At the beginning of the 1960's, Japan had already passed the specialisation profile of the less developed OECD countries. Since then, specialisation in traditional industries as well as natural resource based products has steadily decreased, and the opposite has been the case for engineering. Specialisation in chemicals has *decreased* in most of the period. The Japanese pattern is illustrative as, so to speak, a stylised reference case showing how a national system of innovation may be structurally upgraded from a profile of specialisation above 1 only in traditional industries and natural resource based products – which at first glance may hint to less developed features – at the beginning of the 1960's to a highly developed NSI a quarter of a century later.

On the other hand, the international specialisation index of the Japanese engineering sector of nearly 1 at the beginning of the 1960's (0.91 in 1961 and 1.02 in 1965) indicates that it is certainly not correct to use the term less developed as a characteristic of the Japanese NSI in 1961. Earlier studies of specialisation in engineering (Kjeldsen-Kragh, 1973, Dalum et al., 1978) show that the catch-up of Japanese specialisation in engineering was a phenomenon of the 1950's.[23]

Whether the specialisation profiles have been stable, have changed somewhat or have gone through dramatic structural transformation, it is a salient feature that almost all countries exhibit distinctly different development patterns. In his comprehensive study of international specialisation patterns of engineering, Kjeldsen-Kragh (1973, 1981) pointed towards convergence between the countries, as far as the aggregate engineering sectors are concerned in the period 1954–69. At the same time, his disaggregation to six subgroups showed highly different patterns country by country – with no evident converging features.

The updating of this material to 1975 (Dalum et al., 1978) did indicate, that this convergence had been ended. The empirical material of the present chapter, although the set-up is slightly different, does not point to further convergence either. If anything, the impression of the diagrams indicate renewed divergence from the mid-late 1970's.[24] As discussed in Dalum et al. (1978 and 1981), this aggregate pattern is in accordance with the Cornwall (1977) catching-up growth model – convergence until the late 1960's, and emerging divergent features in the 1970's and 1980's. One main characteristic of this development may be the dominance of catching-up through international diffusion of technology in the 1960's, followed by a renewed emphasis on technological innovation as a major determinant of competitive advantage and the pattern of international specialisation after the early 1970's (cf. the discussion of the dichotomy between convergent and divergent features by Dosi, Pavitt and Soete op. cit.).

10.4.4. Strength of NSI's

According to the empirical studies of the Heretic approach where technology output variables (patents) or input variables (R&D expenditure) have been the core indicators, the so called High Innovative Performers among the large OECD countries are the US, Japan and West Germany. While the Japanese pattern has changed dramatically, the German and, to a lesser degree, the US patterns have been fairly stable. Their specialisation profile had already reached a stage of maturity in the early 1960's. Besides the three economic superpowers, two small countries have usually been added to the group of High Innovative Performers – i.e. Switzerland and Sweden. Together, these five countries constitute a group '1. division clubs'[25] among the OECD countries, while the UK, France and the Netherlands were on their way down to the 2. division already in the 1970's.[26]

Compared to the diagrams presented here, these five countries (the US, Japan, West Germany, Sweden and Switzerland) coincide with those of our sample with a specialisation in engineering above 1. On the other hand, specialisation above 1 in chemicals is not a common feature of this group. Japan and Sweden have, thus, not been specialised in that sector.

When we focus on France, the UK and the Netherlands, lack of specialisation in engineering and specialisation in chemicals has been the case for the two first mentioned since the mid 1970's,[27] and for the Netherlands in the whole period. Thus, among the eight countries mentioned so far, the export specialisation pattern in engineering, as a proxy for an internationally competitive capital goods sector, appears to be a distinguishing feature for the membership of the 'club of 1. division countries'; and the opposite for those moving down.

For the other countries in the sample, the long term development of their specialisation in engineering (level and direction of change) also appears to be a useful indicator of change of strength of their NSI. This is illustrated on the one hand by Finland and Spain in terms of the significant increase in their specialisation; and the sustained low levels for Turkey, Greece, Iceland and, to a lesser degree, Portugal.

However, the Irish and Canadian cases show significant increases in their specialisation in engineering – to a level not far from 1 in the latter case. Both economies are characterised as typical hosts for foreign direct investment, with a fairly low degree of technological spill-over to their respective NSI's, especially in the Irish case. This pattern indicates that our proxy for strength may be too broad. A more disaggregate analysis of the Canadian case indicates that foreign assembly and subsequent exports of cars is a major part of the explanation. In the Irish case, the same aggregate feature is caused by foreign assembly of especially computers and telecommunications equipment.

At this stage, it is evident that our approach leads to substantially different conclusions about the ranking of countries compared to the Leamer study (1984); and much more in line with the Heretic tradition. The top ranking of the Netherlands and the fairly low and even decreasing ranking of Japan in Leamer's analysis illustrate these differences.

10.5. Conclusions

The purpose of the empirical illustrations of this chapter is to bring some, admittedly incomplete, support for the applicability of the National System of Innovation approach in studies of the structural foundations for long term economic performance of OECD countries. There appears to be a certain amount of support for the view that an internationally specialised engineering sector has been a major, though not sufficient, condition for successful long term economic strength of the OECD countries.

This feature, on the other hand, may be of more significance in the past than in the future. An interesting recent piece of work on international specialisation by Storper (1991b) states in the introduction:

> *There is now widespread agreement that the forms of production organization which characterized the most dynamic industries of the post-war period in the advanced economies, i.e. mass production in the consumer durables sectors and their associated capital goods, are no longer central to economic growth, change, and capital accumulation as they once were.*

The empirical material of this chapter indicates that this statement may be slightly premature. However, Storper focuses, as an alternative, on a Product Based Technological Learning (PBTL) sector, which is illustrated empirically by trade data for the US, France and Italy. The PBTL sector is characterised by, among other features, continued product development. This line of work may be promising in the future, although it does not appear to be fully elaborated at the present stage.

Another critical point is the increasing importance of the service sector, which has been entirely neglected in this admittedly 'hardware biased' approach. International trade data of this sector are, though, still of a highly aggregate nature and far from being an applicable analytical tool, such as the data for trade by commodities. Finally, it is also important to bear in mind that the observations of this chapter have primarily focused on the pattern of arms length trade with commodities (visibles). The important impact of MNE's has been more or less neglected.

Before we broaden the analysis to include the latter issue in chapter 13 by Chesnais, the following chapter 11 by Fagerberg will proceed to an in depth analysis of that part of trade theory which has a specific importance for the development of the concept of NSI – the home market theory, originally introduced by Linder in 1961. In terms of the Dosi, Pavitt and Soete model, referred to above, we shall try to introduce one of the *Oij* variables of major importance for further understanding of the different characters of the NSI's, i.e. the historical development of domestic linkage patterns of significant importance for a substantial share of international competitive strength of industries.

Appendix 10.1

The trade data are based on the taped version OECD's *Trade by Commodities, Series C*, which has been published annually since 1961. The data cover trade by 'visible' goods; trade in services ('invisibles') are not included.

The OECD tapes consist of exports from and imports to 23 OECD countries in current US $. They also contain information of the quantities of trade (tons, liters, etc.); these data have not been used in our analyses. The data are delivered at their most detailed level according to the Standard International Trade Classification (SITC). Basically, the tapes consist of matrices for each country with commodity groups as the rows and partner countries as the columns. For each OECD member country exports to and imports from any country in the world are registered – in principle at the most disagregated SITC level.

The tapes are unmanageable in their 'raw' version. During the 1980's the annual amount of information has, thus, been approximately 500 Megabytes. It is necessary to aggregate the information to a certain extent, depending on the available computer resources.

The *IKE trade database* at the Institute of Production, Aalborg University was initiated in the early 1980's for studies of long term structural features of OECD trade. Construction of comparable time series data was from the beginning the major practical aim. This has been realised through long standing collaboration with, Aalborg Universitetsdatacenter (AUD) – especially with Uffe Møller.

The first step of handling the data consists of aggregating the 'raw' tapes to country matrices with 625 rows (the amount of commodity groups at the 4-digit SITC, Revision 1 level) and 33 coloumns (23 OECD countries, the World,

OECD, the Nordic countries and 7 groups of non-OECD countries). Then several steps of checking for confidentiality clauses in the tapes, whether at the commodity or the country level. The tapes, thus, contain a large amount of so-called alphanumeric codes (instead of the usual numeric SITC codes) for which the trade information is omitted *at the given level of disaggregation*. This information is, however, included in the SITC codes at a more aggregate level. The OECD (and the national statistical bodies who deliver the basic information) does not supply any systematic information on these potential pitfalls; researchers have to develop procedures to detect them.

To illustrate the size of the problem – concentrated to certain commodity groups (especially chemicals) and certain countries – 10 to 12 per cent of Swedish exports (in current US $) is missing around 1980 if total exports is calculated 'bottom up' – i.e. from the lowest level of disaggregation. As part of the routinised translation of the tapes to manageable entities, AUD developed software capable to register the size and the position of the alphanumeric codes.

This is the background for aggregating the data first to 41 commodity groups, and then further to 5 sectors as shown in the appendix table – on which the analysis of the specialisation patterns is based. The appendix table was developed and implemented by Bent Dalum and Jan Fagerberg in 1983 based on detailed registration of the alphanumeric codes 1961–80 (see also Fagerberg, 1988c). When total country exports and imports are aggregated from the 41 commodity groups, the difference is usually less than 0.5 per cent compared to the total value published by the OECD.

It is also important to notice that only SITC, Revision 1 is used. In 1961–77 Revision 1 is applied in the tapes. But in 1978–87 the data are published according to SITC, Revision 2. The latter has been converted to the previous classification in order to construct comparable time series. From 1988 the data are published according to SITC, Revision 3; data from this period have not been included in the analysis.

The database only covers selected years 1961–87. As a criterion for selection we have chosen the 'peak years' used by Kjeldsen-Kragh (1973) – i.e. 1961, 1965, 1969. Then 1973, 1979, 1984 have been chosen as the following peaks in the 'average' OECD business cycles. 1987 was the last year available. 1988 would have been a better choice; but these data have not been available for this study.

Australia and New Zealand have been omitted from the group of OECD countries because data are not avaiable for the 1960's. Data for Japan and Finland in 1961 are not present in the tapes either, but have been reconstructed (with some approximation for Finland, but rather precise for Japan) from national statistical sources.

The Balassa Revealed Comparative Advantage (RCA) Index is defined as:

$$\frac{\dfrac{X_{ij}}{X_j}}{\dfrac{X_i}{X}}$$

where X_{ij} are exports from country j of commodity i; X_j are total exports from country j; X_i are total OECD exports of commodity i; and X are total OECD exports.

Appendix Table

Products Based on Natural Resources

1. Animals, meat and meat preparations	00, 01, 091.3, 411.3,
2. Dairy products and eggs	02
3. Fish and fish preparations	03, 411.1
4. Cereals and cereal prep.	04
5. Feeding-stuff for animals	08
6. Skins and leather manufactures	21, 61
7. Wood and wood manufactures	24, 63
8. Pulp and paper	25, 64
9. Textiles	26, 65
10. Iron ore	281
11. Iron, steel and ferro-alloys	67
12. Aluminium	684
13. Other products based on natural resources	Rest 0–4 (excl.33, 34) 62, 66 and rest 68

Oil and Gas

14. Oil and gas	33, 34

Chemicals

15. Organic chemicals	512
16. Inorganic chemical	513, 514
17. Dyestuffs, colouring materials	53
18. Pharmaceuticals	54
19. Fertilizers	56
20. Plastic materials	581.1, 581.2
21. Other chemicals	Rest 5

Engineering, Electronics and Transport Equipment

22. Power generating machinery	711
23. Machinery for special industries or processes	712, 715, 717, 718, 719.3, 719.5, 719.8
24. Heating and cooling equipment	719.1
25. Pumps and centrifuges	719.2
26. Typewriters and office machines	714.1, 714.9
27. Computers and peripherals	714.2, 714.3
28. Semiconductors	729.3
29. Telecommunications equipment	724.9
30. Machinery for production and distribution of electricity	722, 723, 729.9
31. Consumer electronics	724.1, 724.2, 891.1
32. Domestic electrical equipment	725
33. Scientific instruments, photographic supplies, watches and clocks	726, 729.5, 729.7 861, 862, 864
34. Road motor vehicles	732
35. Aircraft	734
36. Ships and boats (& oilrigs)	735
37. Other engineering prod.	Rest 7 (excl.719.4)

Other Industrial Products

38. Manufactures of metal	69, 719.4, 812.1, 812.3
39. Furniture	82
40. Clothing	84
41. Industrial products, n.e.s.	Rest 8–9 (excl. 861, 862, 864, 891.1)

Chapter 11

THE HOME MARKET HYPOTHESIS RE-EXAMINED: THE IMPACT OF DOMESTIC USER-PRODUCER INTERACTION ON EXPORT SPECIALISATION[1]

Jan Fagerberg

11.1. Introduction

Part I of this book focuses on the relation between the economic structure, user-producer interaction and learning. It is argued (chapter 4) that learning through interaction between actors from different parts of the economy may have important implications for competitiveness and comparative advantage. However, these insights have largely been ignored by 'mainstream' economic theory. Traditionally, textbook explanations of specialisation patterns in international trade have focused on differences in supply conditions. Countries, it is argued, tend to specialise in areas of production that make intensive use of factors of production with which the country is relatively well equipped. However, empirical research has shown that the explanatory power of this type of theory is limited. This initiated an active search for alternative approaches from the early 1960's onwards. Many of the new theories which were developed (often labelled 'neo-technological'[2] theories) came to focus on differences in technological capabilities across countries and sectors as the main explanatory factor behind the observed differences in patterns of export specialisation. This focus is now widely shared, also among many 'mainstream' economists, and is supported by a large amount of empirical research.[3] However, *what causes technological capabilities to differ often remains unexplained*. Thus, in this sense, existing theories fail to provide a definite answer to the question of 'why patterns of export specialisation differ'. This chapter discusses to what extent the theoretical perspective of this book, with its emphasis on the relation between the structure of the domestic economy and its learning capability may throw some further light on this question.

11.2. Structure, Learning and Export Specialisation

The idea that the structure of the domestic economy, or links between firms from different sectors of the economy, may have a say for competitiveness/ comparative advantage has a long tradition in economics. Already List (1841/1959) in his famous defence for protectionism pointed to the positive impact that such relations may have in the process of industrialisation. Perroux (1955), combining a Schumpeterian and 'structuralist' perspective, arrived at similar conclusions in his analysis of industrial development ('growth-poles'). Hirschman (1958) made 'linkages' one of the most influential concepts in development economics. Linder (1961), to whom we will return below, discussed the implications of such relations for trade theory. Mistral (1982), working in the French structuralist-institutionalist tradition, coined the concept 'structural competitiveness' to cover the positive impact that relations between different sectors of the economy have on national export performance. More recently Porter (1990), in his widely read book 'The Competitive Advantage of Nations', has presented similar views and evidence.

The precise nature of the assumed relationship between 'structure' and competitiveness is of course not the same in all these contributions. Nor is it always clear why some links have a greater positive impact than others. An interesting interpretation, which fits the approach presented in part I of this book, was presented by Linder (1961).[4] His argument runs as follows. First, a need that cannot be sufficiently satisfied by existing products arises on the demand side. Since entrepreneurs for various reasons (culture, language, proximity) tend to be better informed about the developments in the home market than in markets elsewhere, they will usually be the first to react to demand for new or improved products arising from the domestic market. The outcome of this activity, i.e. the innovation, then enters a period of testing and revision in which the home market is assumed to play a critical role:

> *Whether it is a question of 'critical revision' of an invention or a product development work in general, it must be carried out in close contact with the market....If, for some odd reason, an entrepreneur decided to cater for a demand which did not exist at home, he would probably be unsuccessful as he would not have easy access to crucial information which must be funnelled back and forth between producer and consumers. The trial-and-error period which a new product must almost inevitably go through on the market will be the more embarrassing costwise, the less intimate knowledge the producer has of the conditions under which his product will have to be used. And, if*

there is no home demand, the producer will be completely unfamiliar with such conditions. (Linder 1961, 89).

Linder assumes that the introduction of the product in the export market will have to wait for this testing in the home market to be completed. However, if the product is successful at home, it will probably be a success on the export market too (Linder, 1961, 88).

The evolutionary flavour of the argument is quite obvious: entrepreneurs strive to solve problems that arise in their environments (domestic market), learn as possible solutions (innovations) are proposed, tested and improved, and eventually – on the basis of accumulated experience – penetrate foreign markets as well. Theoretically, this has much in common with the approach presented in part I and II of this book, stressing the importance of 'user-producer relationships' (chapter 3) and 'networks' (chapter 6, see also Håkansson, 1987). In these analyses stable relations between users and producers of technology are seen as a way to minimise costs related to information and communication and internalise positive external effects. This is viewed as especially important in cases where technology is complex (and changing) and the need for close communication and interaction between users and producers of technology is large (Lundvall, 1988). This process involves learning and – in many cases – the modification of an existing or the creation of an entirely new technology. When this happens, the competitive position of the firms involved will normally improve. Since, for a variety of reasons (culture, language, proximity etc.), such relationships are more likely to be established within than across borders,[5] this should be expected to affect patterns of export specialisation (or comparative advantage) of countries as well. However, Lundvall is careful in pointing out that not all 'user-producer relationships' promote innovation to the same extent: 'Being closely linked to conservative users having a weak technical competence might be a disadvantage for a producer, and vice-versa' (Lundvall, 1988, 356). *Thus, the mere existence of a home market for a particular product or technology is not enough to generate the necessary innovations and, hence, comparative advantage. A necessary condition is that the domestic users are both sophisticated and demanding.*

Linder also pointed out that the importance of 'the home market', as discussed above, varies across countries, sectors and products. For instance, he did not expect this to be very important in developing (or semi-industrialised) countries, nor did he expect it to contribute much to the explanation of differences in trade performance in standardised (or, more generally, 'non-innovative') products (Linder 1961, 90). In these cases he expected other factors to be more important. Thus, what is discussed here is *not* a general theory of export specialisation, but a partial one that may (and should) be combined with other approaches.

11.3. Empirical Methods and Evidence

Andersen et al. (1981a and b) chose the label 'the home market hypothesis' for the approach to export specialisation outlined above. We will follow their choice, although one may object that only one particular aspect of the home market is taken into account. What we will do in this section is to discuss the available evidence and problems related to empirical testing.

First, it may be noted that 'the home market hypothesis' commands considerable empirical support at a descriptive level. Table 11.1, extracted from Andersen et al. (1981a), gives a good illustration of this point. In the case of Denmark, which is a large exporter of agricultural products, the three engineering products with the highest specialisation-indexes[6] all belong to the group 'agricultural machinery'. Similar examples can be found for other countries. For instance, Sweden has been shown to be specialised in both pulp and paper and machinery for that sector, Norway in both shipping/fishing and ship building etc (Andersen et al., 1981a). More recently, Porter (1990) has presented a large amount of historical evidence and descriptive statistics on export specialisation that can be interpreted in support of 'the home market hypothesis'.

In spite of the large amount of descriptive evidence available, there appears to be little statistical work done to test the hypothesis. This is not surprising, given the complexities involved. To test the hypothesis, a relatively large number of exporting sectors, as well as domestic users of the products from these sectors, must be identified and defined. While this may be easy in theory, it is more difficult in practice, since the available statistics are not

Table 11.1. **Danish Export Specialisation in Engineering Products (1975)**

Rank	SITC Rev. 1	Product Group	RCA-Index
1.	712.3	Milking machines, dairy farm equipment	13.2
2.	718.3	Food processing machinery	4.1
3.	712.1–2	Agricultural machinery for cultivating soil and harvesting	3.4
4.	735	Ships and boats	3.1
5.	725	Domestic electrical equipment	3.1
6.	712.9	Agricultural machinery and appliances, n.e.s.	2.9
7.	729.1	Batteries and accumulators	2.9
8.	719.1	Heating and cooling equipment, non domestic	2.7
9.	729.5	Electrical measuring and controlling instruments	2.4
10.	719.2	Pumps and centrifuges	2.0

Source: Andersen et al. (1981a).

collected for this purpose: most 'advanced' products are not classified according to users, and even when this is the case it is not always easy to find internationally comparable data for users on a sufficiently disaggregated level. Furthermore, assuming that these problems can be solved, we have to establish what we mean by an 'advanced user sector', and decide how this empirically can be distinguished from a less advanced one. To the best of our knowledge, the only attempt to face these problems is the one by Andersen et al. (1981a and b) which we will discuss below.

The hypothesis tested by Andersen et al. was the following: If internationally competitive producers exist in one sector of the economy, and these producers buy their technology from another sector of the economy, the latter sector should be expected to be internationally competitive. For instance, if a country is export specialised in agricultural products, it should be expected to be export specialised also in agricultural machinery too.[7] Thus, in the interpretation of Andersen et al. 'advanced user sectors' are identified as sectors in which the country has a comparative advantage. This interpretation has the advantage that it enables us to use the same data source, trade statistics, and the same index, revealed comparative advantage (Balassa, 1965), to measure the strength of both *'producer' (export) sectors* and *'user' (home market) sectors*. The problem, of which Andersen et al. were well aware, is that this interpretation introduces a bias towards products where the trade statistics allow a link to be made. For 'producer' sectors (or products) this implies that most of them belong to the group 'specialised machinery' (SITC 71), where users in many cases are relatively well specified. On the user side the consequence is that users in the non-trading sectors of economy (or in other sectors not covered by the international trade statistics) are excluded from the investigation. For instance, the link between technology producers and public-sector users, which is discussed in chapter 7 of this book, cannot be taken into account. Letting X denote exports and S the index for revealed comparative advantage, RCA, the model considered by Andersen et al. may be presented as follows:

$$i = 1.. n \quad \text{(Countries)}$$
$$j = 1.. m \quad \text{(Commodities)}$$
$$\text{('export')}$$
$$k = 1.. m \quad \text{(Commodities)}$$
$$\text{('home-market')}$$

$$(1) \quad S_{ij}^{t} f\left(S_{tk}^{t}\right)$$

where

$$(2) \quad S_{ij} \, \frac{\dfrac{X_{ij}}{X_{ij}}}{\dfrac{{}_{j}XX_{ij}}{{}_{ij}X_{ij}}}$$

The exact form of the functional relationship was not specified by Andersen et al. They chose instead to use the Spearman rank correlation coefficient to test the hypothesis of a positive correlation between export specialisation in selected engineering products and their associated 'user sectors'. The data set consisted of data for 13 pairs of products/user sectors for 9–11 OECD countries and for selected years 1954–1972. In general, a positive correlation was found to exist between the two rankings, but the level of significance was in most cases rather low. Of the 13 pairs included in the main test presented by Andersen et al., only three turned up with significant correlations following traditional statistical criteria: Aircraft engines/aircraft, agricultural machinery/food and textile machinery/textiles.

Thus, the results presented by Andersen et al., although not inconsistent with the tested hypothesis, cannot be interpreted as being very supportive. One reason for this somewhat disappointing result may be that some explanatory variables have been omitted. If, as argued earlier, the home market hypothesis is only a partial theory of comparative advantage, the rank correlation test used by Andersen et al. may be misleading, since the rankings may also be affected by other variables not included in the test. In this case, a more appropriate method would be to use a multivariate test where 'the home market variable' is included together with other variables assumed to affect export specialisation.

Another problem, discussed also by Andersen et al., is the possibility of a significant time lag between the interactive learning process and its impact on comparative advantage. For instance, the original stimulus to a high degree of specialisation in textile machinery may have come from a domestic textile industry that later disappeared. In other cases both sectors continue to be strong. It is only in this latter case that a regression between the comparative advantages of the producer and user sectors (and other relevant variables) *at a particular point of time* is the appropriate method. Thus, this method is likely to underestimate the total, long-run impact of 'the home market' on comparative advantage.

11.4. Testing the Hypothesis

In this section we present the results of a test of 'the home market hypothesis' on a new and larger data set consisting of data for 23 pairs of products, 16

Table 11.2. **Export Products and Home Market Indicators**

SITC (REV1)	Export Product	SITC (REV1)	Home Market Indicator
54	Pharmaceuticals		Health[A]
6291	Rubber tyres and tubes	732–734	Road motor vehicles, aircheft
6951	Hand-tools for agriculture and forestry	04–08(–0814), 24	Agricultural products, wood products
7114	Aircraft engines	734	Aircraft
7115	Internal comb. engines	732	Road motor vehicles
7121	Agr. machinery for preparing		
7122	soil and harvesting	04–08(–0814)	Agricultural products
7123	Milking machines	02	Dairy products
7125	Tractors	04–08(–0814)	Agricultural products
7129	Agr. machinery n.e.s.	04–08(–0814)	Agricultural products
7151	Machine tools for working	69	Metal manufactures
7152	metals		
7171	Textile machinery	65	Textiles
7172	Leather machinery	61	Leather
7173	Sewing machinery	84	Clothing
7181	Paper working machinery	25, 64	Pulp and paper, paper products
7182	Printing machinery	829	Printed matter
7183	Food processing machinery	0–(00)	Food
7184	Construction and mining	27, 28	Crude minerals and
7185	machinery, machinery for mineral crushing, etc.		metals
7191	Heating and cooling equipment	01–03	Meat, diary products, fish and eggs
7249	Telecommunications		Tele[A]
726	Electromedicals		Health[A]
7294	Automotive electrical equipment	732	Road motor vehicles
735	Ship and boats		Shipping[A]
8617	Medical instruments n.e.s.		Health[A]

A For the definition of this indicator, see appendix.

OECD countries and selected years 1965–1987. Table 11.2 lists the 23 pairs of products included in the test.

Generally, the methodology is the one proposed by Andersen et al. An attempt was made to make the definition of the home market sector more precise by use of more disaggregated statistics.

Three new 'home-market-indexes' were introduced representing three of the most important service sectors of the economy: health care, telecommunications and shipping. Since two of these are dominated by public sector services, the results may have some bearing on the question discussed in chapter 7. The resulting sample is larger than that of Andersen et al. (23 compared to 13), but it still has a strong bias towards the group 'specialised machinery' (SITC 71) which accounts for around two thirds of the 'export products' included in the test. By comparison, there is only one chemical product included in the sample (pharmaceuticals).

The new 'home-market-indexes' were calculated in a way that made their structure as close as possible to the RCA-index. For instance, if the index for a specific country for shipping exceeds one, this implies that the market share of the country for shipping services exceeds the market share of the country for goods and services in general. For health services and telecommunication services, which are not traded on the world market to the same extent, the population was used as deflator. Thus, in these cases, a value larger than one implies that the 'quality' of these services in the country is higher than the OECD average. For a more detailed account on how these indicators were constructed, the reader is referred to the appendix.

Since, according to Linder, the theory does not hold for developing or semi-industrialised countries, we excluded the industrially less developed of the OECD countries from the sample: Greece, Iceland, Portugal, Turkey and Yugoslavia. Australia and New Zealand were excluded due to lack of data for the earlier years. 1965 was chosen as the first year (this was the first year with data for Japan and Finland). In addition we included one year from the early 1970's (1973) and the last year available (1987).

The specification of the model departs from the one used by Andersen et al. As mentioned, they chose to test the hypothesis using an univariate test (rank correlation). However, for the reasons pointed out in the previous section, we prefer a multivarate test. The problem then is what additional variables to choose. Since the countries of the sample are relatively developed, we did not find it natural to include a 'development' variable (GDP per capita, wage-level, capital/labour-ratio etc). However, although these countries are all rich by world standards, the sources of 'richness' are not always the same. For instance, some countries may be better endowed with natural resources than others. By definition, countries with a comparative advantage in products based on natural resources (raw materials and semi-finished products), will not have a comparative advantage in manufacturing. The dependent variable in the test is a manufactured product. Hence, we should expect – all other variables assumed the same – countries with a comparative advantage in manufacturing to have a higher value (RCA index) for the dependent variable than countries with a comparative advantage in products based on natural resources. To account for this 'natural resource effect' we included a the RCA index for SITC 0-4, named

'NATURAL', as one of the independent variables. This variable should be expected to take on a negative sign. We also included a variable reflecting the domestic opportunities for exploitation of economies of scale:[8] the share of the country in the total population of the OECD countries (POP). The scale variable was included because it suggests an alternative way in which the domestic market may affect export specialisation.

Two different sets of tests are reported, one for the whole data set and one for each export sector or product. First, we pooled all the data (all years, countries and products combined) and estimated one equation for the whole sample, using ordinary least squares (equation 3 below). A linear formulation was used. No attempt was made to test for other functional forms.

$$(3) \quad S_{ij}^{t} \quad a_0 \quad a_1 HOME_{ij}^{t} \quad a_2 NAT_i^{t} \quad a_3 POP_i^{t} \quad U_{ij}^{t}$$

The result is reported in Table 11.3 (A) below. The scale variable turned out to be totally insignificant, and was therefore omitted. The two other explanatory variables both turned up with the expected signs, significantly different from zero at the 1% level. However, the fit was modest, around 20%, and there were signs of autocorrelation. Since the latter is what should be expected if the model

Table 11.3. The Home Market Hypothesis Tested: General Results

A) S =   0.89 + 0.42 HOME − 0.33 NATURAL
     (13.89)   (15.67)   (7.03)
   $R^2 = 0.19 \ (0.19)$
B) S = 0.81T1 + 0.87T2 + 1.00T3 + 0.42 HOME − 0.34 NATURAL
     (10.49)   (11.52)   (12.53)   (15.79)   (12.53)
   $R^2 = 0.20 \ (0.20)$
C) S = PRODUCTDUMMIES + 0.42 HOME − 0.33 NATURAL
                (15.35)   (6.99)
   $R^2 = 0.22 \ (0.20)$
D) S = COUNTRYDUMMIES + 0.43 HOME − 0.13 NATURAL
                (16.24)   (1.16)
   $R^2 = 0.26 \ (0.24)$
E) S = 0.78 + 0.42 HOME − 0.30 NATURAL − 0.25 CANADA − 0.41 BELGIUM
     (9.25)   (16.18)   (5.02)   (1.85)   (3.16)
   + 0.71 DENMARK + 0.41 GERMANY + 0.39 SWITZERLAND + 0.48 UK
     (5.11)   (3.06)   (2.86)   (3.68)
   $R^2 = 0.26 \ (0.24)$

N = 1104 (16 countries, 23 products, 3 years).
Method of estimation: Ordinary least squares.
Absolute t-values in brackets.
R^2 *in brackets is* R^2 *adjusted for degrees of freedom.*

differs across countries, products or time periods, we proceeded to test for the impact of such differences by introducing dummy variables.

The impact of possible differences across time periods was tested by allowing the constant term to take on different values in the three years covered by the investigation. Although some differences were found (see B in Table 11.3), these were not large (or significant) enough to reject the hypothesis that the three estimates are equal to a common constant term. The increase in fit was almost negligible. This also applies for the test with product dummies (different constant terms across product groups – see C in table 11.3).[9]

The introduction of country dummies (i.e. one constant term for each country) increased the fit to around 25%. Moreover, the impact of 'Natural', or the general comparative advantage of a country, was much reduced. This is not surprising: what the dummy variable test does is to remove the part of the total variance that can be attributed to within-country means (Johnston, 1984). Variables that change relatively little through time – such as, for instance, the patterns of comparative advantage – will as a consequence tend to lose much of their impact. However, on closer inspection, only 6 of the 16 estimated country dummies were found to be significantly different from the mean (or a common constant term) at a 10% level of significance. When reestimated with constant term and the significant country dummies, the 'Natural' variable regained its significance, without any reduction in the explanatory power of the model.

Thus, so far the tests give strong support to the hypothesis of a positive impact of the 'home market' on export specialisation. However, to assume that one model works equally well for all sectors (or products) is an 'heroic' assumption that may be difficult to defend. Therefore, the second set of tests that will be reported was carried out at the sector (or product group) level (equation 4 below).

$$(4) \quad S_{ij}^t \quad a_{j0} \quad a_j \, {}_1HOME_{ij}^t \quad a_j \, {}_2NAT_i^t \quad a_j \, {}_3POP_i^t \quad U_{tj}^t$$

The model was tested with the scale variable included, but without dummies, using a backward search for the best model (the model with least variance). It should be noted that the sample in these tests is rather small (48 observations) and that the results therefore must be interpreted with some caution. The smaller the sample, the greater the problem of multicollinearity tends to be. In the present case this is especially evident for product groups where the 'Home' sector belongs to the 'natural resource base' part of the economy, SITC 0-4, in which case multicollinearity between 'Home' and 'Natural' is to be expected.

Detailed results from these tests, using ordinary least squares, can be found in table A1 in the appendix. Table 11.4 below presents a summary of the results with respect to the impact of the 'Home' variable. The hypothesis that this impact is positive, is tested against the alternative hypothesis that the two variables are

Table 11.4. **The Home Market Hypothesis Tested: Sector Results**

Significant Results[A]	HOME	R^2 [B]	R^2(adj.)
1. Ships and boats	1.04 (10.26)	0.70	0.69
2. Paper working machinery	0.37 (7.72)	0.60	0.58
3. Heating and cooling equipment	0.21 (5.74)	0.43	0.39
4. Leather machinery	0.79 (4.25)	0.31	0.28
5. Automotive electrical equipment	0.50 (4.10)	0.58	0.55
6. Milking machinery	0.79 (4.09)	0.27	0.25
7. Food processing machinery	0.54 (3.85)	0.27	0.22
8. Aircraft engines	0.62 (3.63)	0.22	0.21
9. Medical instruments n.e.s.	0.63 (3.58)	0.42	0.43
10. Telecommunications	0.50 (2.56)	0.21	0.17
11. Electromedicals	0.58 (2.25)	0.10	0.08
12. Internal combustion engines [C]	0.29 (1.93)	0.26	0.21
13. Pharmaceuticals	0.87 (1.85)	0.19	0.13
14. Hand-tools for agriculture and forestry	0.53 (1.83)	0.08	0.02
Non-significant Results:[A]			
Machine tools for working metals[C]	0.48 (1.38)	0.40	0.37
Printing machinery[C]	0.19 (1.36)	0.28	0.25
Rubber tyres and tubes	0.32 (1.26)	0.03	0.01
Textile machinery[C]	0.26 (0.77)	0.31	0.26
Agricultural machinery for preparing Soil and harvesting[C].	–	0.21	0.19
Agricultural machinery n.e.s[C]	–	0.13	0.11
Construction and mining machinery[C]	–	0.23	0.20
Sewing machinery	–	0.45	0.42
Tractors[C]	–	0.35	0.32

Notes:
A Significance level: 5% at a one-tailed test.
B Coefficient, absolute t-value in brackets.
C Multicollinearity caused by correlation between HOME and NATURAL.
For more details, see table A 1 (appendix).

uncorrelated. The results show that the alternative hypothesis can be rejected in 14 out of 23 cases (5 % level of significance, one-tailed test). Thus, for the large majority of the sectors, the test suggests that the 'home market hypothesis' should be accepted. One reason for the weak or lacking correlation in the remaining cases may be multicollinearity problems. In fact, this was a significant problem in 7 out of 9 sectors where the 'home market hypothesis' lacked support. An attempt to remedy this problem was made by using univariate tests. These suggested that two other sectors, machine tools for working metals and textile machinery, may be added to the list of significant correlations.

As in the tests discussed earlier (Table 11.3), there were signs of autocorrelation in many sectors. Earlier, we identified (see E in Table 11.3) a set of countries deviating from the specialisation pattern that should be expected from the model. We therefore reestimated the equations with these six country dummies, using the same technique as above (a backward search for the model with least variance). In qualitative terms, the results were the same as earlier, but the problem of autocorrelation was much reduced. As earlier, the 'Home' variable was found to have a significant positive impact on export specialisation in 14 cases.[10] We also estimated a model with 'Home' and a full set of country dummies. The results now deteriorated significantly. A significant positive correlation between 'Home' and export specialisation was now found for 6 sectors only. However, it should be kept in mind that this test leaves out the impact of the within-country means of the variables. What remains, roughly speaking, is the changes in the variables through time. Thus, it comes close to being a test of the hypothesis that the RCA-indexes increase (or decrease) simultaneously. The results show that this holds only for a minority of the sectors included in the test. One possible explanation could be the one discussed in the previous section: that, in many cases, very long lags are present. No attempt was made to test this possibility.

11.5. Concluding Remarks

The view that the home market may have a positive impact on the competitiveness of domestic producers is by no means a new one. Indeed, it has been widely held for at least a century. In spite of this, neoclassical trade theorists have normally regarded this view as 'theoretically unsound' (a cover for protectionism). This chapter has argued that, based on the theoretical perspective developed in part I of this book, it is possible to give a plausible theoretical foundation for 'the home market hypothesis' However, this is *not a general theory of export specialisation*, but a partial theory about one among several factors that shape comparative advantage. Nor is it equally important for all products and sectors: it is expected to hold only in those cases where innovation and R&D play an important role for the competitive process. And even in these cases the mere existence of domestic demand for a certain range of products is not enough. *A necessary condition for a positive impact of the home market on international competitiveness is that domestic users of the product or technology in question are technologically sophisticated and demanding.*

Patterns of export specialisation are, as pointed out in earlier chapters, relatively stable through time. They are the result of a long-term historical process where interactive learning between domestic users and producers of technology is one feature among several. The long time horizon, combined with the inherent difficulty in empirically identifying the actual links and outcomes of interactive learning processes, poses large problems for empirical work. Indeed, it may be questioned whether the kind of empirical exercise carried out in this chapter is worthwhile at all. For instance, it may be argued that a period of a little more than two decades is much too short to achieve a real insight into processes of interactive learning. The representativity of the sample, severely restricted as it is by statistical classifications made for entirely different purposes, is another critical point, not to mention the econometric problems present.

It is true that the short time perspective only allows a few snap-shots from a short part of a long historical process. However, as argued earlier, this represents a downward bias: we are likely to underestimate the real effect. The fact that a significant correlation was found in the majority of the cases considered here, is therefore not weakened by this problem. No doubt, the representativity of the sample does not allow sweeping generalisations to be made, but this does not undermine the results for those sectors where significant correlations were found. In spite of econometric problems, in a number of cases the results were shown to be relatively robust. Most importantly, perhaps, for a number of specialised engineering products or instruments, a clear correlation was found between the relative export performance of the 'technology producing sector' and the relative performance of its 'home market sector'. This includes some cases where the most important 'home market sector' belongs to the public sector. Thus, the results presented here give some support to the argument (chapter 7) that the public sector, when acting as a *competent user*, may affect industrial development and export performance positively.

Appendix 11.1

The trade data used in this paper were calculated from OECD Trade Series C (value data) using the IKE data base on trade statistics at the Aalborg University. Data for health care were taken from OECD: Health Care Systems in Transition, OECD, Paris, 1990, data for merchant fleets and telephone lines were taken from UN Statistical Yearbook, various editions. Other data from OECD National Accounts.

Construction of home-market indicators. Tele and Health

$$T_j = \text{Telephone lines in country}_j$$
$$j \quad i, i = 1..j..n$$
$$N_j = \text{Number of inhabitants in}_j$$

$$I_j \quad \frac{T_j}{N_j} \frac{{}_iN_i}{{}_iT_j}$$

Similarly for health services, where $T_j =$ health services in country j (in common currency)

Shipping

$$S_j = \text{Fleet of country}_j, 1000 \text{ tons}$$
$$X_j = \text{Total export of country}_j \text{ (goods and services)}$$

$$I_j \quad \frac{S_j}{{}_iS_i} \frac{{}_iX_i}{X_j}$$

Chapter 12

INTEGRATION, INNOVATION AND EVOLUTION[1]

Esben Sloth Andersen and Asger Brændgaard

12.1. Introduction

One of the results of studying national systems of innovation (NSI) from the viewpoint of the production structure (cf. chapter 4) is that emphasis is put on the diversity of the economic system. A simplified system has few possibilities of interactive learning while a diversified system has many innovative possibilities (cf. chapter 2). This result needs some qualification but it may, nevertheless, be the starting point for an exploration of economic processes which involve changes in the degree of diversity. Such changes are at the forefront of international economics and they have indirectly been dealt with in chapters 10 and 11. However, the subject matter of the present chapter, the development and effects of international integration, is especially suited for dealing with the question of diversity. The core thesis of the chapter is that neglected but important effects of integration on innovation can be brought into focus by the approach developed in this book. The main line of argument is theoretical, but in section 12.4 some of the points are related to the competitiveness problems of EC's information technology sector.

Our starting point is the recent 'Cost of Non-Europe' analyses of the effects of the European Single Market (already mentioned in chapter 10) which have revitalised the age-old debates on international economic integration. As in the case of earlier debates there have been many verbal arguments on the innovative and evolutionary effects of the new increase in the degree of integration, but nearly all systematic studies neglect such arguments and stick to the productivity gains which can be obtained with the given products and processes. However, the 'dynamic' or evolutionary effects of the integration process are so obvious that they are reintroduced in the conclusions of the studies (EC Commission, 1988a). But the way they are reintroduced is unsatisfactory because 'dynamic' effects are, so to say, added to 'static' effects. There are no clear arguments why and to which degree the effects are additive. This problem becomes especially evident when we consider the two different conclusions (cf., e.g. Cecchini, 1988, EC Commission, 1988a): existing diversity must be reduced in order to promote the best-practice technology and the highest-quality products; but diversity-creation must be increased in terms of new products and processes. This analytical conclusion may be appropriate for many cases but the possible link between existing diversity and the creation of new diversity casts some doubts on the general validity of this way of analysing the effects of economic integration.

The independent ways in which the two subquestions are treated is underlined in the 'Costs of Non-Europe' studies: practically all the underlying studies are related to the question of reduction in the existing diversity and this fact is clearly emphasised. On the other hand, it is pointed out that it has been necessary to exclude the diversity-creating effects of integration which should be subjected to dynamic analysis. These latter effects are only given few remarks which emphasise that they are difficult to judge but thought to be large and positive:

> *Examples of this [other type of effects] include product and process innovation which will modify – upwards – the entire trajectory of EC growth and economic welfare throughout the 1990's and beyond into the twenty-first century.* (Cecchini, 1988, 104)

In the systematic exposition of Single Market study the argument goes:

> *It has long been recognised that changes in the market and trading environment can have an important impact on the continuing, 'dynamic' evolution of the economy, this contrasting with the 'comparative static' approach that underlies the larger part of microeconomic studies and partial and general equilibrium analysis. Unfortunately, these dynamic features are extremely difficult to explain with scientific rigour. ... There appear none the less some studies of how market conditions appear to influence the trend rate of technological progress and innovation in enterprises.* (EC Commission, 1988a, 37)

A similar verbal emphasis on innovation appears to be the outcome of the academic discussion (cf., e.g. Jaquemin and Sapir, 1989), and some efforts have been made to include 'dynamic evolution' into standard presentations (Robson, 1987, Jovanovic, 1992). A primary reason for the conclusion is that integration is believed to lead to an increase in Schumpeterian competition among firms which will create the dynamic or, rather, evolutionary effects of integration. But here the studies stop and leave further work on these important effects of integration to future analysis.

Even if the analytical framework of the present book is developed for other purposes, it may help to understand aspects of the interaction between existing diversity and the process of diversity-creation and the related changes of the competitiveness of an array of industrialised national economies which are integrating into a single system, E. The integration process among the members of E may provide a new framework for creative producer-user linkages, for the signpost function of institutions, for the exploitation of innovative development blocks, etc. Thus E may function as a system of innovation which to a smaller or larger degree supplements or substitutes the respective NSI.

However, the integration process may also create an environment which curbs diversity-creation by weakening old structures of production and institutions which are important for certain types of innovation without compensating by creating new or promoting other old structures which can take over their functions. In this respect one might ask the proponents of the Schumpeterian view (Schumpeter, 1942, chapter 7) whether and when the 'creative destruction' of existing structures can (in some sense) be larger than the 'destructive creation and expansion' of successful firms and other new structures.

However, it is not such a grand question which will be dealt with in the present chapter. Instead we will discuss some more limited questions of the possibilities and constraints on innovation created by the integration within E. By the very naming of the area of integration by E, the reader is warned that the argument is primarily made in the form of theoretical sketches. However, we believe that some further development of our approach is made possible by relating it to one of the difficult areas of the concrete EC-integration, namely the area of information and communication technology (the IT area). In the present chapter those possibilities can be exploited to only a limited degree. But the case story of IT and EC illustrates some of the problems which underlie the present argument and some of the difficult tasks in relation to its further development.

12.2. Diversity and Evolution

In an evolutionary perspective the integration of an array of national economies $(E_1, E_2, \ldots, E_m)$ into one 'single market' with related institutional structures, E, may be considered in (at least) three major ways: the reallocation approach, the diversity approach and the diversity-creation approach. We will discuss these approaches one by one.

12.2.1. The Reallocation Approach

According to a radical version of the reallocation approach each of the m national markets have been supporting n different industries, each of which is producing a (basically) homogeneous product. Through integration we get instead of mn individual markets only n markets. The original selection environment formed by the *mn* individual markets gave raise to *mn* national industries with different peculiarities with respect to, e.g. unit costs. The selection environment of only *n* markets (selection environments) forms the basis of only *n* industries.

But there is a period of transformation: The creation of *E* starts a process of change due to the increased selection against low productivity firms within each of the *n* industries. The average productivity level of each of *E*'s *n* industries will gradually increase towards a level of saturation (with respect to the existing best-practice technology). If (with some caution) we define an aggregate measure of *E*'s productivity, we may discuss the S-shaped progress of productivity in terms of the level of saturation as well as the intrinsic rate of growth towards this level.

The saturation level (with respect to existing technology) is basically influenced by the degree to which *E* is actually able to replace the *m* national selection environments. If this is not fully the case, there may still be some 'niches' for low-productivity firms and this will influence the overall productivity level. The rapidity of the progress towards the saturation level is influenced by a great many factors including the strength and financial support behind the expansion of the high-productivity firms, the mechanisms supporting the transfer of resources from low- to high-productivity firms and other mechanisms for coping with resistance to change.

This version of the reallocation approach is critically dependent on several contestable assumptions. First, the question of diversity is related to a very simplified 'ecosystem' in *E* where there is only *n* niches. Each such niche only allows the long-term survival of one variant of the techniques of production (according to 'principle' of niche exclusion). In the reality of economic evolution with long-term coexistence of very different techniques within the industries, this picture seems inadequate. Second, the analysis is made in terms of the existing range of techniques even if technology is known to be radically changing during the prolonged process of approaching the saturation level of productivity. There is no guarantee that the firm which has the highest productivity before *E*-integration is also the firm which is most suited to adapt to future changes in technology. In some cases high productivity reflects the exploitation of an established technological trajectory to which the firm becomes bound in some way (Arthur, 1988). In contrast, the technology of the firms of the future has not yet matured and many show slow initial productivity gains. Third, it is assumed that the reallocation mechanisms will be sufficient to keep down the level of unutilised resources, especially unemployment. These and other limitations call for supplementary approaches.

12.2.2. The Diversity Approach

The diversity approach to the study of the effects of E-integration differs from the reallocation approach by considering the number of products and, indirectly, the number of industries, as central variables in the process of integration. This approach may be related to Linder (1961) and has some affinity to the many empirical studies of intra-industry trade (which place the relevant diversity beneath the empirically defined 'industry' level). The idea is that n is changing as a consequence of the creation of a larger and, perhaps, more complex selection environment.

Such changes have already occurred due to earlier waves of trade liberalisation but the creation of E represents a new step in the process. The effects of this step are seen in the changes of the number of species of products and related (sub)industries from a point of time t before to a point t' after the (prolonged) process of integration; moreover, the proposition is that $n(t') > n(t)$. This proposition may appear difficult to understand. Why should the defragmentation of national economies (their number is reduced from m to 1) lead to an increased fragmentation in terms of the types of products and related (sub)industries? The answer may be related to one of the interpretations of Adam Smith's famous dictum 'that the division of labour depends on the extension of the market'.

According to this interpretation, the process of specialisation around a specific need or technique is not only taking place within firms but also between firms. The possibilities for a division of labour (measured in terms of the number of well-established specialities for workers and for firms) are dependent on the existence of a sufficient number of customers.

If the actual number is not sufficient for a certain speciality, the supply has to be made by generalists and thus at a lower level of quality and at a higher price. If we assume that the needs of the customers are, in principle, infinitely heterogeneous, we see that a national economy of a large aggregate size may support a larger number of specialities than a small economy. Any degree of trading between the economies will, of course, increase the possibilities for developing specialities. But a full integration will maximise the number of sustainable specialities, although not in a proportionate manner. The progress towards $n(\max)$ will probably be quite different from the progress towards the maximum level of (sustainable) productivity discussed above since there must both be an extinction of some general purpose products and a creation of a lot of new products which exploit the new economic possibilities.

This diversity-oriented interpretation of the process of integration resembles the results of the biological studies on the number of species sustainable on islands of different size (cf. May, 1976/1981, chapter 10). Here it is found that the number of species increases in proportion to the logarithm of the area of the island. An analogous phenomenon in economic evolution (where we can bring the 'economic islands' together) would be that the long-run equilibrium degree of product diversity is dependent on aggregate income, perhaps as $n = aY^b$, where Y is national income, a and b are constants, $b < 1$.

Economic integration is hence seen as a radical increase in the selection-revelant Y through the creation of E. But here the biological analogy breaks down in several important respects. First of all, the specialisation of a group of firms is not only dependent on the relevant demand in their own (extended) nation but also on the possibilities to export to other nations. Second, economic life is influenced by rapid changes in technologies and even shifts in techno-economic paradigms (Perez and Soete, 1988) which may increase or decrease the numbers of products in a more rapid way than the integration within E. Third, economic diversity is influenced by the strategies of the agents and the resultant major changes in product differentiation or standardisation. These lacking analogies suggest that the comparative-static approach to the diversity of E is much too restricted.

12.2.3. The Diversity-Creation Approach

The limitations of the diversity approach lead us to explore the possibility of a diversity-creation approach. According to this approach, the central effects are not the productivity gains due to simple reallocation and the increasing number of products due to the simple increase in the size of the economic niches but the changes in the capacity and inducement to product and process innovation. This shift of emphasis is combined with a broadening of the study from E to the whole world. Thus the central selection environment for new products and processes is seen as the world market.

The world except E is, of course, extremely heterogeneous, but we will emphasise the aspects of it which select vigorously among new products and processes. For this reason we will in this chapter (regrettably) have to ignore the weaker competitors and only consider the 'rest of the world' as consisting of one sophisticated trading partner, J.[2] To prepare the ground for the discussion of integration and diversity-creation, we will also introduce a few other distinctions into the picture.

First, we will distinguish between two classes of industries: T is the industries which are related to a relatively stable set of products and H is the industries which are related to most of the introduction of new products. We may think in terms of the traditional T-industries and the high-tech creating H-industries. Second, we will distinguish between two classes of potential customers: G is the general customers who react on offers of well specified products with well specified prices. S is the, supposedly small, class of sophisticated customers who with respect to at least one product area will react upon loosely defined proposals to buy new products or products with no kind of routine pricing; S-users may also ask a specific firm to develop such products. In this framework we have the following matrix of possibilities:

	G-users	S-users
T-industries	(1)	(2)
H-industries	(3)	(4)

In relation to the diversity-creation approach to integration we are especially interested in case (4), i.e. sophisticated users for the highly innovating class of industries. But our interest in this case is dependent on the spread of the results of the innovative interaction between H-industries and S-users to quantitatively important parts of the economy. In other words, the demand of the S-users must relate to the potential demand of the G-users. A further impact will, of course, arise if the new products supplied from the H-industries influence the productivity level of the T-industries. Another possibility for an increase in the importance of the new products of the H-industries of E is that they may be able to penetrate the whole world market.

A little reflection will show that the framework which is now outlined may have major influences on the study of the effects of the process of integration of E. First of all, the framework is well suited to take into account one of the central ideas of the present book, namely that the matching of innovative (H-)producers and S-users plays a crucial role in the process of innovation. The question in the present chapter is how the process of integration within E influences the possibilities of match-making.

Second, the need for coping with the integration effects as a whole puts emphasis upon the relationships between the innovative demand of the small class of S-users and the demand of large groups of G-users. Similarly, any relationships between the, possibly, small class of H-industries and the productivity (and product development) of the large class of T-industries is of central importance to the study.

Third, the framing of the argument in terms of the competitiveness of E's industries on the world market removes much of the autonomous relevance of the two comparative-static approaches sketched in sections 12.2.1 and 12.2.2. Their economic meaning must primarily be derived from a more developed evolutionary analysis which evaluates and includes their results in a more comprehensive framework.

12.3. Integration and Changes of Comparative Advantage

12.3.1. Relative Fitness and Integration

The first appearance of an innovation does not denote a significant amount of evolution. In the beginning it has (normally) practically no influence on the change of the frequency of other commodities not to talk of the overall state of the economy. To have an economic impact the routines underlying the innovation must show a supernormal competitiveness or fitness, i.e. they must help to increase the relative share of the innovation at the market. After a shorter or longer period of supernormal fitness, the economic importance will become clear. In the simplest case of a supernormal fitness the number of applications of the innovation follows an S-shaped curve which starts near zero and ends at some saturation level.

The result of market selection may be expressed in terms of changes in market shares of different types of commodities characterised by different sets of routines. This conception can give raise to different measurements of competitiveness or relative fitness based on, e.g. production capacity, quantity of production and quantity of export. In relation to the present discussion of E-integration (and the empirical material presented in section 12.4), the last measure may appear the most appropriate.[3] However, the core of the argument can be presented in the simpler terms by concentrating on shares in the total quantity produced. Thus, if we ignore measurement problems, inventory changes etc., we consider the change in the world market share of E in product i as our proxy for fitness, i.e.:

$$F_{iE}(t_0 t_1) = [Q_{iE}(t_1)/Q_{iE}(t_0)]/[Q_{iW}(t_1)/Q_{iW}(t_0)],$$

where $Q_{iE}(t_0)$ is the quantity of product i produced by the firms located in E in period t_0. The definition fails in the case of a new product in E in period $t1$ (we must not divide by zero). The formula distinguishes between three main possibilities of the fitness, $F_{iE}(t_0 t_1)$. If the fitness is one, the market share is unchanging; if it is above one, the market share is increasing; if it is below one, the market share is decreasing.

The question is now how we should expect the fitness of the groups of firms producing the different products within E to be influenced by the integration process. First, we may refer to the reallocation approach to integration and say that not all industries will reap the same relative decreases in unit costs. Assuming that the relative industry situation in J is unchanged, the E industries may be ranked according to their productivity gains which the theory assumes to be reflected in changes in observed fitness. If there were no balancing mechanisms between E and J, all the E-industries would gain in fitness. In the existence of such mechanisms (e.g., changes in the exchange rate between E and J), the price of some E-industries will increase in the J-market and thus they will lose fitness in export terms and maybe also in production terms.

Second, in relation to the diversity approach we should first of all emphasise that industries are not homogeneous with respect to their product mix. Furthermore, we may assume that some industries have larger potentials for developing a wide variety of products in relation to the different niches of an integrated E than other industries. The former will increase their fitness more than the latter.

Third, in relation to the variety-creation approach to integration we may say that some industries are increasing their capability and propensity to innovate in an irrevocable way and this may give raise to increases in fitness which may be supposed to be much more wide-ranging than the types of fitness-increase studied in relation to the two other approaches. In the latter case the supernormal fitness created by integration will gradually move towards normal fitness while recurrent innovation helps to recreate supernormal fitness in new situations and areas. It is this innovation-related cause of increased fitness which shall especially be discussed in the rest of this chapter.

The above discussion of fitness has clear implications for a long-standing issue in international economics: comparative advantage. In the classical formulations this concept is defined as the relative levels of unit costs in the different industries of a nation before trade has begun. In an evolutionary context where the target is always moving, this version of the idea of comparative advantage is only a very first approximation to a much richer concept. What we are trying to approach is a concept of dynamic comparative advantage which will help to understand the mechanisms behind the development of the market shares in an ever-changing world economy. However, we have to leave these possibilities as an implicit theme underlying the discussion.

12.3.2. The Possibility of Negative Dynamic Effects of Integration

The traditional analysis of economic integration has almost exclusively studied the effects of jumps in the degree of integration in terms of once-and-for-all-gains. This kind of comparative static analysis has indicated relatively small effects (less than 1% increase in GNP). The 'Cost of Non-Europe' project has (as mentioned in chapter 10) adopted the same method but included the influence of 'barrier removal' on the exploitation of scale economies and changes in price due to changes in the degree of imperfect competition. By taking these microeconomic effects into account (together with less important macroeconomic effects), the expected growth in EC GNP is increased to 5%. But still the effects on the dynamic development path of the industries located in the EC is not considered.

Even in the extended form, the study of integration effects only deals with the top of the iceberg. What really matters in the present conception of long-term growth performance is the influence of integration on the propensity to learn and innovate (cf. part I). Here the argument has often been phrased in terms of dynamic economies of scale and the 'Schumpeter hypothesis' of the highly innovative performance of large firms. *Ceteris paribus*, integration increases the specialisation and the scale of production and firms, and thus learning and innovation. However, this argument does not treat the problem of 'lock-in' of the structure of production and the different learning/innovation possibilities and income elasticities of the demand of different industries. From this 'structuralist' point of view, there is no reason to presuppose that the evolutionary effects of integration will simply increase the positive static effects of integration. On the contrary, one would assume that the evolutionary effects of integration are sometimes negative.

Within the framework sketched in section 12.2.3 we may look more closely at this claim in terms of trade creation and trade diminution between the E-members $E_1, E_2, \ldots, E_m$ as well as J. Trade may be divided into intra-E-trade between the members and extra-E-trade between E and J. In static terms, the increased integration results in an increase of intra-E-trade but partly this may be the result of a diminution of extra-E-trade (because of technical and other trade barriers around E). In dynamic terms the problem is how E's comparative advantages *vis-à-vis* J are influenced by the static changes.

Which areas are especially gaining from the increased exploitation of scale economies and the increased intra-E competition and thus gaining with respect to comparative advantage? That depends on the initial conditions of the integration project. Let us assume that the starting point is a stronghold in the T-industries and a certain weakness in the H-industries. Furthermore, the H-industries have already internationalised to a considerable extent, and where this is not the case, they face complex markets where integration of standards are a long-term, and highly innovative as well as conflict-ridden process. Under such conditions we expect the result of integration to be a (further) strengthening of E's T-industries *vis-à-vis* J's T-industries while E's H-industries face a sub-normal development in terms of competitiveness and fitness.

If we assume that the income elasticities of 'world' demand of the products from the H-industries are larger than from the T-industries, and if we assume that E's demand is as sophisticated as J's, then E is facing a problem. E's long-run growth may be curbed by a balance-of-payments-constraint while J is in a much more favourable position. Furthermore, the propensity to learn and innovate is higher for H-firms than for T-firms, and thus E's vicious and J's virtuous circles are reinforced. In the end some kind of balance must be reestablished, but the way this is done is probably not favourable to E.

In economic evolution specialisation is seldom absolute as in Ricardo's famous case of British specialisation in an H-industry and Portugal's specialisation in a T-industry (– and in the principle of niche exclusion). The integration effect is rather expressed in terms of the relative weight of and the types of differentiated market niches exploited by each type of industry. Thus E's H-industries may be supposed to retreat to relatively narrow strongholds and protected areas while J's firms are expanding in large, profitable and innovative niches. Such a behaviour would explain some of the 'stylised facts' of the EC in IT which are recorded in section 12.4. In any case we see that integration projects are not necessarily adequate means of changing a given 'lock-in' into weakly performing parts of the H-industries.

12.3.3. Producer-User Linkages in an 'Extended Home Market'

Nearly all discussions of economic evolution have put a strong emphasis on the simple competitive relationship between firms or industries. In this context, the supernormal fitness of one party must, by definition, imply the subnormal fitness of other parties in the same market. However, in a complex and ever-changing environment where new niches are constantly emerging, there is a need to complement this competition-oriented view of the evolutionary process with other possibilities. Actually, a central theme in the present book (cf. part I as well as the other chapters of part III) is the possibility that mutualism (but also asymmetric relationships) may play a central role in the evolutionary process.

In fitness terms we may define mutualism as the case where the fitnesses of two industries (or products or groups of firms etc.) are positively correlated, i.e. if the fitness of one party increases, the fitness of the other party will also increase (and *vice versa*). Such cases have been reported many times in the present book, as in the cases of producer-user relationships and development blocks.

Let us introduce this perspective of mutualism into the discussion of the effects of E's integration. In relation to our reference case, we know that the existence of an apparently matchable pair of users and producers does not necessarily imply the development of a positive relationship. Thus we know that the EC's huge demand for computers has not changed the relatively weak performance on the part of the EC's computer producers. Such a kind of mismatch is partly a natural reflection of international specialisation, but the weakness of major parts of EC's IT industries and the corresponding weakness of intra-EC links between producers and users of IT products appear to create problems. These problems may be formulated in terms of the lack of innovative mutualism in an important area, the relationship between the fitness of E's H-industries and the fitness of E's users of H-products.

There are several reasons for emphasising the lack of symbiosis in this area. First, what is of primary importance for E is not E's fitness in individual H-products but rather the possible positive effects of this fitness upon the fitness of the rest of the H-industries as well as on the fitness of the T-industries in areas of high income elasticities of demand. Second, the possibility of (re-)building a knowledge base is much better in areas which are not at the centre of the competence of the competitor. Third, different types of industrial competence and competitiveness are normally built in a sequential manner. One stronghold may serve as a base for creating (or re-creating) another stronghold. This can clearly be seen from the industrial history of Europe and from present-day changes which are reflected in the discussion of development blocks.

In this connection the basic question is not whether E's 'single market' creates possibilities for obtaining 'minimum efficient scale' in the production of well-established products. The question is rather whether E can function as an 'extended home market' in relation to the interchange of learning experiences between innovative producers and sophisticated S-users (firms and households). The latter has to be lead-users (chapters 3 and 11, Hippel, 1988) in the sense that their sophistication is representative of the potential demand of significant groups. There are, of course, multinational corporations for which this question may be (partially) resolved without much consideration about 'localised interaction' between producers and users. However, in the majority of cases we still think that new producer-user relationships are difficult to establish between firms from different countries, especially when culture, language and life-style as well as more technical norms and standards differ substantially. (chapter 3 and Lundvall, 1988)

Furthermore, there are still many products which fail in their international marketing due to the lack of substantial adaptation and a subnormal level of 'de-bugging' because the product is not supported by a closely knit web of informational and other contacts within nations. The reason why so many products fail to penetrate the whole of E's market may be related to these problems just as much as to deliberately created non-tariff barriers to trade which have been at the centre of attention in the creation of the Single Market of the EC.

The question is therefore whether a further integration of E will create an extended home market which provides a base for the creation of new products and industries, for the long-term development of new areas of E's comparative advantage in international trade. In other words, can E supplement or replace the nation in Linder's somewhat dated statement about the importance of the home market (cf. chapter 11)? Even if we know that there are today many other circumstances influencing the creation of comparative advantage (e.g. information flows in and around multinational corporations), there are still great difficulties in creating a successful process of 'commoditisation' without the support of an (extended) home market. The argument may still be (Linder, 1961, 90):

> ... *(1) that it is unlikely that an entrepreneur will ever think of satisfying a need that does not exist at home; (2) that, even if this alien need was seen, the basically correct product to fill it might not be conceived of; and (3) that, even if the basically correct product was conceived of, it is still improbable that the product could be finally adapted to unfamiliar conditions without prohibitive costs being incurred.*

The question is now whether the sophisticated firms and households of E can exploit the integration in the ways envisaged by Linder. If so, there are plenty of possibilities for demand-enhancing innovations which will also be relevant for international demand. Even most T-industries may give raise to a large number of demand-enhancing as well as labour-saving H-based innovations which cannot be thought out in laboratories but have to go through a stage of initial design and debugging in close interaction with the S-users of the T-industries. The problem may be phrased in terms of 'diffusion' of generic technologies. However, we should not think of diffusion in simple terms but rather as a process which takes place in immature form and with innovative participation of the adopter of the innovation.

Thus we cannot do with the picture of a simple 'epidemic' of innovation-diffusion articulated by the logistic S-curve. In contrast to this and similar mathematical models of innovation-diffusion we do not presuppose a given innovation and a given population of potential adopters. The process of innovation-diffusion is just as well a process of innovation as a process of diffusion. In the beginning of this process, the innovation is often customised to the needs of a small group of adopters. However, due to a lack of debugging, it may nevertheless have a low potential for spreading. Later, the situation changes since the innovation is gradually changed to fit larger groups of adopters (e.g. through price, quality and lower information needs). At the same time, some potential adopters might change their own characteristics (e.g. production and qualification structure) in order to be able to use the innovation. In such a process of successful user-producer interaction plenty of possibilities of change and entry into new product and process areas will show up for both parties.

What we see is evolution through a double-sided change-process: both the innovation's potential for spread and the population of potential adopters increase because of changes during the innovation-diffusion. An alternative form of the diffusion trajectory puts the burden of adaptation more on the side of the innovation than on the side of the adopters: The increase of the potency of spread and of the relevant population involves the splitting up, or the diversification, of the innovation according to the specific needs of subgroups of potential adopters. Thus we have a whole family of innovation-diffusion curves. However, this expansive phase of innovative activity may end up by a 'lock-in' to a given set-up, and it may become obsolete through the development of substitutes and through overall changes of the techno-economic system.

The development of such a process of innovative adaptation is not necessarily promoting the extra-E export performance of the industries involved (possibly both H- and T-industries). The evolutionary process may be quite idiosyncratic with respect to product characteristics and process attributes so that they cannot easily be applied in other nations. The demand and ideas of E's S-users should not only be sophisticated but also be representative of potential and future demand of broad groups of foreign costumers.

12.3.4. Incomplete Commoditisation within an Extended Home Market?

As described in chapter 4, a product life cycle may be analysed in terms of conflictual interactions between producers and users because of the open-ended character of search processes and design criteria (see also Andersen, 1991). They may end up with a (temporary) 'closure of the universe of discourse' by accepting a 'paradigm' in terms of a mutually agreed definition of the producer-user interface which partly takes the form of specifications of the commodities to be delivered. Such specifications tend to become generalised to groups of producers and users of a commodity, which (for reasons to be discussed below) are difficult to change. But the specifications provide a framework which to some extent determines technological improvements performed by producers and users. Radical changes must break with the basic specifications and often involve the setting up of totally new groups of producers and users.

The proposed conception of 'paradigms' is shifting the focus away from a 'community of engineers' involved in the perfection and administration of a particular technology (cf. Dosi, 1984). Instead it is focussing on the 'community of producers and users' of a given commodity and their influence on the related technology. The engineers of the producers and users are not a homogeneous 'community', and many economic considerations are clearly involved. In the present chapter, it is interesting to note that the boundaries of the 'community' shift over time, partly as a result of the decisions taken. These boundaries may be discussed in terms of the H-firms of E and J. But we especially emphasise the

H-firms's customers which is divided into sophisticated users, *S*, and general users, *G*, located in either *E* or *J*.

Apparently, the problem of delimitation of the involved parties is of little importance in the pre-paradigmatic period, since the design of the 'proto-commodity' is open to continued negotiations and experiments. However, only a small group of competent *S*-users can participate in this game and they have to pay a high price for the products delivered. As suggested in chapter 4, there are reasons for upholding this state of affairs: the *S*-users are provided with customised solutions while the *H*-producers of *E* are relatively well-protected against new competition from *J*-firms. The entry of a new *J*-producer into the *E*-network of user-producer relationships would involve investment in an innovation-oriented information channel *vis-à-vis* the *S*-user of *E*. Furthermore, *E*'s *S*-user should be willing to introduce a new *J*-supplier to the finer details of his process of production. Only few *J*-firms are able to overcome such barriers to entry.

However, the pre-paradigmatic state is not a stable one. The *S*-user of *E* may find out that the interface is not as flexible as it was originally designed to be. In an early period, channels of information and agendas of change are established with a clear understanding of their purpose. But gradually they face a 'productivity dilemma' (Abernathy and Clark, 1985). Much investment of human and organisational capital is dependent on the specific set-up. It often becomes a purpose in itself to use the given framework, to formalise informal agreements and to decrease their costs. When a major shift in innovative possibilities occurs, the given structure is very seldom prepared. We have a case of '*E*-sclerosis'. This case was recognised as a general one by Schumpeter who connected (major) innovations with new men and new firms. In well-established but innovative firms (which Schumpeter later realised) change may be supported by the 'circulation of elites'. However, in the case of well-established producer-user relationships changes may be even more difficult since the two parties involved have to make a coordinated move.

From the viewpoint of the *E*-producer there are also other considerations which suggest attempts to go further in the process of commoditisation. The main consideration concerns the limitation of the original market of *E*'s *S*-users. In this context it is the *E*-producer who may attempt to take the initiative to move away from the role of a 'tailor' for advanced *E*-customers towards a broader market of general *G*-users who are unable to digest much information about the product and its continued changes. Now the *E*-producer may look more like a 'king', 'forcing upon the public a new commodity' (Schumpeter, 1928, 32). In this task it is 'the producer who as a rule initiates economic change, and consumers who are educated by him if necessary; they are, as it were, taught to want new things, or things which differ in some respect from those which they have been in the habit of using'. (Schumpeter, 1934, 65).

However, this is a shift in role. Originally, there was a degree of mutualism between E-producers and S-users of proto-commodities. After a period of trial and error commodities which are presented to G-users and unchangeable soluitions may evolve. When the market is saturated, we see yet another inversion in the roles of producers and users. In this case consumers becomes the governors of the allocation between well-established lines of production.

The question is now to which degree these 'role shifts' are supported in different areas of the world. We have no room for a systematic development of the answer in the present chapter but we think there are reasons to believe that the IT-industries of EC have a tendency of getting stuck in the early steps of commoditisation. In this connection we may have some help from the innovation-design dilemma developed in modern theories of the firm (cf. chapter 5). Here it becomes clear that there is no automatic transformation of firms and products from the proto-commodity stage to the stage of standardisation and the stage of well-known and widely acknowledged standards. The overall behavioural rules of the business and engineering communities of E and J as well as the relative strength of different subgroups of H-producers and their S-users and G-users may be supposed to influence the probability that a firm will shift from one stage to another. The relative weakness of this stage-shifting in E may be a major reason why the possibilities implied by the E-integration are weakly exploited.

12.4. 'Stylised Facts' on EC and IT

The character of the analytical framework proposed in the chapter is, of course, dependent on the problem-situation which it is intended to clarify. It is not least the new wave of EC integration and the weakness of EC's IT industries which have been underlying much of the discussion. In this short section we will present a limited amount of information which gives some indications of the possible development of empirically oriented discussions.

But it should be clear from the very outset that the relationship between general evolutionary theory and empirical inquiry must take a stylised form. In the context of growth theory, Kaldor (1960) proposed the articulation of a set of preliminary 'stylised facts' which any framework/model should take into account as a minimum and try to clarify and explain.

In the case of EC's problems with IT there is probably not yet agreement about the basic characteristics of the situation. It is still more difficult to develop a consensus on the conceptual framework used to articulate the problems. We have, however, decided to speak in terms of international trade problems and give a few suggestions of how the evolutionary perspective may be applied in this context. The main reasons are first, that international trade often helps to sharpen (or even dramatise) problems which may seem unclear seen from within the EC and second, that the analysis of international economics has traditionally been somewhat more open to structural problems and structural change than economics in general.

12.4.1. IT as a Key Area of Growth and Innovation

First of all, we should as a first stylised fact note that IT is a key area in many respects, most simply and clearly in terms of its increasing share of overall demand and more specifically of demand for products produced abroad. In Table 12.1 we show the annual average growth rate of OECD's imports of IT products divided into seven commodity groups. Furthermore, they have been aggregated into two larger groups, IT-1 with computers etc. and IT-2 with telecom equipment etc.[4] Both larger groups show growth rates which are more than the double of the aggregate growth rate.

Table 12.1. **Annual Growth Rates of OECD Imports of IT Products (Value), Compared with the Ranking in EC's Export Specialisation**

	Growth of OECD Imports,	Ranking of EC's Revealed Comparative Advantage 1987 (Export Specialisation Figures)	
	1979–87	All Products	Medium and High Tech Products
Computers and peripherals (IT-1)	20.4	33	20
Semiconductors (IT-2)	13.4	39	24
Telecommunications equipment (IT-2)	13.0	36	22
Consumer electronics (IT-2)	12.6	41	25
Electrical instruments for measuring, controlling and medical purposes (IT-2)	12.3	28	15
Scientific instruments, photographic supplies, watches (IT-1)	9.1	32	19
Typewriters and office machines (IT-1)	6.2	27	14
All products	5.9		
IT-1	14.3		
IT-2	12.9		

Source: Nielsen et al., 1991, and the IKE Database described in chapter 10. The figures include intra-EC trade. Low tech products are primarily consisting of raw materials, metals, agricultural products, textiles, clothing and furniture. Medium and high tech products covers the rest of the commodities of the trade statistics.

Five of the IT commodity groups (including computers and telecom equipment) are placed at the very top of ranked growth rates (not shown here). The last two (scientific instruments etc. and typewriters etc.) have more moderate growth rates, but they really belong to the fringe of the IT sector and are partly included for historical reasons and traditions in the production of statistics.

The growth rate figures in Table 12.1 do not reflect the development of homogeneous product group. On the contrary, even at the level of the seven IT-groups the data reflect a wide range of IT applications. Furthermore, the 'fitness' of IT-products *vis-à-vis* other areas of imports implied by the data probably primarily reflects the large capability and propensity to innovate of the IT-industry.

12.4.2. EC's Weak Export Performance in IT Goods

The second stylised fact is that IT product groups play a modest role in EC's exports. This can be expressed in a great many ways. In Table 12.1 we have given the information in terms of ranked export specialisation figures (defined in chapter 11). Given certain assumptions these figures may be interpreted as revealing the comparative advantages and disadvantages of EC. In Table 12.1 it is made clear that EC does not show any comparative advantages in IT commodity groups. This holds even if low tech commodities are not taken into account. In both cases the IT commodities are placed near the very bottom of the ranked specialisation figures, which indicates a comparative disadvantage. In terms of conventional trade theory, this means that if free trade should

Table 12.2. Export/Import Ratios for the EC Seen as a Whole (Excl. Intra EC Trade)

	X/M-Ratios for EC-12, Excl. Intra-EC Trade			
	1965	1973	1979	1987
Computers and peripherals	1.3	0.6	0.5	0.4
Semiconductors	1.4	0.8	0.6	0.6
Telecommunications equipment	3.9	2.5	2.1	1.3
Consumer electronics	1.8	0.6	0.5	0.2
Scientific instruments, photographic supplies, watches	1.4	1.3	0.9	0.9
Electrical instruments for measuring, controlling and medical purposes	1.3	1.4	1.4	1.4
Typewriters and office machines	1.1	1.2	1.7	1.0
IT-1	1.3	1.0	0.8	0.6
IT-2	2.0	1.1	1.0	0.7

Source: Nielsen et al., 1991, and the IKE Database described in chapter 10.

become freer, then the EC should as a minimum expand production relatively slowly (*vis-à-vis* the trade partners) in weak areas and accelerate the growth in strong areas. This is actually what has happened during the last 25 years and this is partially reflected in the following tables. In relation to our theoretically defined *H*-industries it is important to emphasise that EC is not generally weak in high-tech industries. It has a clear strength in chemicals and even in some specialised IT-areas.

Even if IT goods are not strong areas of specialisation for the EC, they have become a more and more important element in both consumer's and producer's demand and there is no indication that EC citizens should be less interested than their trade partners in using increased real incomes and their real investment to get access to the new technology. On the contrary, in some areas demand seems even more advanced than in the US. If this third stylised fact (of relatively advanced demand) is combined with the weaker production performance, the result is that the balance of trade within the IT groups has become more and more negative. This is shown in Table 12.2 where we are considering the EC as a whole, i.e. we have removed the trade between the individual EC members (and expanded the EC-12 backwards in time). In this way we get an EC region which is comparable to, e.g. the US and Japan. The table shows sharply decreasing export/import ratios for most of the IT groups. The major exception is electrical instruments (and the small and atypical group of typewriters etc.). In the other areas, it has not been possible to uphold traditional positions of the times before the integrated circuit and the microelectronics revolution. However, it should be noted that the performance in telecommunications equipment is still relatively strong.

The relative weakness of the IT exports of the EC to the outside world may, of course, be interpreted in many ways. Earlier the problem was seen as one of strong fundamental science in several EC countries which was unfortunately not transformed into competitive positions because of a weak post-invention and post-innovation performance. This may still be so.

12.4.3. EC's Dominance of the Internal Market

A fourth stylised fact seems to be that the weakening of EC's relative position in IT trade has been much stronger on foreign market than with respect to intra-EC trade. This fact has to be confronted in order to avoid unclear interpretations of trade statistics and of the relative positions of the EC, the US and Japan.

The reason is, of course, that intra-EC trade constitute 24% of total OECD exports (see Table 12.3). Even if the general position of the EC has weakened,

Table 12.3. **Shares of Total OECD-Export of IT-Goods,1965–87, Incl. and Excl. of Intra-EC Trade**

Shares of OECD IT-Exports, Incl. Intra-EC Trade				
	1965	1973	1979	1987
EC-12	52.0	47.6	46.2	41.5
-export to EC12	22.0	24.9	24.2	23.7
United States	25.1	21.8	21.4	19.7
Japan	11.4	20.0	22.8	30.2
Rest E-OECD	9.0	8.2	7.3	6.2
Rest of OECD	2.5	2.4	2.3	2.4
Total OECD	100.0	100.0	100.0	100.0

Shares of OECD IT-Exports, Excl. Intra-EC Trade				
	1965	1973	1979	1987
EC-12	38.5	30.2	29.0	23.3
United States	32.1	29.0	28.2	25.9
Japan	14.5	26.6	30.1	39.6
Rest E-OECD	11.6	11.0	9.6	8.0
Rest of OECD	3.3	3.2	3.1	3.2
OECD excl intra	100.0	100.0	100.0	100.0

Source: Nielsen et al., 1991, and the IKE Database described in chapter 10.

this share has been surprisingly stable. But the reverse side of the coin is that the EC considered as a whole (i.e. without intra-EC trade) has seen a rapid weakening in relation to Japan while the US has performed much better. Once more, we should compare the data from the last 25 years with utmost care, since they try to span over the microelectronics revolution. However, in the last half of table 12.3 we see the relatively stable export shares of the US while there is a radical shift in the Japanese performance.

Today, Japan has its revealed comparative advantage in IT goods. Only consumer electronics is an old stronghold while most of the other IT goods have shown rapidly increasing specialisation figures. The result of this systematic build-up of positions of comparative advantage is that in 1987 we have IT commodities on the four first top positions on the list of Japans specialisation figures (cf. Nielsen et al., 1991). Typewriters and computers are number 7 and 8 while only electrical instruments are placed in the middle of the ranking of all the (42) commodity groups. In comparison, the US has three IT groups which are highly ranked (numbers 5, 6 and 7 on the list which also includes low tech products). But the EC has none.

***Table 12.4.* Shares of Patenting in the US in IT, Foreign Patents Granted, 1973–86**

	Foreign Patents Granted in the US		
	1973	1979	1986
	Digital Computers		
Total numbers of foreign patents	50	43	110
	– Percentage –		
EC-12	60	49	32
Japan	28	44	62
Rest E-OECD	2	0	3
Rest of OECD	8	2	1
Rest of World	2	5	2
Total	100	100	100
	Semiconductor Devices and Prod.		
Total numbers of foreign patents	364	323	678
	– Percentage –		
EC-12	51	46	29
Japan	38	46	68
Rest E-OECD	4	3	1
Rest of OECD	4	1	1
Rest of World	3	4	1
Total	100	100	100
	Telecommunications		
Total numbers of foreign patents	824	743	1861
	– Percentage –		
EC-12	53	47	35
Japan	32	42	55
Rest E-OECD	6	5	4
Rest of OECD	8	4	4
Rest of World	1	2	2
Total	100	100	100

Source: SPRU/MERIT Database, cf. Nielsen et al. ,1991.

12.4.4. EC's Weak Technological Performance in IT

A fifth and final stylised fact completes the picture, namely that EC's position in core areas of IT-technology development appears to be weakening. A somewhat problematic indicator of this weakened position is patenting activities which not only reflect inventive activities but also oligopolistic strategies for erecting barriers to entry in many areas. However, it may still be worthwhile to look at the patent data. In Table 12.4 we have compared the shares of the EC and Japan in the foreign patents granted in the US. The US itself has been left out due to different patenting strategies in domestic and foreign markets. The table shows clearly the fall in the EC share and the raise of Japanese positions.

12.4.5. Problems for Analysis

The stylised facts only show the top of the iceberg. But we think they reflect basic characteristics of what is going on beneath the surface. Other studies reveal much of the same picture even if it must be emphasised that EC is quite competitive in other high-tech areas (Patel and Pavitt, 1991).

The IT indicators represent a challenge which is not without policy relevance, not least because there is a need to evaluate the effects of different kinds of past and future policy initiatives, including technology programmes and the Single Market project. But in relation to the present chapter the supposed stylised facts first and foremost represent a huge array of problems which demand a further development of the tools of analysis for an evolutionary study of the effects of EC-integration.

In other words, we should try to subject the following phenomena to the above framework of evolutionary analysis: 1) The long-term trend of deterioration in the revealed comparative advantages of the EC in most IT goods. 2) The specialisation of the EC in commodity groups with less than average long-term growth, a phenomenon which may be partly induced by the integration process itself. 3) The pressures on the trade balance and possible growth restrictions created by demand being more advanced than supply. 4) The possible vicious circle of weakening extra-EC trade performance, stronger protection and weakening of technological performance. 5) The very long-run policy measures needed to change this evolutionary trend where it is still not clear whether the Single Market will remove or conserve the trend of a relative weakening of EC's IT sector.

Unfortunately, our data do not allow us to confront directly the problems of techno-economic paradigms, producer-user relationships and development blocks. However, through a combination of the stylised data with other kinds of information on EC's IT-sector we may nevertheless approach the issue at the centre of our analytical scheme.

To start on a positive note, we see that at least in some areas of IT-use (telecom, defence, software systems, etc.) the EC-countries have strong, partly publicly supported *S*-users with well-established linkages to producers. These linkages were originally developed within single countries but the relatively strong position of EC's IT-industry in the intra-EC trade (partly reflected in table 12.3) may to a large extent reflect a generalisation of such relationships to cover broader parts of the EC. The reason is probably primarily that EC's IT-firms have become specialists in close user-producer coordination, including the special styles of coordination prevailing in many European countries. Even in areas dominated by mass-produced electronics, EC-firms seem to have specialised in customised, user-near designs. Thus the firms have already overcome many intra-EC barriers to trade and actually changed these barriers to their own comparative advantage *vis-à-vis* Japanese and US firms. However, a simplification of the rule and behaviour system of the EC in relation to the Single Market project may remove some of these barriers and thus imply a relative weakening of the competitiveness of traditional European firms.

The possible bias of EC firms towards pre-paradigmatic types of user-producer interfaces is a mixed blessing in an IT industry facing rapid transformation and rapid expansion of actual and potential demand. This lower-than-average degree of commoditisation may be reflected in the sharp drop in export shares of extra-EC trade in IT goods (table 12.3) and the rapid increase in import penetration in the EC market in most IT groups (Table 12.2). The reason is, of course, that markets characterised by an above-average degree of standardisation have been expanding most during recent years. Furthermore, the IT-technology related to such areas is probably most radically changing so that a system of innovation geared to these areas will perform much better than the part of the IT-industries which is oriented towards customised solutions or, at least, less-than average degrees of standardisation of products. If the patenting data of table 12.4 reveal something about the technological strengths of the EC and Japan, the dramatic shift may be partly related to the different orientations of the respective systems of innovation.

12.5. Perspectives

Public opinion about national and European systems of innovation appears to be swinging much faster than the real phenomenon. After a period of strong build-up of systems of innovation in relation to IT, there was a strong sense of disillusion in the beginning of the 1980's in several European countries

('Eurosclerosis'). At the same time the challenge from Japan and the US was strongly felt. On this background ESPRIT and RACE were developed as large-scale R&D efforts at the EC level based on collaborative R&D between firms and institutions from two or more EC countries (cf. Brændgaard, 1988). The success of these programmes was important for the development of the project of the Single European Act and several related initiatives towards a European system of innovation ('Europhoria'). However, a shift in opinion occurred in 1990, when the weakness and even failures in the IT sector of the EC and the difficulties in many areas of techno-economic harmonisation and unification became apparent. What had earlier seemed to be a rapid catching up with Japan was now seen as a treadmill where the Japanese leader was learning and moving faster. Furthermore, the general trend towards trade liberalisation did not appear to be secured any more. So, the question appeared to be a long-term and difficult combination of national, European and global systems of innovation ('Eurorealism'?).

In this latest perspective, it is important that the evolutionary processes with relation to the IT sector take more time than short-term public discussions. Furthermore, evolution involves 'diversity and variety'[5], 'destructive creation' and 'creative destruction'. In such a context, the preservation of given industrial positions cannot be the goal and there is a need for patience *vis-à-vis* novelties. It is not least this patience with respect to policy and finance we find in the Japanese case (cf. chapters 5 and 8). In this perspective, politics and banking with 'instant response' might strangle innovation. But 'lagged response' may be a sign of 'decision-making sclerosis'. There are no simple answers to the question how one should manoeuvre in this version of Scylla and Charybdis.

In the present chapter we have indirectly argued that a continued debate about how the system of innovation within the EC is evolving is interesting and important. This is the background for a discussion of supranational systems of innovation with special emphasis on the innovative performance of the IT industries within the EC taken as a whole. In other words, we have used the analytical tools of the book in an analysis of the general relationship between integration and innovation and thus pointed to the question whether and in which way EC contains or is developing a single 'NSI'. In this way we stretch the concept of 'nation' even more than in the previous chapters and in the present context it might better be abandoned.

However, there are still an array of nation-like structures, E_1, E_2, ... ,Em, which are not likely to disappear and which may have important roles in different aspects of the evolutionary process. Of course, their policies may look like attempts to keep the fruits of the evolutionary process or specific development blocks within their own boundaries. But this is not a necessary consequence. Even if individual countries are trying to secure that 'their' firms will exploit possibilities of symbiosis, this does not mean that the broader process of evolution is only competitive or even less a zero-sum game. Furthermore, the local authorities and groups *within* these countries try to play the same game. And so on.

The conclusion of evolutionary thinking is thus not only the Schumpeterian dictum: 'never trust in aggregates'. The conclusion is rather: 'never trust in unchanging aggregates'. In some periods, we have seen a conspicuous build-up of national systems of innovation, in other periods emphasis is put on the build up of multinational or transnational or regional systems of innovation (cf. chapter 13). But underlying them all is a certain degree of unpredictability as to the course of the broad evolutionary process and lack of computability of the concrete development of the fitnesses of individual products. The evolutionary perspective may thus create humble policy-makers. But, as argued in chapter 14, evolutionary arguments against active policy making should not be taken to far, and there is a wide range of problems to be tackled even in an area as apparently homogeneous as the EC. The major problems of evolution are, however, neither related to the EC nor to its major competitors but in a very concrete sense to the rest of the world.

Chapter 13

NATIONAL SYSTEMS OF INNOVATION, FOREIGN DIRECT INVESTMENT AND THE OPERATIONS OF MULTINATIONAL ENTERPRISES

François Chesnais

13.1. Introduction

In this chapter, the analysis moves from the area of foreign trade to that of foreign direct investment (FDI). The purpose of the chapter is to discuss the ways in which the operations of multinational enterprises may have influenced the structure and organisation of national systems of innovation first during the previous, now 'classical' period of MNE expansion (1955–1975) and how they may be impacting on these systems today within the new phase, often referred to as 'globalisation', which began in the course of the 1980's.

The analytical approach adopted is historical. The underlying hypothesis is that as a result of capital accumulation, income growth and technological change, the substantive dimensions and the organisational forms of international production and the other operations of MNEs undergo over time significant and at some moments qualitative changes.

Along with some other factors, the same processes which offer new, enlarged opportunities for MNEs will have impacts on the economies and social institutions *largo sensu* of nation states. The level of inward and outward foreign direct investment (FDI) as well as the forms investment take and more generally the changes occurring in the operations of MNEs, represent one broad avenue through which such impacts occur. The overall context of the changes which have affected the economy of the nation state during the last decade is of course much wider: it includes *inter alia* the increasingly close interdependencies created by international trade, and more important still some key dimensions of financial globalisation, notably the truly global character of monetary markets and the world-wide impacts on the level of interest rates in dominant economies, along with their limiting effects on the autonomy of domestic macro-economic management in all other countries. During the 1980's, the relationship between national economies and globalisation was also strongly influenced by the political processes which led to the economic policies associated with 'Thatcherism', the net effect of which has been to dismantle many of the policy instruments used by governments to monitor economic, technological and social change.

13.1.1. The Differentiated Impacts of Trade and Investment

The term internationalisation has a generic content (see Chesnais, 1988a). It encompasses all the processes whereby previously fairly separate national economies have become increasingly interrelated and are now economically interdependent to an unprecedented degree. In this sense internationalisation is not simply the result of FDI and the establishment of international production controlled by MNEs, but also the consequence of international trade, transnational communication systems and the international flow of scientific and technological knowledge.

International trade has received infinitely more attention from economic theory and applied analysis than FDI and international production as organised by MNEs. Although the two processes have become more and more closely intertwined and are harder and harder to disentangle in their effects, it is worth attempting to point to some differences between them.

International trade theory postulates the existence of separate, clearly identifiable national economies (even if, as in the case of neo-classical theory, countries are only defined by their overall factor endowment). Trade can be viewed as pertaining to a logic of the extension of the productive forces and the full exploitation of the potentialities of an international division of labour. The logic is that of the 'Wealth of Nations' and Adam Smith's central proposition that the division of labour is dependent on 'the extent of the market'. Considered in isolation from the process of concentration and centralisation of capital and the formation of very large firms, this logic points to processes such as the growth in international trade, the increasing complexity of patterns of international trade specialisation, arm's length trade in technology, and the constitution of a common pool of scientific knowledge at the international level open to all those with the level of competence required to understand it. All these processes undeniably call for the adjustment of domestic industrial structures and inter-industry patterns, but do not imply per se a serious reduction in the cohesion of national productive systems.

In contrast with trade created internationalisation, multinationalisation pertains to the accumulation, centralisation and deployment of capital across national borders within large corporations and to the formation of transnationalised internal corporate markets organised within the structure of large multinational firms and banks operating in a number of countries. One moves from the logic of the Wealth of Nations to that of the chapters on the concentration and centralisation of capital of Marx's theory of long-term capital accumulation. Once capital becomes centralised within large profit-making centres, a number of consequences will follow. In particular, the subsequent deployment of this capital will be commanded by strictly defined criteria of profitable value creation and/or rent-based value appropriation and so to the conditions (both geographically and activity-wise) which appear to fit this requirement best at any given moment. The MNE examines the allocation of productive and R&D resources between the different countries where it operates and the type of operations assigned to each plant or laboratory from its own centralised viewpoint and strategy (Michalet, 1985).

The growth of strongly concentrated capital has its own internal logic which *combines* the search for industrial *profit* through industrial production, the reaping of *rent* from corporate assets in various forms including technology and numerous forms of speculative gains and interest earning operations associated with concentrated money capital, and the high premium place on the mobility of operations leading to constant reviewing of the possibilities of modifying industry specific and location specific involvements. Highly concentrated capital possesses a capacity not open to smaller firms for reaping 'appropriable rents' or 'quasi rents' exerting numerous forms of monopolistic and monopsonic market power and exploiting situations where, as Dunning (1981) puts it, the deliberate organisation of 'market failure' and the extension of 'internalisation' has to be seen as 'a powerful motive for takeovers or mergers and a valuable tool in the strategy of oligopolists'. Once it consolidates its international operations, the MNE acquires what Dunning defines as the specific ownership advantage stemming from 'the ability to organise related productive activities more efficiently than the market' (Dunning, 1988a, 11).

13.1.2. National Systems and Structural Competitiveness

The notion of 'structural competitiveness' (see Chesnais, 1986, for a full discussion) is a convenient way of expressing the fact that, while the competitiveness of firms will obviously reflect successful management practices by entrepreneurs or corporate executives, their competitiveness will also stem from economy-specific long-term trends in the strength and efficiency of a national economy's productive structure, its technical infrastructure and other factors determining the externalities on which firms can build. Early fairly well researched aspects of economic structure which were relevant to the 'structural competitiveness' of countries included the size and sophistication of domestic markets, the related 'internal market' hypothesis developed by Mistral and discussed by Fagerberg in chapter 11, the structure of domestic production relationships between the different sectors and industries (as captured in part through input-output analysis) and the size distribution and market power of supplier firms.

Newer aspects on which analytical progress was made during the 1980's include the characteristics and size distribution of buyers, the quality of interfirm user/producer relationships (Lundvall, 1988 and 1991), and the efficiency of non-market relations between firms and production units (integration, quasi-integration and the numerous modes of organisation among firms which have developed with and in complement to the market). The important role played by generic technologies implies likewise that the competitiveness of most industrial sectors and a large part of the service sector now depends on the extent to which inter-industrial and inter-sectoral transfers of technology occur, and on the extent to which technological opportunities, created by R&D undertaken in specific parts of the economy, lead to innovations and increased competitiveness by firms in other parts of the system. These different forms of interconnection and interactivity are strongly facilitated when technology-related institutional learning processes (see chapters 1 and 2) rest on sound foundations.

13.1.3. The Main Issue

Collectively firms and institutions, along with the linkages they have built, represent the foundation upon which the complex 'learning processes' analysed in the first chapters of this book are built. These learning processes are inherently social processes which can only take place on the basis of interactive processes occurring within organisations and through co-ordination and co-operation among them (Hollingsworth, 1990, Ferguson, 1991). In a production and linkage approach, national systems of innovation exist to the extent that economic and institutional developments of an evolutionary type, aided in some cases by conscious institutional building by public and private agents, have led to the emergence of an identifiable set of linkages and feedback relationships tying together the numerous profit and non-profit institutions and organisations which concur to technological innovation in ways which lead to positive direct and indirect effects on the competitive process.

The inclusion in this book of a chapter on globalisation is a response to a major concern or question which probably encompasses two related but nonetheless distinct hypotheses. The first is that the process of globalisation may be weakening or indeed severely impairing the overall capacity and political willpower of governments to continue enhancing many of the institutions supporting innovation at the national level as well as to go on ensuring the cohesion of domestic competitive environments. The second is that within this process, some of the operations of MNEs, notably their investment and disinvestment decisions, the steps that they take following the take-over of domestic firms, and their strategies regarding the location of R&D, production and other activities affecting innovation and learning, may be having identifiable impacts on some specific component elements of NSI (in particular those embedded in domestic firms, notably the smaller ones). This chapter has sought to collect and discuss data and analytical material mainly aimed at addressing the second hypothesis. However, the broader macro-social and macro-economic processes now being experienced by nation states, notably in Europe represent the setting of the analysis.

One major difficulty in this discussion is that the economies of nation-states are separated by qualitative differences (in some cases really huge ones) with respect to the size of their population, natural resources, built up industrial capacity, financial wealth and of course their scientific and technical capacities. Genuine 'small country' specificities and problems exist (Walsh, 1987, O'Doherty, 1990), even if economic and technological change is continually modifying the cut-off points between the 'small' and the 'large countries'. Through a long history, countries have also established very different relations to the world economy. The United Kingdom and the Netherlands for instance have experienced a multisecular process of internationalisation which other countries have only started to follow over the last thirty years. Finally, one should not forget what neo-classical liberal economists seek to hide, namely that the world economy is structured hierarchically through a whole set of economic, financial and political processes and institutions. This implies that it is in fact very difficult to talk in a general manner about national systems of innovation in relation to globalisation: every situation has its particularities; country-specific analyses must complete what is said here.

13.2. MNEs Technological Transfer and Domestic R&D Capacity: The Evidence from the 1960–75 Period

Much of the available knowledge concerning the effects of MNEs on the industrial R&D component of national systems of innovation results from work carried out in the 1970's and is certainly prior to the onset of 'globalisation' with its specific characteristics. It tends to reflect the features of the internationalisation process during the 1955–75 period of 'classical multinationalisation'. However, some forms of organisation, in particular the world or regional product mandate subsidiary and the internationally integrated laboratory, are now basic MNE institutions (see sections 13.5 and 13.6).

13.2.1. MNEs in the Period of Classical Multinationalisation

'Classical multinationalisation' corresponds to the phase during which international trade still grew faster that FDI and so seemed, in appearance at least, to remain the strongest driving force behind the overall movement of internationalisation. During this period furthermore, FDI was still guided to some significant extent by considerations related to the characteristics of host economies, what Dunning's eclectic theory calls their 'location advantages'. These include 1) the possession of particular immobile natural resources (mining and agriculture), 2) availability of given types of labour and attractive labour costs, 3) markets marked by some degree of protection and national specificity, and 4) external economies to firms stemming from product specialisation and concentration of production in certain production sites. Up to the beginning of the 1980's, government policies could effectively act to increase some of these locational advantages, for instance by increasing the incentives and/or constraints on firms to resort to FDI. The use of import substitution policies aimed at making FDI more attractive than exports as a way of supplying domestic markets was not confined to Latin America. These policies were also practiced in Europe, in a variety of ways, at a smaller scale and with wider and more uniformly positive effects, since trade liberalisation was taking place at the same time (notably after the signature of the Rome Treaty), thus increasing the degree of domestic competition.

As far as intra-OECD relationships were concerned, the international pattern of FDI during this period was dominated by very strong flows of outward US investment directed towards productive activities in particular manufacturing, coupled with smaller investment flows within Europe both inside and outside the Common Market. European investment into the US only began to be significant at the end of the period. Japanese FDI in the US and Europe was very small. At a time when the US technological lead was still very strong, but many technologies becoming rapidly mature thus leading to product life cycle driven FDI (Vernon, 1966) and at a time when US outward investment was also largely an international extension of US domestic oligopolistic competition, US firms were content in establishing international production on a 'multidomestic' basis and adapting their operations to the characteristics of host economies. While this was not the case in other continents, in northern and western Europe US investment remained on the whole fairly respectful of national economic sovereignties. It did not impair the cohesion of national production structures nor the capacity of host economies to accumulate either capital or technological skills. In many cases, it had beneficial effects: the arrival of US firms forced the pace of domestic industrial restructuring; their presence reduced the level of monopoly in domestic markets and represented a spur to adopt more efficient techniques and forms of production.

13.2.2. Traditional Distinctions between Subsidiaries and Laboratories

An examination of the available evidence (from Cordell, 1971, Ronstadt, 1977, to Pearce, 1989) shows that during the 1955–75 period, MNEs generally established in host countries two only very partially inter-related sets of affiliated organisations and so of intra-group linkages. MNEs invariably set up manufacturing subsidiaries. To a much lesser extent, they established specialised affiliates devoted to R&D and innovative or adaptive technological activities.

Most authors identified *three forms of manufacturing subsidiaries* – 'replica' subsidiaries, rationalised product subsidiaries and world product mandate subsidiaries – and *three forms of affiliate laboratories* – support laboratories, locally integrated laboratories and independent internationally integrated laboratories (IIL's). *Support* laboratories tended to be set up and owned by subsidiaries of the *replica type*, but this does not imply that all such subsidiaries would have a support laboratory. Two quite distinct sets of internal corporate relationships usually coexisted within MNEs. One was managed by the International Division; the other by the Director for Corporate R&D or the head of the largest corporate laboratory situated in the vicinity of headquarters.

13.2.3. MNEs and the Transfer of Technology

To make sense, transfer of technology implies the transfer to the recipient not only of the technical knowledge needed to produce the products, but also of the capacity to master conceptually, develop and later produce autonomously, the technology lying behind these products. For firms which own it, this asset is the outcome of costly investments and complex firm-specific assimilation processes. It represents an important specific ownership advantage which the firm normally seeks to appropriate (e.g. keep for itself) as long as it can. This is why firms have inevitably always tended to fix limits on their transfer of technology, to develop complex policies regarding this transfer and to examine closely the conditions within which it takes place.

During the 1955–75 period the product life cycle approach dominated corporate policies for the transfer of technology. It was only once extensive imitation had occurred in the firm's home market that MNEs would be ready to release the technology to foreign firms. Even then the terms on which they were prepared to do so varied significantly according to the bargaining power of firms and host countries. Case studies carried out in Latin America (Vaitsos, 1974) and in the less industrialised OECD countries including Ireland, Portugal and the Mediterranean countries (De Bresson, 1976) showed that when the bargaining power of recipients was weak, the inclusion of export restriction clauses and tie in clauses on purchases tended to be the rule. One of the most frequent clauses encountered in contracts of technology commercialisation was that of export prohibition.

This pattern was observable not only for 'arm's length' operations involving the sale of patents or the licensing of technology, but also for the technology supplied by a parent company to its subsidiary. This technology tended to be tailored to the tasks a subsidiary had been assigned and the particular market it was intended to serve. Since US, UK, German and Swiss data (see Vickery (1986) for a full review) shows that 75% or more of the technology transferred abroad by MNE parent companies during the 1960's and 1970's, as recorded by official balance of payment data, was sold or provided to subsidiaries, the nature of these subsidiaries and their operations must be recalled.

13.2.4. Manufacturing Subsidiaries and Technological Accumulation

FDI can foster technological accumulation, in particular as a consequence of the gradual learning and establishment of local skills and routines which this investment (like all others) entailed. Learning is inherently cumulative, since the capacity for learning depends on the complexity of what is already known. Technology is created and installed in production methods through learning by doing and learning by using, building on what has already been achieved. The extent to which these processes take place depends however on the exact form of subsidiary set up.

The first kind of subsidiary set up by MNEs has always represented in its operations and structure a sort of 'down-scaled replica' of the parent company. It manufactures roughly the same range of products as the parent. Its organisation is also modelled on that of the parent company. The 'replica' subsidiary produces mainly for the local market of the country in which it is established. Criticism of the 'replica' subsidiary has often focused on the lack of innovative capability in such units: the subsidiary produces a product which is already well established within the MNE, with perhaps small amounts of product and process adaptation to the extent deemed necessary. Work on the East Asian and Latin American NIC's has shown that some 'learning by doing' and 'learning to learn' does take place and can be consolidated by domestic policies. Work done at OECD and in many of the UN agencies during the 1970's also showed that technological accumulation was determined by the nature and intensity of the relationships with the host domestic industrial structure: as a result, the scale and scope of local sourcing of industrial components came to be viewed as a significant proxy for the spill over or effective transfer of technology to the host country industry.

The second type of subsidiary has been the '*rationalised subsidiary*'. This type emerged in the late 1960's as MNEs began to establish rather more systematic approaches to their international involvement and development strategies aimed at creating rationalised operations, with individual national subsidiaries fulfilling a specialised role in a broadly defined international strategy. Increasingly an individual subsidiary produced only a limited part of the MNEs product line, possibly not even a part relevant to the demand of the country in which it was located. The aim sought by corporate management is to achieve efficient production, by making optimum use of the distinctive productive capabilities of different locations accessible to the MNE. In some cases, the technological dependence of a 'rationalised product' subsidiary on the parent corporation can be even greater than that of a replica subsidiary.

A third form of subsidiary is '*world product mandate subsidiaries*'. This type of subsidiary will be born out of

> ...*an agreement between a multinational enterprise's parent company and one of its subsidiaries to grant the subsidiary exclusive rights to produce and market a product and, if circumstances warrant, to pursue the necessary research and development activity. As a result of such agreements, the firm generally acquires greater managerial autonomy because it has in fact become the international centre for a product.* (Bonin and Perron, 1986).

The expression 'world product mandate' can be viewed as having a generic context, and be applicable to subsidiaries with exclusive rights for one or several products in large regional markets (e.g. North America or Europe).

13.2.5. The Organisation of R&D by MNEs: Centralised and Decentralised Activities

The third way in which MNEs could be seen to be contributing at least potentially to the strengthening of national systems was by building R&D capacity in host countries and contributing to the training of host country scientific and technical personnel. The data published by the US Department of Commerce from the mid-1960's until the early 1980's (see Table 13.1) shows that a slow but nonetheless regular growth occurred in the share of corporate R&D carried out by US MNEs in foreign locations. It also points to strong differences from one industry to another.

The case studies carried out from the late 1960's (see Cordell, 1971, Ronstradt, 1977, Berhman and Fischer, 1980, Pearce, 1989) onwards yielded useful insights into the way MNEs (Michalet, 1985) organised their R&D at group level. The most general pattern shows a high degree of centralisation of R&D with the corporate management at the MNE headquarters and the location of the most strategic work in the home country of the parent corporation. US surveys showed that US MNEs did carry out some R&D abroad, but that decision-making, organisation and control of R&D and innovation tended in almost all cases to be strongly centralised under the direct

Table 13.1. **The Share of the R&D Expenditure of US Multinational Corporations Located Abroad, Organised by Industrial Group of Parent Company, 1966–82 (Percentage)**[A]

	1966	1977	1982
1. Food products	11.69	15.20	18.22
2. Chemicals nes	4.88	9.56	8.13
3. Pharmaceuticals	7.62	15.72	15.32
4. Metals	3.11	4.26	4.00
5. Mechanical engineering	13.51	7.56	6.25
6. Electrical equipment	5.37	3.38	3.30
7. Office equipment	6.98	4.09	4.68
8. Motor vehicles			
9. Aircraft	5.02	10.07[B]	13.04
10. Other transport equipment			
11. Textiles and wood products	_[C]	5.26	3.66
12. Rubber and plastic products	3.05	17.49	9.47
13. Non-metallic mineral products	3.74	7.69	8.81
14. Coal and petroleum products	N.A.	12.75	11.22
15. Professional and scientific instruments	5.34	9.80	10.97
16. Other manufacturing	6.15	11.03	4.43
Total	6.47	8.77	9.00

A. In 1977 and 1982 expenditure on R & D for the company in question, including that locally subcontracted out by parents or affiliates.

B. In 1977 the proportions were 13.71% for motor vehicles, and 2.62% for aircraft and other transport equipment.

C. The Tarif Commission notes that the proportion of R & D attributed to foreign locations in textiles and wood products in 1966 (e.g. 53%) appears to be dramatically overstated probably due to a misallocation between industries.

Source: US Tariff Commission, Report on the Implications of Multinational Firms for World Trade and for US Trade and Labor, Washington DC, February 1973: US Department of Commerce, Direct Investment Abroad, 1977, Washington DC, April 1981, US Department of Commerce, Direct Investment Abroad:1982 Benchmark Survey Data, Washington DC, December 1985.

control of the parent company's senior management. This was coupled with a clear-cut tendency for the most vital and important part of R&D to be carried out in laboratories located in the home country. Some of the reasons behind this marked tendency towards the location of R&D in the United States were identified in a 1970 report by the NICB (National Industrial Conference Board), based on interviews with the management of American firms. The great majority of firms perceived their R&D activities as aimed primarily at the US market; they considered R&D to be more efficient when scientists were grouped together and communication easy; the problem of co-ordinating programmes became increasingly complex with distance while the cost of duplicating R&D was very high. One further, quite decisive reason US firms had (and still have) for locating their principal R&D facilities at home was that the United States was (and still is) the most advanced science base in the world. Despite the caveats surrounding patent data as indicators for the internationalisation of R&D, these data are correct in showing that with the exception of Japanese firms, US MNEs have delocated their R&D much less than others (see section 13.6).

The rule of centralisation suffered some partial exceptions. MNEs based in home countries with weaker science bases, but also a few US MNEs which were early in developing strategies for getting foot-holds in the most sophisticated markets, broke the dominant pattern in the late 1960's and began to set up or transfer a part of their core corporate R&D to a foreign site possessing strong locational advantages in R&D, trained personnel and/or sophisticated markets. The most frequent exceptions concerned MNEs from some of the smaller home countries of MNEs (Sweden, Netherlands, Switzerland) or those with a weak science base (Canada). Summarising the results of surveys made in Canada in the early 1970's, A.J. Cordell found that many Canadian MNEs had transferred their main R&D activities to the United States. Among the reasons advanced by Canadian executives, many mentioned the necessity of being close to major customers. This was required by the complementary nature of the Canadian subsidiary's product and some other manufactured by an American firm. Cordell considered this situation relevant to many smaller industrialised countries:

When a company in a relatively smaller country expands its international operations into a significantly larger market it finds, over time, that it pays to locate not only production but support and managerial functions including R&D in the larger offshore market area.

The numerous reasons why MNE from large countries with strong science bases might decide to establish R&D facilities abroad explain why from

Cordell onwards the literature recognised three types of foreign laboratory: Case studies made at OECD in the late 1970 illustrate the choices made by MNEs in different industries.

13.2.6. Support Laboratories in the Food Processing Industries

Support laboratories generally corresponded to 'replica' subsidiaries but were also met in some rationalised subsidiaries. In replica subsidiaries *support laboratories* had two main tasks. In the case of process technology the main job of local technicians was to scale down the technology of the parent company and adapt it to the subsidiary's smaller market. The task was one of adapting manufacturing processes. Even if the work of adaptation often calls for much ingenuity, case studies found the creative function of the support laboratory generally to be very limited. With respect to product technology, development activities were aimed at adapting the product to the tastes and conditions of the host country.

In the course of the case study work carried out at OECD, the food processing industry (OECD, 1979) confirmed the validity of this assessment regarding the R&D work of foreign laboratories. Food processing is one of the industries where the share of foreign located R&D as a percentage of total corporate R&D has always been high (see Table 13.1). The study found that basic research and most significant applied R&D, whether on raw material inputs to production, production processes or end products for the consumer, was conducted almost entirely within the central laboratories situated in the MNEs home country.

There were other less expected findings about engineering skills. In food processing, the technological characteristics of production are such that the design of plant and specialised equipment by company engineering departments represent a very significant component of scientific and technological capacity, often as important as R&D *stricto sensu*. It might be expected that these functions would become decentralised relatively quickly, because of the need to adapt processing, packaging and product presentation to local conditions. The OECD case study showed that this was not in fact the case. Engineering was decentralised only where the scale of investment by an affiliate was so high as to require an autonomous engineering capacity. When this was not the case, parent companies were found to resist decentralisation, and act directly or indirectly as the sole suppliers of technical facilities and equipment to their subsidiaries. In some cases, the parent firm itself was the exclusive manufacturer of some of the equipment used by its different subsidiaries. In other cases, it was recognised preferable to conduct overall negotiations with suppliers for the equipment required by all its subsidiaries. In both cases the centralisation of engineering functions ensured a high degree of standardisation of plant used by MNE production units throughout the world.

13.2.7. Internationally Interdependent Laboratories in the Computer Industry

Internationally interdependent laboratories (IIL's) differ from support laboratories in a number of important respects. An IIL carries out R&D projects decided by the group's corporate R&D management in the framework of activities which will involve R&D units in a wide range of locations. Its work is guided by directives from a central coordinating unit (probably, though not inevitably, the parent) to which results will be channelled for evaluation and assimilation with the results obtained through complementary work elsewhere. IIL's were first set up in the 1960's, but remained for many years somewhat exceptional. Today they are the form of foreign laboratory most frequently met. They are generally acquired through a merger or acquisition or (more rarely) set up through new investment, in order to do real R&D as distinct from adaptation down scaling or trouble-shooting and establish real interactions with the local science system. They become part of a specific intra-group network linked to the corporation's main R&D laboratory and managed by corporate headquarters. While IIL's were generally encountered in R&D-intensive industries rather than in other sectors, the choice to set up such laboratories was found to be very much a firm-specific decision which differed significantly from one MNE to another.

In the case of computers and data-processing, the study made by Michalet and Delapierre (1977) found that at the time IBM had pushed the organisation of world-based R&D further than any other group. Few laboratories within the IBM group were engaged competitively or simultaneously in research, and then only in the exploratory stage, before any heavy development expenses were involved. Their work was organised so as to maximise complementarities. At the end of the 1970's, IBM had three laboratories performing fundamental research, two in the United States and one in Switzerland. Development tasks were distributed on a world basis among all the other laboratories, i.e. fourteen major laboratories in the United States and eight in other countries. IBM's laboratories were financed by the corporation's overall research fund which was financed at the time by the royalties paid by manufacturing subsidiaries. When a laboratory was assigned a task for the whole group it became responsible for the product it develops. This meant that together with the production engineers of the manufacturing unit (or units) for that product, it became responsible for the starting up process and for achieving quality standards at industrial level.

13.2.8. The Wide Range of International R&D in Pharmaceuticals

Pharmaceuticals has long been one of the industries characterised by a fairly high level of delocated R&D. The OECD study carried out by M. Burstall, J.H. Dunning and A. Lake (1980) observed a wide range of situations marked by the coexistence of internationally interdependent laboratories and support laboratories, as well as by several quite different firm specific approaches to the role given to the former. A survey carried out by the authors with 31 MNEs showed that while 14 firms still relied only on the research carried out in the home country, 17 possessed another large laboratory in another OECD country. However, only three companies had a co-equal – or nearly co-equal centre outside the parent country. The US, the UK and Germany were the favourite locations; Italy, France and Japan less frequent while the smaller developed countries attracted little attention. The choice of a second country for serious research activity was made on the criteria that the nation should be politically stable, have a large and flourishing scientific community and a record of successful innovation. Less critically, it would be expected to offer the full range of ancillary services necessary for successful R&D and should as far as possible be culturally compatible with the parent country. India was the only developing country in which multinational companies had at that time substantial research activities.

13.3. A Summing up of the 1955–75 Findings and the Transition Towards the New Phase

The conclusions which can be drawn from the findings of the studies we have just examined are somewhat different in the case of formal R&D capacity building and in that of strengthening host national systems of innovation through investment and related technology transfers.

13.3.1. MNEs and the Building of R&D Capacity

The most complete overall assessment is probably the one made by Pearce (1989) on the basis of his wide review of the available case study material. The assessment is fairly pessimistic. In the case of *replica subsidiaries* and their *support laboratories*, Pearce considers that there is little scope for the local R&D staff to gain much knowledge of the wider creative process in a manner likely to significantly enhance the overall domestic R&D capability.

Locally integrated laboratories provide manufacturing subsidiaries with an increased degree of product autonomy. They may also provide the basis for the development of a technical capability of increasing scope. Its R&D projects will probably remain constrained to the development of new products (and/or productive techniques) from the MNEs existing stock of basic knowledge and expertise. To delve effectively into this reservoir the personnel from the LIL will need to establish fairly close contacts with personnel from the MNEs more centralised basic research units. This contact is likely to benefit the personnel of the LIL by enhancing their experience of the more complete R&D/innovation process, this in turn increasing their potential ability to stimulate a more dynamic technical environment in the subsidiary and the host country.

With respect to the work done in *internationally interdependent laboratories*, Pearce suggests that it will almost certainly be of a more basic scientific nature than that of support laboratories, and will certainly be part of a programme whose aims are more fundamentally innovative than those decided by a replica subsidiary and its support laboratory. This does not mean however that it will inevitably provide substantial benefits to its host country. Pearce considers that the available data points to the existence of high opportunity costs for host countries' scientific resources, in particular skilled manpower.

The OECD case studies confirmed this assessment generally with the additional insight that since MNEs adapt the scale and type of R&D investment to host countries technological capacities as they exist prior to their arrival, they may in fact trigger off cumulative processes with 'virtuous' but also with 'vicious' technology accumulation characteristics. This emerged particularly clearly in pharmaceuticals. The Burstall et al. (1980) study identified three categories of countries in respect to the nature of national scientific and technological capacity as shaped by public and private R&D and enterprise embedded technological and marketing capabilities. The study concluded that the impact of MNE investments were different in each case.

In the case of countries with a high technological capacity the effect of the international allocation of R&D by MNEs was to strengthen this capacity and consolidate their position.

In countries with a medium capacity the assessment was less clear-cut. Since foreign affiliates had a high proportion of the domestic market in most such nations, the financial position of the indigenous firms was weakened thus increasing their exposure to take-overs. Conversely the best firms could be stimulated to meet the challenge successfully and increase their capacity for innovation. When take-overs occurred in such countries, they could be followed by the progressive down-grading of R&D activities in the affiliate and their transfer out of the country (this occurred in Italy when Lepetit was taken over). The low capacity countries were the ones where MNEs limited themselves to R&D activities of a supporting nature and to product development for the local market.

13.3.2. Investment and Technology Transfer
in a Dynamic Perspective

Many of the conclusions regarding formal R&D stem from the ability of firms to maintain a strong degree of centralisation over their R&D function. The situation is different with respect to some of the broader dimensions of FDI and the accompanying transfer of technology and their effect on host systems of innovation. Here the quality of indigenous industrial and technological activities in host countries and the strength and innovative ability of domestic firms represent key variables which modify both the content of MNE decisions regarding the quality of the technology transferred, the terms offered in agreements as well as the capacity of host countries to make the best advantage of the presence of foreign firms.

One of the most widely accepted conclusions of studies on the transfer of technology is that the extent and quality of the transfer process depends heavily on the absorptive capacity and structural characteristics of the recipient economy which are an outcome of the growth and technological accumulation which has taken place prior to the arrival of the MNE. These structural characteristics are inherently the outcome of dynamic processes, but in turn they affect the content of foreign corporate decisions. As catching up occurs, it becomes both harder and less rational for MNEs to impose ties in clauses for equipment and intermediate products and easier for host countries (both firms and governments) to negotiate local sourcing. Industrial and technological linkages will start to develop.

13.3.3. Catching up and Technology Sharing in the 1970's

During the first half of the 1970's there was increasing evidence that genuine technology sharing agreements began to be established between US corporations and a number of foreign firms and/or governments. Extensive case study material gathered and analysed by an acute US observer (Baranson, 1978) for a number of high or medium technology sectors industries (computers, aircraft, consumer electronics and cars) concluded that by the mid-1970's the earlier strict product life cycle strategy for managing technological assets on the part of US MNEs had given way to technology sharing through joint ventures and complex licensing agreements.

The new approach to world marketing and production implicit in these new technology-sharing arrangements between US corporations and non-controlled foreign enterprises did not occur suddenly nor in response to an isolated event. It was the result of progressing modifications in the world economy that forced US MNEs to change viewpoints about foreign involvements as well as altering the relative bargaining position of technology purchasers. The factors shaping these changes, identified by Baranson at the time, included the intensified political risks and economic uncertainties of overseas capital investments in plant and equipment in the mid-1970's, the shifting emphasis in certain US firms from production to marketing and R&D functions, the intensified competition experienced by US firm from foreign enterprises as suppliers of industrial technology and the consequent compulsion for them to release proprietary technology early in the product cycle, and the escalation of R&D and capital investment costs connected with the proliferation of world involvements and the ever-increasing sophistication of product systems.

The last point indicates one of the factors which was subsequently to become a driving force behind the establishment of R&D consortia and interfirm technological alliances (Chesnais, 1988b, Mytelka, 1991). The other points all have to do with the progressive exhaustion of the technological trajectories which had carried the post war boom as well as with the collapse in the second half of the 1970's and the early 1980's of the previous régime of US dominated international oligopoly. They characterise what is basically a transition period leading to the subsequent phase of truly international or world oligopoly predicted by Hymer in one of his last essays (Hymer and Rowthorn, 1970).

13.4. Some Distinctive Features of Globalisation

Globalisation is essentially a term coined by journalists and politicians. It has been thrust on academic community. Some economists have rejected it, characterising it simply as a catchword (which is partly true of course). Others have attempted to give the term some scientific meaning (see OECD, 1992, chapter 10). Here we shall argue that the term refers to two related processes. The first concerns some important changes in the organisation, scope and effects of international production, technology sourcing and marketing by MNEs. The second concerns the loss by an increasing number of OECD countries (probably all save Japan, Germany and the US) of many of their attributes of economic sovereignty. It is hard to date very precisely the moment at which these two parallel and partially related processes reached full maturity, but by the late 1980's all the elements which concur in making 'globalisation' a new phase had emerged.

Globalisation is marked by a change in the ranking of the factors creating interdependencies. Today, FDI in manufacturing and services is driving internationalisation more strongly than trade and is determining international location patterns for the production and exchange of goods and services

Figure 13.1. Trends in Foreign Direct Investment (FDI), Gross Domestic Product (GDP), Trade and Gross Fixed Capital Formation (GFCF) in the OECD Area, Current Prices.

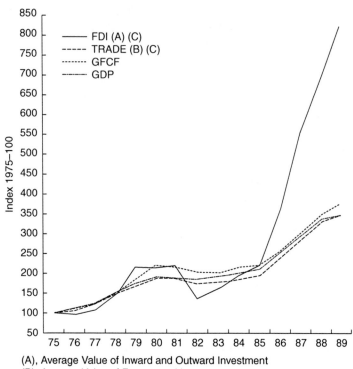

(A), Average Value of Inward and Outward Investment
(B), Average Value of Exports and Imports
(C), Includes Intra–OECD

Source: OECD.

(see Figure13.1). With respect to MNEs, globalisation refers to a set of emerging conditions in which value and wealth are increasingly being produced and distributed within 'networks firms' (see below) world-wide intra-corporate networks. Since the transition from internationalisation to globalisation has gone hand in hand with a process of global concentration in most key industries in manufacturing and services, the prevailing form of supply structure is world oligopoly.

With respect to countries, globalisation is marked by a loss of sovereignty in the area of macroeconomic policy (with the notable exceptions mentioned above), in particular their almost total subordination to levels of interest rates fixed independently of their own requirements or situation. It is also marked by a need to attract FDI, but also simultaneously by important changes in the 'location advantages' which countries can offer MNEs. More generally, it is marked by a significant weakening of the capacity of individual governments to strike 'hard bargains' with MNEs. Today countries are competing to attract and even to keep MNEs (including their own) in conditions where, in terms of industrial employment, the level of industrial competence and the cohesion of industrial structures the outcome of this competition is not a 'zero sum' one, but entails the existence of winners and losers.

The overall effect of the technological changes of the last twenty years has been to modify even further than during the previous period the foundations of what neo-classical theory calls 'endowments', but which can only be properly defined as 'man made competitive advantages', which take the form of socially determined locational advantages, shaped by investment, education, and technological capacity. In the phase of classical multinationalisation, access to large and/or high-income markets, still partially protected by trade barriers, occupied a major place in the strategies of MNEs within the OECD area. Now the emphasis within the OECD area is increasingly on the supply-side features of countries, in particular their potential for science based types of technological development on which MNEs can build. Today, the yard stick for measuring locational advantages of a country will be relative to knowledge-intensiveness, the capacity to participate actively in the production of technology and the possession of agglomeration economies which bring together the complementary assets (Teece, 1986) needed for successful innovation, production and marketing in the 'variety intensive production regime' (Willinger and Zuscovith, 1988).

The technological basis for the shift to *global* as distinct from multidomestic strategies is provided by telematics and the facilities it offers MNEs for establishing world-based intra-corporate IT networks. The new management and control procedures authorise a qualitative increase in the capacity to move specialised productive assets across national frontiers. Globalisation corresponds to a qualitative step in the opportunity offered to large and very large firms to distribute their R&D, manufacturing and marketing facilities world-wide in a number of different national locations, to source key technological and intermediate product inputs internationally and to manage their value and profit creating activities on a global basis.

The advent of a new type of transnational firm, the 'network firm' (Antonelli, 1988, Imai and Baba, 1991) is the organisational expression of a number of these changes. The adoption of new forms of corporate organisation has been hastened by Japanese competition and the demonstration provided by the Japanese Keiretsu that a new approach could be taken to the management and control of manufacturing production with the extensive use of subcontracting and 'just-in-time' delivery. The need for corporations to 'internalise externalities' (Chesnais, 1990) through a wide variety of non-equity interfirm relationships and contractual agreements rather than through classical vertical integration, is also the expression of the need to pool R&D resources and obtain complementary technical assets through external sourcing and co-operation.

Antonelli has shown how network firms are built on a wide range of corporate instruments which resort in a *complementary manner* to the specific

> ...*dynamics of economies of scale and economies of scope, selectively internalized by means of administrative coordination and 'electronic quasi-integration' which is increasingly based on telematics.*

Thus the network firm does not represent a total break with hierarchies (Coase, 1937, Williamson, 1975), but essentially a complementary way, albeit an important one, of organising and managing decentralised but nonetheless strongly hierarchically-controlled value chains. A proof of the very great strength hierarchies still have is, of course, the importance of FDI (UNCTC, 1991).

13.5. National Production Systems in the Context of Global Industries

One dimension of 'globalisation' understood as a process which concerns both firms and countries, is the shift from the earlier situation where the operations of MNE went hand in hand with the existence of 'multidomestic industries' to a new situation where 'global industries' have emerged. In Porter's definition, a global industry

> ...*is an industry in which a firm's competitive position in one country is significantly affected by its position in other countries or vice versa. Therefore, the international industry is not merely a collection of domestic industries but a series of linked domestic industries in which the rivals compete against each other on a truly world-wide basis. Industries exhibiting or evolving toward the global pattern today include commercial aircraft, TV sets, semiconductors, copiers, automobiles, and watches.* (Porter, 1986, 18).

At this stage in our research, we suggest several major points of clarification and qualification. The first concerns the necessary distinction between industries were competition certainly takes place in a world market arena in the strongest sense of the terms as in aircraft, but does so by exports and through a type of competition still waged from a small number of nationally or regionally-based production sites easy to identify (e.g. Seattle), and the growing number of other industries where a very large amount of 'mutual invading' in the form of FDI (Erdilek, 1985) has taken place, leading both to a deep interweaving of previously fairly distinct industries and to highly elaborate patterns of mutual recognition by competitors.

Another point of clarification concerns the need to render explicit a major feature which remains implicit in Porter's definition, namely the onset of a truly international process of capital concentration and centralisation and so the advent of global or world oligopoly as the most characteristic form of supply structure in science based but also in scale intensive industries (in the Pavitt, 1984 classification). This dimension which is not explicitly part of Porter's definition of a 'global industry' is certainly a central dimension of our own. World oligopoly and the 'global competition' or 'cross-border network rivalry' which accompany it, is the outcome of two related but nonetheless distinct processes: the process of internationalisation and the extension of international or delocated production; and the process of industrial concentration resulting from domestic and cross-border acquisitions and mergers. It occurs when industrial and technological development places extremely strong constraints on firms to produce for world markets as distinct from even the largest domestic markets, and when, as a result of cross-entry of home markets by major competitors, concentration becomes a truly international process, with the number of firms effectively capable of waging world, or global competition dropping progressively world-wide to levels which correspond *pari passu* to those previously associated with domestic oligopoly (see OECD, 1992, chapter 10 for figures assessing this situation in a number of industries). The ensuing result is mutual market dependence and mutual recognition between rivals.

The third important clarification which must now be made to the Porter definition is that the 'linked domestic industries' have started to be something more than just 'linked' following a process of widespread restructuring. This process is strongly shaped, in host as well as in home economies, by the strategies of the dominant MNEs in a way which leaves less and less leeway for much more than a purely reactive type of government industrial policy in many sectors.

This restructuring is the outcome first of cross-entry and mutual invasion by rival MNEs, which occurs very often through the acquisition and merger with existing domestic firms. The underlying process is the one highlighted by authors such as Graham (1990) who insist that oligopolistic reaction (previous studies by Hymer and Rowthorn, 1970 and by Knickerbocker, 1973 in the US context) is a now vital dimension of MNE strategic behaviour within the setting of world oligopoly. They have attempted in some cases to use game theory to model the moves by firms. Independently of cross-entry, the shift from multidomestic to global industries necessarily entails the reorganisation and restructuring of production facilities (and also of R&D capacities as discussed in section 13.6) by MNEs. This involves a simultaneous process of focusing and switching of activities by the MNE among its numerous production sites. *Replica* subsidiaries previously set up to cater domestic markets are closed down. Production is organised on the basis of *internationally interdependent* production facilities. The process leads to a situation in which national manufacturing industries are subjected to a process of upgrading, downgrading and hierarchical ranking of which governments may not be aware over a quite long period of time.

Home and host countries to MNEs are also progressively trapped into an increasingly tightly knit set of trading relationships, at the basis of which are intra-firm flows of parts and intermediate goods between MNE subsidiaries. Countries which are not hosts to MNEs will, on the other hand, only be involved in such trade to the extent they supply raw materials or act as second or third tier subcontractors. An exclusion process is at work alongside the increasing interdependency of the major agents. Intrafirm trade (Helleiner, 1979) represents one measure of these flows; another indicator, which reflects these intra-group exchanges as well as global sourcing by MNEs to second or third tier subcontractors, is represented by the level of imports in intermediate goods. Both because it is painstaking and expensive to collect and because they want to stay rather discrete about their MNEs, very few countries publish reliable data on intrafirm trade. Only the US and Japan do so periodically (Julius, 1990). The latest available data for the US (1988) shows that approximately half of US merchandise trade (both imports and exports) was intrafirm trade organised either by US or by foreign MNEs (UNCTC, 1991). Data collected at OECD on trade in intermediate goods (DSTI/STIID, 1992) shed some light on the strength of the trade interdependencies created by FDI and the operations of MNEs. The data shows that the direct import of intermediate inputs (which now represents between 50–70% of all imports by the six largest OECD countries) grew more rapidly than domestic sourcing in all countries, with the greatest growth generally occurring in the most recent years.

13.6. Three Modes of Globalisation in Technology by MNES

MNEs continue to keep in their home countries near their corporate headquarters a much higher fraction of their R&D than of their manufacturing activities (Patel and Pavitt, 1990). However, the global strategies developed by MNEs in the area of science and technology do not reside solely in the organisation of a growing fraction of their corporate R&D in laboratories located abroad. At least two other forms of operations organised on a global scale or in a global setting must be considered alongside the organisation of formal R&D, namely the sourcing of scientific and technological knowledge on a global scale and the establishment by MNEs of strategic alliances in technology with oligopolistic rivals. Cantwell (1990) argues that in any given industry,

> ...technological activity is locationally differentiated, as part of different national systems of innovation. The distinct characteristics of innovations in each country provide MNEs with an incentive to disperse research facilities to gain access to complementary paths of technological development which they can then integrate at a corporate level.

13.6.1. Enlarged Opportunities for the Internationalisation of R&D

The advent of telematics has considerably increased the scope for the internationalisation of R&D by MNEs. Previously (as noted above) one of the reasons often cited by US firms for not spreading their R&D activities abroad was the difficulty of ensuring adequate supervision and control. For obvious reasons, MNEs in the telecommunications and computer and data processing industries were the first to use the new methods of supervision and control. As early as the mid-1970's several large firms in these industries had a kind of international technical system with a foot in several national systems, but with identifiable autonomous features of their own, ensuring the international flow of technology within international group structures. In this respect, IBM was exemplary and had organised its laboratories at an early stage as one single network. With the emergence of world-wide telecommunication networks, IBM's experience was followed by an increasing number of large corporations. A survey (247 respondents) carried out recently at Reading found that parent corporations no longer excluded overseas R&D on account of economies of scale, the vulnerability of such work to security risks when dispersed, or because of excessive communication problems (Pearce and Singh, 1991a, 25).

Studies carried out in Scotland in a small group of US-owned manufacturing plants provided some earlier support for a positive evolutionary hypothesis (Howells and Wood, 1991): the older the overseas affiliate the more likely it was to be R&D intensive. A larger, more recent survey of US subsidiaries also carried out in Scotland found that the number of subsidiaries undertaking some kind of R&D had increased significantly (Young et al., 1987). Evidence of upgrading is also reported by Pearce and Singh who found that

> ...development work replaces adaptation, so that the R&D units work with marketing and/or engineering units to derive distinctive product variants within the context of the group's new technology. (1991b, 21).

Using a typology of innovation related strategies which distinguishes two 'classical' approaches and two 'truly transnational' approaches to the management of innovation by MNEs, Bartlett and Ghoshal (1990) have also noted a move from 'the local-for-local' strategy previously assigned to subsidiaries to a 'locally-leveraged global approach' which involves 'utilising the resources of a national subsidiary to create innovations not only for the local market but also for exploitation on a world-wide basis'. The second of the new 'transnational' approaches to innovation distinguished by Bartlett and Ghoshal also involves the recognition by MNEs of the existence of sources of creative ability in several countries. This globally-linked approach

> ...pools the resources and capabilities of many different components of the MNE at both headquarters and the subsidiary level – to create and implement an innovation jointly. In this process, each unit contributes its own unique resources to develop a truly collaborative response to a globally perceived opportunity (Bartlett and Ghoshal, 1990, 217).

In both cases, however, the process remains under very close central supervision and control (Pearce and Singh, 1991a, 24). Within 'network corporations' even more than in 'classical MNEs', R&D and innovation strategies are functionally related to the central corporate management quite as much as in the case of corporate financial strategy (Antonelli, 1988).

13.6.2. Patenting as an Indicator of Internationalisation

Patent data have been used as a way of measuring the extent to which internationalisation of R&D has occurred. Some lively debates have ensued. Patel and Pavitt (1990) argue that the process can be measured by the proportion of a country's patenting in the US controlled by foreign as distinct from domestic firms, reflecting the capacity of foreign MNEs to monitor and absorb local basic research. Using this indicator, it appears that in most countries, large foreign firms still hold a relatively small position in national technological activities; only in Canada and the United Kingdom do they account for more than 20% of total national patenting in the US, with Belgium standing out as a special case (see Table 13.2). Similarly, the importance of the foreign technological activities of nationally owned firms as measured by patents, would indicate a country's capacity to benefit through its MNEs from the results of research undertaken in other countries. Here, the second column in Table 13.2 confirms that large firms based in small countries undertake a higher proportion of their technological activities, as measured by patenting, outside their home countries. For the Netherlands, patents obtained by firms through foreign affiliated laboratories amount to more than 70% of the

Table 13. 2. **The Geographical Origin of Patenting in the US (1981–86)**

	US Patenting from Inside Country by Foreign Firms (as % of Country's Total US Patenting)	US Patenting by National Firms from Outside Home Country (as % of Country's Total US Patenting)
Belgium	45.7	16.5
France	11.8	3.8
FR Germany	11.5	8.5
Italy	11.2	3.0
Netherlands	9.5	73.4
Sweden	5.4	16.7
Switzerland	12.5	27.8
United Kingdom	22.3	
Europe (average)	7.4	9.3
Canada	28.1	12.5
Japan	1.2	0.5
United States	4.2	4.4

Source: Pavitt and Patel, 1989.

national total, more than 25% for Switzerland and more than 16% for Sweden. Among the large R&D spenders the United Kingdom has the largest figure, also superior to 25%. Given the size of the United Kingdom's technology base and the long tradition of UK science, the two figures indicate in fact a high degree of internationalisation in R&D, both inward and outward.

Using the longest time series available for patents statistics (available only up to 1986), Cantwell and Hodson (1990) are firmer in their conviction about the trend towards internationalisation with some product groups and/or technologies leading the process and others lagging. They also give reasons, however, why patent data may understate the true extent of the internationalisation of R&D. First, whenever the internationalisation of R&D is achieved through acquisition and mergers, it is not recorded as a change in the geographical composition of the firm's technological development since the affiliate is deemed to be a part of the corporate group at both the beginning and the end of the long 1969–1986 period.

Second, where acquisitions have had motives other than the extension of research facilities (and there have been many of these), it is quite possible that the new parent company may close down affiliate R&D. Certainly, any duplication with the work at the MNEs technological headquarters or in other major laboratories is likely to be eliminated. As argued by Cantwell and Hodson, this would appear in the data as a move away from the internationalisation of technological activity. Other key innovation-related functions are generally centralised in the parent company, in particular the legal work preparatory to patenting.

13.6.3. The Global Sourcing of Scientific and Technological Inputs

The internationalised sourcing of technology has been a very under-researched dimension of MNE operations (Chesnais, 1988a). For a long time, MNEs were considered as simply, or any way principally mainly transferring technology outwards and not also transferring it inwards. Discussing overseas R&D spending by MNEs, Caves (1982), for instance, simply mentions in passing that the 'basic research of MNEs is much more footloose than is applied research, and that some of it goes abroad to seek out particular scientific specialists'. This is insufficient. In a number of industries (cf. the studies produced at OECD in the late 1970's, Michalet and Delapierre, 1977, Chesnais, in OECD, 1979, Burstall, Dunning and Lake, 1981), there is evidence that MNEs were early to understand that foreign direct investment and internationalised group structures could form the basis not only for internalised transfer of technology conducive to the most advantageous exploitation of 'firm-specific advantages' across national frontiers, but also for the sourcing and centralisation of scientific and technical knowledge and resources on an international scale. The findings of a US Survey made in the early 1980's (Fusfeld, 1986, 132–133) regarding the motivations of US MNEs for setting up foreign laboratories provided further information regarding the strategies of MNEs in this area. The most frequently quoted objective was the desire to 'have a window on foreign science', first and foremost in Europe. Other objectives included access to special skills not easily available in the home country and the development of technical concepts on the basis of approaches different to those dominated by US technological paradigms. The fact that this foreign sourcing process is a *distinctive* form of MNE operation, even if the 'window' or 'watching post' is located in a formal R&D laboratory (in which case it may in fact be the main objective assigned to the unit) is now slowly being recognised. It represents the fourth motive for setting up foreign R&D facilities listed by Dunning in recent work (1990a and b). As now noted by Dunning,

> *Sometimes, this presence (in the form of delocated R&D facilities) takes the form of the setting up of listening or monitoring posts, sometimes of acquiring firms with complementary R&D activities to those engaged in by the acquiring firm, and sometimes that of specialized R&D facilities intended to produce innovations and ideas for the rest of the organisation. To give just one example, in Japan's Tsukuba Science City a world class center for R&D – no less than eleven foreign owned chemical and pharmaceutical companies have set up research facilities.*

The information available on the technology-related investments and operations of European and Japanese MNEs in the US during the 1980's suggests that getting a foot inside the US science and technology base in order to start this process of identification and acquisition of external knowledge, and to tap into the knowledge existing in the US university and small firm environments in California and New England has become increasingly important. This is especially true for the chemical and chemicals-related firms. Gaining direct access to the US science and technology base in the field of pharmaceuticals and biotechnology motivated much of their US investment (see Howells, 1990, for some evidence on UK pharmaceutical MNEs, Wortmann, 1990, for German corporations and Peters, 1991 for recent evidence about the Japanese firms).

The internationalisation of S&T by MNEs must include the acquisition and appropriation of technology developed by such institutions and small firms. Earlier work on the foreign sourcing strategies of Japanese MNEs in areas where their basic research is weak (Saxonhouse, 1985) was often dismissed either as oriented against the Japanese or as describing a rather marginal phenomenon. Wortmann's (1990) conclusion is also that in the case of German MNEs their US agreements *'can be viewed as part of active R&D internationalization strategies of the commissioning companies'* (1990, 181). Under these agreements, the US biotechnology firm usually does the gene technical research and develops the new production process on a laboratory scale, while the pharmaceutical MNE handles the upscaling into industrial production, conducts the registration procedure and does the marketing.

13.6.4. Strategic Alliances in R&D Intensive Industries

The 'messy' nature of the issues under discussion (Dunning, 1990) is increased still further as soon as one starts to understand that international and domestic interfirm technological agreements cannot be considered in a simple unilateral way and that even in the context of this analysis they must be considered from several standpoints: the acquisition of external knowledge (often underpriced), the pooling of R&D and complementary assets (Teece, 1986); and the perhaps not consciously collusive, but quite definitely collective protection of technological advantage by alliances between firms belonging to international oligopolistic supply structures.

Interfirm agreements possessing this latter feature have, of course, always existed to some degree or another. International cross-licensing between large corporations in concentrated supply structure, which remains a fairly basic form of technical co-operation agreement in some industries, was already a significant feature of the chemical and heavy electrical equipment industries in the 1920's and 1930's (Newfarmer, 1985). Today agreements involving the world's largest firms in strategic industries and R&D intensive product groups and their implications for national systems must necessarily be set in the context of the present trend towards high levels of world concentration. This means that this type of alliance must be identified and submitted to special analysis. This is what J. Hagedoorn and his colleagues at MERIT have started to do (Hagedoorn and Schakenraad, 1990a and b). The emerging pattern of agreements between oligopolists must be examined closely from the stand-point of their effects on entry barriers and the access to technology by firms which are not parties to the complex set of inter-connected and overlapping agreements now occurring between firms that are otherwise competitors. A hold over best practice technology by leading firms in an industry is a component of the industrial barriers to entry by newcomers.

In this respect, contemporary innovation theory (Dosi et al., 1988) stresses the importance of analysing different 'appropriability regimes', e.g. the degree to which an innovation can be protected (ranging from 'tight' regimes where technology is extremely difficult to imitate to very 'weak' regimes where it is almost impossible to protect). The further suggestion made here is that appropriability must now be considered alongside classical entry barrier factors. The effect of rapid, radical and paradigmatic technological change probably works in two opposite directions. On the one hand, they will weaken the previous appropriability regime considerably and destroy previous dominant designs. This will weaken the technological component of entry barriers, although other components, such as a strong hold over distribution networks as in pharmaceuticals still offer oligopolists a considerable degree of protection against would-be entrants, in particular when they are smaller domestic firms. On the other hand, radical technological change recreates the basis for strong appropriability. Today, however, it does so within changed international conditions, marked in particular by the fact that potential competitors fall into different groups, the most important division being the one which occurs between those competing firms who are capable of 'reading' technological trajectories and understanding what the 'other man' is doing, and those which do not have the in-house technological capacity to do this. By pooling some of their R&D, or by organising the two way exchange of key complementary technologies (see studies by Hacklisch, 1986, on cooperation between US and Japanese oligopolists), the firms in the first grouping while still competing between themselves, can nonetheless increase constantly their lead over other firms and raise the technological entry barriers facing potential entrants.

Similarly, in the context of industries such as advanced microelectronics and semiconductors, efforts by leading firms to regain international competitiveness, and to wage global competition now appears to have a chance of success if undertaken collectively. This explains why the largest firms in the electronics industry – be it in Japan with the VLSI project, in the US with Microelectronics and Computer Technology Corporation (MCC) and in Europe with ESPRIT – have been active in setting up large joint R&D and technology creating and sharing agreements (Mytelka, 1991). Further collective action by European oligopolists with the help of large EC support and subsidies is now in preparation in an attempt to 'save' a European technological capacity in these industries.

13.7. Our Conclusion at this Date: The Need for Policy in the Face of Increased Differentiation and Uneven Development

This chapter has attempted to show some key differences between 'classical multinationalisation' and the new phase of globalisation with respect to their impact on national systems of innovation. It has discussed some of the factors which lie behind the present restructuring by MNEs of their manufacturing and R&D operations and facilities among countries. Stress has been laid in particular on the implications for firms and consequently for host and home countries of the oligopolistic rivalry which is now taking place within the highly concentrated supply structures created by intra-Triadic mutual invasion through FDI. The present situation of intense rivalry by Japanese oligopolists in a context of macro-economic depression has aggravated yet further the constraints placed on other MNEs (see Womack et al., 1990, for a discussion of the technological and organisational foundations of this rivalry in the automobile industry). We have also argued that the internationalisation of R&D, or more widely of S&T by MNEs cannot be limited to the internationalisation of their corporate R&D. The process must be seen to include the global scientific and technological sourcing policies of MNEs as well as the strategic alliances they set up globally with their main oligopolistic rivals.

As a result of all these phenomena, a combined process of integration and exclusion is now at work.

13.7.1. Virtuous and Vicious Cycles of Technological Accumulation

As shown in sections 13.6 and 13.7, the emergence of globally integrated MNEs, within which the international dissemination of technology is now more linked to its creation, entails a reorganisation of the group's production and innovation-related activities with an emphasis on manufacturing affiliates with world or regional product mandates and internationally integrated laboratories (IIL's). Some affiliates are being upgraded, and others downgraded, as technologically sophisticated production and assembly tasks have become increasingly geographically separated as a consequence of the new patterns of international specialisation within MNEs.

Cantwell (Cantwell, 1989 and Cantwell and Dunning, 1991) has given reasons why this process '*is likely to reinforce patterns of cumulative causation within countries*' (1991, 53–54, our stress). Countries which are still experiencing growth through upgrading their industrial structures, and devoting more resources to the support of indigenous technological capacity are likely to attract inward MNE investment in R&D intensive activities, and to benefit from technological accumulation in the associated affiliates and some technological dissemination outside them. By contrast, countries which are losing international competitiveness can only expect to attract subsidiaries concentrated in assembly and low value added activities The process is rather similar with respect to outward FDI in industries where domestic MNEs hold an internationally strong competitive position, they can usually afford to invest more in technology creation, which through backward linkages may benefit their domestic suppliers. This, in turn, will strengthen the latter's competitive capacity to supply the affiliates of foreign firms requiring their products. More subcontracting work is then given to domestic suppliers by foreign affiliates which further strengthens their technological capacity. In this setting, outward and inward investment are complementary forces facilitating an improved international competitive situation of the country concerned.

Taken in combination, the result of inward and outward FDI and the operations of foreign *and* domestic MNEs are what Cantwell and Dunning name 'virtuous' and 'vicious' cycles of increasing or declining technological capability. Cantwell's study of European integration (Cantwell, 1987) leads him to conclude that the process is 'further reinforced when operations are located in an economically integrated region'.

13.7.2. Small Countries and International Interfirm Alliances

Firms belonging to the smaller industrialised countries and to other OECD countries with weaker technology bases, may have a particular interest in, and face particular constraints with respect to, international technological co-operation (Walsh, 1987). Concentrated supply structures, and the forms of interfirm agreements associated with such structures, will often lead to a raising of entry barriers. Small country firms will find it increasingly difficult to compete with large firms based in countries possessing large technology bases and greater power in the world market. They will be forced to seek some kind of co-operative agreement with one of the large firms belonging to the concentrated international supply structure (Chesnais, 1988), in order to secure access to a wider market and/or to catch up in some areas of technology – in exchange, perhaps, for the sharing of technological expertise in another area (e.g. manufacturing technology in exchange for design expertise). One of the objectives of the EUREKA project is to facilitate this type of co-operation between large and small European firms. The chance a small-country firm has of achieving this is likely to depend on its bargaining power; this is related to its experience and the degree of dominance it exercises in its market, the appropriability of its technology and the extent to which successful innovation depends on complementary assets which it possesses.

13.7.3. Three Policy Approaches in the Face of Globalisation

If one rules out the policy of head-on confrontation with MNEs which requires political conditions (in particular the support of a wide alliance of social forces in a number of closely interconnected countries) totally lacking today, there still remain at least three broad forms of approaches to policy which governments can adopt.

The first policy is the one which advocates deregulation and privatisation, and calls for the 'primacy of the market' and the ending of all government created forms of market failure, as if the process of concentration and centralisation of capital and the building of extremely powerful MNEs with global reach was not *per se* both the consequence and the cause of deep, pervasive 'market failures'. In the view of the ultra neo-liberal school, governments are by definition incompetent in all areas other than the keeping of 'law and order'. Men and women are likewise presented as being essentially 'consumers' best on getting 'quality for their money' without having first to earn their living as workers, employees or civil servants and so having to be employed. The satisfaction of 'consumers' means that all barriers to trade and investments must be dismantled even if the result is a few prospering sites in one industrial wasteland. Nor are these 'consumers' really seen as citizens with broader aspirations and responsibilities. Increasingly unemployed and more and more disoriented by the world situation, these frustrated mass consumers can only become the easy prey of ultra-nationalist political leaders. Over the last decade, the European Commission has been strongly influenced by this 'neo laissez-faire' approach (see the Cecchini report on the 'cost of non-Europe'), intending to dismantle industrial policy instruments at the national level, and satisfied with heralding a European economy almost totally structured by the decisions of MNEs. Programmes like ESPRIT have tended simply to consolidate a pan-European oligopoly (Mytelka, 1991), and have accelerated the formation of a hierarchically-organised tier structure among European technological regions and sites (Roobeck, 1990).

The second policy argues the need for governments to use a wide range of important policy instruments in order to attract 'the right sort' of MNE dominated activities. The strength of this approach lies in its 'realism': since MNEs now possess a great flexibility and choice in the location of different varieties of activities, and have amply demonstrated their capacity to redistribute their manufacturing and R&D facilities among countries. Then the only sensible and realistic policy is to give MNEs what they are looking for, namely an environment which combines 'law and order' with the provision of a wide range of very important 'externalities', in particular efficient communication and business infrastructures, an educated and trained workforce, efficient local supplier firms and some components at least of a sophisticated innovation system. This approach invites governments, now meaning both national governments and regional (or Länder) authorities, to compete for FDI and to ensure that the foundations and all the public sector ingredients of Porter's 'diamond' of competitive assets are available to firms. If this is the case, then MNEs will perhaps recognise that these assets are available to them locally and not seek to economise transactions costs through internalisation and foreign sourcing (Dunning, 1991b). This approach can easily forgo a holistic approach to national production and innovation system (and of course to the social systems of which they are part). It is satisfied if a given country has a small number of successful sites and is ready to justify domestic economic and social dualism and to let unequal development among regions proceed. This second approach is an improvement of the first in that some very important 'externalities' (including the education system) receive the support of public investment, and that some of the interactive relationships between component elements of the production and innovation system are shown to require monitoring by governments. But because of its intent to woo MNEs, the consequences of this approach may come close to these of the first one.

The third approach considers that both on strictly political grounds and for reasons related to the fabric of production and innovation systems, governments cannot view their role simply as providing decent 'externalities' for MNEs and leave a free hand to the very strong processes working towards increased differentiation (both social and among regions), unequal development and an even more strongly hierarchical domestic and international economic order. The political grounds are both those of equity, solidarity and justice and also the necessary recognition that extreme-right political parties have, as in the 1920's and 1930's, started to grow very rapidly again because of unemployment and social marginalisation. The economic reasons are that however hard governments 'woo' MNEs, the latter will continue to make their strategic decisions on the basis of the considerations discussed in sections 13.4 and 13.5, without countries ever being able to rely firmly on these firms for tangible and intangible investment and employment at home. The remark concerns domestic MNEs as much as foreign ones. Today in a country such as France, the overwhelming part of public funds to industry and technology go to the French participants in the world global oligopolies. Such a policy does not ensure either the efficiency of these firms nor their commitment to public policies which may not correspond to the corporate policies dictated by international oligopolistic reaction.

The only way of attempting to ensure the cohesion and interactiveness of production and innovation systems is to build upon national institutions and on small domestic firms. MNEs can be incorporated into the policy to the extent the national environment has strong elements of cohesion; MNEs should not be given the role of pillars in national competitiveness; in some cases, it may be preferable not to call them in at all. In this approach the enhancement of key externalities is geared to the support of domestic innovation-related institutions and small firms. This must also be backed by a strong government-oriented financial system providing the necessary capital and by bank policies providing innovative firms protection against destructive acquisitions and take overs.

Since competitiveness hinges on the capacity of firms to make their own technology-related investments (in relation with, but also partly independently of public R&D investment) the degree of protection that this investment receives against take-overs may become vitally important. In particular when globalisation is led by financial considerations, the business enterprise-embedded component of NSI which is perhaps the most decisive for the existence and effectiveness of national systems may also be the one which is the most vulnerable. In capitalist economies, there exists a close inter-relation between the overall processes of competition, investment and profitability and the enterprise-embedded components of the national system of innovation. This is why domestic financial institutions, not simply governments but also regional authorities and, more important still, the domestic banking system must play the role of a 'guardian' of the ownership of innovation-related production assets as they do in Japan and also in Germany (see Booz and Allen, 1989). This is now recognised to be an important element of the cohesion of national systems in the medium-to-large EC countries (Muldur, 1990) as well as in the United States (Zysman, 1990). For smaller countries, it is absolutely vital.

Chapter 14

PUBLIC POLICY IN THE LEARNING SOCIETY

Bent Dalum, Björn Johnson and Bengt-Åke Lundvall

14.1. Introduction

Recently, several writers have argued that globalisation erodes national specificity and leads to long term convergence of structure, institutional set up, culture and, as a consequence, economic performance of countries. This does not correspond to observable facts nor has it been the message of this book. One of the most interesting developments of the 1980's is that despite globalisation, the distinctive features of national environments, have attracted much greater analytical attention than previously (Porter, 1990, Butry, 1991) and are seen by many authors as explaining differences among countries in competitiveness, growth and income.

While the post war, 'golden age' growth period from the early 1950's to the early 1970's was characterised by convergence between the OECD countries (Gomulka, 1971, Cornwall, 1977, Maddison, 1982 and Abramovitz, 1989), as well as by a trend towards an increase in economic and social integration and reduction in inequalities inside nations (cf. the small but real closing of the gab between the Mezzogiornio and Northern Italy and a lowering of income distribution inequality in many OECD countries), the diverging features have been significantly more important in the two following decades.

National specificity remains important and appears quite definitely to bear a relation to the capacity to produce, acquire, adopt and use technology. The erosion of the autonomy of national systems through globalisation is not synonymous with convergence and improved integration.

The strong element of cumulative causation in the technological development of countries (stressed in the conceptual chapters in part I) makes it reasonable to assume that foreign direct investment, whether outward or inward, *reinforces* the differences between countries, and inside countries between regions and sites. As stressed by Chesnais in chapter 13, the stronger economies get even stronger (virtuous circles) and the weaker get weaker (vicious circles), while unequal development proceeds inside both, in particular in countries where social cohesion has been weak and the mechanisms for interactive learning less developed.

This points to a need for a reassessment of the role of government in relation both to innovativeness and the capacity to learn and to uneven development, and consequently we close this book with a chapter on the implications for public policy of an interactive learning approach.

In section 14.2, some theoretically based arguments against state intervention will be critically discussed while section 14.3 presents a general approach to policy making based upon the learning perspective.

State intervention may take place within a framework defined by the structure of production and the institutional set up. Or it may represent long term efforts to affect the structure of production and the institutional set up in order to stimulate processes of learning.

The interactive learning approach brings into focus this second kind of long term intervention, and section 14.4 discusses the role of policy in molding and reshaping the production structure, while section 14.5 points to the problems and opportunities involved when institutional borrowing and learning take place between agents from different countries. In this context, it is argued that the further development of analyses of national systems of innovation may give governments a role also in international institutional learning.

14.2. The Limits of the Anti-Interventionist Argument

A classical controversy in political economy refers to the proper role of government in the economy. To a certain degree, the normative conclusions reached by economists will reflect how they define the 'economic problem'. Neoclassical welfare economics, with its focus on allocation of scarce resources, defines the limits for one possible programme for legitimate state intervention. When the market fails government intervention should be called upon in order to correct the failure.[1] Today, most neoclassical economists might be expected to add that the risk for government failure tends to make this programme too ambitious.

Classical Keynesian economics is focused on the problem of underutilising labour. The legitimate programme is extended as compared to the neoclassical one. In order to keep the economy close to full employment, governments should intervene and compensate for the uncertainty inherent in investment decisions and 'socialise investments'.

14.2.1. Some Arguments Against Government Intervention

The approach of this book is neither neoclassical nor Keynesian. Our focus is upon the production and utilisation of new knowledge in the economy. The economic problem focused upon is related to the learning capability of the economy. In this chapter, the policy implications of such a shift in focus will be discussed. Colleagues working along similar lines of thought have been somewhat reluctant to challenge and to develop an alternative to the neo-liberal vogue in policy.[2] This reflects, of course, real difficulties to reach normative conclusions in this area, but we also believe that implicit in evolutionary thinking, there are hidden arguments in favour of non-intervention. Even when these arguments remain tacit in the analysis, they tend to influence the policy conclusions.

First, there is the scepticism to prediction and manageability of processes of change inherent in evolutionary thinking. Evolution is, fundamentally, an open process partly ruled by contingency, and partly by unforeseeable and accidental generation of new knowledge. The importance of unexpected novelty and 'survival of the luckiest' in the evolutionary approach tends to make forecasting and planning for the future rather uncertain affairs and seems to leave little room for effective innovation policies.

Second, there is the 'Austrian' argument that the market mechanism is a very effective discovery process, the results of which cannot be improved by policy makers. The significance of the market is that it coordinates the use of widely dispersed knowledge and during this process, through competitive entrepreneurial entry and intervention, discovers new possibilities. In Hayek's words the market 'turns out to be a more efficient mechanism for digesting dispersed information than any man has deliberately designed' (Hayek, 1975).

Third, the Austrian notion of the market as a discovery process is closely connected to a more general rejection of the possibility of prediction and, hence, effective policy making. When the economy is regarded as a process, time must be allowed to elapse, and this is impossible without something happening. Unexpected novelty is experienced and expectations are confirmed or refuted. In any case, the constellation of knowledge is changed. But knowledge shapes human action and action shapes the world. Hence, it is impossible to predict any future state of the world (Lachmann, 1978). We can't have certain knowledge about the future. This seems to be an argument against the effectiveness of especially long-term economic policy aiming at restructuring and innovation.

Furthermore, the three arguments seem to be related to each other and combine into a warning against intervening in subtle processes whose future directions and results we know very little about. In a caleidic society (Shackle, 1972), where unexpected novelty is, sooner or later, bound to disintegrate, change and rearrange existing patterns into new ones, economic policy is an uncertain affair. The market process of discovery is necessarily decentralised, subtle and surprising. Any attempt to centralise it risks to harm it, it seems.

14.2.2. The Evolutionary Argument

These anti-interventionist arguments are less devastating for economic policy than they might seem, however. They certainly raise well motivated doubt about the possibility for government to fine-tune the economy towards an equilibrium state. Neither does it seem possible to design the institutions and technologies of a future society with anything that resembles precision. Many important institutional innovations (money, the banking system, the public firm, the market etc.) are 'self grown', unplanned results of human action and not consciously designed. Radical technological innovations (the electric motor, the computer, plastics etc.) are often not foreseen, neither as pure technical break-throughs, nor as economic innovations with a great economic impact.

But these doubts do not apply generally, to all kinds of economic policy. There is still, and in some cases more than ever, room for economic policy in relation to long term economic development and growth.

First, the evolutionary argument is not only underlining the unpredictability of the future and the importance of accidental combinations in economic development. As pointed out many times in this book, the evolution of knowledge is not only accidental in its character. It is also cumulative and often developing along 'trajectories' which may remain quite stable for long periods. This transmission and reproduction of knowledge over time makes evolution predictable to a certain degree. This perspective makes it clear that the role of policy might be twofold. Either, it might stimulate the progress along the prevailing trajectories – and this is what industrial policies often end up doing – or it may take on the more demanding task of making it easier for agents to shift from one trajectory to another.[3]

This cumulativeness and path-dependency of innovation also highlights the risks of lock-in into technological and institutional cul de sacs. In such a context, there is a need for economic policy to keep options open: to stimulate and protect technological and institutional diversity. (This can be done through the educational system, the research system, the system of technological service, etc.).

According to the evolutionary argument, the uncertainty of future paths of development is partly a result of economic agents' persistent but normal acting and intervening in market processes. This is no argument, however, for the superfluity of political action – some things still have to be done politically, if they are to be done at all – only that policy makers should recognise the uniqueness of their position in terms of information and power.

14.2.3. The Austrian Argument

Second, the argument that the market is a subtle discovery process does not mean that unregulated markets will necessarily, by themselves, discover everything worth discovering, and that any government regulation will necessarily harm the discovering ability. The latter seems to be Kirzner's (1978) position. He actually states the proposition that nothing can be gained by regulation: 'When a better state of affairs is indeed feasible, the market probably would have discovered how to achieve it'.[4]

This argument is not convincing, however, since there is no such thing as an unregulated market. Markets are always embedded in sets of institutions, which differ from country to country and from period to period; for example, in chapter 3, it was demonstrated that markets for products characterised by innovation are 'organised markets'. Only few of the rules regulating markets are government regulations. Furthermore, not all non-government rules are self-grown, undesigned. Many are deliberately manipulated by private actors. There are no strong reasons to believe that politically determined rules – for example rules for environmental protection today, or rules against child labour during the industrial revolution – will necessarily harm market discovery processes more than they stimulate them. It is not at all obvious that a government supported technological service system, for example, will hamper entrepreneurial action.

Third, the impossibility of any certain knowledge about the future state of the world does not mean that, for example, safeguards against risks and incentive mechanisms for stimulating learning cannot be, productively, designed. After all, the fact that you do not know tomorrow's weather is a poor argument against building a house today. Long term economic growth has been proved possible under different forms and degrees of market regulation and, in fact, also in pre-industrial non-market economies.[5]

In addition, the argument that unregulated market processes are invincible mechanisms for discovering new knowledge does not distinguish clearly enough between different kinds of knowledge. The Austrian argument is mostly about coordinating already existing but dispersed knowledge and about discovering persistently emerging imbalances between prices, costs and wants; knowledge about changing market conditions, about unused opportunities, about 'which things or services are wanted and how urgently they are wanted' (Hayek, 1978). It shares with the neo-classical tradition the focus on the allocation of scarce resources. In this sense, the Austrian learning process is subordinated to the allocation process. It is much less about institutional and technological learning. Hayek himself explicitly excludes 'the undoubted role competition plays in the advance of technological knowledge' from the argument (Hayek, 1975).

14.2.4. The Choice of Perspective

The anti-interventionist argument is not irrefutable and there seems to be some room for an evolutionary enlightened policy which interacts with the dynamics of the market processes. In the rest of this chapter, the role of government intervention will be discussed from the specific perspective of interactive learning. This does not take into account all possible complications. For instance, the fact so strongly emphasised in chapter 13 that global oligopoly is becoming the predominating form of competition, and the ensuing power concentration might seem difficult to reconcile with our emphasis on honesty and trust within national systems. We believe that there is a permanent conflict between different rationalities at all levels of the world economy and, perhaps somewhat naively, that national systems reinforcing discursive rationality based upon honesty and trust will take the upper hand in the learning process in the long run.

14.3. The Interactive Learning-Approach and Public Policy

Through out this book we have argued that the technological capability of a national system of innovation is rooted in processes of interactive learning. We have also stated that these processes are conditioned by the economic structure and the institutional set up. In this perspective the crucial role of government becomes a didactic one, to support learning processes and, sometimes, processes of forgetting.

Seen from this perspective, the neoclassical rules for intervention are not very useful.[6] Market failure is ubiquitous when it comes to learning; knowledge cannot easily be traded on markets. Neither is the favoured solution to market failure – the definition of property rights – a workable alternative when it comes to knowledge.[7]

The Austrian tradition is closer to our own in its emphasis upon learning as a fundamental process in the economy. But the fact that Hayek and Kirzner have not integrated Schumpeter's innovating entrepreneur in their theoretical schemes gives their learning process a one-way bias towards a constantly moving and never realised equilibrium and, as already mentioned, it results in a narrow definition of what learning is about.

Our perspective, according to which the economy is a system in historical change, has much in common with the evolutionary approach in economics, but our focus upon learning makes it extra important to define the limitations of evolutionary analogies. In a sense, it is reasonable to regard routines as genes, and search and learning as a process of variety creation and selection. But, at the same time, it is crucially important to take into account that in social evolution human beings are creating and shaping their own conditions in a way which has no immediate counterpart in biological evolution. For example, animals do not learn very much compared to people, and with a few exceptions they do not pass on very much of what they have learnt to the next generation.[8] They do not innovate a lot and they certainly do not debate, how they should organise innovation. In human society, on the other hand, social communication is extremely important because it results in collective action forming new institutions which affect both the variety creation, the reproduction and the selection of knowledge and technology.

Human intelligence is bounded when confronted with the complex and changing environment, but it is not totally without power. Therefore, neither is it reasonable to assume rational expectations nor is it wise to assume human individuals or collectives to be totally driven by waves of accident. Learning – both intra-cultural and cross-cultural, to which there is no counterpart in biological evolution – is the main characteristic of social and economic evolution and learning can be affected by policy-making and, deliberately, institutionalised in more or less efficient ways. Also in policy-making, itself, learning may be more or less efficiently institutionalised.

14.3.1. Basic Dimensions of Learning

Five different topics will be discussed in connection with the role of the state in the learning economy:

- The means to learn
- The incentive to learn.
- The capability to learn.
- The access to relevant knowledge
- Remembering and forgetting.
- Utilising knowledge

It should be taken into account that national systems differ in all these respects. In some systems one or the other of these mechanisms is already well taken care of by private interests or efficiently managed by the government, while in others there are neither public nor private institutions able to cope with the tasks involved. The need for and role of state intervention will therefore differ drastically between national systems but fundamentally the role will, in addition to providing the means to learn by public investment in education and training, be one of stimulating creativity and the generation of novelty, preserving knowledge and keeping technological options open, and dispersing the personal and social costs of change. These tasks may, as already mentioned, be affected either by direct state intervention or government may support the creation of non-governmental institutions which can help to solve the problems.

14.3.2. The Means to Learn

As pointed out in the introductory chapter, the national education and training system is of central importance for the innovation system and we will return to it under several of the subheadings in what follows. The most important and obvious way public policy can strengthen the capability to learn and to innovate is through investing in education and training, and through continuously renewing the form and content of these activities. The following brief remarks do not give justice to the extreme importance of policies for education and training.

First, it must be recognised that building specific competencies, as well as the fundamental ability to learn in the formal education system, demands substantial public investments which provide the means to learn. There is a need for physical infrastructures in terms of buildings and equipments and for human resources in terms of teachers and students. This is true for all levels of the education system from nurseries to the training of engineers and scientists. Adequate public investments in education and training is a necessary (but not sufficient) precondition for sustaining the competitiveness of any national system of innovation. Saving public expenditure by reducing the quantity and quality of education is therefore as a rule a myopic and dangerous strategy.

Besides building specific and general competencies, the school system has other important functions. The basic social values and the capability to communicate of national citizens are developed in the formal education and training system, especially at the early stages. The ideals, in terms of respectively élitisme and equality, built into the system of education will be reproduced and implanted in the whole society and affect the potentials for and forms of interactive learning in the economy. For example, both the British and the French education systems seem to foster rather closed élites and hereby delimit the learning capability in the economy.

The relative emphasis on respectively 'classical education' and abstract reasoning versus practical know-how and engineering in the school system and the priorities given to different kinds of professional training will also affect the learning potential of the economy. For example, Germany and the Scandinavian countries have well developed systems for training skilled workers, while the Anglo-Saxon countries seem to be handicapped by their less developed systems.

Education policy is not just a question of the quantity of government funding. The ability of the national education and training system to adapt to new social and technological developments is extremely important in the present era. The increasingly systemic character of new technologies, where old borders between technical and scientific disciplines are broken down, makes it necessary to review the traditional departmentalised organisation of academic training and research. New organisational forms in firms, which have increased flexibility as their goal, point to a need to review the specialisation within the systems for industrial training. Old distinctions between respectively unskilled, semiskilled and skilled workers become less relevant in knowledge-intensive production. Public policies should aim at building into the institutions of the education and training system a capability to change when confronted with such new challenges.

14.3.3. Incentives to Learn

Incentives to engage in learning may be of a pecuniary kind. At the level of the individual, systems of salaries and wages and income taxes may be designed to promote learning and creative efforts. At the level of the firm, patent laws and tax rules, including depreciation allowances for investment in tangible and intangible resources, may affect the learning activities and efforts.

One of the conclusions of our analysis is that the importance of pecuniary incentives may be overstated, however. In the present period, individual entrepreneurship plays a more limited role than it has done and 'collective entrepreneurship' has become much more important. First, the cooperation between departments within the firm has become crucial for innovative success (chapter 5). Second the cooperation and interaction between firms in industrial networks has become an important source of innovation (chapter 6). Third, the public sector has an important role to play as a professional user interacting with private firms (chapter 7).

Individualised pecuniary incentive systems will hamper processes of interactive learning, if they reinforce instrumental rationality, weaken the capability to engage in open communication with other parties and foster opportunism, making all kinds of cooperation burdened by high transaction costs.

Incentive systems which reinforce communicative rationality and cooperative behaviour are more efficient in this respect but also less simple to design. The incentives of the formal system of education and training may be designed in order to affect the social norms, for example incentives which emphasise the individual's contribution to group performance rather than his/her individual results. In the short run, systems of non-pecuniary and collective rewards at the firm level and government programmes supporting projects of cooperation and networks between firms may help to establish a more efficient communication between parties otherwise reluctant to cooperate.

14.3.4. The Capability to Learn

The learning capability of the individual is, of course, affected by experiences made in the formal education and training system and this is an old theme which has been revived in recent OECD work on the new technologies (OECD, 1988). More than ever it has become important to design systems of education and training so that they give the trainees a capability to learn. Expert knowledge is needed but it becomes rapidly obsolete in the learning society. A specific problem to be tackled by most national systems in the OECD-area is the training needs of the adult population. Here, there is a need for very substantial national efforts both in terms of resources and institutional design.

The firm's capability to learn reflects the way it is organised. The Japanese archetype model of firm organisation, as discussed in chapter 5 seems to be especially well-suited for supporting interactive learning and innovation. The movement away from tall hierarchies with vertical flows of information towards more flat organisations with horizontal flows of information is one aspect of this model. Other elements relate to the circulation of personnel between departments and functions and the broad definition of jobs. Is it possible for government to intervene in order to promote organisational change in this direction? One obvious way to do this would be systematically to study, how domestic firms advance in this area, to diffuse information about experiences made by 'lead firms' to laggards and to give financial support to organisational innovations and experimenting.

The capability to learn for the system as a whole or for sub-systems will depend upon the existence of environments where different kinds of knowledge, skill, competence and experience can be combined and allowed to generate new knowledge. It will depend on interfaces between firms and between firms and public organisations. In section 14.4 the importance of the production structure will be discussed from this perspective.

14.3.5. Access to Relevant Knowledge

There are many different sources of knowledge which enter into the innovation process. Old and new scientific results may be inputs to this process at different stages. Here the access to universities and technical institutes is of importance. One of the main problems in this context is the communication between industry and university. Big science-based firms in fine chemistry, biotechnology and electronics might be well prepared to communicate with universities knowing their codes and their culture, while smaller engineering firms may have great difficulties in this respect. When there are 'bridging' problems, agents translating between knowledge producers and knowledge users may be established by government. Public and semi-public technological service institutions and libraries etc. are also important in this connection.

Another kind of knowledge source is the informal, not codified and more or less tacit knowledge accumulated through learning inside the firms. One of the reasons why firms establish network relationships is that these relationships give access to such knowledge. Network formation may be stimulated by government programmes supporting projects of cooperation.

Finally, governments will still have an important role in maintaining and improving the telecommunication infrastructure although some competition from private network operators might be useful. To secure a broad access to relevant data bases through such networks may be another task not automatically solved by the market. The increasing importance of information and communication technology raises new problems. As information increasingly becomes electronically stored, the risk for a sudden loss of data access may actually increase. A change in the configuration of information systems may make large quantities of data inaccessible. Another side of the increasing use of information technology is a growth in the amount of storable data which is out of proportion with what will ever be needed. To develop and implement a policy (including considerations of privacy and security) for the use of information technology is an important task for government.

14.3.6. Remembering and Forgetting

One important aspect of the innovation system is its capacity to preserve and store the knowledge obtained through learning. Again, government agencies may play a role together with private consultants and institutes.

But it is also important that the innovation system is able to forget, both in the literal meaning of forgetting and with a broader interpretation. At all levels it is important that there is room for change in the collective memory of organisations – i.e. in routines related to technology and organisation.

For the individual, the broader interpretation of forgetting relates to the abandoning of obsolete skills and professional expertise. Within firms it is a question of having mechanisms putting an end to outmoded activities, projects and products. Between firms it is a question of having a mechanism which helps to select the firms with a future from those with no learning capability. The most apparent mechanism in this context is the market but in some national systems (Japan and South Korea) the state has played an important role also in the closing down of ailing industries.

It is also important to be able to preserve knowledge and competence which is presently going out of use in the economy, but still may have a future, yet unknown, value; to forget temporarily while keeping options as open as possible.

Since remembering is costly and has a higher social than private value, this has to be a responsibility for public educational and research institutions.

For all kinds of forgetting, people are burdened with costs of change. These may be very unevenly distributed and may provoke resistance. One obvious way to support 'creative forgetting' is a system of redistribution which compensates the victims of change and makes it easier for them to move ahead into more promising activities. This will typically involve different kinds of social security arrangements, active labour market and retraining policies.[9]

14.3.7. Utilising Knowledge – the Normative Dimension

Expanding knowledge is not necessarily to the benefit of society. Most people would agree that learning by doing and other efforts to develop new techniques in crime does not increase the well-being of the majority of citizens. It might be less simple to agree when it comes to technologies of warfare, genetic engineering and technologies which pollute and use up unrenewable resources. Here the government has an important role to play in organising a democratic process of technology assessment.

The relatively disappointing experiences of the impact of institutionalised technology assessment, so far, points to the need to find new forms which emphasise the discursive aspects of technology assessment. Technology assessment which mobilises a broad spectrum of economic agents may be more efficient than direct government intervention because it establishes a degree of consensus among different interest groups which makes the regulation of unwanted technologies possible and effective. As a result of technology assessment governments may institute rules and regulations limiting the use of certain technologies.

The other side of the coin is that many of the most obvious problems of mankind can be attacked only by a systematic increase in and use of knowledge. Environmentalists argue more and more strongly these days that economic growth is incompatible with ecological considerations. What they may rightly argue is that economic growth without technical and institutional innovation will bring us closer to a break-down of the ecological system. The same is true for the global problems of poverty, hunger and disease. Therefore one of the most important tasks of the government is to guide the search for new knowledge into trajectories which lead towards solutions to these problems. This may be done either by supporting the potential demand for solutions – for instance subsidising advanced users of renewable energy sources – or by direct government demand (cf. chapter 7).

So far, this kind of government intervention has been developed primarily in relation to military technology and in relation to national prestige projects.

The present era with the new relationships between Eastern and Western Europe should open up for strengthening this kind of guidance and the efforts in other fields (health, nutrition, anti-pollution, renewable energy).

14.3.8. The Didactic Role of the State

Government has an important role to play as the only agency responsible for the overall coherence of the national system of innovation as well as for the cohesion of the social system as a whole. In the earlier sections we have shown that the new arguments against state intervention may be less convincing than they look at first sight.

However, we believe that here is a certain rational core in the neo-liberal scepticism to detailed interventionism and policies of fine-tuning. According to modern didactic principles, students learn best when they search for solutions to problems they regard as important and a wide space for self-organised learning may be preferred to detailed tutoring. But few pedagogical experts would go as far as abdicating from giving the process of learning a direction and from developing a supportive organisational framework.

In order to avoid detailed state intervention into processes of learning government may choose to take an active part in the restructuring of the economy and it might try to stimulate institutional learning including learning from abroad. As long as the production structure includes development blocks with a strong potential and as long as the institutional set-up is well adapted to the prevailing technological opportunities the capability of self-organised learning will be strong. When this is the case there will be little need for government to fine-tune the learning economy and to 'pick technological winners'.

14.4. Shaping the Structure of Production

The specific characteristics of each NSI are, so to speak, the 'superstructure' of its production system. The latter were conceptualised by the IKE-group in terms of the idea of 'industrial complexes', originally introduced in the Andersen et al. studies in the early 1980's. The background of this work has in several chapters been traced back to Dahmén (1950/70), Linder (1961) and Vernon (1966) and others; the micro-underpinnings centred around user-producer interaction are developed further in chapter 3 by Lundvall; and the original empirical tests have been reformulated and updated by Fagerberg in chapter 11.

The basic perspective is one where industries are intertwined and interact in sub-systems of production and where the dynamic potential of such sub-systems have a decisive impact upon the performance of the whole economy. The dynamic potential refers both to the income elasticities of its strategic products and to the opportunities for learning presented by the technologies involved.

What role should governments play in fostering such dynamic sub-systems (industrial complexes, clusters of industries or development blocks)? This question will be discussed first from the micro-perspective of user-producer interaction and second with reference to Michael Porter's (1990) cluster analysis.

14.4.1. User-Producer Relationships and Public Policy

In chapter 3 two different characteristics of user-producer relationships which systematically foster unsatisfactory innovations were mentioned.

One was the asymmetrical power relationships between users and producers which result in biased technical change, and the second the inertia which characterises user-producer relationships. The information technology revolution, and the changes in technological opportunities and user needs it brings along, represents a challenge to the prevailing pattern of user-producer relationships in all countries.

One important conclusion from the analysis in chapter 3 was that there is no single mechanism which rapidly, and automatically, adjusts this pattern when it is confronted with such radical changes in technological opportunities and user needs. Selection through competition might be extremely slow in adjusting the historically established network of user-producer relationships to new conditions. As a first approximation there seems to be a considerable room for policy making and especially for agencies playing the role of match-maker; renovating, or breaking up, old and establishing new user-producer relationships. Such an agency must, in order to be successful, be able to muster a broad acceptance of its legitimacy for intervention and must have a very thorough understanding of the workings of the innovation system, as a whole. On the other hand, such a policy does not, necessarily, involve massive amounts of public subsidies.

Such interventions might aim at strengthening the position and competence of weak parties in biased relationships, breaking down, or renewing, stubborn relationships, and stimulating the establishment of new ones. Among the specific means, might be consultations and mediating between parties, educating parties with a weak competence, and using subsidies to stimulate the formation of new relationships.

Of course, there exists already institutions which more or less efficiently play such a role. In some small countries, as for example Sweden and Switzerland, a few big firms have had their own strategies, concerning the restructuring of the pattern of national user-producer relationships. In Germany, the banks historically have played such a role. In Japan the most important function of MITI might have been to bring together parties which would not have cooperated spontaneously. The military industrial complex in the US has played an important role in organising the US economy. In Scandinavia discussions on the role of the welfare state, as a coordinator of a social need-oriented process of innovation have been coming up, time and again.

But current discussions of industrial policy are usually expressed in more primitive terms. Often a choice is presented between massive financial support to 'winners'; specific branches, to be picked by amateurish government authorities on the one hand, and a laissez-faire strategy where markets are assumed to be pure, and thus presented as totally flexible, on the other hand. Given this choice, many governments have ended up, supporting ailing industries, and pre-competitive research, but neglecting the possibility of influencing the patterns of user-producer relationships.

The fact that the big multinationals especially in small countries now tend to loosen their roots in their home-base national innovation system (cf. chapter 13) implies that interest of MNEs in the coherence and restructuring of the pattern of national user-producer relationships is weakened. This increases the responsibility of government in this respect.

14.4.2. Porters Cluster Analysis

Porter's (1990) study of the competitive advantage of nations contains an international comparison of national production systems based on his 'diamond' approach as the conceptual basis for industrial 'clusters' (as discussed in chapter 10 by Dalum). Porter's mix-of-clusters study shows that a few clusters often cover more than 50% of a country's exports. However, his concluding policy chapters are of a fairly general nature and do not take the full consequences of the analytical results. In our interpretation, the existence of such 'industrial complexes' may form an important point of departure for formulation of a specific kind of technology policy programmes, which aim at coordinating education and training efforts, R&D-efforts and the technological service with the interactive learning taking place inside the industrial complexes. The conceptual basis for such a policy were discussed in chapters 4 and 10.

A simple classification exercise appears helpful. What comes out of Porter's case studies is primarily the 'visible' *well established complexes* associated with the risks of lock-in in the old existing order (e.g. the Danish agro-industrial complex). Another category, potentially more relevant for policy considerations, may be the *emerging complexes* – i.e. those which are hardly 'visible' as yet and the take-off of which may be doubtful without deliberate policy initiatives. Examples of the latter are typically associated with such areas as environmental protection and energy production/distribution. These are areas, where it appears fairly evident that government regulation and institutional learning often play important roles for the possibilities to realise technological innovation (for the case of the Danish windmill industry, see e.g. Karnøe, 1991).

As mentioned in the last section, the structural adaptation of the economy will be a slow and painful process if left to itself in a period of radical change in the techno-economic foundation of the economy. The predominance of mature development blocks locked into old technological trajectories will hamper learning in the whole system, while the establishment of new interfaces and linkages would be a way of increasing the learning capability of the innovation system.

Technology programmes aiming at supporting emerging industrial complexes may, as suggested in chapter 13, put a special emphasis on involving the most dynamic small and medium sized enterprises in interactive learning, rather than try to foster a few national 'champions'. The smaller dynamic firms are very active in terms of product innovation and they are also more dependent in these activities on government support than the big firms (Kristensen and Lundvall, 1990). Finally, they are strategic in creating new employment.

More recently industrial and technology policy programmes, taking more or less explicitly their point of departure in such concepts, have been launched in Denmark – however only on a small scale (e.g. a food-processing technology programme and an environmental technology programme).[10]

14.5. International Institutional Learning

One of the basic arguments for studying national systems of innovation is that the studies may stimulate institutional learning across countries. Institutional learning is important for different reasons. As argued in chapter 2 the institutional set-up is important for technical learning. Even more important, one might argue that several of the most serious unsolved problems of the world (as those mentioned in section 14.3.6) reflect institutional barriers to change rather than a lack of technical knowledge. To promote international institutional learning among domestic agents is one way for governments to limit the need for detailed state intervention.

14.5.1. Technological Borrowing and Technological Learning

It is obvious and well known that in most nations only a small part of the total technical learning is really home spun. To be sure (and as repeated many times throughout this book), since innovation is a cumulative process, there almost always occur national, home spun, adaptations and improvements during the diffusion of foreign inventions. This does not change the fact, however, that both the product and process innovations diffusing through most national economies are, normally, to a large extent developed abroad.

A lot of technical learning in a national economy is relatively easy, because the hardest work – the development of new knowledge – is already done abroad. To borrow and absorb technical knowledge developed and already used abroad often involves more limited efforts than to develop it from scratch. This is often regarded as the main factor behind the catching up growth during primarily the 1950's and 1960's, when labour productivity was growing more rapidly in Japan and the Western European countries than in the technology leading USA.

Of course, to borrow product and process techniques from abroad is not an entirely automatic process without frictions. Even importing new, ready-made, stand-alone machines, like for instance when a firm wants to invest in cnc-machines for the first time, gives rise to, often substantial, information- and transaction costs. In addition, there are, often unforeseen or underestimated, costs of training and education and of organisational change as a consequence of the introduction of the new machinery and sometimes the machines themselves have to be adapted to fit into the new context.

14.5.2. Interdependence Between Technologies and Institutions.

So, despite the fact that it is often much easier to borrow technology from a country near the front than to develop it oneself, and despite an often surprisingly rapid imitation between countries of incremental product and process innovations, technical knowledge does not float freely across national borders. It takes time and effort for laggards to emulate best practice techniques from technology leaders.

One important reason for this is the fundamental interdependence between technology and institutions. Technology (which is normally considered a very practical thing, which has to work to be meaningful) does not exist all by itself, but is embedded in an institutional set-up. The capabilities of a firm reside not only in its machinery and in its individual employees, but also, and primarily, in its organising capability to transform inputs into output. And this capability, in turn, depends on its institutional relationships with suppliers, customers, public agencies, research institutes and on the domestic institutional set-up as a whole.

Product or process technologies borrowed from abroad do not automatically fit into new institutional set-ups. Since institutions are cultural phenomena and as such local in character, this problem emerges, whenever one tries to borrow technologies across national borders. The institutions of a nation are the sets of habits, routines, rules, norms and laws, which regulate the relations between people and shape human interaction (chapter 2). Since technology always has to function in firms or other organisations in contexts where people and groups relate and communicate in order to carry out production, institutions necessarily affect how, and with which results, technologies are used. Thus, when technological innovations are diffused across national borders, it usually involves some adaptations: Either parts of the receiving institutional system, or the innovation itself (or perhaps more likely both), have to adapt. Learning becomes an extension of borrowing. Borrowing becomes a part of learning.

14.5.3. Institutional Borrowing and Institutional Learning

Even if several technological gaps are still open and there is ample room for international technological borrowing and learning, institutional borrowing is an integrated part of this and an important part of the international growth and development mechanisms. It is now also entering the economic-political agenda:

The growing interest in the United States for Japanese and European institutional set-ups and a growing self-critique of US economic institutions as reflected in the MIT study 'Made in America' (Dertoutzos et al., 1989) is one indication of this.

Even more obvious, the break-down of the old economic institutions in Eastern Europe and the Soviet Union has been connected to, quite simplistic, ideas of institutional borrowing through an import of the institutions of private ownership and the free market from the West.

Finally, the development of the European Community towards stronger economic, political and social integration brings closer together, national systems with very different institutional set-ups established through long historical processes. How to exploit this institutional diversity as a source of institutional learning, is becoming a key question for present, as well as potential, members of the Community (Bruno et al., 1991).

Comparative studies of different institutional set-ups is of course not a new field in economic theory. Traditionally, it has been handled by the somewhat ambiguous department of 'comparative economic systems'. The focus has normally been on static efficiency and comparisons between rather pure systems of capitalist market economies and socialist plan economies. In the interactive learning perspective of the present book, this is not the most relevant topic, however. The possibility of international institutional borrowing, as an integral element of institutional learning, becomes still more interesting, when questions of how different institutional traits affect the use of new technology and technical learning comes into focus. To what extent, and at what costs, is it possible to increase the technical learning capabilities of an economy by borrowing and learning from the international diversity of institutional set-ups?

14.5.4. Some Problems in Institutional Borrowing and Learning

This is a difficult question. Institutional borrowing, and the modification of the receiving institutional system by adaptations and incremental innovations, is in many respects more difficult than, technological borrowing.[11] This may result in strong resistance to institutional borrowing and learning.

Existing institutions tend to condition new, for instance borrowed, institutions. Due to the largely informal, culturally transmitted, part of a nations institutional set-up, it tends to change rather slowly and incrementally, and new or foreign elements are often easily, and informally, rejected (North, 1990). Information about new ways to communicate and interact can often be interpreted in different ways and is intensely culturally filtered. The historical continuity and enormous complexity of national institutional systems adds to this tendency.

A related phenomenon is that it may be easier to recognise technological than institutional problems. It is, normally, more obvious when technologies do not function, or when there are unutilised technological opportunities. Technological innovations are more salient than institutional innovations and this may lead to a postponement of otherwise obvious institutional and organisational innovations.[12] In this way, institutional rigidities may accumulate in small steps over long periods, while information on the adverse effects of this relative delay of organisational change is selected out.

The non-salient character of institutional innovation is related to the problem of superstitious learning i.e when an outcome is credited with the wrong cause (Kogut, 1991). It is obvious that it is easier to connect cause and effect correctly for technological than for institutional innovations. This again makes rejection of possible institutional borrowing easier, especially in potential conflict situations, where the balance of influence and power between different groups is affected.

Since institutions are about relations between people and people, and technology rather is about relations between people and things, there is usually more resistance to institutional change than to technical change. It is easier both for management and workers to accept changes in the work process, which merely involve that technical things should be done in a different way, than changes resulting in a reshuffling of hierarchical patterns and in the introduction of new ways to communicate. Furthermore, if many interlocking persons and groups feel responsible for, or identify themselves with, a specific organisational form, they may try to resist even minor changes.

It can also be argued that the specialists on technical innovation, i.e. engineers, are educated in a more dynamic spirit than the specialists on organisational and institutional factors. In fact, stability and permanence are important ideals amongst 'transaction costs engineers', for instance amongst lawyers. These people also lack a common, international, professional, language compared to technical engineers, and institutional factors, generally, are much more country specific than technology.

14.5.5. Some Illustrations of Institutional Borrowing

All these difficulties should not give the impression that institutional borrowing is next to impossible. Institutional learning is at the centre of the combined but uneven international growth pattern and institutional borrowing is, as it has always been, an important part of this. Relative changes in international competitiveness between countries is often accompanied, and sometimes generated, by institutional innovations in one country, which then slowly diffuse to other countries through mixed processes of institutional borrowing and learning.

In fact, important parts of western economic history can be understood in terms of institutional borrowing and learning across the Atlantic Ocean, from Europe to America and back again. North (1990) underlines the critical importance of the English institutional heritage for the creation of the thriving American colonial economy, which set the stage for a new phase in capitalist development. The institutions which were shaping this early development and resulted in the institutional set-up of a new nation – for example plantations, merchants, shipping firms, family farms, town meetings and self-government, colonial assemblies, and the intellectual traditions from Hobbes to Locke – were predominantly of English origin.

More than 150 years later Europe enters a period of massive institutional borrowing from the US. After the second world war and connected to the Marshall aid programme, 'productivity delegations' left for the USA to study 'scientific management' and the organisational forms which were connected to the best practice mass production technologies, which, without qualification, were supposed to be American. Not many years later the multi-divisional firm structure, introduced by du Pont and General Motors in the 1930's, with some country-specific modifications spread throughout Western Europe (Williamson, 1985).

As a final illustration of the importance of institutional borrowing, the in-house industrial R&D-laboratory and the Institute of Technology can be mentioned. Chapter 9 of this book discusses how these innovations originated in Germany and in the United States and how they thereafter were, rather quickly, introduced into some countries, for example Sweden and Switzerland, while others, for example Great Britain, were much slower to adapt their institutions.

14.5.6. National Systems of Innovation and Institutional Learning

The institutional consciousness seems now to be increasing in many nations and information about the existence of, supposedly, high performance, dynamically efficient institutions in other parts of the world is a strong incentive for institutional learning. It seems difficult, however, in any precise way to introduce international institutional learning in practical economic policy aiming at economic growth and development. The risks for superstitious learning are obvious. It is, for example, in most cases not correct, when the Japanese system is presented, almost, as an ideal from which all important parts can conveniently be copied.

The general role of government in promoting international institutional learning might be to stimulate an openness to what is going on abroad. The internationalisation of education and training at all levels, including of course an emphasis on foreign cultures and languages, is one important part of such a strategy. The domestic multinational firms are far ahead in the process of international institutional learning and special programmes for giving small and medium sized firms better access to international contacts might be necessary. A very important side-effect of the many EC programmes for international cooperation involving public servants, researchers as well as business men is that it increases and broadens the understanding of the institutional set-up of other countries.

In order to get a more realistic assessment of the potential of institutional borrowing it is, and this is an important message in this book, useful to analyse countries as 'national systems of innovation', where the economic structures and the institutional set-ups are looked upon as forming systemic wholes. In this perspective, we might get a better understanding of when, where and to what extent foreign institutions may be transferable from one system to another. Especially when the focus is to learn how to increase the dynamic efficiency of an economy, the concept of 'national systems of innovation' may have an important role in defining opportunities and limits for institutional borrowing and learning between countries.

14.6. Conclusions

We have argued that government intervention should be oriented primarily at shaping the overall structure of production and the institutional set-up so that these promote self-organised learning and thereby reduce the need for fine-tuning and detailed intervention into the economy. It should promote an openness to the rest of the world in order to support international institutional learning.

In the learning economy, the instrumental rationality of isolated economic agents, acting only in their own interest, may be counterproductive and if society becomes invaded by opportunism and lack of trust, transaction costs will escalate and learning processes will be blocked. As mentioned in section 14.3, an important role of national education and training systems have been the transmission of social norms, including honesty and trust, between generations. This is a very precarious function where a strong and visible state intervention would look very much as indoctrination and as intervening into the privacy of its citizens. At the same time, it is obvious that the function is important. To design an education system which promotes trust and social responsibility, but remains relatively autonomous in relation to the prevailing political system is an important task for government and other public organisations.

More generally, the most fundamental role of government in supporting learning throughout society may be to make sure that the prevailing institutional set up reinforces trust and moral and this will be easier to establish if there is a general feeling among all citizens of belonging to a just society. Equal rights and equal opportunity are elements in such a strategy, as well as the support of weak agents and the restrictions on their exploitation by the strong ones. Social justice is not just a good thing in itself; it might be one of the most important long-term prerequisites for a strong innovative capability in society.

The existence of national systems of innovation, which has been argued throughout this book, is an argument for a continuous need for national policies. This need is in some respects increasing even if the international economic integration significantly changes its character. The process of economic integration at the European Community level will tend to strengthen the forces working towards concentration and uneven developments of sites, regions and countries within the community. At present, it seems as if the realisation of the 'social dimension' will become only a marginal correction to this uneven development.

The process of European integration involves attempts to develop supra-national policies in the field of innovation, but these are not yet close to being efficient substitutes for the functions of the national systems of innovation.

As long as this is the case, it is too early to dismantle national government intervention. The most important aspect of the integration process is that it opens up new avenues for institutional learning and institutional innovation. The countries which are able to combine social cohesion and a reasonably coherent innovation system with an openness to the rest of the world, when it comes to institutional learning, will have the best chances to succeed in this process.

Chapter 15

POST SCRIPT: INNOVATION SYSTEM RESEARCH – WHERE IT CAME FROM AND WHERE IT MIGHT GO

Bengt-Åke Lundvall

15.1. Introduction

When the first edition of this book was published 1992, the concept 'national innovation system' was known only by a handful of scholars and policy makers. Over a period of 15 years there has been a rapid and wide diffusion of the concept. Giving 'Google' the text strings 'national innovation system(s)' and 'national system(s) of innovation' you end up with almost 1.000.000 references. Going through the references you find that most of them are recent and that many of them are related to innovation policy efforts at the national level while others refer to new contributions in social science.

Using Google Scholar (May 2007) we find that more than 2000 scientific publications have referred to the different editions of this book. Economists, business economists, economic historians, sociologists, political scientists and especially economic geographers have utilized the concept to explain and understand phenomena related to innovation and competence building.[1]

In this paper we argue that during the process of diffusion there has been a *distortion* of the concept as compared to the original versions as developed by Christopher Freeman and the IKE-group in Aalborg. Often policy makers and scholars have applied a narrow understanding of the concept and this has gives rise to so-called 'innovation paradoxes' which leave significant elements of innovation-based economic performance unexplained. Such a bias is reflected in studies of innovation that focus on science-based innovation and on the *formal* technological infrastructure and in policies aiming almost exclusively at stimulating R&D efforts in high-technology sectors.

Without a broad definition of the national innovation system encompassing individual, organizational and inter-organizational learning, it is impossible to establish the link from innovation to economic growth. A double focus is needed where attention is given not only to the science infrastructure, but also to institutions/organisations that support *competence building* in labour markets, education and working life. This is especially important in the current era of the *globalizing learning economy* (Lundvall and Johnson 1994; Lundvall and Borràs 1998; Archibugi and Lundvall 2001).

We see one major reason for this distortion in the uncomfortable co-existence in international organisations such as OECD and the EC of the innovation system approach and the much more narrow understanding of innovation emanating from standard economics (Eparvier 2005). Evolutionary processes of learning where agents are transformed and become more diverse in terms of what they know and what they know how to do are not reconciliable with the rational 'representative agents' that populate the neoclassical world (Dosi 1999). Actually, we regard the neglect of 'learning as competence-building' as the principal weakness of standard economics and the narrow definitions of innovation systems as reflecting a negative spill-over from this misdirected abstraction.

Both Mode 2 knowledge production (Gibbons et al 1994) and the Triple Helix approach focus on science and the role of universities in innovation. When they present themselves or are applied by policy makers, not as analysing a subsystem within, but as full-blown alternatives to the innovation system approach (Etzkowitz and Leydesdorff 1995; Etzkowitz and Leydesdorff 2000), these approaches contribute to the distortion. These perspectives capture processes linking science and technology to innovation – below we refer to this as *STI-learning.* The fact that science and codified knowledge become increasingly important for more and more firms in different industries – including so-called low-technology ones – *does not imply that experience-based learning and tacit knowledge have become less important* for innovation. To bring innovations, including science-based innovations, to the market organisational learning, industrial networks as well as employee participation and competence building are more important than ever. We refer to these processes as *DUI-learning.*

Section 2 takes a brief look at how the NSI-concept came about and developed on the general background of the history of innovation research.[2] Section 3 confronts the theoretical foundations of the concept with standard economics; section 4 defines analytical challenges. Section 5 relates the concept to economic development, inequality and sustainability. The chapter ends with the concluding section 6. As mentioned, the literature on innovation systems has grown exponentially over the last 15 years and what follows does not aim at a full and fair survey of the literature. The issues raised and the sources cited reflect my own priorities.

15.2. A Concept with Roots far Back in History

15.2.1. Milestones in the Development of the Innovation System Concept

Basic ideas behind the concept 'national systems of innovation' go back to Friedrich List (List 1841).[3] His concept 'national systems of production' took into account a wide set of national institutions including those engaged in education and training as well as infrastructure such as networks for transportation of people and commodities (Freeman 1995a). To the best of my knowledge, the first written contribution that used the concept 'national system of innovation' was the unpublished paper by Christopher Freeman from 1982 that he produced for the OECD expert group on Science, Technology and Competitiveness (Freeman 1982, p. 18).[4] Here he takes Friedrich List as one central point of reference.

Box 1: Regional, Sectoral, Technological and Corporate Systems

Over the last decade several new concepts representing the systemic perspective on innovation have been developed. The literature on 'regional systems of innovation' has grown rapidly since the middle of the 1990s (Cooke 1996; Maskell and Malmberg 1997). Bo Carlsson with colleagues from Sweden developed the concept 'technological systems' in the beginning of the 1990s (Carlsson and Stankiewitz 1991). While Franco Malerba with colleagues from Italy developed the concept of 'sectoral systems of innovation' (Breschi and Malerba 1997). Ove Granstrand has proposed the corporate innovation system as perspective. Some of the crucial ideas inherent in the innovation system concept such as vertical interaction and innovation as an interactive process are central also in the literature on industrial clusters by Porter and colleagues.

Of these different perspectives the regional system approach is the one that resembles most original versions of the national system of innovation. It has in common with the NSI-approach that it uses the fact that some knowledge is local and tacit to explain that innovation systems are localised. Also, both approaches attempt to explain economic performance of geographical entities. The corporate system perspective may also have economic performance at focus at the level of the single enterprise.

The other perspectives aim at explaining the innovation process in relation to specific technologies and sectors. The analysis of technological systems has been especially useful in analysing how new technologies emerge. The sectoral system approach is unique among the different approaches in not defining as analytical object a vertically integrated system. The approach may be seen as the outcome of a cross fertilisation between industrial and innovation economics.

In the beginning of the 1980s, the idea of a national system of innovation was immanent in the work of several economists studying innovation. Richard R. Nelson together with other US scholars had compared technology policy and institutions in the high technology field in the US with Japan and

Europe (Nelson 1984). SPRU at Sussex University pursued several studies comparing industrial development in Germany and the UK covering for instance differences in the management of innovation, work practices and engineering education.

The idea of a national system of innovation was immanent also in the research program pursued by the IKE-group at Aalborg University.[5] In several working papers and publications from the first half of the 1980s we referred to 'the innovative capability of the national system of production'. The handier 'innovation system' appears for the first time in Lundvall (1985) but without the adjective national. Again, it was Christopher Freeman who brought the modern version of the full concept 'national innovation system' into the literature. He did so in 1987 in his book on innovation and innovation policy in Japan (Freeman 1987).

When Freeman collaborated with Nelson and Lundvall in the IFIAS-project on technical change and economic theory the outcome was a book (Dosi et al. 1988) with a section with several chapters on 'national systems of innovation' (Freeman 1988; Lundvall 1988; Nelson 1988). After followed three major edited volumes on the subject (Lundvall 1992; Nelson 1993; Edquist 1997).[6]

The innovation system concept may be regarded as a practical tool for designing innovation policy. But it might also be seen as a synthesis of analytical results produced by scholars working on innovation. In this section we give a brief review of the history of innovation research with focus on how different generations of economists have contributed to the modern understanding of innovation systems.

15.2.2. Innovation Research Starting with Adam Smith

The idea that innovation matters for economic development is present in the work of the classical economists. Innovation plays an important role in the introduction to Adam Smith's classical work on the Wealth of Nations. It is especially interesting to note that he identifies and distinguishes *two different modes of innovation* (see Box 2 below).

The first mode is experience-based and I will refer to it as the DUI-mode – learning by doing, using and interacting. The other mode refers to science-based research processes and I will refe to it as the STI-mode – science is seen as the first step toward technology and innovation. In this chapter we will argue that this distinction is fundamental when it comes to analyzing modern innovation systems and also when it comes to design management strategy as well as public policy.[7]

Box 2: Adam Smith on Innovation and Modes of Learning

Adam Smith (1776: p. 8) on the DUI-Mode of Learning:

A great part of the machines made use of in those manufactures in which labour is most subdivided, were originally the inventions of common workmen, who, being each of them employed in some very simple operation, naturally turned their thoughts towards finding out easier and readier methods of performing it. Whoever has been much accustomed to visit such manufactures, must frequently have been shown very pretty machines, which were the inventions of such workmen, in order to facilitate and quicken their own particular part of the work. In the first fire-engines, a boy was constantly employed to open and shut alternately the communication between the boiler and the cylinder, according as the piston either ascended or descended. One of those boys, who loved to play with his companions, observed that, by tying a string from the handle of the valve which opened this communication, to another part of the machine, the valve would open and shut without his assistance, and leave him at liberty to divert himself with his play-fellows. One of the greatest improvements that has been made upon this machine, since it was first invented, was in this manner the discovery of a boy who wanted to save his own labour.

Adam Smith (1776: p. 9) on the STI-Mode of Learning:

All the improvements in machinery, however, have by no means been the inventions of those who had occasion to use the machines. Many improvements have been made by the ingenuity of the makers of the machines, when to make them became the business of a peculiar trade; and some by that of those who are called philosophers or men of speculation, whose trade it is not to do any thing, but to observe every thing; and who, upon that account, are often capable of combining together the powers of the most distant and dissimilar objects. In the progress of society, philosophy or speculation becomes, like every other employment, the principal or sole trade and occupation of a particular class of citizens. Like every other employment too, it is subdivided into a great number of different branches, each of which affords occupation to a peculiar tribe or class of philosophers; and this subdivision of employment in philosophy, as well as in every other business, improves dexterity, and saves time. Each individual becomes more expert in his own peculiar branch, more work is done upon the whole, and the quantity of science is considerably increased by it.

15.2.3. Friedrich List on the Need for an Active State to Build Innovation Systems

While Adam Smith was propagating free trade and a liberal economy the German economist Friedrich List disagreed. He characterized Adam Smith's theory as 'cosmopolitan' and argued that if followed by other countries, it would just confirm and reinforce the dominance of the British Empire in the world economy (Reinert 1999).

He argued that for countries such as Germany, trying to 'catch up' with the leading economy, there was a need for government intervention. List presented a broad agenda for government in the building of infrastructure that could contribute to technical advance. It is interesting to note that he referred to

NATIONAL SYSTEMS OF INNOVATION

'mental capital' as the most important kind of capital. He argued that the wealth of nations more than anything else reflected '*the accumulation of all discoveries, inventions, improvements, perfections and exertions of all generations which have lived before us*' (Freeman 1995a, p. 6).

15.2.4. Karl Marx on Technological Progress

The historical parts of Das Kapital give deep insights in how new technologies shape the economy and society. The basic assumption in his historical analysis that new productive forces may get into conflict with 'production relations' is a useful guideline for how to study innovation systems. At the micro-level this corresponds to the fact that radically new technologies cannot flourish in firms 'locked in' into old organisational forms and competence sets. At the aggregate level it corresponds to the need to transform societal institutions, competences and organizations in order to reap the benefits of technological revolutions.[8]

Marx is a pioneer also when it comes to emphasize the importance both of 'science as a force of production' and 'technological competition' where firms need to engage in innovation in order to gain markets and reduce costs. Many of his insights on the role of science and technology in relation to the economy are very advanced for his time (Rosenberg 1976).

15.2.5. Marshall's Contribution

Marshall (Marshall 1919; Marshall 1920) is known as one of the founding fathers of modern neo-classical economics. He was also the one who introduced the concept 'the representative firm' – a concept that has contributed to the lack of understanding of economic development in modern neo-classical economics. But as documented by Metcalfe (2006) in a different reading Marshall may be seen as contributing not only to evolutionary understanding of industrial dynamics in general, but also to the idea of a national system of innovation (Metcalfe 2006: p.17). He links innovation to management competences, brings the wider institutional setting in terms of different types of research laboratories into the analysis and recognises that the overall system and mode of innovation may differ across national borders (ibid. p.19).

Marshall's focus on incremental innovation – rather than on the radical innovations as emphasized by Schumpeter – may be seen as an important inspiration for modern innovation research. As will be argued below, any attempt to link innovation to economic growth and development needs to capture radical and incremental innovation but also the on-going processes of imitation and learning (Arocena and Sutz 2000a).

As with Adam Smith it is possible to discern two types of mechanisms for the advancement of knowledge and technology and in the case of Marshall they are linked to two types of 'innovation systems'. One refers to industrial districts where the focus is on experience-based learning (DUI) and the other refers to the national system of research (STI).

Marshall is unique in being a potential source of inspiration both for mainstream and evolutionary economics. This reflects his ambition to develop a theory that explains fluctuations in supply and demand with a theory that explains economic development. His method to try to combine the short-term static analysis and the evolutionary development where innovation takes place and agents become more competent is to introduce the distinction between short period, long period and secular period. Metcalfe argues that this should be seen primarily as an attempt to link order and change.

While the national innovation system approach assumes innovation to be a ubiquitous and on-going process, not to be relegated to 'the secular period', it also operates with a distinction between order and change. It assumes that for national economies there are systemic features in terms of economic structures and relationships as well as institutions that represent continuity and order and that form the environment for innovation processes where technical knowledge and the competence of individuals and organisations change.

15.2.6. Joseph Schumpeter as the Grandfather of Modern Innovation Theory

Joseph Schumpeter is generally seen as the founder of modern innovation research and many scholars who work on innovation would accept to be classified as Neo-Schumpeterian.[9]

In *Theory of economic development* (Schumpeter 1934) innovation is seen as the major mechanism behind economic dynamics. The dynamo of the system is the individual entrepreneur who introduces innovations in markets and creates new enterprises. After the pioneers follow imitators and gradually the profits created by the original wave of innovation are eroded.

In *Capitalism, Socialism and Democracy* (Schumpeter 1942) the innovation mechanism is quite different. Here the major source of innovation is not the brave individual entrepreneur but the big company with experts working together in R&D teams searching for new technological solutions. The distinction between the two ways to present the motor of innovation has led scholars to refer to *Schumpeter Mark I* and *Schumpeter Mark II*.

We can use some of Schumpeter's ideas to inspire our analysis of innovation systems. First, we might note the important role of imitation. The overall performance of an innovation system will reflect not only the pioneers but also the capability of followers. Second, we might revise his analytical scheme and regard the total population of firms in a system as including both Mark I- and Mark II-firms. We may characterise specific national system as being more or less dominated by one type or the other.

But at one very important point Schumpeter's ideas deviate from the basic insights behind the innovation system concept. Schumpeter took an extreme position assuming *that the demand side would simply adjust to the supply side.*[10] It is true that he defines the opening of new markets as one kind of innovation. But, in general, consumers and users are assumed to be ready to absorb whatever new innovations is brought to them by entrepreneurs or firms. Actually, it might be argued that the innovation system perspective came out of a criticism of Schumpeter's relative neglect of the demand side.

Schmookler (1966) opened the debate with taking almost the opposite view of Schumpeter. He used a host of empirical data on inventions as well as secondary sources to demonstrate that inventions and innovations tend to flourish in areas where demand is strong and growing. One important outcome of the ensuing debate was *a new perspective on innovation as reflecting the interplay between technology-push and demand-pull.* The critical debate of Schmookler's empirical results confirmed this new perspective (Mowery and Rosenberg 1979).

The Chain-Linked model, where both supply push and demand pull are analysed in relation to scientific knowledge, may be seen as one contribution to the new perspective (Kline and Rosenberg 1986). The perspective on innovation as a process of interaction between producers and users may be seen as a micro-dimension of this new perspective (Lundvall 1985).

15.2.7. Christopher Freeman as the Father of Modern Innovation Theory

Christopher Freeman played a key role in stimulating these new theoretical developments, especially in Europe.[11] In the early 1980s, his lectures to Ph.D.-students were on Schumpeter Mark I and Mark II and on the controversy between Schumpeter and Schmookler regarding the role of supply and demand in the innovation process.[12] His founding of Science Policy Research Unit (SPRU) at Sussex University 1966 was a major step toward giving innovation studies a more permanent institutional foundation.

One important reference in his lectures in the beginning of the 1980s was to the *Sappho-study* organised at SPRU (Rothwell 1972; Rothwell 1977). This study was simple but original in design. The research team located a number of innovation pairs – 'twins' in terms of major characteristics – where one of the two was a success while the other was a failure. The two innovations were then compared in terms of characteristics of the 'host' organization. The most important result was that *interaction* within and between organizations came out as a prerequisite for success in innovation. Innovations that took place in firms where divisions operated without interaction with each other and firms that did not interact with suppliers, users and customers were less successful than the more interactive firms.[13]

Freeman pioneered the vision that innovation should be understood as an interactive process; not as a linear one where innovation automatically comes out of R&D efforts. As mentioned above, Freeman was also the pioneer when it came to introduce the concept of 'national system of innovation' (Freeman 1982/2004).

15.2.8. The Flourishing 1980s

The 1980s was a period when innovation research became 'emancipated' and more ambitious also in confronting basic assumptions in standard economics. Important work took place in different areas both in Europe and in the US. Dosi, Pavitt and Soete made important contributions to the role of innovation in relation to foreign trade (Dosi, Pavitt and Soete 1990). Christopher Freeman and Soete analyzed employment issues in relation to technical innovation (Freeman and Soete 1987). Giovanni Dosi established his hypothesis on shifts in technological paradigms (Dosi 1984).

Box 3: Different Perspectives on National Systems

Scholars, comparing national systems in terms of how they differ in qualitative terms and in terms of how they perform, have developed and made use of different perspectives. The analysis of the *national competitive advantage* by Michael Porter borrowed some ideas from the innovation system tradition – especially the importance of domestic demand and domestic user for product innovation. But he also added unique ideas about the positive impact of domestic competition on innovation in specific sectors of clusters.

Whitley's analysis of *national business systems* offers important inspiration for the analysis of innovation systems (Whitley 1994). The basic idea that match and mismatch between different elements of the system affect performance and that it is possible to develop a typology of national systems are in line with Freeman's comparison between the Japanese and the Anglo-Saxon systems. But Whitleys analysis is broader and it introduces cultural and social dimensions in the analysis.

Similar intentions lie behind the concept Social Systems of innovation (Amable, Barré and Boyer 1997). Recent work on the micro-organisational basis for learning by Lorenz and Valeyre indicates that the systemic features distinguishing the taxonomic categories are rooted in different types of micro-organisational structures.

In the US, the Nelson and Winter's evolutionary economic approach to economic growth signalled a more ambitious agenda for innovation research (Nelson and Winter 1982). Rosenberg and Kline presented the Chain-linked model (Kline and Rosenberg 1986). Freeman and Lundvall developed further ideas about innovation as an interactive process and innovation systems together with Richard Nelson.

Box 4: Does the Innovation System have a Function?

Edquist (2005) argues that the NSI-concept is diffuse and calls for making it more rigorous, systematic and 'theory-like' concept. This is always a legitimate concern but it is not obvious that the direction he recommends for the effort would bring us in this direction.

Edquist argues that the innovation system has 'as general function' to pursue innovation processes. His functionalist approach seems to emanate from a version of system theory as is practiced among engineers (Rickne 2000). *We would argue that social systems only have the functions that we assign to them.* If I were to assign a function to the national system of innovation I would be more specific than defining it as just 'pursuing innovation' and propose that the function is to contribute to economic performance on the basis of processes of creation and diffusion of knowledge. This corresponds to the normative focus of those who pioneered the NSI-concept.

Edquist lists ten *activities* (also referred to as 'functions' on p. 189) that should be studied in a systematic manner in terms of their respective 'causes and determinants'. The list encompasses quite disparate elements including for instance forms of knowledge creation and learning, organizational forms, market demand and public policy instruments.

The idea that studying separately each of the listed activities reminds somewhat of Edward Denison's attempt to reduce the growth residual through growth accounting. We can see the listing of a number of 'activities' as being potentially useful as establishing a checklist for managers and policy makers (Rickne 2000). It might also be helpful when comparing market with non-market economies (Liu and White 2001).

But in terms of theoretical understanding, it represents a step backwards since much of what we already know about the innovation process is neglected. For instance the distinction made between the three kinds of learning neglects that one of them (innovation) comes out of practising the other two (R&D and competence building) (Edquist op.cit., pp. 191–92). It is therefore not obvious how studying them separately would lead to more rigorous theory.

These different efforts merged in two different major projects. One was a major book project led by a team consisting of Dosi, Freeman, Nelson, Silverberg and Soete (1988). The other major project took place in the policy realm and was organized by the Directorate for Science Technology and Industry at OECD. Director Chabbal initiated the TEP-project and Francois Chesnais was the intellectual dynamo of the project. The TEP-report integrated many of the most advanced ideas developed among innovation scholars in the 1980s and it gave innovation policy as well as innovation studies a new kind of legitimacy in all OECD-countries (OECD 1992). The idea that innovation is an interactive process and that it is useful to analyse 'national innovation systems' was spread to policy makers.

While the TEP-project gave legitimacy to the innovation system concept among policy makers it did not result in a clean break with the linear model where innovation is seen as emanating more or less automatically from science. In international organisations, as in national governments, the strong position of expertise based upon standard economics contributed to a narrow interpretation of the national system of innovation. Triple Helix and Mode 2 theories also tend to support a perspective where the DUI-mode of innovation is neglected.

15.2.9. Intentions Behind the Original Conceptualisation of National Systems of Innovation

As we have seen, the innovation system perspective integrates principal results from innovation research. For several of the protagonists of the concept, including Freeman and myself, it was seen not only as a tool to explain innovation. It was also seen as constituting an alternative analytical framework and a challenge to standard economics when it comes to explain competitiveness, economic growth and development. In the next section we compare the NSI-perspective with the basic assumptions of standard economics.

Many recent contributions to innovation systems have different and in a sense more modest ambitions 'to explain innovation' by linking inputs in terms of investment in R&D to outputs in terms of patents or new products. They may emanate from scholars connected to technical universities and business schools and have as principal aim to give good advice to business managers or specialised government agencies. Other contributions, emanating from international economic organisations analysing national growth performance combine the system perspective with elements of neo-classical economics. Some even utilise production function techniques based upon standard economics assumption, including agents acting on the basis of rational expectations. In this post scriptum I will stick to the original ambitions when discussing how to study national systems of innovation.

15.3. National Innovation System as Analytical Focusing Device

The innovation system framework is in direct competition with standard economics when it comes to give advice to policy makers. In this section we will try to present the core theoretical ideas behind the innovation system perspective and confront them with those of standard economics. Our main conclusion is that the neglect in standard economics of 'learning as competence building' is a major weakness that makes it less relevant for understanding innovation and dynamic economic performance, especially in the current era of the learning economy.

15.3.1. Theoretical Elements Entering into the Innovation System Concept

As indicated in the first section the national innovation system approach is grounded on empirical findings through the 1970s and 1980s many of which emanated from scholars connected to SPRU. Of special importance were the Sappho-study and the Pavitt taxonomy (Rothwell 1977; Pavitt 1984). The Sappho-study demonstrated that interaction and feedbacks are crucial for the innovation performance of the firm while the Pavitt taxonomy helped to see how different sectors interact and fulfil different functions in the overall innovation process.

But, the concept also reflects deductive reasoning explaining the stylized facts observed in empirical studies. For instance, on reflection, it is obvious that product innovation could not thrive in an economy with 'pure markets' characterized by arm's length and anonymous relationships between the innovating producer and the potential user (Lundvall 1985; Lund Vinding 2002; Christensen and Lundvall 2004).

The only solution to the paradox that product innovations are quite frequent in the market economy is that most markets are not 'pure'; rather they are 'organized' and include a mix of trust, loyalty and power relationships. To establish these durable relationships it is necessary for the parties involved to invest in codes and channels of information – and to build 'social capital'. When it is realized that actual markets are mixed with organizational elements, it opens up the possibility that the elements of organization will differ between national and regional systems. This may be seen as constituting a micro-foundation for the innovation systems concept and it was presented as such by Nelson in Dosi (1988) and in Nelson (1993).[14]

Evolutionary economics constitutes a general theoretical framework for the analysis of innovation systems. It is a key assumption in evolutionary economics that agents and organisational routines differ and that *diversity* is fundamental for the dynamics of the system. Innovation creates novelty and diversity in the system, competition is a selection process that reduces diversity, while some routines are reproduced over time. In what follows we will assume that evolution in terms of what people and organisations know and in terms of how they learn is especially important for the dynamic performance of the national innovation system.

Box 5: Is Innovation System a Theory?

Edquist has raised the question if innovation is 'a theory' and his response has been in the negative. In a sense it is obvious that 'innovation system' is a concept rather than 'a general theory'. It is certainly true that it does not specify general laws of cause and effect. But nonetheless this way of putting the question may lead to misleading conclusions for how to proceed research and analytical work in relation to innovation systems.

One problem with posing and answering the question is that it is far from clear what should be meant with 'theory' in social science. As indicated in the earlier section, the innovation system perspective is built upon a series of coherent assumptions. It is also true that most of these assumptions are rooted in systematic empirical work and that they can be tested as well as rejected by further empirical work. Using the perspective helps to see, understand and control phenomena that could not be seen, understood or controlled without using this (or a similar) concept. In this sense it does what theory is expected to do: it helps to organize and focus the analysis, it helps to foresee what is going to happen, it helps to explain what has happened and it helps to give basis for rational action.

The fact that different scholars work with different delimitations of the components of the system and with different focus on elements and relationships does not make the concept less theoretical or scientific. In this paper I have argued in favour of a 'broad definition of the NSI'. But this argument reflects a specific purpose – i.e. to link innovation to economic performance at the national level. It is equally legitimate to pursue the analysis with a more narrow perspective – such as the one implicit in the triple-helix approach – if, for instance, the purpose is to analyse international differences in the emergence of science-based technologies.

A more realistic and fertile approach for social science than the aim to develop general theory is to combine attempts to build general, valid and reliable knowledge about causalities with the insight that social science, by definition, always will remain historical. In such an endeavour heuristic concepts and focusing devices such as national systems of innovation may play a major role since they offer a broad and flexible framework for organizing and interpreting case studies and comparative analyses (Mjøset 2001; Mjøset 2002). To develop a 'general theory' of innovation systems that abstracts from time and space would therefore undermine the utility of the concept both as an analytical tool and as a policy tool (Shin 2004).

15.3.2. Knowledge and Learning

In the very beginning of this volume we stated that 'the most fundamental resource in the modern economy is knowledge and, accordingly, the most important process is learning.' But at the time (1992) our use of the concepts of knowledge and learning were not at all well developed. Over the last 15 years the attempts to get a better understanding of the knowledge-based economy and the learning economy have created a more satisfactory theoretical foundation for the understanding of innovation systems (see for instance Lundvall and Johnson 1994; OECD 2000; Foray 2004; Amin and Cohendet 2004).

The understanding has been developed using the basic distinctions between information and knowledge, between 'knowing about the world' and 'knowing how to change the world' and between knowledge that is explicit and codified versus knowledge that remains implicit and tacit (Johnson, Lorenz and Lundvall 2003). In Lundvall and Johnson (1994) we introduced a distinction between Know What, Know Why, Know How and Know Who that has proved to be useful in understanding knowledge creation and learning in innovation systems. These distinctions are especially helpful when it comes to contrast the theoretical micro foundations of innovation systems with those of standard economics.

If neo-classical models include learning, it is understood either as getting access to more information about the world (know what) or it is treated as a black-box phenomenon as in growth models assuming 'learning by doing'. The very fundamental fact that agents – individuals as well as firms – *are more or less competent* (in terms of know-how and know-why) and are *more or less integrated in knowledge-based networks* (know-who) is abstracted from in order to keep the analysis simple and based upon 'representative firms' and agents. *This abstraction is most problematic in an economy where the distribution of competence becomes more and more uneven and the capability to learn tends to become the most important factor behind the economic success of people, organizations and regions* (Lundvall and Johnson 1994).

15.3.3. The Theory Behind Innovation Systems

As pointed out, List was critical to the exaggerated focus on allocation as opposed to knowledge creation and growth. Table 15.1 illustrates how the analytical framework connected to innovation systems relates to mainstream economic theory. The theoretical core of standard economic theory is about rational agents making choices to which are connected well-defined (but possibly risky) alternative outcomes and the focus of the analysis is on the allocation of scarce resources. As illustrated by the following table the emphasis is different in the innovation system approach.

The analysis of innovation systems is based upon a two-dimensional shift of focus toward the combination of innovation and learning. While standard economics is preoccupied with specifying the institutional set-up that results in an optimal allocation of existing resources we are concerned with how different

Table 15.1. **The Two-Dimensional Shift in Perspective**

	Allocation	Innovation
Choice making	Standard neoclassical	Project management
Learning	Austrian Economics	Innovation systems

institutional set-ups affect the creation of new resources. While standard economics analyse how agents make choices on the basis of given sets of information and competences, we are interested in how the knowledge – including both information about the world and know-how of agents – change in the economic process.

This double shift in perspective has implications for innovation policy. Just to take one example, a policy analysis of patent races where 'winner takes it all' will, as far as it neglects the learning and competence building that takes place during the race, end up with too restrictive conclusions regarding the role of government in stimulating R&D.

15.3.4. The NSI-Perspective is More Complex – Not Less Theoretical – Than Standard Economics

What has been said obviously implies a more complex theory than standard neoclassical economics where it is assumed that all agents have equal access to technologies and are equally competent in developing and utilizing them. But it would be wrong to conclude that the theory behind innovation systems is 'less theoretical'.

Basically, the theory underlying innovation system analysis is about learning processes involving skilful but imperfectly rational agents and organizations. It assumes that organizations and agents have a capability to enhance their competence through searching and learning and that they do so in interaction with other agents and that this is reflected in innovation processes and outcomes in the form of innovations and new competences.

The methodological dictum within neo-classical economics that theory should be both general and abstract sometimes takes Occam's razor too far leading to negligence of the concrete and historical. But the most important weakness of neo-classical theory is not that it is too abstract. *It is rather that it makes the wrong abstractions.* In a context where knowledge is the most important resource and learning the most important process neo-classical theory tends to abstract from the very processes that make a difference in terms of the economic performance of firms and for the wealth of nations.

Processes of competence building and innovation are at the focal point in innovation system analysis. The focus is upon how enduring relationships and patterns of dependence and interaction are established, evolve and dissolve as time goes by. New competences are built while old ones are destroyed. At each point of time discernable patterns of collaboration and communication characterize the innovation system. But, of course, in the long term these patterns change in a process of creative destruction of knowledge and relationships. A crucial normative issue is how such patterns affect the creation of new resources and to what degree they support learning among agents.

Box 6: Different Meanings of Learning

As any everyday concept learning has several different connotations. In the literature on learning organizations it is often referred to as *adaptation*: as a process where agents when confronted with new circumstances register and internalize the change and adapt their behaviour accordingly.

In education we see learning also as a process of *competence-building*. We assume that new competences can be established through education and training and thereafter mobilized when coping with and mastering theoretical and practical problems.

In our analysis of innovation systems we see learning as referring both to adaptation and competence building. And we emphasize that competence building takes place on-the-job through learning by doing, learning by using and learning by interacting.[15]

15.3.5. Standard Economics Favours Narrow Interpretation of Innovation Systems

Standard economics tends to stick to the idea that only quantitative as opposed to qualitative concepts can be accepted as scientific (Georgescu Roegen 1971). One reason for the bias toward narrow interpretations of innovation systems is that it is much easier to develop quantitative analysis of R&D and patents, than it is to measure organizational forms and outcomes of organizational learning.

Standard economics will typically focus on potential market failure and on choices to be made between different alternative uses of scarce resources. In the context of innovation policy the concern will be, first, if public rates of return are higher that private rates and, second, if the rate of return of public money is higher in investing in R&D than it would be in other areas of public investment.[16] The very idea that there might be organizational forms that are more efficient than the ones already in use cannot be reconciled with the basic analytical framework where it is assumed that agents, including firms, are equally rational and competent.

Standard economics will tend to see the market as the 'natural', if not optimal, framework of human interaction and economic transaction. This leads to biased conclusions when considering how to organize the economy (Nelson 2006). The concept 'market failure' reflects this bias since it indicates that other institutional set-ups should be considered only when it is obvious that the market cannot do the job.

15.4. Challenges for Innovation System Research

15.4.1. Causality in a Systemic Context

A major challenge for innovation system analysis is to avoid thinking in terms of mechanical models of causality and develop theory as well as analytical techniques that make it possible to study how different factors interact in a systemic context.

When studying national systems it is a specific challenge for statistical analysis that the 'population' is so small and heterogeneous. Some statistical procedures will as first approximation look for causality patterns that are general for the whole population – for all national systems of innovation. Such procedures are sometimes used in empirical analysis of determinants of economic growth. We believe that other methods are more useful when it comes to study national systems of innovation. Clustering procedures that result first in dividing the population into different 'sub-species' or 'families' with common characteristics (level of development, size, continental belonging etc.) and second in looking for patterns of interdependency for each of the different families and finally relating this to multidimensional indicators of economic performance.

It is for instance common to rank the US at the top of performance together with the small Nordic countries. But it is also well known that the US-system is fundamentally different from the small Nordic countries in terms of institutions and characteristics (population size, size of the public sector, degree of inequality, industrial structure and mode of innovation). Therefore, in spite of the fact that both categories belong to the same species, 'national systems of innovation', there is no reason to assume that the mechanism linking R&D effort to innovation and economic performance is the same in the two countries.

The idea that the aim of innovation research is to end up with general laws that can be applied equally in all national systems is mistaken. There are certain activities that can be linked to innovation and that link innovation to economic growth in all systems. But the mechanisms differ across different national systems. This is why theoretical work on national innovation systems cannot dispense from historical analysis.

15.4.2. Understanding Knowledge and Learning

One important challenge for innovation system analysis is to deepen the understanding of how different kinds of knowledge are created and used in the process of innovation. Some elements of knowledge are local and tacit, embodied in people and embedded in organizations. Other elements are global, explicit and can easily be transferred from one part of the world to another. Different sectors in the economy and in society make use of different mixes of local and global knowledge and in some areas, such as education and business consulting, it is especially difficult to codify the know-how that consultants and teachers make use of when they give advice and teach (OECD 2000).

To understand how learning takes place within organizations as well as in the interaction between organizations is a key to understand how systems of innovation work. While it is important to study national characteristics in terms of organisations that pursue R&D, it is equally important to understand national characteristics in terms of how firms interact with customers and to what degree different firms give employees access to competence-building in connection with on-going economic activities.

15.4.3. The Co-Evolution of the Division of Labour, Interaction and Cooperation

As pointed out by Adam Smith, a fundamental process in economic development and economic growth is the deepening and extension of the division of labour. Specialization within and between organizations makes it possible to exploit scale economies and also to focus on competence building so that it can advance more rapidly.

As the horizontal and vertical division of labour evolves it contributes to *diversity* and diversity feeds innovation. But the growing specialisation also creates new barriers for communication and interaction. This is highly relevant because innovation is the outcome of combining knowledge located at different sites in a specialized innovation system. It is well documented that different departments (R&D, production, sales etc.) within a firm have difficulties to understand and communicate with each other. At the individual level, experts with different specialties have difficulties to interact and understand each other. The ease to communicate across such barriers in a national system with vertical disintegration between organizations is especially interesting because it is here product innovations are developed in an interaction between users and producers (Lundvall 2006).

It is a major challenge to understand the co-evolution of the division of labour and the interaction that takes place within and between organizations.

In some countries it is much easier to establish co-operation within and/or between organizations than it is in other countries. This will be reflected in the actual division of labour and affect the kind of learning and innovation that takes place in the system.

15.4.4. Firms as Sites for Employee Learning

Innovation indicators reflect outputs such as number of patents or inputs that are easy to measure such as R&D expenditure. When it comes to indicators of knowledge there is a strong bias in favour of knowledge that is explicit. Investment in scientific knowledge is measured by surveys on R&D and innovation. The know-how built up through learning by doing, using and interacting is much more difficult to measure. Human capital measurements may register formal investment in education but what people learn at the workplace or as consumers is not easy to capture through standard measurements.

The absence of indicators makes the area less visible for policy makers and this contributes to a bias in innovation policy toward promoting STI- rather than DUI-activities (see Table 15.2 below).

In recent empirical work by Lorenz and Valeyre it has been shown that there are dramatic differences between Europe's national systems in terms of how and how much the average employee learns at his/her workplace (Lorenz and Valeyre 2006). While in Denmark a majority of workers are engaged in 'discretionary learning' where they combine learning through problem solving with a certain autonomy in their work situation, the majority of workers in countries such as Greece and Spain are engaged in taylorist type of work with much more limited opportunities for learning and with very little autonomy (See Box 7).

In a follow-up to the analysis of these national patterns of workplace learning they have been combined with innovation indicators. The analysis shows, first, that on average countries that make intensive use of discretionary learning are most prone to engage in 'endogenous innovation' (defined as innovations that emanate from in-house R&D efforts and result in products new to the market). But, second, it shows that strong economic performance may emanate from quite different combinations of innovation and learning modes. For instance Denmark is not very strong in endogenous innovation but very strong in discretionary learning while the opposite is true for another Nordic country, Finland (Arundel, Lorenz, Lundvall and Valeyre 2006).

The national differences in what people do and learn at their workplace is a major factor structuring the national innovation system and affecting its performance: It is certainly more fundamental and difficult to change than for instance R&D intensity. In countries such as Finland and Korea these favoured

BERD-measures of 'performance' reflect the propensity to do research within one big corporation such as Nokia and Samsung. This contrasts with indicators of competence building in working life since these refer to how competence building takes place in all parts of the economy.

Box 7: National patterns in Work Organisation[17]

	Discretionary Learning	Lean Production Learning	Taylorist Organisation	Simple Organisation
North				
Netherlands	64,0	17,2	5,3	13,5
Denmark	60,0	21,9	6,8	11,3
Sweden	52,6	18,5	7,1	21,7
Finland	47,8	27,6	12,5	12,1
Austria	47,5	21,5	13,1	18,0
Centre				
Germany	44,3	19,6	14,3	21,9
Luxemb.	42,8	25,4	11,9	20,0
Belgium	38,9	25,1	13,9	22,1
France	38,0	33,3	11,1	17,7
West				
UK	34,8	40,6	10,9	13,7
Ireland	24,0	37,8	20,7	17,6
South				
Italy	30,0	23,6	20,9	25,4
Portugal	26,1	28,1	23,0	22,8
Spain	20,1	38,8	18,5	22,5
Greece	18,7	25,6	28,0	27,7
EU-15	39,1	28,2	13,6	19,1

Source: Lorenz and Valeyre (2006).

The Table 1 shows that people working in different national systems of innovation and competence building *have very different access* to learning by doing. It also shows that at lower income levels the bigger proportion of the workforce that work in either simple or Taylorist organizations. The richer the country the more workers are employed in discretionary learning contexts. But it is also important to note that countries at similar income levels – Germany and the UK – have quite different distributions of workers between the four forms. While the proportion of workers operating in the lean production is more than 40% in the UK, it is less than 20% Germany. The micro foundation of national systems of innovation differs not only because of levels of income but also because of other systemic features.

15.4.5. The Weak Correlation between Strength of the Science-Base and Economic Performance

Over the last century there has been a certain focus on the European Paradox referring to the assumed fact that Europe is strong in science but weak in innovation and economic growth.[18] Similar paradoxes have been argued to exist in countries such as The Netherlands, Finland and Sweden. In a recent OECD-report a *general result* is that for the countries included in the study it can be shown that those that 'perform well' in terms of STI-indicators do not perform well in terms of innovation (OECD 2005, p. 29).[19] This indicates that what is registered is not so much a paradox as it is a systematic weakness in the theoretical analysis and the indicators upon which it is built.

We would argue that these apparent paradoxes emanate from a narrow understanding of the innovation process. They demonstrate that heavy investment in science in systems where organizational learning within and between firms is weakly developed and where there is a weak focus on user needs has only limited positive impact upon innovation and economic growth.

This can be illustrated by data on innovation performance at the firm level – see Table 15.2. In a series of recent papers based upon a unique combination of survey and register data for Danish firms we have demonstrated that firms that engage in R&D without establishing organizational forms that promote learning and neglect customer interaction are much less innovative than firms that are strong both in terms to STI- and DUI-learning (Jensen, Johnson, Lorenz and Lundvall 2007).[20]

Table 15.2 refers to the outcome of an analysis of survey and register data for almost 700 Danish firms and it presents different variables related to the propensity to introduce new products or services. We use sector, size and form of ownership as control variables but the focus is upon a variable indicating *the mode of innovation* in the firm. We distinguish between firms that are strong in science-based learning, firms strong in organizational learning, firms that are strong in both respects and we use those firms that are weak in both respects as the benchmark category. To construct this variable we pursue a cluster analysis grouping the firms in the four categories.

We use firms that only make weak efforts to support science-based and experience-based learning as benchmark and the odds ratio estimate indicates how much higher the propensity to innovate is among firms strong in respectively one or both of the modes of learning. The results reported in Table 15.2 show that firms that combine the two modes are much more prone to innovate than the rest. It shows that the effect remains strong also after introducing control variables related to size and sector.

Box 8: How to Study National Systems?

Our interest in utilizing the innovation system perspective is not purely academic. We use this concept as a focusing device in order to better understand how innovation affects economic development at the national level. Within this broad view many factors contribute to innovation and it might be seen as a problem that almost all aspects of society need to be brought in to explain the actual pattern of innovation. To structure the analysis it is useful to distinguish between the *core* of the innovation system and *the wider setting*. Both need to be included in the analysis since the aim is to link innovation to economic development.

Firms and the knowledge infrastructure constitute the core of the system. In principle we include all firms in the core since every firm has a potential for developing, absorbing or using new technology.

The wider setting refers to institutions that contribute to competence building and institutions that shape human interaction in relation to innovation. These include, first, family pattern, education system, career patterns in labour markets, inequality and social welfare systems. Second, they include the historical record of macroeconomic stability and the access to finance. Third, they include the final demand from households and public sector organizations. Fourth, they include government and public policy directly aiming at stimulating innovation, including diffusion and efficient use.

This way of setting the scene indicates a marginal role for public policy. What is intended is rather to see public policy mainly as intervening in relation to the core and the wider setting of the national innovation system . Alternatively we could see public policy as endogenous. To some degree we take this perspective in Edquist and Lundvall (1993) where we demonstrate how innovation policy in Sweden and Denmark tends to reproduce rather than renew the strengths of the respective system.

As indicators of strong science-based learning we use the R&D expenditure, presence of employees with academic degree in natural science or technology and collaboration with scientists in universities or other science organizations. As indicator of experience-based learning we take the use of certain organizational practices normally connected with learning organizations such as 'interdisciplinary workgroups' and 'integration of functions' together with 'closer interaction with customers' – to signal learning by interacting and a focus on user needs.

The analysis and results reported above point to the need to develop our understanding of how different forms of knowledge and different modes of innovation are combined in different national innovation systems. The analysis also explains why narrow definitions of national innovation systems that focus only upon science-based innovation are of little relevance for the economic performance of firms and national innovation systems. This is not least important when it comes to analyse the barriers and opportunities for economic

Table 15.2. **The Probability that Firms Develop a New Product or a New Service**

Variables	Odds Ratio Estimate	Coefficient Estimate	Odds Ratio Estimate	Coefficient Estimate
STI Cluster	3.529	1.2611**	2.355	0.8564**
DUI Cluster	2.487	0.9109**	2.218	0.7967**
DUI/STI Cluster	7.843	2.0596**	5.064	1.6222**
Business services			1.433	0.3599
Construction			0.491	−0.7120*
Manuf. (high tech)			1.805	0.5905*
Manuf.(low and med. tech)			1.250	0.2229
Other services			0.747	−0.2923
100 and more employees			1.757	0.5635*
50–99 employees			0.862	−0.1481
Danish group			0.859	−0.1524
Single firm			0.521	−0.6526*
Customised product			1.378	0.3203
Pseudo R^2	0.1247	0.1247	0.1775	0.1775
N	692	692	692	692

** = significant at the .01 level.
* = significant at the .05 level.

development in poor countries, another challenge for innovation system research (Arocena and Sutz 2000b; Cassiolato, Lastres and Maciel 2003).

15.5. National Systems of Innovation and Economic Development

While the modern version of the concept of national systems of innovation was developed mainly in rich countries (Freeman 1982; Freeman and Lundvall 1988; Lundvall 1992; Nelson 1993; Edquist 1997) some of the most important elements actually came from the literature on development issues in the third world. For instance the Aalborg version (Andersen and Lundvall 1988) got some of its inspiration concerning the interdependence between different sectors from Hirschman (1958) and Stewart (1977). Other encouragements came from Myrdal (1968). Applying the systems of innovation approach to economic development brings into focus other research issues of general interest such as the need to understand how innovation relates to sustainable development, economic welfare and the role of government in commodifying knowledge.

Most chapters in this book treat the innovation system as an ex-post rather than as an ex-ante concept. The concept refers to relatively strong and diversified systems with well-developed institutional and infrastructural support of innovation activities. The perspective is one where innovation processes are evolutionary and path dependent and systems of innovation evolve over time in a largely unplanned manner. The system of innovation approach has not, to the same extent, been applied to system building. When applied to the South the focus needs to be shifted in the direction of system construction and system promotion – something that was central in List's ideas for catching up – and to the fact that public policy is a conscious activity that needs to stimulate and supplement the spontaneous development of systems of innovation (Muchie, Gammeltoft and Lundvall 2003; Lundvall, Interakummerd and Lauridsen 2006).

Box 9: A Method to Study National Innovation Systems

In what follows I sketch a method to study national systems of innovation that moves from micro to macro – and back again to micro. The 'model' starts from the following stylized facts:

1. Firms play the most important role in the innovation system. Firms innovate in an interaction with other firms and with knowledge infrastructure.
2. Firms' mode of innovation and learning reflects national education systems, labour markets, etc.
3. Firms belonging to different sectors contribute differently to innovation processes.

Therefore the *first step* would be to analyze what takes place inside firms in terms of innovation in the light of organizational set-up and human resources while taking into account sector specialization.

A *second step* would be to analyze the interaction among firms and with knowledge infrastructure, including both domestic and international linkages.

A *third step* would be to explain national specificities in these respects with reference to national education, labour markets, financial markets, welfare regimes and intellectual property regimes.

A *fourth step* would be to use firm organization and network positioning as factors that explain the specialization and performance of the innovation system.

This method focuses the analysis on the central motor in the innovation system, i.e. the total population of firms, their linkages to each other and to the knowledge infrastructure. But it also recognizes that most parts of the socio-economic system may influence how this motor works and not least how it affects the performance of the economy as a whole.

Another weakness of the system of innovation approach is that it is still lacking in its treatment of the power aspects of development. The focus on interactive learning – a process in which agents communicate and cooperate in the creation and utilization of new economically useful knowledge – may lead to an underestimation of the conflicts over income and power, connected to the innovation process. In a global context where the access to technical knowledge is becoming restricted not only by weak 'absorptive capacity' but also by more and more ambitious global schemes to protect intellectual property this perspective gives a too rosy picture. Post-colonial and class privileges may block

---

Box 10: Innovation Systems and Development Thinking

As pointed out in the text the SI literature builds upon conceptual pillars rooted in the development discussion. The role of technology was an important part of the post-war debate on development. Schumpeter's (1934) concept of development contributed with two central ideas for this debate. One was the positive effects of generating new products and new processes. The other was the disruptive character of development. These two notions shaped the subsequent contributions, with Prebisch's (1950), Singer's (1950) and Myrdal's (1958) analyses of the long-term deterioration of terms of trade for primary products and of the distribution of gains between developed and developing countries.

In Latin America, a number of development studies followed Prebisch, arguing about the central role played by technical change in explaining the evolution of the capitalism and in determining the historical process of hierarchy formation of regions and countries. Furtado (1964), for instance, established an express relation between economic development and technological change pointing out that the growth of an economy was based on the accumulation of knowledge and understood development within a systemic, historically determined, view.

Inspired by Schumpeter an important and influential literature about how firms in the developing world acquire and develop technological capabilities unfolded during the 1970s and 1980s. Key concepts were the notions of technological capabilities and learning. Several empirical studies have shown how less developed countries have managed to develop significant skills, which have led to 'efficient' production, at least in the short term. These studies focused mostly on the capabilities of producers, e.g. knowledge and skills required for production (Katz 1984; Dahlman et al. 1987).

In the same period (1970s and 1980s), in Latin America, authors inspired by the Latin American Structuralist School (LASA) literature, developed a number of firm-level studies where the second of Schumpeter's ideas – the disruptive character of development – was taken into account. This work was instrumental in showing, not only successful stories of technological up-grading, but also important limitations of the capabilities and learning approach to technology and development; precisely because this approach left behind key elements, such as the role of institutions, of the macroeconomic regime and of power conflicts.

In East Asian economies, empirical investigation of successful evolution of innovation systems also helped to link the innovation systems perspective to development analyses. For example, case studies of the textile and clothing and electronics industries in the Taiwan Province of China and the Republic of Korea confirmed that inter-firm linkages, including subcontracting arrangements, were crucial channels of technological learning, in some cases, even more important than direct channels such as foreign direct investment (San Gee and Kuo 1998; Ernst, Ganiatsos and Mytelka 1998).

learning possibilities and existing competences may be destroyed for political reasons related to the global distribution of power.

Furthermore, the relationships between globalisation and national and local systems need to be further researched. It is important to know more about how globalisation processes affect the possibilities to build and support national and local systems of innovation in developing countries (Lastres and Cassiolato 2005). 'Borrowing' and adapting technologies that the technological lead countries control today is an important key to development. The combination of reverse engineering, licensing, sending scholars abroad, inviting foreign firms and experts and engaging in international scientific collaboration may be difficult to achieve but all these elements need to be considered in building the national innovation system. When building such systems it is a major challenge to develop national strategies that make it possible to select technologies and institutions from abroad that support innovation and competence building.

It is thus clear that the innovation system approach proposed here needs to be adapted to the situation in developing countries, if it is to be applied to system building. It is also clear that what is most relevant for developing economies is a broad definition of the NSI including not only low-tech industries but also primary sectors such as agriculture. Activities contributing to competence building needs to be taken into account and narrow perspectives that focus only on the STI-mode needs to be avoided.[21]

15.5.1. Welfare and Inequality in the Context of Innovation Systems

A promising line of research is to link the perspective of Amartya Sen (1999) on welfare and inequality to the national system perspective. Sen presents a capability-based approach where development is seen as an expansion of the substantive freedoms that people enjoy. Substantive freedoms are defined as the capabilities people have to live the kind of lives they have reason to value. They include things like being able to avoid starvation and undernourishment, diseases and premature mortality. It also includes the freedoms of being literate, able to participate in public life and in political processes, having ability and possibility to work and to influence one's work conditions, having entrepreneurial freedom and possibilities to take economic decisions of different kinds. Enhancement of freedoms like these is seen as both the ends and means of development.

This way of looking at development refers to the capabilities people have to act and to choose a life they value, rather than to their level of income and possession of wealth. Poverty, for example, is in this perspective more a deprivation of basic capabilities than just low income. Human capabilities rather than resource endowments are the fundamental factors of development.

Sen's approach fits well into a system of innovation approach. It is noteworthy however that learning and innovation capabilities generally do not seem to be explicitly included in this capability -based approach to development. Extending capabilities may be the result of changing the setting in which the agent operates, but even more important in the learning economy is whether the setting gives access to and stimulates a renewal and upgrading of the competence of agents.

The learning capability is thus one of the most important of the human capabilities and it is conditioned by national institutions and forms of work organisation (see for instance Box 7 for the case of Europe). It does not only have an instrumental role in development but also, under certain conditions, substantive value. When learning takes place in such a way that it enhances the capability of individuals and collectives to utilize and co-exist with their environment, it contributes directly to human well-being. Furthermore, to be able to participate in learning and innovation at the work place may be seen as 'a good thing' contributing to a feeling of belonging and significance.

15.5.2. On the Sustainability of Innovation Systems

National Systems of Innovation may be regarded as a tool for analysing economic development and economic growth. It aims at explaining how systemic features and different institutional set-ups at the national level link innovation and learning processes to economic growth.

But such a perspective may be too narrow. As pointed out by Freeman and Soete (1997) the ecological challenge ought to be integrated in any strategy for economic development and here we will argue that in the learning economy not only intellectual capital but also social capital is an important element in the development process. The extended perspective can be introduced as in diagram 3 below.

The diagram illustrates that economic growth is faced with a double challenge in terms of sustainability and that there is an immanent risk of undermining not only the material basis of material production (Segura-Bonilla 1999), but also the knowledge base. The creation of tangible capital may be

Diagram 3. Resources Fundamental for Economic Growth – Combining the Tangible and Reproducible Dimensions.

	Easily Reproducible Resources	Less Reproducible Resources
Tangible resources	1. Production capital	2. Natural capital
Intangible resources	3. Intellectual capital	4. Social capital

threatened by a neglect of environmental sustainability. We will argue that the production and efficient use of intellectual capital is fundamentally depending upon social capital (Woolcock 1998). A development strategy that focuses only on production capital and intellectual capital is not sustainable.

This is equally true for developed as for developing economies. But in most developed economies there has been a long history of institution building that helps to cope with sustainability (Russia is a case where there is imbalance between the level of technical development and institutions checking unsustainable development). Even if they are insufficient in many respects this kind of institutions are more developed than in the developing part of the world. A success in terms of economic growth in a less developed economy may therefore create extreme tension between growth and sustainability. Directing the efforts of the innovation system toward solving crises in ecological and social terms may be necessary in order to avoid real 'limits to growth'.

Innovation may have a positive role in bolstering sustainability. Technical innovation, for instance in terms of developing substitutes to naturally scarce raw products, may help to overcome the fact that natural capital cannot always be reproduced. In a similar vein new social institutions may help to overcome a crisis where social capital gets fragmented. In both cases it is important to note that the workings of unhampered market forces may in the longer term erode the basis of economic growth.

This perspective indicates a broader and more interdisciplinary approach to national innovation systems.

15.5.3. The Role of the State and the Commodification of Knowledge

As explained, the modern version of the innovation system concept was developed in the middle of the 1980s. It is important to note that the early versions were *critical* both to mainstream economics and to the prevailing economic policy where weak competitiveness was seen as primarily reflecting high costs and especially high wage costs.

The wide diffusion of the concept among policy makers took place in the 1990s. At the beginning of the new millennium most OECD countries had adopted the concept to support the design of innovation policy. In order to understand the interpretation of the concept in policy circles it is important to take into account the ideological and political climate that reigned during this diffusion process.

Basically the 1990s was a period with strong emphasis on market regulation and on private property rights as ideal institutions – the break-down of the centrally planned economies in Europe gave new impetus to neo-liberal strategies developed in the 1980s. This resulted in a certain degeneration of the concept. Analytical aspects of the concept that might lead to conclusions that went against the logic of markets and free trade were suppressed.

The original innovation system approach emphasized that knowledge and learning are crucial for economic performance in the current era (Lundvall 1992). But it does not follow that all knowledge should be 'commodified' and this is what seems to have become the major tendency. There is a growing trend in political circles to regard *all knowledge* as a potential commodity and to subordinate *all knowledge production* under the logic of international competitiveness. This is reflected in a movement in favour of expanding and strengthening intellectual property rights to the extreme and far beyond what promotes socio-economic progress and as well in a strong drive toward colonizing academic knowledge and make it subordinate to market demand.

To make universities more open to society is a necessary process and expectations that the knowledge produced at universities should contribute to economic welfare are legitimate. But the current drive toward the market is driven by the lop-sided understanding of innovation as emanating almost solely from science and therefore it goes too far.

The long-term implications and costs of making scholars and universities profit-oriented seem to be neglected among the protagonists of university reforms in the Bayh-Dole spirit.[22] Scholars who are stimulated to act strategically on their own behalf and on the behalf of their institution will certainly become less engaged in sharing their knowledge with others. Private companies might, in the short run, appreciate that universities become more profit-oriented but they will soon experience that the barriers around the knowledge accumulated will become higher and that access to the most relevant knowledge will become more difficult.

It is even more intriguing to reflect on what awaits at the end of the current trajectory; at the point in time where the entrepreneurial university has become truly a business corporation operating in international markets. At that point we must expect that WTO restrains the current freedom of national governments to subsidize basic research taking place within universities by competition laws and trade regulations. How could it be argued that private firms (universities) that compete on global markets should be subsidized by national government? To establish controls that make it certain that government support only goes to basic research without affecting services sold internationally would open up for complex legal processes. If governments wanted to go on subsidizing basic research they might need to establish a new set of institutions.[23]

Finally, there is a need to think about the implications for the role of universities of the fact that knowledge becomes more and more fundamental for the economy as for society as a whole. The historical role of universities has been an institution that 'validates' knowledge. It has been an institution that, while aiming at the full truth of matters, at least systematically tries to establish what 'reasonably reliable knowledge' is. This is also one reason why it has been an institution with a relative autonomy in relation to the state as well as in relation to economic interests. This function is even more important in a knowledge-based society.[24]

As a kind of countervailing power to the colonizing tendency emanating from market-oriented innovation policy we see a need to develop a wider field of politics – *knowledge politics* – that covers all aspects of knowledge production and takes into account that the production of knowledge has much wider scope than just contributing to economic growth. This includes of course knowledge necessary for social and ecological sustainability but not only that. In rich societies it should be possible to afford culture, ethics and knowledge for its own sake, not only knowledge that promotes innovation and economic growth. This implies that there might be a need for establishing a new kind of 'academy of science and knowledge' that has as one of its dedicated tasks to set the limits for how far innovation policy may influence knowledge production and use.

15.5.4. Higher Education, Innovation and Economic Development

In the context of poor countries the idea of a relative autonomy for universities may appear as a luxury that cannot be afforded. In a recent paper (Lundvall 2007) I have made an attempt to link higher education to innovation and economic development.

In less developed countries as in rich countries the most important function of universities remains to train academic personnel and give them competences so that they can be absorbed in meaningful employment where they solve problems that are so complex that less-skilled workers would fail. Such problems will appear more frequently in economies where innovation is frequent (Nelson and Phelps 1965; Schultz 1975). Therefore the design of the university system needs to be seen as an integrated part of the formation of a national system of innovation.

The idea that universities should serve as direct sources for innovation through their 'third mission' and that this mission should involve the creation of markets for knowledge implicit in much of the triple-helix literature is problematic in poor as in rich countries (Arocena and Sutz. 2005). To establish a closer interaction with the rest of society is especially important in less developed countries where the distance between academia and real life is often very big. But rather than creating market-oriented universities, what is needed is educational reform including the wide introduction of problem-based learning as teaching method and, in general, a closer interaction between theory and practise.

Box 11: The Globelics Experience

Globelics is a global research community combining scholars working on innovation studies with scholars working on development studies. It has been characterised as a network for 'researchers without borders' (www.globelics.org). The Globelics annual conferences take place in developing countries and the finance has been raised within the hosting country.

Besides the annual conferences, regional and national networks have been established in Asia, Latin America and China (see www.cicalics.org). Each year 40 Ph.D.-students, coming equally from Asia, Africa, Latin America and Europe, are invited to Globelics Academy in Lisbon where world-leading scholars in innovation studies for a 10 days period give lectures and methodological advice for their thesis work. A similar Cicalics Academy takes place in China every year with a majority of Chinese students and with international lecturers. New initiatives in Africa and India may soon result in similar activities in these areas.

The purpose of Globelics is to counterbalance the increasingly uneven global access to research networks. It gives scholars in less developed countries access to the most recent research and it opens up channels for publication of their work. It also makes it possible to share experiences among scholars from different parts of the developing world, by-passing the metropoles in the North. Several major research projects with global scope use Globelics as host – the Catch-Up project coordinated by Richard Nelson, The Brics-project co-ordinated by Jose Cassiolato and the Unidev project co-ordinated by Claes Brundenius.

Globelics has a scientific board with distinguished scholars such as Christopher Freeman and Richard Nelson and with leading scholars from the South. But basically Globelics is a self-organising global network. It draws its energy mainly from the fact that scholars from the North and the South find it highly rewarding to work together and learn from each other in a seriously committed but friendly atmosphere.

One major long term positive effect is that young scholars from all parts of the world, sometimes working in isolation and under difficult conditions, get inspiration and support in their effort to do good research on innovation. There is already a lively 'Globelics community' of young scholars who correspond regularly on both a scientific and a social basis.

Investment in higher education may not give substantial rates of return in a technologically stagnant economy. Since the alternative to invest in higher education is to remain in stagnation forever, our analysis needs to focus on two questions. First, how to design higher education in such a way that it helps to break the vicious circle of stagnation and stagnating demand for graduates? Second, how to design a general strategy for vitalising national innovation systems that includes investment in higher education as important element?

15.6. Conclusions

In this paper we went back to the origin of the concept of the national innovation system. We have argued that the original versions as developed by

Christopher Freeman and the Aalborg-group are more adequate tools when it comes to link innovation to aggregate national economic performance than narrow versions that focus mainly on the science base. In the current era there is a need both for strengthening the science base and for promoting experience-based learning. This is absolutely fundamental when it comes to link the analysis of national innovation systems to economic development.

This implies new directions for research on innovation systems. First, it is necessary to develop a better understanding and more efficient analytical techniques to study institutional 'complementarity' and 'mismatch' in innovation systems. Second, there is a need to deepen the understanding of the production, diffusion and use of knowledge. In this connection the focus should be on interactive learning processes and upon how 'social capital' evolves as a basis for interaction within and across organisational boundaries. Third, there is a need to understand and develop indicators of how and to what degree work places function as learning sites in different national systems. Fourth, a promising research strategy is to link organisational learning, mobility of people and network formation. Networks will always involve interaction between people and the specific career will have an impact on with whom and how agents interact.

Universities play an important role in the innovation system but the triple-helix perspective, with its neglect of DUI-mode of learning, may have led to exaggerated expectations of what can and should be expected from them. Universities need to be guaranteed a minimum autonomy in order to give long term contributions to knowledge creation and the idea that they should be completely subsumed to market forces and political control is incompatible with their role as guardians of what is 'reasonably reliable knowledge'. Their most important role in the national innovation system is not to be incubators for start-up firms or for patents, it remains the training of graduates for the labour market.

Today, as compared to the original 1992-approach, we would emphasize even more the importance of human resources. While one aspect of globalization is that codified knowledge moves quickly across borders, the most localized resource remains people, their tacit knowledge, their network relationships and their accumulated organizational experiences. Therefore all parts of the innovation system that contribute to competence building are becoming increasingly important for national performance.

Over the last decade there has developed a big lively and productive research community primarily studying industrial dynamics in the business sector and often the contributing scholar are employed at Business Schools or Technical Universities (compare for the annual Druid and the bi-annual Schumpeter conferences– www.druid.dk). There might be falling marginal returnt to this kind of research and seen from the point of view of the innovation system approach there are important issues not given sufficient attention. Five themes that have been touched upon in this post-script need to be further developed in future research:

- Implications of the NSI-approach for economic theory.
- NSI and economic development.
- NSI welfare states and inequality.
- Environmental sustainability of national innovation systems.
- Innovation in the public sector.

Most of these themes will require transdisciplinary efforts combining economics with management, sociology, political science and engineering.

NOTES

Chapter 1. Introduction

1 The IKE-group has through the last decade cooperated with Christopher Freeman from Science Policy Research Unit, Sussex University, Jan Fagerberg, from the Institute of Foreign Affairs, Oslo and Francois Chesnais, University of Paris and OECD, and we are happy to enrol all three of them as co-authors in this book. Previous contributions from the IKE-group on national systems of innovation are to be found in Lundvall (1988), Andersen and Lundvall (1988) and Johnson and Lundvall (1991).

2 Knowledge does not decrease in value when used. On the contrary, its use increases its value; i.e. knowledge is not scarce in the same sense as other natural resources and technical artefacts. Some elements of knowledge may be transfered, easily, between economic agents while others are tacit and embodied in individual, or collective, agents. Knowledge is not easily transacted in markets and not easily privately appropriated. In spite of attempts to find institutional solutions to the problem (patent laws etc.) property rights to knowledge are not easily defined. When it comes to knowledge market failure is the rule rather than the exception.

3 This implies, for example, that a foreign-owned firm will be part of two different national systems – its home country and its host country.

4 For the case of Denmark versus Sweden see Edquist and Lundvall (1992). A number of different European countries are compared in Bruno et al. (1991).

5 One specific illustration of this general phenomenon is that countries strongly specialised in exports of, for example, agriculture and food products will also be strongly specialised in machinery for agriculture and food industry. The explanation of this pattern is that export oriented users often are both competent and demanding, and that the feed-back of knowledge from the users forms a critical input to the innovation process of producers of specialised machinery (Andersen et al., 1981b). For a follow-up of this work see chapter 11 by Fagerberg.

6 In this context we use the concepts technological trajectories and paradigms in the sense they where introduced in Dosi (1982). For a discussion of different uses of these concepts see Dosi (1988a, 223–228).

7 The distinction between 'learning' and 'searching/exploring' may seem somewhat awkward; in everyday language 'searching/exploring' will result in 'learning' and this is why searching and exploring in chapter 2 are treated as sub-categories to 'learning'. The terminology chosen in this chapter reflects our wish both to distinguish clearly between, and to combine two different perspectives; a structuralist oriented (learning) and an action oriented (searching/exploring). This combined perspective has much in common with recent developments in social theory such as structuration theory (Giddens, 1984).

8 This corresponds to the central behavioural assumption in the evolutionary model of economic growth developed by Nelson and Winter (1982).

9 The OECD-publication 'New Technologies in the 1990s' represents a step towards such an integration (OECD, 1988).

10 For an overlapping but more detailed discussion see McKelvey (1991) who compares some of the recent literature on national systems of innovation.

11 One problem with Porter's approach, discussed by Dalum in chapter 10, is that it is unclear how he moves from the analyses of cases, at the industry level to his conclusions, which refer to national systems as a whole.

Chapter 2. Institutional Learning

1 Learning is used here in a broad sense, including both processes leading to new knowledge or new combinations of old knowledge, and processes putting old knowledge into new heads. In section 2.4.4, a distinction between learning, searching and exploring will be introduced, but until then this is not necessary.

2 This clear-cut distinction between institutions and technologies is sometimes referred to as the 'Veblen dichotomy', even if it is not possible to find it in such a crude form in the writings of Veblen himself.

3 In Johnson (1988) some reasons for the relative stability and inertia of institutions are discussed.

4 Economists are no exception in this respect:
> Like other men the economist is an individual with but one intelligence. He is a creature of habits and propensities given through the antecedents, hereditary and cultural, of which he is an outcome: and the habits of thought formed in any one line of experience affect his thinking in any other. (Veblen, 1898)

5 For Hayek this was the most important aspect of social institutions. He considered human knowledge to be the most fundamental of all scarce resources, and the problem of how to cope with this scarcity as the central problem in both society and economic theory (Gray, 1988).

6 Even if lost knowledge can often be reconstructed, it can sometimes only be done at considerable cost, and it may be almost impossible for some types of tacit knowledge.

7 For some brave scholars the costs of the quest for increased knowledge came high: Giordano Bruno (1548–1600) and Lucilo Vanini (1585–1619), early pioneers in 'evolutionary' thinking were both cleansed by the fire after having got their tongues hooked to the jaw and cut out, respectively, to prevent them from taking a last chance of spreading their 'false knowledge'.

8 These three forms of learning are discussed by Boulding (1985).

9 Aoki (1990b) shows
> ...that the cost of producing a certain mix of outputs through a complex process involving interrelated activities of many shops cannot be regarded exogenously given by a technological blueprint, but should be regarded as partly contingent on a co-ordination mode internalized within the firm.

From an institutionalist perspective it is just as likely that the costs and results of learning and forgetting in a firm depend on the organisational coordination of the activities of the firm.

10 An interesting variant of the proposition that pure market economies don't have the capacity to survive because of a lack of institutional diversity can be found in Polanyi (1957). He argues, that completely free market economies, with totally

unregulated goods-, labour-, land-, and money markets, would tend to over-exploit and destroy the labour power and the environment and destabilise the money – and credit system.

Chapter 3. User-Producer Relationships, National Systems of Innovation and Internationalisation

1 In Choi (1991), Klamer argues for shifting the perspective away from decision-making and towards regarding the economy as a locus for conversation and discourse. Our discussion reflects similar intentions. It is interesting to note that Klamer, in this context, points to differences in national culture as a factor influencing economic behaviour (133).

2 This is a theme which I have pursued elsewhere (Lundvall, 1985, Lundvall, 1988, Lundvall, 1991 and Lundvall, 1992.). What is new in this chapter is the discussion of how norms and rules of behaviour interact with geographical space and the discussion of their combined impact upon processes of intranational and international learning.

3 But it is important to realise that these institutional set-ups involve either qualitative exchange of information between agents (about the reputation of other individual agents) or the establishment of an agency outside the market gathering and disseminating information about reputations. Therefore, this kind of approach raises a fundamental methodological question. Why do agents take part in building a reputation system and how come they are willing to cooperate in establishing new institutions enforcing honesty? If we point to the common interest of the parties as the motive and include cooperation and communication between agents as the mechanism at this stage – which would be sensible – do we not leave the theoretical universe of methodological individualism? And, why should we at the next stage of the analysis, in order to prove the stability of an equilibrium state fostered by the specific institutional set-up, assume agents to act in isolation?

4 In many contributions to innovation theory, engineering activities and technical change are thought of only in terms of innovation and the creation of increasing diversity. In order to understand the dynamics involved, it is important to recognise the other side of technical change which relates to standardisation, and to the development of a stable nomenclature, making communication simpler and less costly. This tendency towards 'commodification' is an important element in the discussion of linkage structures in chapter 4.

5 In this context, the 'interpretative grid', developed in Dosi (1982), and the further discussion in Archibugi (1985), is useful. One important activity in 'normal science' is the standardisation of terminology, increasing the possibility for communication, over long distances, between scientists. Some of the characteristics of competing new paradigms in science will appear akin to, but different from when we observe radical innovations.

6 As pointed out by Dieter Ernst in comments to an earlier version of this paper, it is not obvious that honesty versus opportunism is the most interesting and relevant dimension in which to analyse international differences in rationality. Differences in time perspective, the degree of universality in economic relationships and concentration on financial variables and incentives, may be more easily related to empirically observed international differences. The main reason for sticking to the honesty/opportunism dimension in this context is thus methodological rather than empirical. To develop the analysis of the other dimensions is a task for future research.

7 At this point, it becomes clear that the transaction cost analysis, sometimes, involves a contradiction. The approach is, often, used to explain the actual institutional set up, in terms of markets versus vertical integration. It is assumed that the actual set-up reflects

a selection process, tending to select the most efficient institutional set-up; the set-up involving the lowest production and transaction costs. But, when it comes to behaviour only one specification of rationality (opportunism) is stated. And, this specification is, obviously very 'inefficient' both in terms of transaction costs and in terms of learning capability. The contradiction reflects its focus upon transactions of given bundles of goods and its neglect of product innovation.

One alternative interpretation of the Williamsonian transaction cost approach, would be to regard it as a theory rooted, strongly, in US-culture, where the 'quid pro quo'-logic, for different reasons, may have a stronger grip on all kinds of social relationships than anywhere else in the world. If this is true, the Williamson analysis takes for granted the most problematic institutional aspect of the US-system, while trying to demonstrate that the system selects a reasonably efficient institutional set up on this basis.

8 Our discussion gives a rosy picture of the H-economy and a sombre one of the O-economy. This reflects a ceteris paribus-approach. In the real world, a social norm inducing 'honesty' may be strongly embedded in a broader set of traditional social norms; for example norms inhibiting social advance and weakening the incentives to engage in learning and norms imposing such a high degree of loyalty that they result in very rigid organisational forms etc. The main purpose of the discussion of honesty is to illustrate the more general phenomenon that national culture and social norms tend to invade the economic scene and affect the process of innovation.

Chapter 4. Approaching National Systems of Innovation from the Production and Linkage Structure

1 The unrealistic conception of the search space led to serious misconceptions of the policy implications of the growth pole theory, both in regions and in developing countries. To put the problem sharply: the experience of interdependent and dynamic development based in the steel production of the Ruhr area in the nineteenth century (which was Perroux's paradigmatic example) did not help in providing rapid development in Algeria of the 1960's and 70's (where one of Perroux's students was the chief advisor, cf. Abrahamsson and Hedman 1981).

2 Figure 4.1 does not describe the constants of the model, including the exogenous cost and market conditions, firms's capacity utilisation rules, behavioural rules of banks, the disembodied character of technical change, and the structure of the search space in terms of search costs and productivity of (probabilistic) search results.

3 In other models labour productivity is also taken into account.

4 This proposition is especially designed with respect to homogeneous nations.

5 The reason is that national culture and informal networks help to provide, e.g., the degree of 'interface protocols' which are needed for making the information flow suitable for supporting the learning and innovation of the receiver.

6 Often it is not given which types of relationships are necessary to cope with a new situation. Provided that the nation contains a broad set of advanced producers and possible 'lead users', there are good possibilities of exploiting the national context innovatively.

7 The notion of development blocks may throw some light on the functioning of 'technology systems' and 'techno-economic paradigms' (Freeman and Perez 1988, 46 f), even if the pervasive effects of the latter seem far from Dahmén's original concept.

Chapter 5. Work Organisation and the Innovation Design Dilemma

1 Thompson (1967) mentions scientific management, administrative management and bureaucracy as examples of a closed-system strategy, and the theories of informal organisation and organisational interaction with the environment as examples of an open-system strategy. The closed-system strategy deals with determinate systems, while the open-system strategy deals with systems containing variables subject to influences not controlable by the researcher – hence, we have to accept that uncertainty in the form of synergy and dysfunctions intrude upon the model of an organisation in which 'the parts and their relationships presumably are determined through evolutionary processes' (ibid., 6).

2 Reproductive problem-solving may be defined as a process of 'searching the memory in a relatively systematic fashion for solutions that are present there in nearly finished form', while productive problem-solving may be defined as a process in which 'the construction of new solutions out of more or less 'raw' material is involved' (March and Simon, 1958, 117). In this chapter I define 'memory' at the level of the organisation, i.e. in the sense of of the 'organisational memory' proposed by Nelson and Winter (1982, 99–107).

3 Cyert and March (1963,121) define problemistic search as 'search that is stimulated by a problem (usually a rather specific one) and is directed towards finding a solution to that problem. In a general way, problemistic search can be distinguished from both random curiosity and the search for understanding. It is distinguished from the former because it has a goal, from the latter because it is interested in understanding only insofar such understanding contributes to control'. Thompson (1967, 151), apparently inspired by the duality in the quotation above, proposes an alternative to problemistic search, i.e. opportunistic surveillance defined as

    monitoring behaviour which scans the environment for opportunities – which does not wait to be activated by a problem and which does not therefore stop when a problem solution has been found. … it is the organizational counterpart to curiosity in the individual.

4 For instance, while centralised networks of communication facilitate effective performance in routine problem-solving, communication networks low in centralisation facilitate innovative non-routine solutions (Burns and Stalker, 1961). An intra-unit solution to this problem is that the unit employs different structural configurations at different points in time, while an inter-unit solution would propose the delegation of initiation to one unit and the ensuing implementation to another unit (Holbek, 1988).

5 Zaltman et al. (1973, 143) elaborates on this point: 'A strict emphasis on hierarchy of authority often causes decision unit members to adhere to specific channels of communication and selectively to feed back only positive information regarding their job'. At the same time, it is easy to find cases in which management do not want to be informed about performance gaps at all. For instance, Hage and Aiken (1970, 38–40) invoke the iron law of hierarchy arguing that those in power seek to preserve their power. In cases where a performance gap induces changes threatening the hierarchical structure of the organisation, innovation might be vetoed.

6 The focus on short-run financial performance is, especially, associated with national systems of innovation where the financial system is based on market operations rather than lender-borrower relationships, i.e. a credit-based financial system. The ensuing consequences for the proliferation of technical innovations are discussed at some length by Christensen in chapter 8.

7 The deduction of these features rely on a host of various sources such as Leibenstein (1987), Freeman (1987), Urabe (1988), Dertouzos et al. (1989), Dunning (1990c) and Aoki (1984, 1990a, 1991).

8 However, the Japanese approach has not always been an integrative one. The reverse engineering learning process has played an important role in the enactment of the integrative approach. Furthermore, the development of the integrative model has partly been a managerial response to strong industrial tensions following both world wars (Urabe, 1988). Actually, the pursuit of the ideal-type Japanese management principles, e.g. the principle of permanent employment and seniority wages, has often been forced upon firms by Japanese unions (Lincoln, 1990).

9 It is easily inferred from this that the open-system logic of the JMS requires a high degree of motivation of the employees to adapt to changing circumstances, placing a heavy burden on the incentive system. However, following Shimada (1991, 466), motivation to adapt to changing circumstances seems to be affected by wages only to a very limited degree, while the promotion component of the JMS reward system is much more important:

> Reward systems such as this doubtless not only have a significant impact on worker motivation; they also stimulate the adaptability of workers, while basic wages are not affected much by transfers or rotation among different job assignments. To the extent that scheduled transfers are used as an instrument for worker's career formation, the promotional reward may well foster greater adaptability of workers.

10 The just-in-time concept of the kanban system has the important effect of making small-lot production economically feasible. Small lot production contributes to low inventory costs and provides the whole production system with an ability to respond quickly to changes in demand.

11 This process of incremental improvements of hardware emerging from the experiences of production workers is, in Japanese plants, often called 'giving wisdom to the machines'. Given the self-generating innovative nature of the system, a set of production equipment is no longer simply subject to automatic decay and depreciation, but rather can be an asset the capacity of which may improve and appreciate over time as a result of the interaction with human resources (Shimada, 1991, 462).

12 Whittaker (1990) undertook 18 case studies, matching 9 British and 9 Japanese firms in pairs of equal size, product and batch size.

13 Note that the degree of supervision was higher in the Japanese firm, and that the Japanese operators held a higher level of education than their British counterparts and were expected to learn operating skills directly from manuals (ibid.). These features support the feasibility of the technical approach.

14 However, there are, of course, limits to the degree of 'bottom-upness' in the decision-making process. For instance, the ringi practice, as described by Leibenstein (1987), can only induce changes within the general strategical course of the firm, which is still decided at the top management level.

15 This conclusion is purposively stated in terms of relative frequencies, because all four kinds of search obviously must be expected to take place in both management systems.

16 Hofstede (1980b) define uncertainty-avoidance as the need of the individuals in a society to avoid situations of uncertainty and role conflicts. This need is reflected in a high degree of formalisation of behaviour and intolerance of deviant behaviour, and societies characterised by a high degree of uncertainty-avoidance exhibit a high level of aggression and anxiety, inducing incentives of the individuals to work hard.

17 Hofstede (1980a), studying nation-specific differences in norms, values, and beliefs, among other things, reports on 3 large questionnaires performed in the period of 1967–73. The first questionnaire aimed at 116.000 employees and managers in a large American multinational corporation with units in 40 different countries and was performed during the years of 1967–69. It was repeated in 1971–73, and in the same period Hofstede undertook a third questionnaire aiming at 400 public and business managers, which participated in management courses in Lausanne, Switzerland. Hofstede has summarised his work in Hofstede (1980b).

18 There are three dimensions involved in this description: Uncertainty-avoidance (defined earlier), collectivist values, and tolerance towards power distance. Hofstede (1980b, 45) defines collectivist values in terms of a dimension called 'individualism-collectivism', where individualism 'implies a loosely knit social framework in which people are supposed to take care of themselves and of their immediate families only, while collectivism is characterised by a tight social framework in which people distinguish between in-groups and out-groups'. Further, power distance 'indicates the extent to which a society accepts the fact that power in institutions and organisations is distributed unequally'.

Chapter 6. Innovation and the Development of Industrial Networks

1 The industry-life-cycle model was developed in Gelsing (1988) and draws heavily on works of C. Freeman (1982) and Ann R. Markusen (1987) representing respectively 'economics of industrial innovation' and 'regional economics'.

2 Scott and Storper (1987) criticise life-cycle-models along these lines.

Chapter 8. The Role of Finance in National Systems of Innovation

1 Financial support from The Danish Social Science Research Council is gratefully acknowledged.

2 An important question is of course to *whom* the uncertainty is relevant. A small change in the products might give a large uncertainty with the R&D engineer, but if the change appears to be minor to the lender, there will be the same possibilities for obtaining finance.

3 An analogy can here be made to the previously discussed user-producer interaction. The lender can be seen as producing financial services, loans and making financial innovations. The borrower can then be seen as the user of these financial products.

4 See chapter 3 and Lundvall (1988) for a discussion on the concept of distance in the interaction.

5 In recent years an immense amount of literature has appeared in the 'information and economics' tradition. A common feature is that information problems may disrupt financial markets and cause under lending. The impossibility of uncovering the firm's tacit knowledge may cause an adverse selection of projects (see e.g. Stiglitz and Weiss (1981), for an overview of the literature, see Gertler (1988)).

6 This argument has different strength according to which kind of financial system we are talking about.

7 Stiglitz and Weiss (1981) is a classical article in this connection.

8 If the lender is engaged with risk capital and receives part of the profits, the case is somewhat different. High-tech investment projects often have an over-average return, and a few, or perhaps only one, successful contract may compensate losses on defaults.

9 The general view is, that short-termism is most pronounced in the UK and the US, whereas German and Japanese shareholders act more as investors, rather than as traders in shares. An early discussion of the problem is in Dean (1974).

10 In the US there has been a discussion about 'herding' between banks, i.e. that the behaviour of one group of banks becomes a guide-line for the behaviour of other banks. See e.g. Jain and Gupta (1987).

11 In Sweden A.O.Wallenberg was a key person in reshaping the financial institutions in the mid 19th century. He was the founder of Stockholms Enskilda Bank and controlled several big firms. One of his sons was a banker. He put him in charge of the industrial firms. The other was of the entrepreneur kind, and he was put in charge of the bank. This was a deliberate combination of two different types of logics, and this diversity was successful in creating the dynamics of the Wallenberg group as a whole.

12 Cf. Zysman (1983). Berglöf (1990) and Mayer (1990) who discuss the relevance of this grouping and point to the methodological problems that are indeed substantial in this cross-country statistical exercise.

13 Keynes (1936, 160) elaborated on this point, and he suggested, that buying an asset should be made permanent, so that the valuation of the asset would be tied to the performance of the firm and not to the expectation to the future performance of the stock market.

14 In the A. Hirschman-terminology (1970) this is the distinction between influence through 'voice' or 'exit'.

15 This is documented by Sejersted (1988), who uses a comparison of Sweden and Norway as an illustration.

16 In several credit based systems the stock market is even restricted in the sense that there is a division of stocks into A and B, with A-stocks being the only ones to give access to voting. A-stocks are rarely traded in some countries.

17 Net financing is shown as a proportion of capital expenditures and stock building. Gross financing is a proportion of total sources.

18 A number of statistical reservations are not mentioned here. See Mayer (1990, 310).

19 Using gross financing figures reveals roughly the same pattern.

20 Taken as group 5.2.2 'loans from financial institutions' plus 6.2.3 'owed to financial institutions'.

21 For all manufacturing.

22 For all manufacturing.

23 For all manufacturing.

24 Another paradox pops up here. In spite of these apparent advantages, the Japanese financial market has recently been extensively deregulated and internationalised, and firms have increasingly relied on direct finance. At the same time, the deregulation of the US financial market has switched into a reregulation trend (Mishkin, 1990). I shall return to this apparent paradox in the next section.

25 The German economist F. List argued in 1841 for a national, active role of financial institutions in the process of industrialisation, and Prussian bankers recognised the need for a well functioning financial system.

26 The discussion is by no means new. Adam Smith (1776) also treated the subject and wrote

> *The directors…being the managers of other peoples money than of their own, it cannot be well expected that they should watch over it with the same anxious vigilance with which the partners in a private co-partnery frequently watch over their own.*

Furthermore, the distinction between financial logic and industrial logic, originates from Veblen (1898).

27 In Christensen (1991) I give a description of these processes and how they relate to each other.

28 The significant involvement of Japanese financial institutions in firms is a means of preventing hostile take-overs. Deregulation may be a means to transfer protection of firms from the state to financial institutions, as a response to increasing international political pressure on Japan to ease protectionism. Thus, the lack of a developed market for corporate control in Germany and Japan, explains the low degree of hostile take-overs in these countries compared to the US and the UK (Franks and Mayer, 1990).

29 The reregulation trend in the US described in Mishkin (1990) may be an example of the wish to preserve some of the benefits of the regulated, national system.

30 The OECD (1989b) has also advocated increased specialisation of financial institutions to support small and medium sized, innovative firms. On the other hand the pros of specialisation may not add up to the cons, which could be said to be lower flexibility. If the financial institutions are engaged in several different areas the possibilities of switching between areas of business, is likely to be larger.

Chapter 10. Export Specialisation, Structural Competitiveness and National Systems of Innovation

1 Many collegues have commented on previous drafts of this chapter. In particular, I would like to thank Esben Sloth Andersen, Charles Edquist, Jan Fagerberg, Christopher Freeman, Björn Johnson, Bengt-Åke Lundvall and Kim Møller for detailed comments. Also thanks to Uffe Møller, the computer center at Aalborg University (AUD), who has transformed huge amounts of megabytes of information on international trade to a manageable trade database; and to Vibeke Jacobsen and Hans Peter Larsen for programming assistance.

2 The data are described in more detail in the appendix to this chapter.

3 Se also e.g. Krugman (1990) and Helpman and Krugman (1985).

4 Such as the contributions on EC integration in Balassa (1975). See also the survey of the effects of the most important GATT rounds by Baldwin (1984, 586–88).

5 The results are published in EC Commission (1988a) *European Economy*, No. 35. The background research in EC Commission (1988b) *Research on the 'Cost of Non-Europe'* Vol. 1–16. The general analytical foundations are exposed in a series of articles in Vol. 2.

6 For an illustrative example of the attitude among members of the established profession *vis-à-vis* the academic foundations of more unorthodox analysis of industrial development, see Bhagwati's (1989) review of Cohen and Zysman (1987). After an extremely negative judgement of the quality of the arguments in the book, Bhagwati states:

> *Warts and all, however, this book has the considerable merit of being relevant, possessing a clear thesis and an engaging style that practitioners of our dismal science can no longer command and have almost forgotten to value. It is certainly worth your time, if not your money.* (123).

7 See e.g. Ethier (1988) and Kenen (1989). Others may have a somewhat more revisionistic touch, such as Krugman and Obstfeld (1988). Although most of the New factors adopted by the Revisionists have reached the distinguished research surveys several years ago (e.g. Jones and Kenen, 1984), lags to the textbooks appear surprisingly large.

8 Originally introduced by Mistral (1983) and elaborated further by Chesnais (1986).

 9 In Porter (1980) strategies are applied as structural variables in the analysis of the internal substructure of industries, c.f. the concept of 'strategic groups'.

10 Chapter 11 (by Fagerberg) of the present book contains a more rigourous, extensive and updated econometric test of the validity of the 'home market hypothesis'.

11 Other critical points are the lack of depth in his analysis of the multinational enterprises (see e.g. Dunning, 1991a) and the unclear transmission mechanism from the importance of geographical proximity to the role of nations (see also Dalum et al., 1991a).

12 This approach has been used in a country study of Denmark in Dalum et al. (1991b). The cluster analysis is used as a tool to design the content as well as the organisational aspects of large coherent industrial policy programmes. Different stages of clusters are also discussed, such as 'mature' versus 'emerging', leading to highly different contexts for policy discussions.

13 We shall, however, return to some of Porter's conclusions about the importance of nations *vis-à-vis* increasing globalisation in the final policy discussions in chapter 14.

14 For a more detailed description of the data and the classification principles, see the appendix to this chapter.

15 See Leamer (op. cit.) p. 66 and Figure 3.1 on p. 71.

16 See Table 4.4 and 4.5 on p. 87, which contain the sign of the four sector's net exports for approximately sixty countries in 1958 and 1975, respectively. The classification is based on factor content accounts taken directly from Hufbauer's (1970) 'conciliatory' effort. Leamer's MACH and CHEM aggregates are, by the way, fairly close to the engineering and chemicals aggregates in our trade data.

17 For further details, see the appendix to this chapter, as well as the appendix to chapter 11 by Fagerberg.

18 In principle the analysis could have been done more satisfactorily, than presented here. That would, however, have required a time consuming change of the aggregation principles of the data more in line with the division of labour analysis sketched in chapter 4. Resources for that were not available for the present book.

19 For a discussion of the concept of home versus host nations in the field of international business, see e.g. Dunning (1988b).

20 Finland is of special interest because it was less developed than most other OECD countries in 1961. However, during the 1970's and 1980's Finland went through a very rapid transformation process, which may justify grouping it among the small high income OECD countries, such as Denmark, the Netherlands, Austria, etc.

21 It should be noted that oil exports play an increasing role in the Danish case in the 1980's.

22 The Danish competitiveness in chemicals has been especially concentrated in pharmaceuticals (Novo-Nordisk in insulin and enzymes). Although Finland may have had locational advantages for foreign chemical processing industries during the 1960's, the increasing specialisation appears to have been the outcome of efforts made by Finnish owned companies.

23 The sample of both studies is only 11 OECD countries; and the definition of engineering (in SITC, Rev. 1: 69, 7, 861 and 861) is slightly different from the one used in the present analysis. Kjeldsen-Kragh collected foreign trade date for 1954, 1960, 1966 and 1969; in the Dalum et al. study these data were updated to 1975. From this source (Figure V.1, 87) Japanese specialisation in engineering can be found as approximately 0.5 in 1954 and 0.7 in 1960.

24 These remarks are admittedly of a loose character and not proved by rigorous econometric tests.

25 For a recent analysis of decreasing Swedish performance in *product* development, see Edquist and McKelvey (1991). That may point towards problems for the Swedish NSI to sustain its membership of this exclusive group.

26 These concepts were introduced by Pavitt (1979 and 1980). See also Patel and Pavitt (1987), Fagerberg (1988b) and Dosi, Pavitt and Soete (1990).

27 Although the UK pattern must be interpreted with great care, because oil exports have disturbed the picture significantly from the late 1970's. However, the steady decrease of specialisation in engineering 1961–73 was not a consequence of oil exports.

Chapter 11. The Home Market Hypothesis Re-examined: The Impact of Domestic User-Producer Interaction on Export Specialisation

1 This chapter presents some preliminary results from an econometric study of the relation between domestic demand and export specialisation. A more extensive account, including among else tests for other functional forms and lags, will be published later this year (Fagerberg, 1992).

The ideas presented here owe much to discussions with the participants of the IKE group, especially Bengt-Åke Lundvall, Esben Sloth Andersen and Bent Dalum, all at Aalborg University. I would also like to thank Aadne Cappelen, Central Bureau of Statistics, Margarida Ponte Ferreira and Arne Melchior, both at Norwegian Institute of International Affairs, for valuable comments and suggestions. Economic support from the Nordic Economic Research Council is gratefully acknowledged.

2 For an overview, see Dosi and Soete (1988).

3 See, for instance, the results presented in Dosi et al. (1990).

4 Later in the same book Linder developed another (and more well known) hypothesis on trade, relating trade intensities and income-levels. The hypothesis and the resulting controversy (which still goes on) will not be discussed here.

5 Lundvall, chapter 3, cites one study showing that 80% of all cooperation activities involving user-producer interaction are domestic.

6 For an explanation of this index, see below.

7 This has much in common with the so called 'linkage' approach developed by Hirschman (1987). In the vocabulary of the latter this might be described as a 'forward linkage' from agriculture to machinery.

8 There is a long tradition in economics for the assumption that countries with large domestic markets have a potential advantage over small countries in many manufacturing industries. In recent years there has been a revival of interest in how economies of scale in combination with market structure may have an impact on comparative advantage. For an overview, see Helpman (1984).

9 On closer inspection, only 3 of the 23 estimated product dummies were found to be significantly different from the mean (or a common constant term) at a 10% level of significance. These were ships, milking machines and tractors.

10 Compared to table 11.4, four sectors disappeared from the list of significant correlations, and four merged. The four that disappeared were heating and cooling equipment, milking machinery, food processing machinery and pharmaceuticals. The four that emerged were machine tools for working metals, textile machinery, agricultural machinery n.e.s and construction and mining machinery. See Fagerberg (1992) for further details.

Chapter 12. Integration, Innovation and Evolution

1 Parts of this chapter (especially section 12.4) is based on reports produced for an EC-project based at MERIT, University of Limburg, and a related study at the Institute of Production, University of Aalborg, supported by the Danish Ministry of Labour (cf. Freeman and Soete, 1991, Andersen, 1991, Nielsen, 1991, Nielsen et al., 1991) This work draws on the IKE Database of foreign trade statistics and the related study work developed by Bent Dalum and Jan Fagergerg (cf. chapters 10 and 11 and, e.g. Dalum, Fagerberg and Jørgensen, 1988). Dalum and Fagerberg have also taken the initiative with respect to parts of the subject area of the present chapter, cf. Fagerberg, 1988, and Dalum, 1990. Also thanks to Bent Dalum, Bengt-Åke Lundvall and Poul Thøis Madsen for comments.

2 The names E and J may give some immediate associations but it might be helpful to rethink the arguments in terms of the experiences of integration between the Nordic countries during the 1960's (see Fagerberg, 1988). One might, perhaps, also think in terms of E = Eastern Europe and J = Western Europe.

3 However, in empirical studies (e.g., in chapters 10 and 11 and in section 12.4) the at current value of sales and exports is often more relevant than the quantity since the value measure takes into account changes in product quality, etc. This difference is due to the theoretical character of the present chapter while the other chapters are more empirically oriented. Even in the present chapter the export data is presented by at current values (see section 12.4).

4 The IT-groups have been subdivided into two, mainly to relate to EC data. The export specialisation figures (see definition in chapters 10 and 11) are ranked in two ways: first all 42 commodity groups and then only the 25 medium and high-tech groups. Chapters 10 and 11 give a more general presentation of the IKE Database and the related classification scheme.

5 This theme has recently been developed in a FAST project, cf. Bruno et al., 1991, part III.

Chapter 14. Public Policy in the Learning Society

1 An acknowledged example of market failure in relation to innovation is underinvestment in science and basic research reflecting that private firms cannot fully appropriate the benefits from the production of new knowledge. An institutional set-up where firms appropriate all the benefits would, on the other hand, hamper the diffusion of innovations and have a negative impact at the system level.

2 Nelson and Soete (1988) point to the need for experimentation and technology assessment but are quite cautious in their conclusions regarding what governments should do.

3 Studying the local administration in Denmark and the impact of the radical shift in information technology from big mainframe computers to micro-computers, we found that the central public agencies, which had been very successful in stimulating the movement ahead in the old trajectory, only slowly and reluctantly changed their strategies and began to promote the change to the new trajectory. (Brændgaard et al., 1984).

4 This really amounts to an inverted Murphy's law for unregulated markets: 'If things could have been better, they would have been better'.

5 For example, Sung China (tenth to thirteenth centuries AD) and Togukawa Japan (seventeenth to nineteenth centuries AD) (Jones, 1988).

6 In connection with the learning economy the general equilibrium framework becomes rather empty. A modern definition of general equilibrium says that it is a situation in which no signals are generated which can cause agents to change their theories or

policies. This is a situation where nothing important really happens which can change the situation. All kinds of learning, for example, have ceased.

7 It is paradoxical that the definition of property rights is having a revival in a period so obviously characterised by technological competition and knowledge-intensive production. Arrow (1973) gives (from a neo-classical stand-point) some arguments for why it is difficult to regard information and knowledge as a privatised commodity.

8 However, there is no reason to belittle what animals can do in this respect. Chris Freeman has pointed out to us that for example Lesser Black-beeked Gulls have 'learned' to drop shell-fish from a height onto rocks below to break the shells. This behaviour is not inherited. Rather it is taught to young gulls and diffused from colony to colony as birds move to new territories.

9 Katzenstein (1985) explains the relative economic success of small OECD-countries with the fact that they have succeeded in building institutions which compensate the victims of change into their systems. This has made it possible to engage strongly in international competition with its ensuing demands on permanent structural change.

10 For a discussion of industrial policy based on the idea of 'industrial complexes', see Dalum et al., 1991b and Dalum, 1992.

11 Several empirical studies indicate that imitation lags are longer for organisational and institutional than for technological innovations. See Kogut (1991).

12 Akerlof (1991) discusses the relations between salient information and procrastination effects (i.e. irrational postponement of action) in different social and economic situations.

Chapter 15. Post Script: Innovation System Research – Where It Came From and Where It Might Go

1 In economic geography the diffusion of the innovation system perspective has, together with the industrial district and industrial clusters approaches, contributed to the construction of a 'new economic geography' that has changed the way geographical location and agglomeration is explained (Maskell and Malmberg 1997; Cooke 2001; Clark, Feldman and Gertler 2000).

2 Several authors have presented overviews of the innovation system literature and made attempts to classify different approaches. An early contribution is McKelvey (1991). More recent ones are Balzat and Hanusch (2004) and Sharif (2006). The latter's contribution builds upon a combination of littereature survey and interviews with key persons who were involved in coining the concept. An interesting critical contribution is Miettinen (2002). Miettinen points to the problematic and vague character of the concept as it is transferred back and forth between the academic and the public policy sphere.

3 Reinert (2003) argues that many of the ideas go further back to a succession of scholars belonging to 'the other Cannon' starting with Antonio Serra. De Liso (2006) argues that Charles Babbage may be seen as another ancestor for the innovation system concept.

4 The paper was published for the first time more than 20 years later in the journal Industrial and Corporate Change (Freeman 2004).

5 The IKE-group had the privilege to interact with Christopher Freeman in several projects in this period and many of our ideas were shaped in a dialogue with him (see for instance Freeman 1981).

6 For an overview of the current status of innovation research see the new Oxford Handbook on Innovation (Fagerberg, Mowery and Nelson, 2005).

7 Adam Smith's major contribution was to link the evolving and increasingly more developed division of labour to the creation of wealth. In Lundvall (2006) I have tried to reformulate his theory, emphasizing interactive learning in the context of vertical division of labour, so that it becomes more relevant for explaining innovation-based economic growth.

8 For a historical analysis of how match and mismatch is reflected in economic performance of national systems see Freeman (1995b). In (Lundvall 2002) I discuss the role of mismatches in the disappointing performance following 'the new economy' euphoria.

9 Verspagen and Werker (2003) is interesting in showing which scholars that define themselves as 'neo-Schumpeterians'.

10 Another point where Schumpeter's approach differs from the NSI-approach is his neglect of the importance of knowledge and learning for understanding the innovation process. Schumpeter's entrepreneurs are activists who bring new combinations to the market. How the new combinations come about is left in the dark (Witt 1993, p. xiv).

11 In the US Richard R. Nelson and Nathan Rosenberg played the most important role in developing the theoretical, historical and empirical understanding of innovation.

12 The IKE-group had the privilege to have him visiting as guest professor at Aalborg University for periods and there is little doubt that we all became his apprentices. He is not only an outstanding scholar but also a uniquely generous person.

13 Another characteristic of the successful innovations was that the project team leader in charge of developing the innovation had certain seniority and was able to mobilise resources in critical phases of the innovation process.

14 Today we would add to this micro-foundation the nation-specific characteristics of work organisation and learning at the workplace. This will be addressed in section 4 below.

15 In our empirical research on the performance of Danish firms we have found that there is substantial overlap between organizational characteristics that support adaptive capacities and those that support innovation and competence-building (Nielsen and Lundvall 1999; Lundvall 2002).

16 Within this narrow logic the neglect of learning effects from engaging in innovation will underestimate both the private and public rates of return.

17 The data originate from a survey on working condition of workers in 15 European countries gathered by the Dublin Institute for Working and Living conditions. Discretionary learning refers to work situations where workers say that they learn a lot and that they have some freedom to organise their own work. Lean production learning refers to work situations where workers learn but where there is little discretion left for the worker to organise his/her own activities. Taylorist organisation offers little learning and very little freedom for the worker while simple production gives more autonomy in solving simple tasks that offer little learning opportunities.

18 This debate has triggered strong efforts to link universities to firms in Europe sometimes going as far as seeing the ideal university as 'an innovation factory'. Dosi, Llerena and Sylos Labini (2006) raise doubts about the basic assumption behind the paradox that Europe is strong in Science.

19 After comparing the performance of six countries it is stated that 'A striking feature is the apparent missing link between indicators A–E and the overall performance indicators in F. *This suggests that priorities and biases in the STI-policy system are weakly linked to general economic performance and policies.*' (OECD 2005, p.29, italics by this author).

20 The data in table 2 are from Jensen, Johnson, Lorenz and Lundvall (2007).

21 Several authors analysing the situation of less developed countries have been critical to the use of the concept 'national innovation system' and have preferred to work with

concepts such as national technological systems (Lall and Pietrobelli 2003) or national learning systems (Matthews 2001;Viotti 2002). To some degree I see their alternative conceptual proposals as reactions to the use of narrowly defined innovation systems with focus on STI-learning. I strongly support the idea that understanding processes of experience based learning is a key to the understanding of the specificities of national innovation systems (see Lorenz and Lundvall 2006).

22 The Bayh Dole act implemented in the US in the 1980s gives stronger opportunities and incentives to universities to engage in patenting and protecting their knowledge. As documented by Mowery and Sampat (2004) the interpretation of the 'success' of this reform in Europe has been exaggerated.

23 This scenario gains in realism by the fact that some major US universities would dominate 'the level playing field' and by the fact that the US government would still be able to pursue basic research under headings such as health, military defence and space technology since these can be defined as being of strategic importance for its security.

24 In order to explain this to economists who are eager to market orient universities it is useful to point to the relative autonomy of central banks. To make sure that we can trust the value of money it has been accepted that its main guardian is given a certain degree of autonomy. We need a similar guardian for knowledge and it is difficult to find another institution/organization that is better suited to be the central bank of knowledge than the university.

REFERENCES

Abernathy, W.J. and Clark, K.B. (1985), 'Innovation: Mapping the Winds of Creative Destruction', *Research Policy*, Vol. 14.

Abrahamsson, H. and Hedman, S. (1981), *Den algeriska utmaningen*, Lund, Studentlitteratur.

Abramowitz, M. (1989), *Thinking About Growth*, Cambridge, Cambridge University Press.

Akerlof, G.A. (1991), Procrastination And Obedience, *American Economic Review*, Vol. 81, No. 1.

Aldrich, H. and Whetten, D.A. (1981), 'Organization-Sets, Action-Sets and Networks' in Nystrøm, P.C. and Starbuck, W.H, *Handbook of Organizational Design*, Vol. 1, Oxford University Press.

Allen, P. (1988), 'Evolution, Innovation and Economics', in Dosi, G. et al. (eds.), *Technical Change and Economic Theory*, London, Pinter Publishers.

Amable, B., Barré, R. and Boyer, R. *et al.* (1997), *Les systémes d'innovation a l'ére de la globalization*, Paris, Economica.

Amin, A. and Cohendet, P. (2004), *Architectures of Knowledge: Firms, Capabilities and Communities*, Oxford, Oxford University Press.

Andersen, E.S., Dalum, B. and Villumsen, G. (1981a), *International Specialization and the Home Market*, Aalborg, Aalborg University Press.

Andersen, E.S., Dalum, B. and Villumsen, G. (1981b), 'The Importance of the Home Market for Technological Development and the Export Specialization of Manufacturing Industry', in Freeman, C. (ed). *Technological Innovation and National Economic Performance*, Aalborg, Aalborg University Press.

Andersen, E.S. and Lundvall, B.-Å. (1988), 'Small National Systems of Innovation Facing Technological Revolutions – An Interpretative Framework', in Freeman, C. and Lundvall, B.-Å. (eds.), *Small Countries Facing the Technological Revolution*, London and New York, Pinter Publishers.

Andersen, E.S., Lundvall, B.-Å. and Nielsen, K.V. (1990), *Learning, Structural Change, Competitiveness and Employment, With Special Respect to IT and EC*, IKE Småskrift 66, Institute for Production, Aalborg, Aalborg University.

Andersen, E.S. (1991), 'Techno-Economic Paradigms as Typical Interfaces Between Producers and Users', *Journal of Evolutionary Economics*, Vol. 1, No. 2.

Andersen, M.S. (1991), 'Styring med miljøafgifter', *Samfundsøkonomen*, No. 2.

Andersson, Å.E. (1985), *Kreativitet Storstadens Framtid*, Värnamo, Prisma.

Antonelli, C. (1986), 'TDF and the Structure and Strategies of TNC's', *The CTC Reporter*, No. 22, New York, United Nations.

Antonelli, C. (ed.) (1988a), *New Information Technology and Industrial Change: The Italian Case*, Dordrecht, Kluwer Academic Publishers.

Antonelli, C. (1988b), 'The Emergence of the Network Firm', in Antonelli, C. (1988a), *New Information Technology and Industrial Change: The Italian Case*, Dordrecht, Kluwer Academic Publishers.

Aoki, M. (1984), 'Aspects of the Japanese Firm', in Aoki, M. (ed.), *The Economic Analysis of the Japanese Firm*, Amsterdam, North-Holland.

Aoki, M. (1986), 'Horizontal vs. Vertical Information Structure of the Firm', *American Economic Review*, Vol. 76, No. 5.

Aoki, M. (1990a), 'A New Paradigm of Work Organization and Co-ordination? Lessons from Japanese Experiences', in Marglin, S.A. and Schor, J.B. (eds.), *The Golden Age of Capitalism*, Guildford, Clarendon Press.

Aoki, M. (1990b), 'The Participatory Generation of Information Rents and the Theory of the Firm', in Aoki, M. et al. (eds.), *The Firm as a Nexus of Treaties*, London, New Park, New Dehli, Sage Publications.

Aoki, M. (1991), 'Global Competition, Firm Organization and Total Factor Productivity. A Comparative Micro Perspective', in OECD, *Technology and Productivity. The Challenge for Economic Policy*, Paris, OECD.

Archibugi, D. (1985), *Paradigms and Revolutions: From Science to Technology?*, Paper presented at the UNESCO-CNR Workshop on Long-Term Scientific Forecasting, Venice.

Archibugi, D. and Lundvall, B.-Å. (eds.) (2001), *The globalising learning economy: Major socio-economic trends and European innovation policy*, Oxford, Oxford University Press.

Arnold, E. and Guy, K. (1987), *Parallel Convergence: National Strategies in Information Technology*, London, Pinter Publishers.

Arocena, Rodrigo and Judith Sutz (2000a), 'Looking at national systems of innovation from the south', *Industry and Innovation*, Vol. 7, No.1, pp. 55–75.

Arocena, Rodrigo and Judith Sutz (2000b), *Interactive Learning Spaces and Development Policies in Latin America*, DRUID working papers, No. 00–13.

Arocena, R. and Sutz, J. (2005), 'Latin American universities: From an original revolution to an uncertain transition', *Higher Education*, vol. 50, pp. 573–592.

Arrow, K.J. (1962), 'The Economic Implications of Learning by Doing', *Review of Economic Studies*, Vol. XXIX, No. 80.

Arrow, K.J. (1971), 'Political and Economic Evaluation of Social Effects and Externalities', in Intrilligator, M. (ed.), *Frontiers of Quantitative Economics*, North Holland.

Arrow, K.J. (1973), *Information and Economic Behaviour*, Stocholm, Federation of Swedish Industries.

Arrow, K.J. (1974), *The Limits of Organisation*, New York, W.W. Norton&Company.

Arthur, B. (1988), 'Competing Technologies: an Overview', in Dosi et al. (eds.), *Technology and Economic Theory*, London, Pinter Publishers.

Arundel, A., Lorenz, E., Lundvall, B.-Å. and Valeyre, A. (2006), 'The Organisation of Work and Innovative Performance: A Comparison of the EU-15', *DRUID Working Paper* No. 06–14, Aalborg University.

Axelrod, R. (1984), *The Evolution of Cooperation*, New York, Basic Books.

Baba, Y. (1985), *Japanese Colour TV Firms: Decision-Making from the 1950s to the 1980s: Oligopolistic Corporate Strategy in the Age of Micro-Electronics*, PhD dissertation, University of Sussex.

Baily, M. and Chakrabarti, A.K. (1988), *Innovation and the Productivity Crisis*, Washington D.C., Brookings.

Balassa, B. (1965), 'Trade Liberalization and 'Revealed' Comparative Advantage', *The Manchester School*, Vol. 33, No. 2.

Balassa, B. (ed.) (1975), *European Economic Integration*, Amsterdam, North Holland.

Baldwin, R. (1984), 'Trade Policies in Developed Countries', in Jones, R.W and Kenen, P.B. (eds.), *Handbook of International Econmics – Volume 1: International Trade*, Amsterdam, North-Holland.

Balzat, M. and Hanusch, H. (2004), 'Recent trends in the research on national systems of innovation', *Journal of Evolutionary Economics*, 14: 197–210.

Baranson, J. (1978), *Technology and the Multinationals*, Lexington, Mass., Lexington Books.

Barnett, C. (1986), *The Audit of War*, Macmillan.

Bartlett, C.A. and Ghoshal, S. (1990), 'Managing Innovation in the Transnational Corporation' in Bartlett, C.A. et al. (eds.), *Managing the Global Firm*, London, Routledge.

Berglöf, E. (1990), 'Finance and the Political Structure of the Firm', in Aoki et al. (eds.), *The Firm as a Nexus of Treaties*, London, Sage Publications.

Berhman, J.N. and Fischer, W.A. (1980), *Overseas R&D Activities of Transnational Companies*, Cambridge, Mass., Oelgeschlager, Gunn and Hain.

Bernal, J.D. (1939), *The Social Function of Science*, London, Routledge.

Bévort, F., Pedersen, J.S. and Sundbo, J. (1991), *Udfordringer til 90'ernes personalearbejde. På vej mod en ny samarbejdsmodel*, stencilat, Roskilde Universitetscenter. (*Challenges to the human resource management of the 90s. Heading towards a new cooperative model*, Roskilde University, mimeo).

Bhagwati, J.N. et al. (eds.) (1971), *Trade, Balance of Payments and Growth*, Amsterdam, North-Holland.

Bhagwati, J.N. (1989), 'Review of Cohen and Zysman (1987)', *Journal of Economic Literature*, Vol. 27, No. 1.

Bonin, B. and Perron, B. (1986), 'World Product Mandates and Firms Operating in Quebec', in Etemad, H. and Séguin Dulude, L. (eds.), *Managing the Multinational Subsidiary*, London, Croom Helm.

Booz-Allen Acquisition Services (1989), *Studies on Obstacles to Takeover Bids in the European Community*, Executive Summary prepared for the Commission of the European Communities, PGXV-B-2.

Boulding, K.E. (1985), *The World as a Total System*, Beverly Hills, Sage Publications.

Boulding, K.E. (1991), 'What is Evolutionary Economics?', *Journal of Evolutionary Economics*, Vol. 1, No. 1.

Boyer, R. (1988), 'Technical Change and the Theory of Regulation', chapter 4 in Dosi, G. et al. (eds.), *Technical Change and Economic Theory*, London, Pinter Publishers.

Braun, E. and Macdonald, S. (1978), *Revolution in Miniature – The History and Impact of Semiconducter Electronics*, Cambridge University Press.

Broman, S. (1988), *Blåsigt i Frontlinien – Varmt på Bakgården?*, København, Industriministeriet.

Brookfield, H. (1975), *Interdependent Development*, London, Methuen & Co.

Bruno, S., Cohendet, P., Desmartin, F., Llerena, P. and Sorge, A. (1991), *Modes of Usage and Diffusion of New Technologies and New Knowledge*, A Synthesis Report, Bruxelles, Commission of the European Communities, Fast, FOP 227.

Brusco, S. (1982), 'The Emilian Model. Productive Decentralisation and Social Integration', *Cambridge Jounal of Economics*, Vol. 6.

Brændgaard, A. and Gelsing, L. (1987), *Elektronik-industrielle miljøer i Nordjylland (Industrial Networks in Electronics Industry of North Jutland*, Danish only), Aalborg University.

Brændgaard, A, Gregersen, B and Aaen, I. (1984), *Technical Change and Employment in the Public Sector: The Case of Office Automation in Danish Local Gocernment*, IKE-Working Paper, No. 55.

Brændgaard, A. (1988), 'International Technology Programmes and National Systems of Production: ESPRIT and the Danish Electronics Industry', in Freeman, C. and Lundvall, B.-Å. (eds.), *Small Countries Facing the Technological Revolution*, London and New York, Pinter Publishers.

Breschi, S. and Malerba, F. (1997), 'Sectoral innovation systems', in Edquist, C. (ed.), *Systems of innovation: Technologies, institutions and organizations*, London, Pinter Publishers.

Bullock, M. (1983), *Academic Enterprise, Industrial Innovation and the Development of High Technology Financing in the United States*, London, Brand Brothers and Co.

Burns, T. and Stalker, G.M. (1961), *The Management of Innovation*, London, Tavistock Publications.

Burstall, M.L., Dunning, J.H. and Lake, A. (1981), *Multinational Enterprises, Governments and Technology: The Pharmaceutical Industry*, Paris, OECD.

Bush, V. (1946), *Science, the Endless Frontier*, Washington, USGPO.

Cable, J. (1985) 'Capital Market Information and Industrial Performance: The Role of West German Banks', *The Economic Journal*, March.

Camagni, R.P. (1990), 'Local Milieu, Uncertainty and Innovation Networks: Towards a New Dynamic Theory of Economic Space', in Camagni, R.P. (ed.), *Innovation Networks: The Spatial Perspective*, London, Belhaven-Pinter.

Cantwell, J. and Dunning, J.H. (1991), 'MNEs, Technology and Competitiveness of European Industries', *Aussenwirtschaft*, Vol. 1, No. 46.

Cantwell, J. and Hodson, C. (1990), *The Internationalisation of Technological Activity and British Competitivenes: A Review of Some New Evidence*, Discussion Papers in International Investment and Business Studies, No. 138, Series B, Vol.III., University of Reading, United Kingdom.

Cantwell, J. (1987), 'The Reorganisation of European Industries After Integration', *Journal of Common Market Studies*, Vol.XXVI, No. 2, December.

Cantwell, J. (1989), *Technological Innovation and Multinational Corporations*, Oxford, Blackwell.

Carlsson, B. and Stankiewitz, R. (1991), 'On the Nature, Function and Composition of Technological Systems', *Journal of Evolutionary Economics*, Vol. 1, pp. 93–118.

Cassiolato, J. E., Lastres, H. M. M and Maciel, M. L. (2003), *Systems of Innovation and Development*. Edward Elgar. Cheltenham, UK, 2003.

Caves, R.E. (1982), *Multinational Enterprise and Economic Analysis*, Cambridge, Cambridge University Press.

Cecchini, P. (1988), *1992: Benefits of a Single Market*, Aldershot, Wildwood House.

Chesnais, F. (1986) , 'Science, Technology and Competitiveness', *STI Review*, No. 1.

Chesnais, F. (1988a), 'Multinational Enterprises and the International Diffusion of Technology', in Dosi, G. et al. (eds.), *Technology and Economic Theory*, London, Pinter Publishers.

Chesnais, F. (1988b), Technical Co-operation Agreements Between Firms, *STI Rewiev*, No. 4.

Chesnais, F. (1990), 'Accords de Coopération Interfirmes, Dynamique de l'Economie Mondiale et Théorie de l'Entreprise', in Humbert, M. (ed.), *Investissement International et Dynamique de l'Economie Mondiale*, Paris, Economica.

Choi , Y.B. (1991), 'An Interview With Arjo Klamer', *Methodus*, Vol. 3, No. 1.

Christensen, J. L. and Lundvall, B.-Å. (eds.) (2004), *Product Innovation, Interactive Learning and Economic Performance*, Amsterdam, Elsevier.

Christensen, J. (1991), *Financial Systems, Internationalization and Corporate Finance*, Paper for Conference on EC Business and Integration, Gilleleje 18.–30. August.

Christensen, P.R., Ibsen. F., Lundvall, B.-Å and Sverdrup-Jensen, S. (1978), *Lønniveau og konkurrenceevne*, Aalborg, Aalborg Universitetsforlag.

Clark, G. L, Feldman, M. P. and Gertler, M. S. (2000), *The Oxford Handbook of Economic Geography*, Oxford, Oxford University Press.

Cohen, S.S. and Zysman, J. (1987), *Manufacturing Matters: The Myth of the Post-Industrial Economy*, New York, Basic Books.

Commons, J. R. (1931), 'Institutional Economics', *American Economic Review*, Vol. 21.

Cooke, P. (1996), *Regional Innovation Systems: An Evolutionary Approach*, London University Press, London.

Cooke, P. (2001), Regional innovation systems, clusters and the knowledge economy. Industrial and Corporate Change 4 (10), pp. 945–974.

Cordell, A.J. (1971), *The Multinational Firm, Foreign Direct Investment and Canadian Science Policy*, Science Council of Canada, Special Study No. 22, Information Canada, Canada.

Cornwall, J. (1977), *Modern Capitalism – its Growth and Transformation*, Oxford, Martin Robertson.

Cox, A. (1986), *The State, Finance and Industry*, New York, St. Martins.

Cyert, R.M. and March, J.G. (1963), *A Behavioural Theory of the Firm*, Englewood Cliffs, Prentice-Hall.

Daft, R.L. (1982), 'Bureaucratic Versus Nonbureaucratic Structure and the Process of Innovation and Change', *Research in the Sociology of Organizations*, Vol. 1.

Dahlman, C. J., Ross-Larson, B. and Westphal, L. E. (1987), 'Managing Technological Development: Lessons from the newly Industrialized Countries', *World Development*, Vol. 15, No. 6.

Dahmén, E. (1950/1970), *Entrepreneurial Activity and the Development of Swedish Industry 1919–1939*, Homewood, American Economic Association Translation Series.

Dahmén, E. (1988) ''Development Blocks' in Industrial Economics', *Scandinavian Economic History Review*, No. 1.

Dalpé, R. and Debresson, C. (1989), *The Public Sector as First User of Innovations – A Research Note*, Center for Research on the Development of Industry and Technology, Canada.

Dalpé, R. (1989), *Government Procurement and Innovation*, Research Note, Department of Political Science, University of Montreal.

Dalum, B., Fagerberg, J. and Jørgensen, U. (1988), 'Small Open Economies in the World Market for Electronics: The Case of the Nordic Countries', in Freeman, C. and Lundvall, B.-Å. (eds.), *Small Countries Facing the Technological Revolution*, London and New York, Pinter Publishers.

Dalum, B., Gregersen, M., Schmidt, J. and Villumsen, G. (1978), *Nogle ændringer i Danmarks placering i den internationale arbejdsdeling med særlig henblik på maskinsektoren*, Institute for Produktion, Aalborg University , Skriftserie A:2.

Dalum, B, Gregersen, M, Schmidt, J. and Villumsen, G. (1981) *Økonomiers langsigtede udvikling – en struktur– og teknologidiskussion*, Aalborg, Aalborg Universitetsforlag.

Dalum, B., Møller, K., Jørgensen, U. and Valentin, F. (1991a), 'Porter og den erhvervspolitiske debat', *Samfundsøkonomen*, No. 7. København, Jurist– og Økonomforbundets Forlag.

Dalum, B., Møller, K., Jørgensen, U. and Valentin, F. (1991b) *Internationalisering og erhvervsudvikling – Et debatoplæg om fremtidig dansk erhvervspolitik*. København, Industri– og Handelsstyrelsen, Notatserie No. 3.

Dalum, B. (1990), 'Effekterne af EF's indre marked – belyst ved eksemplet mobil radiokommunikation', *Nordisk Tidsskrift för Politisk Ekonomi*, No. 25–26.

Dalum, B. (1992), 'National Systems of Innovation and Technology Policy – The Case of Denmark', in Archibugi, G. and Scienstock, G. (eds.), *Technology Policy Towards an Integration of Social and Ecological Concerns*, Berlin, de Gruyter.

Danziger, J.N. et al. (1982), *Computers and Politics*, New York, Columbia University Press.

David, P.A. (1985), 'Clio and the Economics of QWERTY', *American Economic Rewiev*, No. 75.

David, P.A. (1988), *Path-Dependence: Putting the Past into the Future of Economics*, Technical Report 533, Institute for Mathematical Studies in the Social Sciences, Stanford University.

De Bresson, C. (1976), 'Le Transfert de Technologie dans Trois Pays Mediterranéens : Données Empiriques', *Mondes en Développement*, No. 15.

De Liso, N. (2006), 'Charles Babbage, Technological change and the "national system of innovation"', *Journal of Institutional and Theoretical Economics*, Vol. 162, No. 3, pp.470–485.

Dean, R., Jr. (1974), 'The Temporal Mismatch – Innovation's Pace vs. Management's Time Horizon', *Research Management*, May, 12–15.

Derian, J.-C. (1990), *Financing the Needs of Small Technology Oriented Companies: The Case of France*, Paper for the Conference Technology and Investment, 21–24 January, Stockholm.

Dertoutzos, M.L., Lester R.K. and Solow, R.M. (1989), *Made in America*, Cambridge, Mass., The MIT-press.

Dore, R. (1986), *Flexible Rigidities*, Stanford, Stanford University Press.

Dosi, G., Freeman, C., Nelson, R., Silverberg, G. and Soete, L. (eds.), (1988), *Technical Change and Economic Theory*, London, Pinter Publishers.

Dosi, G., Llerena, P. and Sylos Labini, M. (2006), 'Science-Technology-Industry link and the European paradox: Some notes on the dynamics of scientific and technological research in Europe', in Lorenz, E. and Lundvall, B.-Å. (eds.) (2006), *How Europe's economies learn*, Oxford, Oxford University Press, pp. 203–234.

Dosi, G., Pavitt, K. and Soete, L. (1990), *The Economics of Technical Changeand International Trade*, Hemel Hempstead, Harvester Wheatsheaf.

Dosi, G. and Soete, L. (1988), 'Technical Change and International Trade', in Dosi, G. et al. (eds). *Technical Change and Economic Theory*, London, Pinter Publishers.

Dosi, G. (1982), 'Technological Paradigms and Technological Trajectories: A Suggested Interpretation of the Determinants and Directions of Technical Change', *Research Policy*, Vol.11, No.3.

Dosi, G. (1984), *Technical Change and Industrial Transformation: The Theory and an Applcation to the Semiconducter Industry*, London and Basingstoke, Macmillan.

Dosi, G. (1988a), 'The Nature of the Innovative Process', in Dosi, G. et al, *Technical Change and Economic Theory*, London, Pinter Publishers.

Dosi, G. (1988b), 'Sources, Procedures and Microeconomic Effects of Innovation', *Journal of Economic Literature*, Vol. XXVI, No. 3.

Dosi, G. (1990), 'Finance, Innovation and Industrial Change', *Journal of Economic Behaviour and Organization* , No.13.

Dosi, G. (1999), 'Some notes on national systems of innovation and production and their implication for economic analysis', in Archibugi, D., Howells, J. and Michie, J. (eds.), *Innovation policy in a global economy*, Cambridge, Cambridge University Press.

Douglas, M. (1987), *How Institutions Think*, London, Routledge.

DSTI/STIID (1992), *The International Sourcing of International Inputs*, (DSTI/STIID/IND (92)1), Paris, OECD.

Dunning, J.H. (1988a), *Multinationals, Technology and Competitiveness*, London, Unwin Hyman.

Dunning, J.H. (1988b) *Explaining International Production*, London, Unwin Hyman.

Dunning, J.H. (1990a), 'The Changing Dynamics of International Production: Some Firm and Country Specific Influences', *Discussion Papers in International Investment and Business Studies*, No. 142, Series B, Vol. III., University of Reading, United Kingdom.

Dunning, J.H. (1990b), 'Multinational Experiences and the Globalization of Innovative Capacity', *Discussion Papers in International Investment and Business Studies*, No. 143, Series B, Vol. III., University of Reading, United Kingdom.

Dunning, J.H. (1990c), *The Governance of Japanese & U.S. Manufacturing Affiliates in the U.K.: Some Country Specific Differences*, Workshop on the Organization of Work and

Technology: Implications for International Competitiveness, EIASM & The Wharton School, Brussels, May 31–June 1.

Dunning, J.H. (1991a), 'Dunning on Porter: Reshaping the Diamond of Competitive Advantage', *Business and Economic Studies on European Integration*, Working Paper 6–91. Copenhagen Business School.

Dunning, J.H. (1991b), 'Governments, Economic Organisation and International Competitiveness', in Matsson, L.G. and Stymme, B. (eds.), *Corporate and Industry Strategies for Europe*, The Netherlands, Elsevier Science Publishers.

EC Commission (1988a), *European Economy*, No. 35.

EC Commission (1988b), 'Studies on the Economics of Integration, Research on the 'Cost of Non-Europe'', *Basic Findings*, Vol. 2.

Edquist, C. (ed.) (1997), *Systems of innovation: Technologies, institutions and organizations*, London, Pinter Publishers.

Edquist, C. (2005), 'Systems of Innovation: Perspectives and Challenges', in Fagerberg, J., Mowery, D. and Nelson, R.R. (eds.), *The Oxford Handbook of Innovation*, Norfolk, Oxford University Press.

Edquist, C. and Jakobsson, S. (1988), *Flexible Automation – the Global Diffusion of New Technology in the Engineering Industry*, Oxford, Blackwell.

Edquist, C. and Lundvall, B.-Å. (1989), 'Comparing Small National Systems of Innovation', Contribution to the Nelson-project on *National Systems Supporting Technical Change*, mimeo.

Edquist, C. and Lundvall, B.-Å. (forthcoming, 1992), 'Comparing the Danish and Swedish Systems of Innovation', in Nelson, R.R. (ed.), *National Systems of Innovations: A Comparative Study*, Oxford University Press.

Edquist, C. and McKelvey, M. (1991) 'The Diffusion of New Product Technologies and Productivity Growth in Swedish Industry – A Study for the Swedish Productivity Delegation', Department of Technology and Social Change, University of Linköping, Sweden. Published in Swedish as 'Högteknologiska produkter och produktivitet i svensk industri' in *Forskning, teknikspridning och produktivitet*. Expertrapport No. 10 til Produktivitetsdelegationen, Stockholm, Allmänna Förlaget.

Edwards, J.S.S. and Fischer, K. (1991), *Banks, Finance and Investment in West Germany Since 1970*, CEPR Discussion Paper No. 497.

Elster, J. (1989), 'Social Norms and Economic Theory', *The Journal of Economic Perspectives*, Vol. 3, No. 4.

Eparvier, P. (2005), 'Methods of evolutionism and rivalry with neoclassical analysis. The example of the National System of Innovation concept', *Journal of Economic Methodology*, vol. 12, no. 4, pp. 563–579.

Erdilek, A. (ed.) (1985), *Multinationals as Mutual Invaders: Intra-Industry Direct Foreign Investment*, London, Croom Helm.

Ethier, W.J. (1988), *Modern International Economics*, 2nd ed., New York, W.W. Norton & Company.

Etzkowitz, H. and Leydesdorff, L. (1995), 'The Triple Helix – University-Industry-Government Relations: A Laboratory for Knowledge-Based Economic Development', *EASST Review 14*(1), 14–19.

Etzkowitz, H and L. Leydesdorff (2000), 'The dynamics of innovation: from National Systems and 'Mode 2' to Triple Helix of university-industry-government relations', *Research Policy*, Vol. 29, No. 2, pp. 109–123.

Fagerberg, J. (1987), 'A Technology-Gap Approach as to Why Growth-Rates Differ', *Research Policy*, Vol. 16.

Fagerberg, J. (1988a) 'International Competitiveness', *Economic Journal*, Vol. 98.

'Fagerberg, J. (1988b), 'Why Growth Rates Differ', in Dosi, G. et al. (eds.), *Technical Change and Economic Theory*, London, Pinter Publishers.

Fagerberg, J. (1988c), *Technology, Growth and Trade: Schumpeterian Perspectives*, unpublished D.Phil thesis, University of Sussex.

Fagerberg, J. (1992), *User-Producer Interaction and Export Specialization*, Report, Norwegian Institute of International Affairs, Oslo.

Fagerberg, J., D. Mowery and R.R. Nelson (eds.) (2005), *The Oxford Handbook of Innovation*, Norfolk, Oxford University Press.

Ferguson, C.H. (1991), 'Macroeconomic Variables, Sectoral Evidence and New Models of Industrial Performance', in OECD (1991), *Technology and Productivity: The Challenge for Economic Policy*, Paris.

Foray, D. (2004), *The Economics of Knowledge*, Cambridge, Mass., The MIT Press.

Franks, J. and Mayer, C. (1990): 'Capital Markets and Corporate Control: A Study of France, Germany and the UK', *Economic Policy*, No.10.

Freeman, C. and Perez, C. (1986): *Business Cycles, Long Waves, Investment Behaviour and Technological Changes*, SPRU, mimeo.

Freeman, C. and Perez, C. (1988), 'Structural Crisis of Adjustment: Business Cycles and Investment Behaviour', in Dosi, G. et al., *Technical Change and Economic Theory*, London, Pinter Publishers.

Freeman, C. and Lundvall, B.-Å. (eds.) (1988), *Small Countries Facing the Technological Revolution*, London: Pinter Publishers.

Freeman, C. and Soete, L. (eds.) (1987), *Technical change and full employment*, Oxford, Basil Blackwell.

Freeman, C. and Soete, L. (1991), *Macro-Economic and Sectoral Analysis of Future Employment and Training Perspectives in the New Information Technologies in the European Community: Synthesis*, Report, MERIT, University of Limburg.

Freeman, C. (ed) (1981), *Technological Innovation and National Economic Performance*, Aalborg, Aalborg University Press.

Freeman, C. (1982), *The Economics of Industrial Innovation*, London, Pinter Publishers.

Freeman, C. (1982), 'Technological infrastructure and international competitiveness', Draft paper submitted to the *OECD Ad hoc-group on Science, technology and competitiveness*, August 1982, mimeo.

Freeman, C. (1987), *Technology and Economic Performance: Lessons from Japan*, London, Pinter Publishers.

Freeman, C. (1988), 'Japan: a New National System of Innovation?', in Dosi, G. et al., *Technical Change and Economic Theory*, London, Pinter Publishers.

Freeman, C. (1990), 'The Third Kondratieff Wave', in Kihlström et al. (eds.), *Festschrift in honour of Lars Herlitz*, Gothenburg (forthcoming).

Freeman, C. (1991), 'Networks of Innovators: a Synthesis of Research Issues', *Research Policy*, Vol. 20, No. 5.

Freeman, C. (1995a), 'The National Innovation Systems in historical perspective', in *Cambridge Journal of Economics*, vol. 19, no. 1.

Freeman, C., (1995b), 'History, co-evolution and economic growth', in IIASA Working Paper 95-76, Laxenburg, IIASA.

Freeman, C. (2002). Innovation systems: City-state, national, continental and sub-national, Mimeo, Paper presented at the Montevideo conference, *Research Policy* 31 (2): 191–211.

Freeman, C. (2004), 'Technological infrastructure and international competitiveness', *Industrial and Corporate Change*, Vol 13, No. 3, pp. 540–52.

Furtado, C. (1964), *Development and Underdevelopment: A Structural View of the Problems of Developed and Underdeveloped Countries*, Berkeley, University of California Press. Freeman, C. and Soete, L. (1997), *The Economics of Industrial Innovation*, Pinter, London.

Fusfeld, H.I. (1986), *The Technical Enterprice: Present and Future Patterns*, Cambridge, Mass., Ballinger.

Galbraith, J.K. (1969), *The New Industrial State*, Harmondsworth, Penguin.

Gelsing, L. (1988), *Local Industrial Networks – From Production Complexes to Knowledge Networks*, Paper for RSA-Conference in Stockholm, August.

Gelsing, L. (1990), *Udviklingssamarbejde i Industrien – Hovedrapport fra SAMOVID-projketet,(Cooporating on development in industry*, Danish only), Aalborg University.

Georgescu-Roegen, N. (1971), *The entropy law and the economic process*, Harvard, Harvard University Press.

Gertler, M, (1988), 'Financial Structure and Aggregate Economic Activity: An Overview', *Journal of Money, Credit, and Banking*, Vol. 20, No. 3.

Gerybadze (1982), *Innovation, Wettbewerb und Evolution*, Tübingen, J.C.B. Mohr.

Gibbons, M. and Johnston, R. (1974), 'The Roles of Science in Technological Innovation', *Research Policy*, Vol. 3, No. 3.

Gibbons, M., Limoges, C., Nowotny, H., Schwartzman, S., Peter Scott, P., and Trow, M. (1994), *The new production of knowledge: the dynamics of science and research in contemporary societies* London: Sage.

Giddens, A. (1984), *The Constitution of Society*, Cambridge, Polity Press.

Gjerding, A.N., Johnson, B., Kallehauge, L., Lundvall, B.-Å. and Madsen, P.T. (1990), *Den forsvundne produktivitet*, Charlottenlund, Jurist– og Økonom Forbundets Forlag. (*The Missing Productivity*, forthcoming in English).

Gjerding, A.N. (1992), 'Virksomhedsledelsen står i et organisatorisk vadested' (Midstream Management), *Ledelse i dag (Management Today)*, No. 2.

Glimell, H. (1989), *Going Flexible: The Penetration of New Management Practices and the Growth of a New Workplace Politics in Sweden*, Paper presented at the Conference on 'A Flexible Future? Prospects for Employment and Organization in the 1990's', Cardiff Business School, September 19–20.

Gomulka, S. (1971), *Inventive Activity , Diffusion , and the Stages of Economic Growth*, University of Århus.

Gouldner, A.W. (1959), 'Organizational Analysis', in Merton, R.K. et al. (eds.), *Sociology Today*, New York, Basic Books.

Graham, E.M. (1990), 'Strategic Management and Transnational Behavior: A Formal Approach', in Pitelis, C. and Sugden, R., *The Nature of the Transnational Firm*, London, Routledge.

Grandstrand, O. and Sigurdson, J (eds.) (1985), *Technological Innovation and Industrial Development in Telecommunications. The Role of Public Buying in the Telecommunication Sector in the Nordic Countries*, Lund, Nordforsk and Research Policy Institute.

Granovetter, M. (1973), 'The Strength of Weak Ties', *American Jounal of Sociology*, Vol. 78.

Granovetter, M. (1985), 'Economic Action and Social Structures: the Problem of 'Embeddedness'', *American Journal of Sociology*, Vol. 91, No. 3.

Granstrand, O. (2000), Corporate Innovation Systems A Comparative Study of Multi-Technology Corporations in Japan, Sweden and the USA, *Chalmers University of Technology*.

Gray, J. (1988), 'Hayek, the Scottish School, and Contemporary Economics', in Winston, G. and Teichgraeber III, *The Boundaries of Economics*, Cambridge, Cambridge University Press.

Greenaway, D. and Milner C. (1986), *The Economics of Intra-industry Trade*, Oxford, Blackwell.

Gregersen, B. (1988), 'Public-Sector Participation in Innovation Systems', in Freeman, C. and B.-Å. Lundvall (eds.), *Small Countries Facing the Technological Revolution*, London and New York, Pinter Publishers.

Gregory, G. (1986), *Japanese Electronics Technology: Enterprise and Innovation*, New York, Wiley.

GRESI (1976), *La Division Internationale du Travail*, 2 Vols., Groupe de Reflexion pour les Strategies Industrielles, Paris, La Documentation Française.

Habermas, J. (1984), *The Theory of Communicative Action*, Vol. I, Boston, Beacon Press.

Hage, J. and Aiken, M. (1970), *Social Change in Complex Organizations*, Clinton, Mass., Random House.

Hagedoorn, J. and Schakenraad, J. (1990a), *Leading Companies and the Structure of Strategic Alliances in Core Technologies*, MERIT Working Paper, Maastricht.

Hagedoorn, J. and Schakenraad, J. (1990b), 'Interfirm Partnerships and Co-operative Strategies in Core Technologies', in Freeman, C. and Soete, L., *New Explorations in the Economics of Technological Change*, London, Pinter Publishers.

Haklisch, C.S. (1986), *Technical Alliances in the Semiconductor Industry*, Centre for Science and Technology Policy, New York University, mimeo.

Hall, B. (1991), *Corporate Restructuring and Investment Horizons*, NBER Working Paper 3794.

Hallén, L., Johanson, J., and Nazeem, S.M. (1987) 'Relationship Strength and Stability in International and Domestic Industrial Marketing', *Industrial Marketing & Purchasing*, Vol. 2, No. 3.

Hamel, G., Doz, Y. and Prahalad, C.K. (1989), 'Collaborate With Your Competitors – and Win', *Harvard Business Rewiev*, No. 1.

Hannah, L. (1983), *Entrepreneurs and the Social Sciences*, Inaugural Lecture, London School of Economics and Political Science.

Hayek, F.A. (1948), 'Economics and Knowledge and The Use of Knowledge in Society', in Hayek, F.A., *Individualism and Economic Order*, Chicago, University of Chicago Press.

Hayek, F.A. (1975), *The Pretence of Knowledge*, Nobel Memorial Lecture, December 1974, Stockholm, Les Prix Nobel en 1974.

Hayek, F.A. (1978), 'Competition as a Discovery Procedure,' in Hayek, F.A., *New Studies in Philosophy, Politics, Economics and the History of Ideas*, Chicago, University of Chicago Press.

Heertje, A. (ed.) (1988): *Innovation, Technology and Finance*, Oxford, Blackwell.

Helleiner, G.K. (1979), 'Transnational Corporations and Trade Structure: The Role of Intra-firm Trade', in H. Giersch (ed.), *On the Economics of Intra-Industry Trade*, Tübingen, J.C.B. Mohr.

Helpman, E. and Krugman, P.R. (1985). *Market Structure and Foreign Trade*, Cambridge, Mass., MIT Press.

Helpman, E. (1984), 'Increasing Returns, Imperfect Markets and Trade Theory', in Jones, R.W and Kenen, P.B., *Handbook of International Economics*, Vol. 1, Amsterdam, North-Holland.

Hirschman, A.O. (1958), *The Strategy of Economic Development*, New Haven, Conn., Yale University Press.

Hirschman, A.O. (1970), *Exit, Voice and Loyalty*, Cambridge, Mass., Harvard University Press.

Hobsbawn, E.J. (1968), *The Age of Capital, 1848–1875*, London, Abacus.

Hodgson, G. M. (1988), *Economics and Institutions, A Manifesto for a Modern Institutional Economics*, Cambridge, Polity Press.

Hofstede, G. (1980a), *Culture's Consequences: International Differences in Work-Related Values*, Beverly Hills, Sage Publications.

Hofstede, G. (1980b), 'Motivation, Leadership, and Organization: Do American Theories Apply Abroad?', *Organizational Dynamics*.

Holbek, J. (1988), 'The Innovation Design Dilemma: Some Notes on Its Relevance and Solutions', in Grønlaug, K. and Kaufmann, E. (eds.), *Innovation: A Cross-Disciplinary Perspective*, Oslo, Norwegian University Press.

Hollander, S. (1965), *The Sources of Increased Efficiency: A Study of DuPont Rayon Plants*, Cambridge, Mass., MIT Press.

Hollingsworth, R. (1990), *Variation among Nations in the Logic of Manufacturing Sectors and International Competitiveness*, Paper Presented to the Paris TEP Technology and Competitiveness Conference, June.

Hoshi, T., Kashyap, A. and Scharfstein, D. (1989), *Bank Monitoring and Investment: Evidence From the Changing Structure of Japanese Corporate Banking Relationships*, NBER Working Paper 3079.

Hoshi, T., Kashyap, A. and Scharfstein, D. (1990): *The Role of Banks in Reducing the Costs of Financial Distress in Japan*, NBER Working Paper 3435.

Howells, J. and Wood, M. (1991), 'The Globalisation of Production and Technology', *Prospective Dossier* No. 2, Vol. 2, Monitor-FAST Programme.

Howells, J. (1990), 'The Location and Organization of Rersearch and Development: New Horizons', *Research Policy*, Vol. 19, No. 2.

Hufbauer, G.C. (1970) 'The Impact of National Characteristics & Technology on the Commodity Composition of Trade in Manufactured Goods', in Vernon, R. (ed.), *The Technology Factor in International Trade*, New York, Columbia University Press.

Hughes, T.P. (1989), *American Genesis*, New York, Viking.

Hymer, S.H. and Rowthorn, R. (1970), 'Multinational Corporations and International Oligopoly: The Non-American Challenge' in Kindleberger, C.P. (ed.), *The International Corporation*, Cambridge, Mass., Institute of Technology.

Håkansson, H. (ed.) (1987): *Industrial Technology Development – a Network Approach*, London, Croom Helm.

Håkansson, H. (1989), *Corporate Technological Behaviour – Co-operation and Networks*, London, Routledge.

Hirschman, Albert, O. (1958), *The Strategy of Economic Development*, Clinton: Yale University Press.

Imai, K and Baba, Y. (1991), 'Systemic Innovation and Cross-Border Networks, Transcending Markets and Hierarchies to Create a New Tecno-Economic System', in OECD (1991), *Technology and Productivity: The Challenge for Economic Policy*, Paris.

Imai, K. (1986), Chapter 4 in Patrick, H. (ed.), *Japan's high technology industries: Lessons and limitations of industrial policy*, University of Washington Press, University of Tokyo Press.

Industrirådet (1986), *Ny Teknologi. Forskning og Udvikling*, København.

Insley, S. (1989), 'The Honda Way: An Innovative Approach to Management and Production', in Lundstedt, S.B. and Moss, T.H., *Managing Innovation and Change*, Dordrecht, Kluwer Academic Publishers.

Irwin, A. and Vergragt, P. (1989), 'Re-thinking the Relationship Between Environmental Regulation and Industrial Innovation: The Social Negotiation of Technical Change', *Technology Analysis & Strategic Management*, Vol. 1, No. 1.

Itami, H. (1988), 'The Japanese Corporate System and Technology Accumulation', in Urabe, K. et al., *Innovation and Management: International Comparisons*, Berlin, Walter de Gruyter.

Jain, A.K. and Gupta, S. (1987), 'Some Evidence on 'Herding' Behavior of U.S. Banks', *Journal of Money, Credit and Banking*, Vol. 19.

Jaquemin, A. and Sapir, A. (eds.) (1989), *The European Internal Market: Trade and Competition*, Oxford, Oxford University Press.

Jensen, M. B., Johnson, B., Lorenz, E. and Lundvall, B.-Å. (2007), 'Forms of Knowledge and Modes of Innovation', forthcoming in *Research Policy*.

Jewkes, J., Sawers, D. and Stillerman, J. (1958), *The Sources of Invention*, London, Macmillan.

Johanson, J. and Mattsson, L.-G. (1989), 'Internationalisation in Industrial Systems – A Network Approach', in Hood and Vahlne J.-E. (eds.), *Strategies in Global Competition*, London, Routledge.

Johnson, B. and Lundvall, B.-Å. (1991), 'Flexibility and Institutional Learning', in Jessop, B. et al. (eds.), *The Politics of Flexibility*, Aldershot, Edward Elgar.

Johnson, B. and Lundvall, B.-Å. (forthcoming, 1992), 'Closing the Institutional Gap?', *Revue d'Economie Industrielle*.

Johnson, B. (1974), 'Jämförelse av ekonomiska system', *Nordisk Tidskrift för Politisk Ekonomi*, No. 2.

Johnson, B. (1981), *Aktuelle Tendenser i den Økonomiske Politik under Krisen. Den Nyliberale Tendens*, Aalborg, Aalborg Universitetsforlag.

Johnson, B. (1986), 'Marknaden som Patentløsning – En Kritik av Nyliberalismen', From NFS, *Utmaning för Norden*, Nordens Fackliga Samorganisation.

Johnson, B. (1988), 'An Institutional Approach to the Small Country Problem', in Freeman, C. and Lundvall, B.-Å. (eds.), *Small Countries Facing the Technological Revolution*, London and New York, Pinter Publishers.

Johnson, B. (1992), 'Institutional learning', in Lundvall, B.-Å. (ed.), *National Innovation Systems: Towards a Theory of Innovation and Interactive Learning*, London, Pinter Publishers.

Johnson, C. (1986), 'The Institutional Foundations of Japanese Industrial Policy', in Barfield and Schamrei (eds.), *The Politics of Industrial Policy*, Washington, American Enterprise Institute for Public Policy Research.

Johnson, B. and Lundvall, B.-Å. (1991), 'Flexibility and Institutional Learning', in Jessop, B. et al. (eds.), *The Politics of Flexibility*, Aldershot, Edward Elgar.

Johnson, B. and Lundvall, B.-Å. (forthcoming, 1992), 'Closing the Institutional Gap?', *Revue d'Economie Industrielle*.

Johnson, B. and Lundvall, B.-Å.. (2003), 'National Systems of Innovation and Economic Development', in Muchie, M., Gammeltoft, P. and B.-Å. Lundvall (eds), *Putting Africa First, The Making of African Innovation Systems*, Aalborg University Press.

Johnston, J. (1984), *Econometric Methods*, Duckworth, McGraw-Hill.

Jones, E. L. (1988), *Growth Recurring. Economic change in World History*, Clarendon Press.

Jones, R.V. (1978), *Most Secret War: British Scientific Intelligence 1939–1945*, London, Hamilton.

Jones, R.W. and Kenen, P.B. (eds.) (1984), *Handbook of International Econmics – Volume 1: International Trade*, Amsterdam, North-Holland.

Jovanovic, M.N. (1992), *International Economic Integration*, London and New York, Routledge.

Julius, D. (1990), *Global Companies and Public Policy: The Growing Challenge of Foreign Direct Investment*, London, Royal Institute of Foreign Affairs.

Jørgensen, U. (1986), *Elektronikbranchens etablering og strukturelle udvikling*, Forskningsrapport No. 11, Institut for Samfundsfag, DtH, København.

Kaldor, N. (1960), *Essays on Economic Stability and Growth*, Glencoe, Ill., The Free Press.

Kaldor, N. (1978), 'The Effect of Devaluations on Trade in Manufacturers', in *Furthers Essays on Applied Economics*, London, Duckworth.

Kaldor, N. (1981), *The Baroque Arsenal*, New York, Hill and Wang.

Karnøe, P. (1991), 'Technological Innovation and Industrial Organization in the Danish Wind Industry', *Entrepreneurship & Regional Development*, No. 2.

Katz, R. (1984), *Organizational Issues in the Introduction of new Technologies*, working paper, Alfred P. Sloan School of Management, Massachusetts Institute of Technology.

Katzenstein, P.J. (1985), *Small States in World Markets*, Itacha, Cornell University Press.

Kenen, P.B. (1989), *The International Economy*, 2nd ed., Englewood Cliffs, New Jersey, Prentice Hall.

Keynes, J.M. (1936), *The General Theory of Employment, Interest and Money*, Cambridge, Cambridge University Press.

Kirzner, M.I. (1978), 'Government Regulation and the Market Discovery Process', in Kirzner, M.I., *Perils of Regulation: A Market Process Approach*, Law and Economics Center Occasional Papers, University of Miami School of Law.

Kjeldsen-Kragh, S. (1973), *Specialisering og Konkurrenceevne*, København, Nyt Nordisk Forlag/Arnold Busck.

Kjeldsen-Kragh, S. (1981), 'The Specialization Pattern in the Danish Machinery Sector', in Freeman, C. (ed.), *Technological Innovation and National Economic Performance*, Aalborg, Aalborg University Press.

Klamer, A. (1989), 'An Accountant Among Economists: Conversations with Sir John Hicks', *The Journal of Economic Perspectives*, Vol. 3, No. 4.

Kline, S. J. and Rosenberg, N. (1986), 'An overview of innovation', in Landau, R. and Rosenberg, N. (eds.), *The positive sum game*, Washington D.C., National Academy Press.

Kogut, B. (1991), 'Country Capabilities and the Permeability of Borders', *Strategic Management Journal*, Vol. 12, No. 1.

Kornai, J. (1971), *Anti-equilibrium*, Amsterdam, North-Holland.

Kristensen, A. and Lundvall, B.-Å. (1990), *Innovationsaktivitet i dansk industri 1984–88*, København, Industri og Handelsstyrelsen, notat november 90.

Kristensen, A. and Lundvall, B.-Å. (1991), *Den Nordiske Innovationsundersøgelse*, København, Industri– og Handelsstyrelsen.

Krugman, P.R. and Obstfeld, M. (1988), *International Economics: Theory and Policy*, Glenview, Illinois, Scott Foresman/Little Brown.

Krugman, P.R. (1990), *Rethinking International Trade*, Cambridge, Mass., MIT Press.

Lachmann, L.M.(1978), 'An Austrian Stocktaking: Unsettled Questions and Tentative Answers', in Spadaro (ed), *New Directions in Austrian Economics*, Kansas City, Sheed, Andrews and McMeel.

Lackmann, L.M. (1970), *The Legacy of Max Weber*, London, Heinman.

Lall, S. and Pietrobelli, C. (2003), 'Manufacturing in Sub-Saharan Africa and the Need of a National Technology System', in Muchie, M., Gammeltoft, P. and B.-Å. Lundvall (eds), *Putting Africa First, The Making of African Innovation Systems,* Aalborg, Aalborg University Press.

Lane, J-E (1988), 'Public and Private Leadership' in Kooimann, J. and Eliassen, K.A. (eds.), *Managing Public Organizations, Lessons from Contemporary European Experience*, Oxford, Sage Publications.

Lastres, H. M. M. and Cassiolato, J. E. (2005), 'Innovation systems and local productive arrangements: new strategies to promote the generation, acquisition and diffusion of knowledge'. In *Innovation: Management, Policy & Practice*, Vol. 7, No. 2.

Leamer, E. (1984), *Sources of International Comparative Advantage – Theory and Evidence*, Cambridge, Mass., MIT Press.

Leibenstein, H. (1987), *Inside the Firm. The Inefficiencies of Hierarchy*, Cambridge, Mass., Harvard University Press.

Lester, R.K. and Crocker, M.B. (1987), *The Economic Organisation of Nuclear Plant Projects: Some Cross-National Comparisons*, Center for Energy Policy Research, MIT.

Lester, R.K. (1989), *Determinants of US Productive Performance: Findings of the MIT Commission on Industrial Productivity*, Paper presented at the OECD International Seminar on Science, Technology and Economic Growth, Paris, OECD, mimeo.

Lewis, W.A. (1978), *Growth and Fluctuations 1870–1913*, London, Allen and Unwin.

Lincoln, J.R. (1990), *Work organization in Japan and the United States*, Workshop on the Organization of Work and Technology: Implications for International Competitiveness, EIASM & The Wharton School, Brussels, May 31–June 1.

Linder, S.B. (1961), *An Essay on Trade and Transformation*, Stockholm and New York, Almquist & Wiksel and Wiley.

List, F. (1841/1959), *Das Nationale System der Politischen Oekonomie*, Basel, Kyklos-Verlag.

Liu, X. and White, S. (2001), 'Comparing innovation systems: A framework and application to China's transitional context', *Research Policy*, Vol. 30, No. 7, pp. 1091–114.

Lockett, M. (1987), *The Factors Behind Successful IT Innovation*, Oxford, Templeton College, mimeo.

Lodge, G.C. and Vogel, E.F. (eds.), (1987), *Ideology and National Competitiveness. An Analysis of Nine Countries*, Boston, Mass., Harvard Business School Press.

Lorenz, E. and Lundvall, B.-Å. (eds.) (2006), *How Europe's economies learn*, Oxford, Oxford University Press.

Lorenz, E. and Valeyre, A. (2006), 'Organizational forms and innovation performance: A comparison of the EU15', in Lorenz, E. and Lundvall, B.-Å. (eds.), *How Europe's Economies Learn*, Oxford, Oxford University Press, pp. 140–160.

Lundberg, E. (1961), *Produktivitet och räntabilitet: Studier i kapitalets betydelse inom svenskt näringsliv*, Stockholm, Studieförebundet Näringsliv och Samhälle.

Lundvall, B.-Å (1985), *Product Innovation and User-Producer Interaction*, Aalborg, Aalborg University Press.

Lundvall, B.-Å. (1988), 'Innovation as an Interactive Process – from User-Producer Interaction to the National System of Innovation' in Dosi, G. et al. (eds.), *Technical Change and Economic Theory*, London, Pinter Publishers.

Lundvall, B.-Å. (1991), *Innovation, the Organised Market and the Productivity Slow-down*, Paper Presented at OECD's International Seminar on Science, Technology and Economic Growth, Paris June 6–9, mimeo.

Lundvall, B.-Å. (1992), 'Explaining Inter-Firm Cooperation – the Limits of Transaction Cost Approach', in Grabher, G. (ed.), *The Embedded Firm; On the Socioeconomics of Industrial Networks*, London, Routledge.

Lundvall, B.-Å. (ed.) (1992), *National Innovation Systems: Towards a Theory of Innovation and Interactive Learning*, London, Pinter Publishers.

Lundvall, B.-Å. (2002), *Innovation, Growth and Social Cohesion: The Danish Model*, Cheltenham, Edward Elgar.

Lundvall, B.-Å. (2006), 'Interactive learning, social capital and economic performance', Foray, D. and Kahin, B. (eds.), *Advancing Knowledge and the Knowledge Economy*, Harvard University Press, US.

Lundvall, B.-Å. (2007), 'Higher Education, Innovation and Economic Development', Paper presented at the World Bank's *Regional Bank Conference on Development Economics*, Beijing, January 16–17, 2007.

Lundvall, B.-Å. and Borras, S., (1998), 'The Globalising Learning Economy – Implications for Innovation Policy', *The European Commission*, DG XII-TSER, Bruxelles.

Lundvall, B.-Å., Intarakumnerd, P. and Vang, J. (eds.) (2006), *Asia's Innovation Systems in Transition*, London, Elgar.

Lundvall, B.-Å. and Johnson, B. (1994), 'The learning economy', *Journal of Industry Studies*, Vol. 1, No. 2, December 1994, pp. 23–42.

Lundvall, B.-Å., Johnson, B., and Lorenz, E. (2002), 'Why all this fuss about codified and tacit Knowledge?', *Industrial and Corporate Change*, No. 2, pp. 245–62.

Lundvall, B.-Å., Johnson, B., Andersen, E. and Dalum, B. (2002), 'National Systems of Production, Innovation and Competence-building', *Research Policy* 31 (2): 213–231.

Maddison, A. (1982), *Phases of Capitalist Development*, Oxford, Oxford University Press.

March, J.G. and Simon, H.A. (1958), *Organizations*, New York, John Wiley & Sons.

Markusen, A.R. (1987), *Regions – The Economics and Politics of Territory*, New Jersey, Rowman & Litt lefeld.

Marshall, A. (1919), *Industry and Trade: A Study of Industrial Technique and Business Organisation*, Macmillan, London.

Marshall, A. (1920), *Principles of Economics*, 8th edn., Macmillan, London.

Maskell, P. and Malmberg, A. (1997) Towards an explanation of regional specialization and industry agglomeration. *European Planning Studies*, 5: 1 pp. 25–41.

Mathews, J.A. (2001), 'National systems of economic learning: The case of technology diffusion management in East Asia', *International Journal of Technology Management*, 22 (5/6): 455–479.

May, R.M. (ed.) (1976/1981), *Theoretical Ecology: Principles and Applications*, Sunderland, Mass., Sinauer Associates.

Mayer, C. (1988), 'New Issues in Corporate Finance', *European Economic Review*, Vol. 32.

Mayer, C. (1990), 'Financial Systems, Corporate Finance and Economic Development', in Hubbard, R.G. (ed.), *Asymmetric Information, Corporate Finance and Investment*, Chicago, NBER, The University of Chicago Press.

Mayhew, A. (1987), 'Culture: Core Concept Under Attack', *Journal of Economic Issues*, Vol. XXI, No. 2.

McKelvey, M. (1991), 'How Do National Systems of Innovation Differ? A Critical Analysis of Porter, Freeman, Lundvall and Nelson', in Hodgson, G. and Screpanti, E. (eds.), *Rethinking Economics: Markets, Technology and Economic Evolution*, London, Edward Elgar.

Metcalfe, J. S. (2006), 'Marshallian economics', paper presented at the International Schumpeter Society, 11th Conference, Sophia Antipolis 2006, June 21–24.

Michalet, C.A. and Delapierre, M. (1977), *The Impact of Multinational Enterprises on National Scientific and Technical Capabilities in Computing*, CEREM, Paris. X University, mimeo.

Michalet, C.A. (1985), *Le Capitalisme Mondial*, Paris, Presses Universitaires de France.

Miettinen, R. (2002), *National Innovation System, Scientific Concept or Political Rhetoric*, Helsinki, Edita.

Milgrom, P.R., North, D.C. and Weingast, B.R. (1990), 'The Role of Institutions in the Revival of Trade: The Law Merchant, Private Judges, and the Champagne Fairs', *Economics and Politics*, Vol. 2.

Mishkin, F. (1990), *Financial Innovation and Current Trends in U.S. Financial Markets*, NBER Working Paper 3323.

Mistral, J. (1982), 'Matrise du Marché Intérieur, Compétivité et Redéploiment', in Bourguinat, H. (ed.), *Internationalisation et Autonomie de Décision*, Paris, Economica.

Mjøset, L. (ed.) (1986), *Norden dagen derpå*, Oslo, Universitetsforlaget.

Mistral, J. (1983), *Competitiveness of the Productive System and International Specialization*, Paris, OECD, DSTI/SPRU/83.31.

Mjøset, L. (2001), 'Theory, understanding of in the Social Sciences', in N. J. Smalser and P. B. Bates (eds), *International Encyclopedia of the Social and Behavioral Sciences*, Pergamon/Elsevier, Amsterdam.

Mjøset, L. (2002), 'An Essay on the Foundations of Comparative Historical Social Science', Working Paper No. 22, ARENA, Oslo.

Mowery, D. and Sampat, B. N. (2004), 'The Bayh-Dole Act of 1980 and University–Industry Technology Transfer: A Model for Other OECD Governments?', in *The Journal of Technology Transfer*, Vol. 30, No. 1–2.

Mowery, D. and Rosenberg, N. (1979), 'The Influence of Market Demand upon Innovation: A Critical Review of Some Recent Empirical Studies', *Research Policy*, Vol. 8, No. 2.

Muchie, M., Gammeltoft, P. and Lundvall, B.-Å. (eds.) (2003), *Putting Africa First: The Making of African Innovation Systems*, Aalborg, Aalborg University Press.

Muldur, U. (1990), 'Fusions et Acquisitions dans le Secteur Financier Européen', *Revenue d'Economie Financière*.

Mullineux, A. (1987), *International Banking and Financial Systems: A Comparison*, London, Graham & Trotman.

Murray, R. (1987), 'Den offentliga sektorn – produktivitet och effektivitet', *Långtidsutredningen '87*, Stockholm.

Musson, D.E. and Robinson, E. (1969), *Science and Technology in the Industrial Revolution*, Manchester, Manchester University Press.

Myrdal, G. (1958), *Economic Theory and Underdeveloped Regions*, Duckworth & Co.

Myrdal, G. (1968), *Asian Drama*, New York, Pantheon.

Mytelka, L.K. (1991a), 'States, Strategic Alliances and International Oligopolies: The European ESPRIT Programme', in Mytelka (ed.) (1991b), *Strategic Partnerships: States, Firms and International Competition*, London, Pinter Publishers.

Mytelka, L.K. (ed.) (1991b), *Strategic Partnerships: States, Firms and International Competition*, London, Pinter Publishers.

National Science Foundation (NSF) (1969), *Report on Project TRACES*, Washington.

Nelson, R. R (1984), *High-technology policies – A five-nation comparison*, Washington, American Enterprise Institute.

Nelson, R. R. (1987), *Understanding Technical Change as an Evolutionary Process*, Amsterdam, North-Holland.

Nelson, R. R. (forthcoming, 1992), *National Systems of Innovation; A Comparative Study*, Oxford, Oxford University Press.

Nelson, R. R. (ed.) (1993), *National Innovation Systems: A Comparative Analysis*, Oxford, Oxford University Press.

Nelson, R. R. (2006), 'What makes an economy productiven and progressive? What are the needed institutions?', *Columbia University*.

Nelson, R. R. and Phelps, E. S. (1965), 'Investments in Humans, Technology Diffusion and Economic Growth', in *The American Economic Review*, Vol. 56, No. 1/2.

Nelson, R. R. and Winter, S.G. (1978), 'Forces Generating and Limiting Concentration under Schumpeterian Competition', *Bell Journal of Economics*, Vol. 9.

Nelson, R. R. and Winter, S.G. (1982), *An Evolutionary Theory of Economic Change*, Cambridge, Mass., The Belknap Press of Harvard University Press.

Newfarmer, R.S. (1985), 'International Industrial Organisation and Development: A Survey', in *Profits, Progress and Poverty: Case Studies of International Industries in Latin America*, Indiana, University of Notre Dame Press.

Nielsen, P. and Lundvall, B.-Å. (1999), 'Competition and Transformation in the Learning Economy: The Danish Case', Revue d'Economie Industrielle 88, 67–90.

Nielsen, K.V. (1991), *Informationsteknologi, beskæftigelse og færdigheder i EF: Paradigmer og metoder i udredningsarbejdet*, Aalborg, Aalborg Universitetsforlag.

Nielsen, K.V., Mortensen, J. and Andersen, E. S. (1991), *Intra and Extra EC Trade in Information Technology from 1965 to 1987. Background Materials for a Study of Employment and Training*, IKE Småskrift 73, Institut for Produktion, Aalborg, Aalborg University.

Nordic Industrial Fund (1991), 'Innovation Activities in the Nordic Countries', *Newsletter*, No. 4, Oslo.

North, D.C. (1990), *Institutions, Institutional Change and Economic Performance*, Cambridge, Cambridge University Press.

NSF (1973), *Interactions of Science and Technology in the Innovative Process*, NSF 667, Washington.

O'Doherty, D. (ed.) (1990), *The Co-operation Phenomenon: Prospects for Small Firms and the Small Economy*, London, Graham and Trotman.

OECD (1963), *The Measurement of Scientific and Technical Activities*, (Frascati Manual) and Revised Editions, 1970 and 1981, Paris.

OECD (1979), *Impact of Multinational Enterprises on National Scientific and Technical Capacities: The Food Industry*, Paris.

OECD (1988), *New Technologies in the 1990s. A Socioeconomic Strategy*, (The Sundqvist Report), Paris.

OECD (1989a), *Economic Instruments for Environmental Protection*, Paris.

OECD (1989b), *Financial Market Trends*, No. 44.

OECD (1991), *Technology and Productivity: The Challenge for Economic Policy*, Paris.

OECD (1992), *Technology and the Economy – The Key Relationships*, Paris.

OECD (2000), *Knowledge Management in the Learning Society*, Paris, OECD.

OECD (2005), *Governance of Innovation Systems*, Volume 1: Synthesis Report, Paris, OECD.

OECD – Canada (1991), *Summary of Discussions*, The Conference on Technology and the Global Economy, February 1991, Montreal.

OECD CSTP-Secretariat (1987), *The Contribution of Science and Technology to Economic Growth and Social Development*, Paris, mimeo.

Ostry, S. (1990), *Governments and Corporations in a Shrinking World: Trade and Innovation Policies in the United States, Europe and Japan*, New York, Council of Foreign Relations.

Papachristodolou, C. (1988), *Inventions, Innovations and Economic Growth in Sweden*, Stockholm, Almquist and Wiksell International.

Pasinetti, L.L. (1981), *Structural Change and Economic Growth*, Cambridge, Cambridge University Press.

Patel, P. and Pavitt, K. (1987) 'Is Western Europe Loosing the Technological Race?', *Research Policy*, Vol. 16, No. 2–4.

Patel, P. and Pavitt, K. (1988), *The International Distribution and Determinants of Technological Activities*, Brighton, SPRU, University of Sussex, September, mimeo.

Patel, P. and Pavitt, K. (1989), *Do Large Firms Control the World's Technology?*, University of Sussex Science Policy Reseach Unit Discussion Paper, January. YEAR????

Patel, P. and Pavitt, K. (1991), 'Europe's Technological Performance', in Freeman, C. et al. (eds.), *Technology and the Future of Europe: Global Competition and the Environment in the 1990s*, London and New York, Pinter Publishers.

Pavitt, K., Robson, M. and Townsend, J. (1985), *The Size Distribution of Innovating Firms in the UK, 1945–1983*, DRC paper, SPRU, University of Sussex.

Pavitt, K. (1979) 'Technical Innovation and Industrial Development: 1. The New Causality', *Futures*.

Pavitt, K. (1980) 'Technical Innovation and Industrial Development: 2. The Dangers of Divergence', *Futures*.

Pavitt, K. (1984), 'Sectoral Patterns of Technical Change: Towards a Taxonomy and a Theory', *Research Policy*, Vol. 13.

Pavitt, K. (1987), 'Uses and Abuses of Patent Statistics', *University of Sussex Science Policy Reseach Unit DRC Occasional Paper*, No. 41.

Pavitt, K. (1991), 'What Makes Basic Research Economically Useful?', *Research Policy*, Vol. 20, No. 2.

Pearce, R.D. (1989), *The Internationalisation of Research and Development*, London, Macmillan.

Pearce, R.D. and Singh, S. (1991a), 'Global Strategy and Innovation: The Role of Internationalised Research and Development', *Discussions Papers in International Investment and Business Studies*, No. 156, Series B, Vol. IV, University of Reading, United Kingdom.

Pearce, R.D. and Singh, S. (1991b), 'Internationalisation of Research and Deveopment Among the World's Leading Enterprices: Survey Analysis of Organisation and Motivation', *Discussions Papers in International Investment and Business Studies*, No. 157, Series B, Vol. IV, University of Reading, United Kingdom.

Penrose, E. (1980), *The Theory of the Growth of the Firm*, Oxford, Blackwell.

Perez, C. and Soete, L. (1988a), 'Catching Up in Technology: Entry Barriers and Windows of Opportunity', in Dosi et al. (1988), *Technical Change and Economic Theory*, London, Pinter Publishers.

Perez, C. and Soete, L. (1988b), *Technical Change and Economic Theory*, London, Pinter Publishers.

Perez, C. (1983), 'Structural Change and the Assimilation of New Technologies in the Economic and Social System', *Futures*, Vol. 15, No. 4.

Perez, C. (1985a), 'Long Waves and Changes in Socioeconomic Organization', *IDS Bulletin*, Vol. 16, No. 1, Sussex, Institute of Development Studies.

Perez, C. (1985b), 'Microelectronics, Long Waves and World Structural Change: New Perspectives for Developing Countries', *World Development*, Vol. 13, No. 3.

Perez, C. (1988), 'New Technologies and Development', in Freeman, C. and Lundvall, B-A. (eds.), *Small Countries Facing the Technological Revolution*, London and New York, Pinter Publishers.

Perez, C. (1989a), 'Technical Change, Competitive Restructuring and Institutional Reform in Developing Countries', *SPR Publications, Discussion Paper* No. 4, December, The World Bank, Washington D.C.

Perez, C. (1989b), *Equipment, Services and Organizational Change: Three Moving Frontiers for Telecommunication Managers to Handle*, Draft Notes, Keynotes Speech at the Canto Conference, Santo Domingo, June 4–9.

Perroux, F. (1950/1969), 'Les Espaces Economiques', in Perroux (1969), *L'Économie du XXᵉ Siècle*, 3rd edn., Paris, Presses Universitaires de France.

Perroux, F. (1955), 'Note sur la Notion de Pole de Croissance', *Economie Appliquéé*, Paris. Reprinted in Perroux (1969).

Perroux, F. (1969), *L'Économie du XXᵉ Siècle*, 3rd edn., Paris, Presses Universitaires de France.

Peters, L.S. (1991), *Technology Strategies of Japanese Subsidiaries and Joint Ventures in the United States*, Center for Science and Technology Policy, New York, Rensselaer Polytechnic Institute.

Polanyi, K. (1957), *The Great Transformation*, Boston, Beacon Press.

Porter, M.E. (1980), *Competitive Strategy – Techniques for Analyzing Industries and Competitors*, New York, The Free Press.

Porter, M.E. (1985), *Competitive Advantage – Creating and Sustainaing Superior Performance*, New York, The Free Press.

Porter, M.E. (1986), 'Competition in Global Industries: A Conceptual Framework' in M.E. Porter (ed.), *Competition in Global Industries*, Boston, Harvard Business School Press.

Porter, M.E. (1990), *The Competitive Advantage of Nations*, London, MacMillan.

Prebisch, R. (1950), *The Economic Development of Latin America and its Principal Problems*, United Nations, Department of Economic Affairs, Economic Commission for Latin America.

Reinert, E. (1999), 'The Role of the State in Economic Growth', *Journal of Economic Studies* 26 (4/5): 268–326.

Reinert, E. (2003), 'The Other Canon: The History of Renaissance Economics', *Evolutionary Economics and Income Inequality*, edited by E. Reinert. Northampton: Edward Elgar Publishing.

Reppy, J. (1990), *Military Research and Economic Performance*, Paper Prepared for the Colloquim on Technology and Competitiveness, TEP/OECD, Paris, June 24–27.

Rickne, A. (2000), *New Technology-based Firms and Industrial Dynamics: Evidence from the Technological System of Biomaterials in Sweden, Ohio and Massachusetts*, Göteborg, Chalmers University of Technology.

Robson, P. (1987), *The Economics of International Integration*, 3rd ed., London, Allen & Unwin.

Ronstadt, R.C. (1977), *Research and Development Abroad by US Multinationals*, New York, Praeger.

Roobeek, A.J.M. (1990), 'The Technological Debacle: European Technology Policy from a Future Perspective', *Futures*, Vol. 22, No. 9.

Roos, D. (1991), 'The Importance of Organizational Structure and Production System Design in Deployment of New Technology', in OECD, *Technology and Productivity. The Challenge for Economic Policy*, Paris.

Rosenberg, N. (1976), *Perspectives on Technology*, Cambridge University Press, Cambridge.

Rosenberg, N. (1982), *Inside the Black Box: Technology and Economics*, Cambridge, Cambridge University Press.

Rothwell, R. (1972), *Factors for Success in Industrial Innovations: Project SAPPHO – A Comparative Study of Success and Failure in Industrial Innovation*, Science Policy Research Unit, University of Sussex, Brighton.

Rothwell, R. (1977), 'The characteristics of successful innovators and technically progressive firms', R&D Management, No 3, Vol. 7, pp. 191–206.

Rothwell, R., Freeman, C., Jervis, P., Robertson, A. and Townsend, J. (1974), 'SAPPHO Updated – Project SAPPHO Phase 2', *Research Policy*, Vol. 3, No. 3.

Rothwell, R. and Zegfeld, W. (1981), *Industrial Innovation and Public Policy*, London, Pinter Publishers.

Russo, M. (1985), 'Technical Change and the Industrial District: The Role of Interfirm Relations in the Growth and Transformation of Ceramic Tile Production in Italy', *Research Policy*, Vol. 14, No. 6.

Rybzinsky, T. (1984): 'Industrial Financial Systems in Europe, U.S. and Japan', *Journal of Economic Behavior and Organization* , Vol. 5.

Sabel, C. (1987), *The Reemergence of Regional Economics – Changes in Scale of Production*. Paper Prepared for the SSRC Western European Committee Volume Experimenting with Scale.

Sabel, C. (1990), *Shades of Trust: The Construction and Destruction of Regional Economies*, Paper Presented to the Paris TEP Technology and Competitiveness Conference, June.

Sako, M. (1989), *Neither Markets nor Hierarchies: A Comparative Study of the Printed Circuit Board Industry in Britain and Japan*, Paper for the 2nd Conference of the Project 'Comparing Capitalist Economies: Variation in the Governance of Sectors', Bellagio, May 19 – June 2.

San Gee and Kuo, W.-J. (1998), 'Export Success and Technological Capability: Textiles and Electronics in Taiwan, Province of China', in Ernst, D., Ganiatos, T. and Mytelka, L. (eds), *Technological Capabilities and Export Success in Asia*, Routledge, London.

Savary, J. (1989), *Les Groupes Industriels et Financiers er l'Intégration Européenne – Des Stratégies Multinationales aux Stratégies Globales des Groupes en Europe*, Paper Presented at the International Seminar organised by the LEREP, 28–30 September, Toulouse.

Saxenian, A. (1991), The Origins and Dynamics of Production Networks in Silicon Valley, *Research Policy*, Vol. 20, No. 5.

Saxonhouse, G.R. (1985), 'Biotechnology in Japan: Industrial Policy and Factor Market Disortions', *Prometheus*, Vol. 3, No. 2.

Schackle, L.S. (1972), *Epistemics and Economics: A Critique of Economic Doctrines*, Cambridge, Cambridge University Press.

Schmookler, J. (1966), *Invention and Economic Growth*, Harvard University Press.

Schultz, T.W. (1975), 'The Value of the Ability to Deal with Disequilibria', *Journal of Economic Literature*: 827–846.

Schumpeter, J.A. (1928), 'The Instability of Capitalism', in Schumpeter, J.A. (1951), *Essays on Economic Topics*, (ed.) R.V. Clemence, Port Washington, N.Y., Kennikat.

Schumpeter, J.A. (1934), *The Theory of Economic Development: An Inquiry into Profits, Capital, Credit, Interest and the Business Cycle*, London, Oxford University Press.

Schumpeter, J.A. (1939), *Business Cycles: A Theoretical, Historical and Statistical Analysis of the Capitalist Process*, 2 Vols., New York, McGraw Hill.

Schumpeter, J.A. (1942), *Capitalism, Socialism and Democracy*, London, Unwin, 1987.

Scott, A.J. and Storper, M. (1987), 'High Technology Industry and Regional Development: a Theoretical Critique and Reconstruction', *International Social Science Journal*, May.

Segura-Bonilla, O. (1999), 'Sustainable Systems of Innovation: The Forest Sector in Central America', *SUDESCA Research Paper No. 24*, PhD dissertation, Department of Business Studies, Aalborg University.

Sejersted, F. (1988), 'Bank og Samfunn', *Bergen Bank Kvartalsskrift*, No. 4.

Sen, A. (1999), *Development as Freedom*, Oxford: Oxford University Press.

Sharif, N. (2006), 'Emergence and development of the National Innovation Systems concept', *Research Policy*, Volume 35, No. 5, pp. 745–766.

Shimada, H. (1991), ''Humanware' Technology and Industrial Relations', in OECD, *Technology and Productivity. The Challenge for Economic Policy*, Paris.

Shin, J.-S. (2004), 'Studies of National Innovation Systems – Which Way to Go?', Working Paper, *National University of Singapore*.

Silverberg, G. (1990) in Freeman, C. and Soete, L., *New Explorations in the Economics of Technological Change*, London, Pinter Publishers.

Singer, W.H. (1950), 'U.S. Foreign Investment in Underdeveloped Areas – The Distribution of Gains between Investing and Borrowing Countries', in *The American Economic Review*.

Smith, A. (1776/1904), *An Inquiry into the Nature and Causes of the Wealth of Nations*, London: Methuen and Co., Ltd., ed. Edwin Cannan, 1904, 5th edition.

Smith, A. and Venables, A. (1988), 'The Costs of Non-Europe: An Assessment Based on a Formal Model of Imperfect Competition and Economies of Scale', in EC Commission (1988b), 'Studies on the Economics of Integration, Research on the 'Cost of Non-Europe'', *Basic Findings*, Vol. 2.

Stewart, Frances (1977), *Technology and Underdevelopment*, London: Macmillan.

Stiglitz, J. and Weiss, A. (1981): 'Credit Rationing in Markets with Imperfect Information', *American Economic Review*, Vol.71.

Storper, M. (1991a), *Production Organisation, Technological Learning and International Trade*, mimeo.

Storper, M. (1991b), *Technology Districts and International Trade: The Limits to Globalization in an Age of Flexible Production*, Graduate School of Urban Planning & Lewis center for Regional Policy Studies, Los Angeles, University of California, mimeo.

Suzuki, Y. (1990), *The Japanese Financial System*, Oxford, Clarendon Press.

Teece, D.J. (1986), 'Profiting from Technological Innovation', *Research Policy*, Vol. 15, No. 6.

Thirlwall, A.P. (1986), *Balance-of-Payments Theory – and the United Kingdom Experience*, 3rd ed., London, Macmillan.

Thompson, J.D. (1967), *Organizations in Action*, New York, McGraw-Hill.

Thomson, G. (ed.), (1989), *Industrial Policy – USA and UK Debates*, Routledge.

Tylecote, A. and Demirag, I. (1991): *Short-termism: Culture and Structures as Factors in Technological Innovation*, Research Project on 'Performance pressures and technological progress in British industry', mimeo.

UNCTC (1991), *World Investment Report 1991. The Triad in Foreign Direct Investment*, New York, United Nations.

Urabe, K. (1988), 'Innovation and the Japanese Management System', in Urabe et al., *Innovation and Management: International Comparisons*, Berlin, Walter de Gruyter.

Vaitsos, C.V. (1974), *Intercountry Income Distribution and Transnational Enterprices*, Oxford, Clarendon Press.

van de Donk, W.B.H.J. and Snellen, I.T.M. (1989), 'Knowledge-Based Systems in Public Administration: Evolving Practices and Norms' in Snellen, I.T.M. et al. (eds.), *Expert Systems in Public Administration – Evolving Practices and Norms*, Amsterdam, Elsevier.

Veblen, T. (1898), 'Why is Economics not an Evolutionary Science?', *The Quarterly Journal of Economics*, Vol. XII,.

Veblen, T. (1919), *The Place of Science in Modern Civilization*, Reprint, Augustus M. Kelley, New York, 1965.

Vernon, R. (1966), 'International Investment and International Trade in the Product Cycle', *Quarterly Journal of Economics*, Vol. 80, No. 1.

Verspagen, B. and Werker, C. (2003), 'The invisible college of economics pf innovation and technological change', *Estudios de Economia Aplicada*, Vol. 21, No. 3, 203–220.

Vinding, A. L. (2002), *Interorganizational Diffusion and Transformation of Knowledge in the Process of Product Innovation*, PhD dissertation, Department of Business Studies, Aalborg University.

Viotti, E.B. (2002), 'National learning systems: A new approach to technological change in late industrialising countries and evidence from the cases of Brazil and Korea', *Technological Forecasting and Social Change*, 69 (7), pp. 653–680.

von Hippel, E. (1976), 'The Dominant Role of Users in the Scientific Instrument Innovation Process', *Research Policy*, Vol. 5.

von Hippel, E. (1988), *The Sources of Innovation*, New York and Oxford, Oxford University Press.

Wallmark, J. and McQueen D. (1988), *100 Important Swedish Technical Innovations from 1945 to 1980*, Studentlitteratur, Lund and Chartwell-Bratt, Bromley, Kent.

Walsh, V. (1987), 'Technology, Competitiveness and the Special Problems of Small Countries', *STI Rewiev*, No. 2.

Whitley, R. (1994), 'Societies firms and markets: The social structuring of business systems', in Whitley, R. (ed.), *European business systems*, London, Sage Publications.

Whittaker, H. (1990), *New Technology and the Organization of Work: British and Japanese Factories*, Workshop on the Organization of Work and Technology: Implications for International Competitiveness, EIASM & The Wharton School, Brussels, May 31–June 1.

Williamson, O.E. (1975), *Markets and Hierarchies: Analysis and Anti-trust Implications*, New York, The Free Press.

Williamson, O.E. (1985), *The Economic Institutions of Capitalism*, New York, The Free Press.

Willinger, M. and Zuscovitch, E. (1988), 'Towards the Economics of Information Intensive Production Systems: The Case of Advanced Materials', in Dosi et al. (1988), *Technical Change and Economic Theory*, London, Pinter Publishers.

Winter, S.G. (1987), 'Natural Selection and Evolution', in Eatwell, J. et al. (eds.), *The New Palgrave: A Dictionary of Economics*, London and Basingstoke, Macmillan, Vol. 3.

Witt, U. (1993), *Evolutionary Economics*, Aldershot, Edward Elgar Publishers.

Womack, J.P., Jones, D.T. and Roos, D. (1990), *The Machine that Changed the World*, New York, Rawson Associates.

Woolcock, M. (1998), 'Social capital and economic development: toward a theoretical synthesis and policy framework', *Theory and Society*, No. 2, Vol. 27, pp. 151–207.

Wortmann (1990), 'Multinationals and the Internationalisation of R&D: New Developments in German Companies', *Research Policy*, Vol. 19, No. 2.

WS Atkins Management Consultants (1988), 'The 'Cost of Non-Europe' in Public-Sector Procurement', *Research on the 'Cost of Non-Europe', Basic Findings*, Vol. 5 Part A, Commission of the European Communities, Luxembourg.

Young, S., Hood, N. and Hamill, J. (1987), *Foreign Multinational and the British Economy*, London, Croom Helm.

Zaltman, G., Duncan, R. and Holbek, J. (1973), *Innovations and Organizations*, New York, John Wiley & Sons.

Zysman, J. (1983), *Governments, Markets and Growth – Financial Systems and the Politics of Industrial Change*, Cornell University.

Zysman, J. (1990), *Trade, Technology and National Competition*, Paper for OECD Conference in Paris 24–27/6.

Lightning Source UK Ltd.
Milton Keynes UK
25 February 2010

150568UK00001B/57/P